TEAM OF VIPERS

MR. SIMS

WELCOME
ABOARD

Air Force One

TEAM OF VIPERS

MY 500 EXTRAORDINARY DAYS

IN THE TRUMP WHITE HOUSE

CLIFF SIMS

THOMAS DUNNE BOOKS 🐊 ST. MARTIN'S PRESS

NEW YORK

THOMAS DUNNE BOOKS.
An imprint of St. Martin's Press.

TEAM OF VIPERS. Copyright © 2019 by Cliff Sims. All rights reserved. Printed in the
United States of America. For information, address St. Martin's Press,
175 Fifth Avenue, New York, N.Y. 10010.

www.thomasdunnebooks.com
www.stmartins.com

Designed by Steven Seighman

The Library of Congress Cataloging-in-Publication Data is available upon request.

ISBN 978-1-250-22389-0 (hardcover)
ISBN 978-1-250-22390-6 (ebook)

Our books may be purchased in bulk for promotional, educational, or business
use. Please contact your local bookseller or the Macmillan Corporate and
Premium Sales Department at 1-800-221-7945, extension 5442, or by email
at MacmillanSpecialMarkets@macmillan.com.

First Edition: January 2019

10 9 8 7 6 5 4 3 2 1

For James Breland, my granddaddy:
Like everything worthwhile I've ever done or ever will do,
I wrote this book hoping that it will make you proud.

CONTENTS

AUTHOR'S NOTE

Not long after he entered the White House in 2017, a study proclaiming Donald J. Trump the most famous person on the planet was passed around among those of us working in the West Wing. I'm not sure how scientific this study was, but it estimated that Trump might even be the most famous person in history, at least in terms of the total number of living people who knew who he was. When I mentioned this to the President, he smirked and raised his eyebrows quickly. But he didn't say a word.

The news didn't seem to surprise him. *Of course* he was the most famous person on earth. After all, this is what he'd been working for all of his life. Unlike most human beings, his greatest fear wasn't death or failure or loss. It was obscurity. If he was noticed, he mattered. And he didn't much care if the attention was good or bad, as long as it wasn't indifferent. Mentions in the press had long been his oxygen. Another "Page Six" scoop, another breath. A *Time* magazine cover, a shot of adrenaline. He spent his adult life keeping the brand going, whatever it took. He couldn't just own a nice hotel, but the most beautiful hotel ever built. He couldn't have a difficult divorce, but the most sensational ever to hit the tabloids. He couldn't just have a popular TV show, it had to be the most highly rated in history. He couldn't be a good president, he'd have to be as great—greater, even—than Lincoln. The most famous person in history? Of course he was. Donald J. Trump wouldn't settle for anything less.

It's anyone's guess whether Trump will be better known to history than Aristotle, Michael Jackson, or Napoleon, but one thing is certain: ever since he glided down the Trump Tower escalator and announced he was running for President of the United States in June 2015, he has been the most watched, most debated, most polarizing person in the country—probably the world. How and why we as a nation put him in office at this time in our country's history will be questioned, studied, and debated for the rest of our lives, and probably well beyond. After spending a majority of my waking hours for nearly two years working alongside Donald Trump and his senior staff, I keep coming back to the same question: What was *that* all about?

Which is why I wanted to write this book. For one of the most talked-about people on this planet, I have found almost everything written or said about President Trump—by sympathizers as well as critics—to fall woefully short. This is in part because Trump is almost always viewed through a distorted prism. Different people can witness the same events, hear the same words, and digest the same facts, and still walk away with dramatically different opinions on what it all meant. Those who know him best want to stay on his good side and spin all of his actions in the most positive light; it's good business for them. The same holds true for his most bitter critics—there's a big market for Trump hatred, too. Even the best reporters at the best media outlets are beholden to their sources, and the sources within the Trump White House are often self-serving or duplicitous. As for the most recent Trump biographies—some written by sycophants, others by haters, and even those by famous journalists: Each offers a glimpse of the real Donald Trump—the genius, the impulsive risk taker, the hothead, the insurrectionist, the hypocrite—because he can be all of these things. But none tells the full story.

That is where I hope this book will be different. I want to show you the unvarnished Donald Trump, a man whose gifts and flaws are both larger than life, written by someone with an appreciation of both. You may love him; you may hate him. I'm not trying to change your mind either way. But in reading my firsthand account, I hope you will gain a deeper, more complete understanding of Trump and those of us who served him.

The inner circle of Trump World was not always a pretty picture. Too often it was a portrait of venality, stubbornness, and selfishness. We leaked. We schemed. We backstabbed. Some of us told ourselves it was all done in the service of a higher calling—to protect the President, to deliver for the people. But usually it was for ourselves. Most of us came to Washington convinced of the justice of our cause and the righteousness of our principles, certain that our moral compasses were true. But proximity to power changes that. *Donald Trump* changes that. The once clear lines—between right and wrong, good and evil, light and darkness—were eroded until only a faint wrinkle remained.

I suspect that posterity will look back on this bizarre time in history as if we were living in the pages of a Dickens novel. *It was the age of wisdom, it was the age of foolishness.* Some of us on both sides of that blurry divide were young, wide-eyed, and seeing the real world for the first time. Others were battle weary, watching with great cynicism the twisting of the American experiment. Those of us who were there were part of a unique moment in time when the greatest nation on earth wrestled with its better angels and its nagging demons. We will hold tight to the triumphs, lose sleep over the failures, and perhaps shed tears over what could have been. Some of us will be proud of what we did. Others will be ashamed and never speak of it again. Some will remember this as the best work we ever did. Others will wish it could all be deleted from the record.

Lincoln famously had his Team of Rivals. Trump had his Team of Vipers. We served. We fought. We brought our egos. We brought our personal agendas and vendettas. We were ruthless. And some of us, I assume, were good people.

I was there. This is what I saw. And, unlike the many leakers in the White House, I have put my name on it.

—Cliff Sims
Washington, D.C.
October 2018

INTRODUCTION: ELECTION NIGHT

"The peso is plummeting!" Trump exclaimed at 10:16 P.M. on Election Night, a broad smile creasing his ever-tanned face. "That's the best news I've heard all day."

As we stood in the campaign war room on Trump Tower's fourteenth floor, the global markets were reacting to a reality that the top reporters in the country and political figures on both sides of the aisle could not yet absorb: Donald J. Trump was going to be President of the United States. All the prognosticators and bloviators who'd predicted his doom were being humiliated, and he was loving every minute of it.

Going into Election Day, *The New York Times* had given Trump a 15 percent chance of winning. If he was honest about it, Trump probably had a similar view as the night began. We all did. Those of us working on the campaign knew the momentum was with us, but it was hard to tell if the surge of support came too late.

The war room, typically the campaign's central hub of activity, was sparsely populated for most of the early evening. Then, to everyone's surprise, Mr. Trump walked in, flanked by campaign manager Kellyanne Conway. His first comments, predictably, were about his favorite medium. "Nowhere else on earth has this many TVs where I can watch it all at once," he smiled, pointing to the wall full of televisions with both hands like a conductor overseeing a symphony. And it was a symphony—a symphony of Trump. His face was on every screen.

Election Night was one of the rare moments when I was cognizant in real time of the fact that I was witnessing a significant historical moment firsthand.

With that realization, I planted myself beside Mr. Trump and refused to move the entire night, even as dozens of people crammed into the room in the coming hours, trying to get in his orbit—campaign staff, volunteers, various surrogates, the mega-rich Mercer family, Mike Pence, Ben Carson, and, of course, Omarosa, beaming with pride.

Ever the TV critic, the candidate was engaged throughout the night in a running commentary on the quality of the programming. He addressed no one in particular, and he didn't care who was listening. Trump talked like other people breathed. It was like a form of exercise for him—an endless exertion of words, phrases, asides, and observations. Sometimes he'd start a sentence and figure out the point he wanted to make along the way. Lacking any filter, he'd make the same observation to the Queen of England that he'd make to a construction worker at one of his hotels. To those open to him, this can be one of his most endearing qualities—he just is who he is.

"The graphics on Fox are the absolute worst—are you looking at this?" he said at one point. "CNN and MSNBC are both so much better. I hate to say it—honestly, I *really* hate to say it—but MSNBC has the best graphics. Fox is the best—they have the best talent. I mean, look at the rest of these people. They can't believe what's happening right now. But Fox's graphics are terrible. They've got to do something about it."

CNN's John King was working the interactive map—or "Magic Wall"—throughout the night, turning states red and blue as results came in and playing out different electoral scenarios. "They've got John King on the maps again," Trump quipped. "I used to hate him on the maps, then the maps started turning red and I started liking him. But he wants the map to be blue. And everyone knows he should be an anchor by now. But [CNN president Jeff] Zucker has him on the maps, and we all know what that means." I actually wasn't entirely sure what that meant, but no matter. I nodded knowingly just the same.

At one point, with Fox News back on the main screen, frequent Trump critic Karl Rove came on to lambaste both Clinton and Trump. "Rove is a dope," Trump said, turning away from the screens for the first time. "How many times has he been wrong about everything but they still put him out there? This guy spent a half-billion dollars and didn't win a single race. But they don't say anything about that. He wants people to forget. I don't forget, that I can tell you."

But it wasn't all hot takes and criticism. "There's my Jeffrey," he said as CNN commentator Jeffrey Lord came on screen as a panelist. "Someone turn up CNN, Jeffrey is on. They're always beating the hell out of him and he just keeps on fighting." Then he said to no one in particular, "Tell Jeffrey he's doing a good job—somebody call Jeffrey and let him know he's doing a good job." I'm not sure anyone did. When Fox News commentator Tucker Carlson complimented Trump's ability to articulate an antiwar vision to Republican voters, Trump said, admiringly, "He totally gets it."

Eventually, Melania Trump and their ten-year-old son, Barron, came into the war room to join the crowd. Melania was wearing a white designer dress with flowing fabric draped over her left shoulder and falling diagonally across her neckline, leaving her right shoulder exposed. An enormous diamond ring on her left hand glistened under the fluorescent lighting. Barron was wearing a black suit without a belt, with a white tie draped over his shoulder.

"Hey, baby," Trump said, giving his wife a kiss. "We're looking a lot better than they said we would." Then he added his usual "Let's see what happens."

All eyes were on Florida, which the campaign viewed as a must-win state. In the last ten days of the race, our internal polling numbers had improved in every single battleground state. But for some unknown reason, the momentum in Florida seemed to have stalled about forty-eight hours before Election Day. Brad Parscale, the campaign's digital director, was optimistic. There was no question that the race was tightening and, in most states, we had the wind at our back. But in Florida, he felt like it was a toss-up, at best. "Have you seen the numbers in Florida?" became a running joke inside the comms team.

Between 7:52 P.M. and 8:05 P.M., the vote deficit we were facing in the Sunshine State had shrunk from 193,000 to 87,000. Vote tallies from the reliably Republican Florida Panhandle—which resides in the Central Time Zone, while the rest of the state is in the Eastern—were yet to come in. Though the rest of us were almost manic with tension, Trump was casually rolling through calls on his beloved Android cell phone.

Very few of the incoming calls had a name attached to them in his phone, but Trump answered them all anyway.

Almost every caller was a household name—from media, entertainment, politics, corporate America. Matt Drudge, the reclusive conservative media giant, updated Trump on what he was hearing from around the country. He was bullish on Trump's chances. He predicted states that had been out of the GOP's reach for decades would swing Republican as a result of Trump's hardline immigration and trade positions.

POLITICAL MAP COULD BE RESHAPED, the headline blared atop Drudge's site. I showed it to Mr. Trump on my cell phone and he smiled. "We're about to find out how smart he really is," he said.

He didn't look nervous, but resigned to whatever fate had in store. And why not? He was going to be rich and famous, no matter what. The only question was whether he'd also be the most powerful person on the planet.

Drudge was also raising the alarm about illegal voting, an issue that had long been of concern to Trump, who fixated on the idea that someone, somewhere, might "steal" his victory. LEAKED DOCUMENTS REVEAL SOROS FUNDING TO MANIPULATE ELECTION, read one Drudge link. PA VOTERS REPORT SEEING TRUMP VOTES SWITCH TO CLINTON BEFORE THEIR EYES, added another.

At 9:35 P.M. *the New York Times* updated its projections and, for the first time, gave Trump a better-than-even shot at winning. Florida was looking good, with the Panhandle poised to deliver a stunning victory.

But while things were on a positive trajectory down south, Trump was coming unglued about reports streaming in from Virginia. This wasn't a state we were counting on, but the race was tight enough that Trump launched into a tirade about Virginia's Democratic Governor, Terry McAuliffe, a close ally of the Clinton family. McAuliffe had restored voting rights to tens of thousands of felons in a controversial move that sparked outrage among law-and-order conservatives, and Trump was now convinced that might be enough to swing the election. To Trump, the fix was in.

"He pardoned sixty thousand criminals—a bunch of hardened felons; they probably killed their neighbors—just in time for the election so they could go vote for Crooked Hillary," the candidate grumbled as New Jersey Governor Chris Christie came into the room for the first time. Once the GOP's brash, straight-talking golden boy, Christie had passed on a presidential run in 2012, only to see Trump, his longtime friend, swoop in and fill that lane in 2016. He had still given it a shot, but dropped out of the race in February 2016 and endorsed Trump. Since then, he had been leading a quixotic effort to organize a presidential transition, just in case Trump pulled off an improbable victory. Christie's typically bombastic personality seemed more subdued than usual. He was smiling and wearing an American flag lapel pin in the shape of his home state, but he seemed to be just soaking in his surroundings.

At 10:20 P.M., Secretary Clinton was up by forty-five thousand votes in

Virginia and Trump got spun up further. For the first time that night, I saw his paranoia threaten to get the best of him. He pulled out his phone to tweet that he was prepared to protest the results if he didn't win—an impulsive act of pique that could have sparked a major political disaster.

Standing near Trump, campaign strategist Steve Bannon found himself in an unfamiliar role—the voice of reason. "Don't tweet about it," Bannon pleaded. "We've got to be patient tonight—we've really got to be patient."

Trump was not easily calmed in such moments. "Well, it'll just look like sour grapes if I do it after," Trump retorted. Finally he came up with a compromise. Referring to the Fox News chairman, he yelled, "Somebody get Rupert on the phone and tell him to get ready to make this a big deal if we need to."

Fortunately, at that moment Ohio was called for Trump, sending the room into an uproar and putting Virginia out of the candidate's mind.

David Bossie, the deputy campaign manager, walked over between Mr. Trump and the wall of TVs and said out loud what no one else had yet had the courage to voice. "Sir," he said, looking the candidate right in the eyes, "you're going to win this thing."

I watched the soon-to-be President digest this new reality. Trump nodded, but didn't speak. His hands were clutching his belt buckle, like a cowboy who'd just slain a legendary gunfighter. In the midst of the euphoria around him, it was as if everything had gone silent for him. And then he returned to the moment. There was a telling gleam in his eye. On the verge of his ultimate victory, a historic repudiation of all of his critics, a moment when he could have taken the high road as his place in history was assured, his first thought was retribution.

"When I get to Washington I'm gonna shove it up Kasich's a—!" he declared of Ohio's vehemently anti-Trump Governor and Trump's former presidential rival, John Kasich. It was the first time that night that I had heard him say "when" rather than "if."

Kasich, who had snubbed the Republican National Convention nominating Trump even though it was held in his home state, was now all but completely out of the news. But he was not out of Trump's memory. Trump wanted him relegated to a life of obscurity—which, to him, would be the ultimate degradation.

Governor Christie by now had nudged his way through the crowd and ordered several interns sitting just to Mr. Trump's left to move out of the way so he could take a seat next to the candidate. Trump took a seat as well, placing his Android phone on his left leg and leaning back in the black office chair long used by the campaign's war room director, Andy Surabian. Christie occasionally leaned over to whisper something to Trump, who was polite but didn't seem particularly interested.

Mike Pence sat down immediately to Trump's right, phone pressed to his ear, covering his mouth and the phone's microphone so that whoever he was speaking with could hear him through the clamor.

At 10:34 P.M. the *Times* finally called Florida for Trump, and three minutes later, famed political statistician Nate Silver updated his projections to give Trump an 86 percent chance of winning. I pulled up the projection on my phone and showed it to Eric Trump, who was standing directly to my right, and Jared Kushner, whose eyes grew larger as a grin engulfed his face. "What's it say?" asked Donald Trump Jr. Kushner showed him the screen, then turned to show it to the soon-to-be President-Elect.

The atmosphere in the room was euphoric. In the span of about ninety minutes, most people there had gone from thinking there was very little chance we would win to daydreaming about what it was going to be like to work inside the fabled West Wing. Each time positive vote tallies from various states were splashed across the wall full of television screens, the assembled crowd of Trump and Pence family members and campaign staff would erupt in applause.

In the midst of the chaos, Trump bent down to talk to his son Barron, tied his necktie for him, and kissed him on the forehead.

At 10:45 P.M., Fox News called North Carolina for Trump, and the entire family simultaneously cheered and looked toward Eric Trump's wife. Lara, a native North Carolinian, had spearheaded campaign operations in her home state. Trump garnered over ninety-two thousand more votes in the state than Republican nominee Mitt Romney had four years earlier. Mr. Trump leaned back as far as his chair would go to look at her sitting behind him and held out his hand to take hers. "So proud," he said.

At 10:55 P.M., Stephen Miller placed "Speech Number 2"—a draft victory speech—in front of Trump. I wondered to myself if Speech Number 1 had been a concession speech, or just an earlier draft of the victory speech. But Trump didn't even finish reading the first paragraph before he turned the paper facedown, right next to a copy of his campaign platform book, *Crippled America,* one of the many copies that were strewn about the campaign offices.

Jared watched the scene carefully—as he always did. "That's right," he said, "don't jinx it."

Trump, who has always been extraordinarily superstitious, echoed that sentiment at 11:13 P.M. when Rupert Murdoch called his phone to congratulate him. "Not yet, Rupy," he said. "We have a three-stroke lead with one hole left. We can't celebrate until we're in the clubhouse."

For the next several hours, battleground states continued to be called in Trump's favor, culminating after 2 A.M. when Wisconsin officially put him over the 270 Electoral College vote threshold.

Throughout the night, at least in public, Trump stayed true to his persona: boastful, friendly, talkative, and confident. Always confident. There was never a moment when he seemed awed by what was about to happen to him, about the responsibility he would soon undertake. He's the most self-assured person I've ever been around. He's the alpha dog in every conversation I've ever seen him engage in, and he owns every room. Except for one moment that night, in private.

As Trump and the next First Lady of the United States entered the Trump Tower elevators, and the doors closed in front of them, he let his guard down. Just for a split second, at least, as a friend who was in the elevator told me soon after. In that instant—the first time on Election Night when they weren't around hordes of aides and friends—the bravado and bragging were gone. For the briefest of moments, the gravity of what was happening hit him. President of the United States of America. Leader of the Free World. Extraordinary power. Mind-boggling responsibility. Heavy, heavy stuff.

The man who is never at a loss for words was rendered speechless by the verdict of history. And he looked, just for the briefest of moments, vulnerable. Sensing this was Melania Trump. Melania was never the person outside observers seemed convinced that she was—a reluctant and put-upon spouse who just wanted to escape him. For good or ill, she was in it with him all the way. In that moment, she reached for her husband's hand and squeezed it.

"We're going to do this together," she reassured him, "and you're going to be a great president."

He stood silently in the elevator as the floor numbers scrolled down.

For the next eighteen months, I was a part of this unusual and extraordinary journey. I would be around Trump nearly every day—serving at various times as a communications adviser, a producer, a confidant, an errand boy, and a punching bag. Sometimes all on the same day. Sometimes all in the same conversation. In an ordinary White House, a young communications staffer wouldn't have such access. But because Trump liked and trusted me, I found myself sitting in on meetings with foreign leaders, private conversations with his family, and discussions with the top leaders of Congress. I was a fly on the wall as history unfolded before my eyes. And I took notes, as part of my job. Lots and lots of notes. A first draft of history written in real time.

This is what I saw. It is the story of an unlikely—and unusual—President, whose extraordinary talents were in constant competition with glaring flaws that sometimes bordered on self-sabotage. I saw that battle firsthand. This is the story of a ragtag band of political outsiders who stormed the White House, and of staffers who couldn't seem to decide whether serving their country meant serving their President or undermining him. And this is also a very personal story of a Southerner who came to Washington with high expectations, only to leave the White House uncertain of whether anything I did really mattered, or whether I lost myself along the way.

In some ways I found Washington to be exactly what most voters seem to think it is: a cesspool of preening and weak politicians, moralizing and selectively outraged journalists, and staffers more worried about the trajectory of their careers than that of the country. Sometimes I was one of them. It was a constant struggle between my conscience, my principles, and a culture that often asked you to compromise both. And sometimes I did. I experienced the intoxicating effects of power and the astonishing lengths to which people, myself included, will go to hold on to it. But I also found public servants, toiling away outside of the spotlight, devoting their lives to the continuation and success of the American experiment. Sometimes I was one of them, too.

I want to show readers how it really was as I saw it firsthand—the highs and lows, the triumphs, struggles, outrages, and embarrassing failures. I experienced them all. And now you can, too.

TEAM OF
VIPERS

A SLOW CLIMB ABOARD
THE TRUMP TRAIN

I sat in silence watching the second hand of a silver clock on the wall spin slowly during a commercial break. It had been a long time since I'd been nervous going into an interview. For some reason, though, this one was different. This one *felt* different.

On August 21, 2015, I was the CEO of a fast-growing Alabama media company called Yellowhammer, which began as my blog when I was a student at the University of Alabama a few years earlier. I focused on state politics and the behind-the-scenes machinations of lawmakers. My biggest weekly feature was "Rumors and Rumblings," giving the scoop on what was really going on inside the Alabama State House. The site initially attracted a hard-core following among state politicos from both parties, but within four years our readership had exploded. Now I was in the Yellowhammer Radio studio in Birmingham, preparing to interview the most unlikely of presidential candidates, Donald J. Trump.

That evening, he was slated to visit the state for the first time for what was predicted to be the largest event in the history of presidential primaries. Tens of thousands of Alabamians were expected to pile into Ladd-Peebles Stadium in Mobile to witness what *The Washington Post* later described as "something between a Lynyrd Skynyrd concert and the Daytona 500." They weren't far off.

I had made several attempts to get the Republican candidate to appear on my radio show in the run-up to the event, but all my calls and emails went unanswered. When a rival radio host did land an interview, I fired off a terse email to the campaign to explain that it made no sense for Trump to do that other show instead of mine because our reach was so much greater, and we also had a large online platform. I figured some staffer would read that email and think, *Okay, big shot, you're definitely not getting an interview now.* But, to my surprise, I was contacted by a press aide named Hope Hicks.

"Eleven-thirty your time, okay?" she asked. Perfect. It was on.

Later, when we met in person for the first time, she laughed when she found out that we were about the same age. "Your emails made me think you were a cranky old man!" she said.

It was still unclear, at least to me, whether the Trump candidacy was a fad—a chance for voters to vent their frustration with political correctness and the status quo before they got serious with another candidate. Predictions of Trump's imminent implosion, over one incendiary thing he said or did after another, were an almost daily occurrence. A pollster I knew who had worked for Trump in the past told me privately that the billionaire tycoon didn't actually want to win the presidency, but rather viewed the race as a once-in-a-lifetime promotional opportunity for his brand.

And yet there was *something*—something that made it hard to pass this all off as a lark. Other presidential contenders had called in to my show before, but none elicited the office-wide response that Trump did. Nearly everyone in the building, it seemed, was gathering around to bear witness to a live interview with "The Donald," an aggressive billionaire real-estate developer turned boisterous reality TV star turned presidential front-runner. He'd be a thousand miles away.

A poll released the week before showed Trump lapping the rest of his Republican opponents in Alabama. But it wasn't his polling numbers that made me nervous. It was his entire larger-than-life persona. I'd watched him steamroll interviewers in the past, some of the best in the business, with long, occasionally rambling, monologues until time was up. I didn't want to be the next victim. I was planning to ask him some tough questions—the kind my mostly conservative listeners were asking themselves.

I was snapped out of my contemplative state by music blaring from the headphones sitting on the table in front of me, signaling the commercial break was over. I looked up at the computer screen, which displayed the phone lines. "TRUMP," my producer had typed on the line identifying the caller. Here we go.

"He's defying political gravity in a way that we've never really seen before," I said. "He is Donald Trump, and he joins us now. Mr. Trump, how're you doing today?"

"Very good, thank you very much, Cliff," he said. "I appreciate it."

There was no denying his popularity in Alabama, nor the fact that his message—particularly on the issue of illegal immigration—was resonating with a wide swath of the electorate.

With that in mind, I started by asking him if, should he win the presidency, he would consider nominating Alabama's popular United States Senator Jeff Sessions—a fellow immigration hard-liner—to serve as his Attorney General. Looking back, I guess you could say that was the first piece of advice I ever gave him.

"He's a great guy, and while it's a little early in the process, I'd like to get there first, and I have to get there," Trump answered. "Alabama is lucky to have him, and he's lucky to have Alabama, but frankly, when I was getting very, very serious on this immigration thing, because as you know it's out of control, I took tremendous abuse. . . . What's happening at the border is a disgrace."

We went on to discuss a variety of issues on which conservatives were hoping to get some assurances, from abortion to gun rights to religious liberty.

"Conservatives around the country really love what you're saying," I told him. "But when I hear criticisms of you from conservatives, and even some of the reservations I have myself, it really comes down to some of the past positions that you've held on issues that we really care about."

"I understand that," Trump replied.

He had come under scrutiny for his many contributions to Democratic candidates over the years—including the Clintons, who were probably two of the most disliked politicians in all of Alabama. He'd also made a number of comments over the years that seemed to put him somewhere between Chuck Schumer and Nancy Pelosi politically.

"So, for conservatives who are trying to give you the benefit of the doubt," I continued, "can you walk us through your personal journey that led to such profound shifts in your philosophy and ideology?"

"Well, it's timing. And you have to understand I was a businessman," he calmly explained. "So I'm pro-life, as an example. But when somebody would say, 'Are you pro-life or pro-choice?' or whatever they might ask, it was, like, something that I never really would express. . . . I'm not sure I was ever asked the question until I was in the world of politics."

That wasn't entirely true. I'd done my research on this point. "Well, somebody asked and you said that you were very pro-abortion at one point," I interjected.

"No," he shot back. "What I said is that I hate the concept of abortion. I think it was the first time it was ever asked of me. Because I hated the concept of abortion."

The quote we were both referencing came from an interview Trump gave to the late Tim Russert on NBC's *Meet the Press* a year before the 2000 election, one of several previous election cycles when he toyed with the idea of running for President. Trump did, indeed, say during that interview that he "hated the concept of abortion." But he had also said he was "very pro-choice"—a fact he now wanted to gloss over as if it never existed. This would, of course, be a recurring habit.

But then he added more to his answer that seemed to suggest he'd given abortion more thought than he'd been given credit for. "Ultimately I changed because I had two friends that were going to have a baby and they were going to terminate that baby—they were going to have an abortion—and they didn't do it," he explained. "And their child has turned out to be so incredible. So every time I see them they say, 'Can you believe that we were thinking of . . .' I know the child, the child is a phenomenal person. . . . I've seen things like this over the years, so I evolved on that. . . . But I'm pro-life." As I got to know Trump, he'd often cite various nameless "friends" whose statements or experiences fit neatly into whatever point he wanted to make. Sometimes reporters wondered if those friends existed. But in this case, I had no reason to think he was being insincere.

I also wanted to get Trump talking more about his faith, which was important to me personally. Like many kids who grew up in the South, I was in church every Sunday morning and Wednesday evening. For me, it was more like every day of the week, though, because my dad was a pastor and my mom was the church pianist. Like many preachers' kids, I'd rebelled in my teenage years, but later returned to my roots.

My granddaddy James Breland was a pastor, too. He was approaching ninety years old and still preached at a country church in the Mississippi Delta every Sunday. Before his wife, my Mimi, passed away in 2015, she had been the volunteer church librarian. She was also an avid note writer. Every photo on the walls of their home was meticulously documented. She wrote down funny things that happened or quotes she wanted to remember, all in the perfect cursive handwriting that could only belong to a schoolteacher. We don't know exactly when she did it, but before she passed away, she left one final note tucked inside her checkbook—but this one wasn't for her, it was for my granddaddy. She knew where to leave it so he would find it, and he did, just a few days after she died.

"Please don't cry because I died!" the note said. "Smile because I lived! Know that I'm in a happy place! Know that we will meet again! I'll see you there!" I wrote an article about the note on *Yellowhammer* and it went viral all over the world, with stories in *People* magazine, on the *Today* show, and dozens more.

Needless to say, I was raised to believe that faith is the foundation of character. At the time, my faith was one of the reasons I struggled with Trump's unexpected rise. The playboy past, the casinos, the profanity, a seeming lack of common decency—all of it was tough to swallow for a Southern boy with Baptist ministers for a father and grandfather.

Ideologically I was more aligned with Ted Cruz, a rock-ribbed conservative who'd been giving the party establishment fits since getting elected to the Senate a few years before. Stylistically I was drawn to the aspirational tone of Marco Rubio. *Time* magazine had dubbed him "The Republican Savior" in 2013, a time when conventional wisdom held that Republicans would struggle to ever win a national election again unless they became a "Big Tent Party." For the GOP establishment, this meant softening the party's stance on immigration. On that point, I couldn't have disagreed more. I know people have different views on this, but without a border, you don't have a country. Without the rule of law, you don't have a republic. Without assimilation, you don't have a culture.

Most candidates seemed oblivious to the power of those issues, which were affecting millions of people, economically and socially. Trump owned those issues, and the intensity around them fueled his meteoric rise. I'd met Alabama coal miners who'd lost their livelihoods and the local steelworkers who blamed the dumping of Chinese steel for their jobs getting cut. I'll never fully understand how a billionaire from Queens intuitively understood Middle America better than Republican politicians who'd spent their entire lives in the heartland—but he did.

Yet I was still concerned about these character questions. Earlier that summer, during an event organized by several faith-based organizations, Trump had identified himself as a Protestant. But when asked whether he had ever felt inclined to ask God to forgive him for any of his mistakes, his answer raised some eyebrows, including mine.

"I don't think so," he said. "I think if I do something wrong . . . I just try and make it right. I don't bring God into that picture."

When I raised the topic, he went straight to one of his favorite tactics: citing polls in lieu of answering the question directly. "There was a recent poll where the evangelicals said that I was their number-one choice."

That gave me an opening to dive in. "There are a lot of evangelicals here in Alabama," I told him. "This is something that really matters to us. Faith is an important part of our lives."

"Yes," he said. "For me, too."

"Tell us a little bit about your stance on religious liberty," I continued. I told him many of my listeners were alarmed by details of recent Supreme Court decisions that found a church, a mosque, a synagogue, or another faith-based nonprofit could lose their tax-exempt status or be compelled to act against their sincerely held religious beliefs, such as not providing health care for abortion-inducing drugs or only conducting marriage ceremonies between a man and a woman.

"Talk to us," I went on, "about what a Trump administration would look like with regard to religious liberty."

He basically ignored all of that and went somewhere totally out of left— well, right—field. "There's an assault on anything having to do with Christianity," he replied without hesitation. "They don't want to use the word 'Christmas' anymore at department stores."

I leaned back in my chair and smirked. *Where's he going with this?*

"There's always lawsuits, and unfortunately a lot of those lawsuits are won by the other side. I will assault that. I will go so strongly against so many of these things. When they take away the word 'Christmas,' I go out of my way to use the word 'Christmas.'"

Whether someone agreed with this position or not—and my listeners loved it—it was easy to see the genius behind it. He'd taken a complicated subject and instead of discussing what he undoubtedly thought were boring things—like Supreme Court cases and the federal judiciary—he turned the issue into something people could instantly relate to.

Why don't "they" let us say "Merry Christmas" anymore? Trump's constant railing against "them" helped create a deep connection between himself and his fans. They were in this fight together—against the elites, the Republican establishment, the Democrats, or whoever else they believed was holding them down.

The clip went viral, sweeping across the internet in spite of the fact that we were talking about Christmas in the middle of the summer. And also despite the fact that just six months earlier President and Mrs. Obama had sent out a message from the White House wishing Americans a "Merry Christmas." This was my first direct exposure to Trump's ability to distill an argument down into a bite-sized nugget packed with symbolism, even if it wasn't entirely aligned with the facts. It was a speaking style built for the age of social media and 24/7 cable news. In a world of "Happy Holidays," he was a "Merry Christmas" missile, locked and loaded on the politically correct elites.

This was far from the only example of Trump's marketing genius. I also believed that "Make America Great Again" was perhaps the single most brilliant piece of political branding in modern American history. Though many on the left characterized the term as having racial undertones, not everyone saw the phrase that way. After all, even then-President Bill Clinton said in a 1991 speech, "I believe that together we can make America great again." The idea tapped into a deep-seated belief and anxiety among many Americans—people I knew growing up in the Deep South—that the country they had grown up in was slipping away from them. It reminded me of a scene from AMC's hit TV show *Mad Men,* which dramatized the inner workings of a Madison Avenue ad agency in the 1960s. In one of the show's most poignant scenes, Don Draper, played by actor Jon Hamm, introduces his plan to market a home slide projector made by Kodak.

With the lights in the room dimmed, Draper flips through photos showing pivotal moments in the life of his family—his wedding day, his pregnant wife, his young children playing together. "There's the rare occasion when the public can be engaged on a level beyond flash," he began. "If they have a sentimental bond with the product . . . nostalgia. It's delicate, but potent. . . . In Greek, 'nostalgia' literally means the pain from an old wound. It's a twinge in your heart, far more powerful than memory alone."

As the room sits in rapt silence, Draper explains that the slide projector is "a time machine. It goes backwards, forwards. It takes us to a place where we ache to go again. . . . It lets us travel the way a child travels—round and round, back home again, to a place where we know we were loved."

While Donald Trump would never speak in such sentimental terms, his political slogan was channeling a profound sense of nostalgia that lived inside millions of Americans. And much like Barack Obama's "Hope" and "Change" slogans, the power of MAGA was that each person could define the ambiguous phrase in whatever way suited them personally.

After our thirteen-minute interview ended, I pushed the Trump campaign to the back of my mind. The 2016 presidential race was a peripheral concern for me, especially as I was embroiled in a political circus much closer to home.

In March of 2016, a source contacted me with a tip. They had a thumb drive for me, which I could only retrieve if I was willing to meet behind an obscure Birmingham gas station at midnight.

As I drove up U.S. Highway 280, swerving in and out of traffic and making my way from suburban Birmingham toward the city's center, I thought about the events of the past year that had led up to this moment.

For many months the hottest rumor in Alabama politics was that long-married Republican Governor Robert Bentley, seventy-seven, had engaged in a long-running extramarital affair with his senior political adviser, Rebekah Caldwell Mason, forty-four, herself a married mother of three. At first the idea seemed so absurd, I dismissed it as politically motivated nonsense.

For the week prior to this midnight meeting, I had been in discussions with confidential sources who claimed to be in possession of secret audio recordings of Governor Bentley and Mrs. Mason. The recordings, I was told, contained explicit details of the Bentley-Mason affair. The sources were wary of their identities being revealed, and one of the sources expressed concerns about the Bentleys' grandchildren having to endure such embarrassment.

But they agreed on three key points:

Number one, that Bentley—the husband, father, church deacon, dermatologist, and now Governor—had allowed his once-sterling character to be corroded by power.

Number two, that Mason—the former local TV news anchor, small-time communications consultant, and now senior adviser to the Governor—had willfully destroyed the Bentleys' marriage of fifty years (they ultimately divorced) while simultaneously consolidating near-full control of the executive branch of Alabama's state government.

And number three, that the evidence they held could spark a seismic event in Alabama politics and bring the Bentley-Mason house of cards crumbling down.

In spite of their reservations about releasing the recordings, it was Governor Bentley's arrogance, one of the sources said, that was too much for them to endure. While Mrs. Bentley struggled to understand what all had happened and mourned what she felt like was catastrophic damage to her "Christian witness," her husband continued to give his mistress unfettered access to every part of his life.

As he walked down the center aisle of the Old House Chamber after delivering the State of the State address, Mrs. Mason was by his side. When he was photographed at a swanky Washington, D.C., gala typically reserved for only governors and first ladies, she was his date. And when any meeting in the capitol was concluded, she was always the last one left in the room with him. The frustration and anger simmered for months, but it was now boiling over.

I pulled behind the gas station to find my source waiting exactly where they said they would be. The episode felt like a dramatic scene out of a spy movie, complete with me hopping out of my black sedan, 9mm pistol tucked in my waistband. Not a single word was spoken. My source handed me the thumb drive, and we both turned around, stepped back into our vehicles, and sped away. When I made it home fifteen minutes later, I plugged the drive into my computer, opened the file, and within a few minutes knew it would change the course of Alabama's political history.

"You'd kiss me?" Bentley could be heard saying on the recordings. "I love that. You know I do love that." He went on to describe—in explicit detail—touching her, pulling her "in real close," and more. A lot more. "Hey, I love that, too," he said.

As I listened to the roughly forty-five minutes of conversations between the two lovers, I cringed. I also felt a strange sense of sadness about what had happened and what was surely to come. Families would never be the same. The Bentley and Mason children would endure undeserved ridicule. And the state that I loved would weather yet another torrent of embarrassing head-lines.

The next morning, I spoke on the phone with Mason for almost an hour. It was a roller-coaster conversation that made it abundantly clear that, in spite of her communications background and the obvious dangers of carrying on an intimate relationship with the Governor, there had not been much thought given to what they would say if they were ever caught red-handed.

Then came the excuses.

"Sometimes when you're a woman working in politics," she said, "you have to just let inappropriate comments roll off you like water off a duck's back." I stopped her from continuing and told her the recordings did not support that narrative. I could feel her anxiety growing.

"What should I do?" she asked. My advice was very simple: tell the truth.

It became clear that she was deeply conflicted. She did not want her children to hear what must be on the recordings. She did not want to be a front-page headline and the butt of every joke, like Alabama's version of Monica Lewinsky. But she also did not want to give up just yet. Her unlikely rise from small-town television anchor to the most powerful political operative in the state had not come easy, and she was not convinced the ride was over.

She asked for an hour to think. I agreed.

She texted me several times asking for more details about the recordings. She said that she and the Governor were meeting about what to do.

One hour turned into several hours, and I texted her one last time saying I could not wait any longer to run the story, even though I wanted to include their side—whatever that could be.

Silence.

I hit "publish," closed my computer, and sat back in my chair. My phone buzzed a few minutes later. It was a text from Rebekah Mason: "I'm sorry."

Yellowhammer became the first news outlet to publish the complete audio recordings. The story was international news within the hour, and was soon accompanied by allegations of corruption, that the Governor was abusing his office and taxpayer dollars in part to carry on this affair. It consumed Alabama for weeks.

Who made the tapes?

As it turns out, Bentley's wife of fifty years, Dianne, had grown suspicious of her husband. So while at their beach house one weekend, she hit "record" on her cell phone, set it down on a table, and went for a walk alone on the beach. The Governor took advantage of his sudden alone time by calling Mason. It was like a couple of high schoolers hiding their relationship from their parents, who just wouldn't understand the depths of their endless love.

In the coming months, I broke numerous other stories on the Bentley-Mason saga. They had a secret safe-deposit box together. He'd sometimes ditch his security detail to meet her in complete privacy as state troopers were left desperately searching for the "lost" Governor. He'd dispatched a state helicopter to retrieve his wallet from his home in north Alabama and fly it to him at his beach house. We dubbed that scandal "#WalletCopter," and Bentley defiantly admitted to it by saying, "I'm the Governor and I had to have money. I had to buy something to eat." A year later he resigned in disgrace, cutting a deal with prosecutors to avoid jail time after multiple charges were filed against him.

Yellowhammer had helped take down a creepy Governor. I was a conservative Republican, but proud that we had helped rid our party of one of its corrupt leaders. We had made a name for ourselves as investigative journalists.

But slowly, over the course of 2016, my attention was being pulled back into what was happening at the national level. Little did I know how deeply I'd become embedded in that story.

Day after day I would make the drive from my home in suburban Birmingham to Yellowhammer's downtown offices and marvel at "Teflon Don's" seeming invincibility in the face of nonstop media fury. It was fun to watch, but the furor surrounding his candidacy didn't fully hit home for me until the early fall of 2016.

Football season was under way and the Briarwood Christian School Lions, from suburban Birmingham, were slated to take on the inner-city Fairfield High School Tigers.

Just prior to the game, the Briarwood cheerleaders raised a banner for the football team to run through onto the field. MAKE AMERICA GREAT AGAIN—TRUMP THE TIGERS! the banner declared.

The seemingly innocuous play on words sparked an immediate—and furious—backlash.

"It's ridiculous. To me, it's an insult because I don't like Trump and Trump doesn't like my people either," an African American Fairfield student told a local television station, which was breathlessly covering the supposed scandal.

"This should not be going down this close to me!" another student added.

In response to the blowback, Briarwood, a private, predominantly white school, immediately backed down. "Briarwood Christian School desires to publicly apologize for any understandable offense caused by the sign used during a recent football game," they said in a statement released to local media. "Above all we desire to seek forgiveness of any who were offended."

This was a silly banner, not an endorsement of a political campaign. To me, the whole fiasco looked like the scourge of political correctness that Trump had been railing against, and the faux outrage over the banner compelled me to personally incentivize schools to stand up to the PC police. I relished being a political troublemaker.

At the time, the Clinton campaign was struggling to explain why Secretary Clinton had set up a private email server to house her communications—including some of a classified nature—while serving as Secretary of State. Additionally, tens of thousands of the emails had inexplicably been deleted, apparently lost forever. So, maybe just to be a malcontent, I offered to donate one thousand dollars to the first high school football team who ran through a pregame banner that said HILLARY WOULD DELETE THIS BANNER IF SHE COULD.

The episode drove local media coverage for several days, and was generally amusing to me, but it also came at a time when I was starting to really consider what the 2016 presidential race meant for the country. I stumbled across a pseudonymous essay titled "The Flight 93 Election" in *The Claremont Review of Books,* published by the conservative think tank the Claremont Institute. It was driving a lot of conversation online and I wanted to see what all the fuss was about.

2016 is the Flight 93 election: charge the cockpit or you die. You may die anyway. You—or the leader of your party—may make it into the cockpit and not know how to fly or land the plane. There are no guarantees.

Except one: if you don't try, death is certain. To compound the metaphor: a Hillary Clinton presidency is Russian Roulette with a semi-auto. With Trump, at least you can spin the cylinder and take your chances.

That struck me as roughly correct. Yes, America is bigger than any single election, and no, I didn't think we had al-Qaeda terrorists in the pilot's seat in Washington. But I was deeply concerned about the country's trajectory. I was—and am—a conservative. But, as I demonstrated during the Bentley case, I was more than willing to see the faults in the Republican Party or its leaders. What bothered me the most in 2016 was not just a dispute between political parties, or ideologies, but something larger.

Like many Bernie Sanders supporters who still hadn't gotten behind the Democratic nominee, I thought Hillary Clinton was a corrupt member of America's ruling class—the "masters of the universe," as Jeff Sessions liked to call them. This included leaders of both parties in Washington, D.C., who made all sorts of promises, got richer and more powerful as they went along, and never actually delivered for the people they were supposed to represent.

As I snaked my way up Highway 280 from my house to the office, I considered the moment in American history, and whether I was doing enough myself. Did the challenges facing our country—on which I believed Donald Trump was generally correct from a policy perspective—supersede the significant character concerns I had with him as a human being?

This was a question that Senator Jeff Sessions had clearly wrestled with to some degree as well. I'd asked him about it during an interview on my radio program.

"I think good people in Alabama are concerned about [Trump's character and integrity]," he had told me. "I've tried to think about it, and none of us are perfect, but . . . anybody who wants to be president needs to conduct himself . . . as a person of character. He does seem to have a good family . . .

the kind of people that must have had some good values when they were raised. He doesn't drink. So I understand and I'm hearing that, and I appreciate the concerns."

As I drove toward my office and thought about whether I wanted to have a role in the 2016 race, I decided to call Senator Sessions on his cell to get his advice.

Although many people have taken issue with some of his positions on various issues, particularly his hard-line stance on immigration, I knew him as a decent and honorable man. My wife, Megan, and I had gotten to know him and his wife of forty-seven years, Mrs. Mary, over long dinner conversations. They loved their family. They weren't engrossed by the trappings of power. Jeff Sessions had a reputation for wanting to do what he believed was the right thing—to the point that his Senate colleagues called him "the Boy Scout" behind his back. Sometimes this was said with genuine respect. Other times it was said in frustration.

I told him that I thought I might want to take a leave of absence to join Trump's campaign for the home stretch—to do my part, whatever I could. I could hear the excitement in his voice.

"If nothing else, it'll be a once-in-a-lifetime experience," he said. "And if he wins, who knows what could happen. I'm happy to call and set it up."

As it turned out, the campaign was excited I was willing to come on board and made me an offer to come join right away as a communications adviser. With the opportunity now in front of me, there was no way I could just sit back and complain any longer. My wife and I discussed it, prayed about it, and decided that if there was an opportunity for me to have any influence, even a small one, on the campaign, on the country's future—on Trump himself—it would be worth the effort.

Days later, I announced I was taking a leave of absence as CEO of Yellowhammer and moved into an apartment in midtown Manhattan. I was officially aboard the Trump train. I didn't know yet whether it would run off the tracks and go down in a blaze of glory, or steamroll the Clinton machine on its way into the history books. And nobody else did, either, not even the candidate himself.

2

THE DEPLORABLES

The first time I ever walked into Trump Tower's marble lobby, I was dragging a rolling suitcase behind me and had a blue backpack slung over my shoulder. I had come straight from the airport, and these two bags contained all of the belongings I had brought to get me through the next few months.

"Fourteenth floor, please," I told the elevator operator.

"Right away, sir," he replied. He was a middle-aged African American man, and he was impeccably dressed: black tuxedo jacket with gold buttons and the letters "TT" embroidered on the sleeves—in gold as well, of course—gray vest, black bow tie.

"Where are you from?" he asked, facing away from me as the doors slid shut and we began our ascent.

"Alabama," I said, laughing. "I only said three words and you could already tell?"

He smiled.

"Well, I knew it wasn't New York. I haven't seen you here before. Do you work for Mr. Trump's campaign?"

"Just started," I said, looking down at the backpack and luggage I'd set down on the floor in front of me. "I got off the plane at LaGuardia and came straight here."

There was a brief silence and I wondered to myself what his day must be like. An elevator operator, dressed to the nines and riding up and down all day—in 2016? His sunny disposition had certainly made my ride more pleasant, and nothing oozed "Trump" more than over-the-top service. But I wasn't sure there was a single elevator operator left in my entire home state.

A bell dinged, bringing the elevator to a stop, and the doors slid open.

"Here we are," he said. His body was still facing away from me, but he turned his head to the left to look me in the eyes for the first time. "Good luck, sir." I thanked him and stepped out of the elevator into a small, empty lobby.

In contrast to its surroundings, the campaign's office space was decidedly less Trumpian. Commercial-grade gray carpet stretched from wall to wall. A standard receptionist's desk sat unoccupied in the middle of the room, and the white walls were bare—no gold or marble in sight. To my right, a large glass wall with magnetic-locking doors separated the lobby from the rest of the offices. I tugged on the handles, but it was clear I would need an ID to swipe in. As I turned back around, a wooden door opened on the other side of the room, and four staffers in their early twenties emerged. I caught the door before it closed and suddenly found myself in a hub of activity.

The room was long—roughly four times as wide as it was deep. Dozens of desks were positioned in two long rows stretching from end to end. All of them were facing a bank of eight flat-screen TVs neatly hanging on the wall with no cords in sight. Seven of the TVs were muted, but one near the center was blaring MSNBC. In the back of the room, giant windowpanes overlooked an atrium down on the ground floor.

Roughly a dozen staffers sat in front of their laptops, most of them alternating between looking at their computers and glancing up at one of the TVs. As I walked past them all, a few peeked up at me, but most didn't pay any attention to the random stranger walking by. It felt a little like my first day of middle school. As I put my bags down on the floor next to a wall, someone in the back of the room piped up.

"Hey, could somebody change this TV over to CNN?" he said to no one in particular.

Nobody moved, but I happened to see a TV remote sitting on the desk right in front of me. Picking it up, I pointed it at the second screen from the left and pressed the channel button "up."

Seven of the eight TVs all changed channels in unison.

"Bro!" a guy in the front row said emphatically as he got out of his seat. Taking the remote out of my hand, he walked right up to each TV's sensor and changed the channels back one by one.

"Don't mess with Surabian's TVs," another staffer in his early twenties said, laughing and sticking out his hand as he approached me. "I'm Kaelan Dorr. And you must be Cliff. I heard you'd be here at some point today."

Surabian, Kaelan explained, was the war room director. I'd come to find out that he was a shrewd political operative with a libertarian streak. His knowledge of American politics—including in-depth and random insight into seemingly every congressional district—was surpassed only by his Rain Man–like knowledge of the history of professional wrestling. "And that's Cheung," Kaelan continued, pointing to the campaign's director of rapid response. I recognized him. There had been a round of stories when he left his job running public affairs for the Ultimate Fighting Championship (UFC) to join the campaign. Coming in at about three hundred pounds, with a shaved head and hands the size of bear paws, Steven Cheung looked like he could cave in a grown man's chest with his fist. "And this is Chris Byrne," Kaelan said. Neatly dressed in an open-collared shirt and blue blazer, Byrne stood up and shook my hand. He'd worked as a producer for Sean Hannity's Fox News show, he explained, but was now spearheading the campaign's regional media operation.

After a few more introductions, Kaelan walked me over to his boss's office. When I walked in, Jason Miller, the campaign's senior communications adviser, was yelling at a TV screen mounted on his wall.

"Come on, Hallie!" he yelled as NBC's Hallie Jackson delivered her latest report direct to the camera. As I would come to find out, one of the ways Trump would test his top communications aide was by telling him what topics he wanted to be highlighted in the media that day. Reporters liked it because they could say, "According to a senior source inside the Trump campaign. . . ." And Trump liked it because he could see that his communications shop was effectively pushing his narrative. This time, however, it looked like Jason had failed to deliver what the boss wanted.

Jason, in his early forties, had spent the previous fifteen years working his way up the ladder of D.C.'s political consulting class. He'd run countless House and Senate races, usually for antiestablishment, "outsider" candidates. In fact, he'd managed to get himself blackballed by the National Republican Senatorial Committee for helping conservatives challenge establishment incumbents. Most recently he'd served as the top comms staffer for Senator Ted Cruz's ill-fated presidential campaign. He'd joined the Trump team just ahead of the Republican National Convention, when it was clear that Trump was going to win the nomination.

As the story was told to me by several people in the coming months, Trump had asked his son-in-law, Jared Kushner, who was leading Ted Cruz's communications. Cruz's campaign was setting him on fire day after day and he wanted to know who was behind it. When Kushner told him it was Miller, whose television appearances had impressed Trump, the candidate asked for him to be brought in for an interview. Once Miller arrived in Trump's office, Trump pushed him to dish on Cruz. Miller deflected at first, but finally said he didn't think it would be right for him to speak ill of his former boss. "That's good," Trump told him. "If you had, I wouldn't have hired you." And with that, Miller—or "my Jace," as Trump would end up calling him—was brought into Trump's tight-knit inner circle.

Miller told me he wanted me to help sharpen the campaign's messaging. So one of my first tasks was to overhaul the way we produced talking points— the playbook for how allies all around the country would talk about the issues of the day. In addition to that, he wanted me to work with Dan Scavino, the director of social media, to help his team develop the campaign's social media reach outside of Trump's massive personal accounts. Other than that, he just wanted me to fill any void I saw in the operation.

"Hey, they're back," Kaelan said, popping his head in as Jason and I wrapped up our first meeting. Trump had just arrived back at the Tower, along with the small group of aides who traveled with him on his Boeing 757 jet. Trump called the plane "T-Bird," but to everyone else it was known as Trump Force One.

Moments later, Stephen Miller entered. I'd known him for years as Senator Sessions's communications director. He was now Trump's speechwriter and often warmed up the crowd for him at rallies. He stood in the doorway staring at me for a moment. "What are you doing here?" he deadpanned. It would have come across as rude if it were anyone else, but I'd known Stephen long enough to understand that it's just how he is. He was often the funniest guy in the room, thriving as the center of attention as he poked fun at people and bragged about his brilliance. Other times it just felt like an act— overcompensation for his own insecurities. He had always been self-conscious about the perception that he was a fringe character, both ideologically and socially. But now he was one of the closest advisers to the Republican nominee for president. Suddenly at the top of this emerging new power structure, Miller's social response was to buddy up to other top aides while harshly condescending to anyone he perceived as being below his newfound status. In short, he was just treating others the way he had been treated for so long.

By the time I met him, in his mid-twenties, he already had a fully formed political ideology and worldview. I often disagreed with him but respected that he knew what he believed and why he believed it. And he could write—I mean *really* write, and fast. While working in Sessions's Senate office, he'd single-handedly written what amounted to the definitive "anti-amnesty" handbook. It was full of statistics and messaging recommendations. Immigration hard-liners had used it as their road map to successfully kill a bipartisan effort to pass so-called "comprehensive immigration reform." Since joining the Trump campaign, he'd helped the candidate flesh out his populist platform, and based on the next conversation I had, he was impressing the people who mattered.

Jared Kushner walked into Jason Miller's office right behind Stephen. Jason told him who I was and what I'd be doing on the campaign. Kushner welcomed me to the team and began introducing me to Stephen, who told him we already knew each other through Senator Sessions.

"This is our key man right here," Kushner told me, putting his hand on Stephen's shoulder. "If we took out key-man insurance on any one person on the campaign, it'd be him. We'd be lost without him."

If Stephen Miller overcompensated for his insecurities, Kushner seemed to take the opposite approach. The candidate's son-in-law had a relaxed vibe that reflected his unassailable position in the Trump orbit. Unlike most of the other men on the campaign, who usually wore suits and ties, Kushner was wearing a chill long-sleeve blue cardigan with a green vest over it. A black leather bag was strapped over his shoulder and hanging at his waist, like someone might wear on a trendy college campus. I'd seen him countless times on television, but I'd never heard him speak. His voice was soft, but there was a quiet confidence in everything he said. Upon finding out I had run a successful digital media company, he immediately wanted to pick my brain to see if anything I'd learned along the way could be useful. While the Trump team was reinventing what a presidential campaign looked like, Kushner was clearly looking to soak up knowledge and information wherever he could.

"We need to get you connected to our digital director, Brad Parscale," he said. "We're killing it on social and digital and small-dollar donations." He was right. It would become public a few weeks later that Trump's small-dollar donations—two hundred dollars or less—were dwarfing every other campaign in history. He'd built a donor base of over two million Americans, a milestone it had taken the Clintons decades and multiple campaigns to reach, and he'd done it in just three months.

Before I left Trump Tower for the first time that night, I wandered around the fourteenth floor to get my bearings. The layout was basically a giant square. If you walked in one direction long enough you would arrive back where you began. Along the way there were several open-concept offices with desks pushed up against the walls. Around the perimeter of the square were glassed-in offices with external views overlooking some of the world's most exclusive real estate. As I walked by them I noticed printouts labeling offices for campaign manager Kellyanne Conway and deputy campaign manager David Bossie. Neither one of them was inside. But as I approached the office of campaign CEO Steve Bannon, I noticed he happened to be standing in there alone.

Bannon looked like he hadn't shaved in weeks. Like Kushner, he was also dressed atypically, but hardly in a style that anyone would characterize as "trendy" or "cool." He was wearing black-rimmed glasses, an army-style jacket over multiple open-collared shirts, and khaki slacks. If he had been wandering around the streets outside Trump Tower, instead of inside it, passersby would have handed him their spare change.

"Steve?" I said, leaning slightly into the room.

"Yeah," he replied without looking up from his phone.

"I wanted to take a second to introduce myself," I continued.

"Give me a minute," he said, still not looking up.

For the next—well, it felt like five solid minutes of silence, I stood patiently as Bannon finished his email. When he finally hit "send," he still didn't look at me, choosing instead to walk over to his external window as if there was something urgent needing his attention down on Fifth Avenue.

"Okay, what's up?" he asked, facing away from me. "Whaddaya got?"

"Uh, I just started on the campaign today and wanted to introduce myself. I'm Cliff Sims, from Yellowhammer News down in Alabama."

He spun around suddenly. His voice was filled with energy. "The f—ing Yellowhammer is here?! The Hammer?! Epic. I know Yellowhammer. I followed it. I want you weaponizing everything. We're not being aggressive enough. F— anyone who tells you not to do something. Let's start wrecking some s——, okay? Good. Go." He buried his head back in his phone and started typing again. The conversation was over. But that was positive, right? We had met for the first time minutes earlier and he sent me on my way like I was his closest confidant and with the fate of the campaign in my hands. Of course, I wasn't entirely sure what to "weaponize," or how to do it, or if my new friend Steve had the authority to offer such direction to me. Or even if he'd remember me the next time I saw him. But I decided to assume that this was Steve's way of giving me the green light to jump in and contribute wherever I could, which was what I planned to do anyway.

When I left Trump Tower that first night, I decided to walk, instead of taking a taxi, to the apartment the campaign had secured for me at the corner of Sixth and Forty-fifth Street, twelve blocks away. As I walked down Fifth Avenue, I saw St. Patrick's Cathedral lit up in spectacular fashion. Its marble spires stretched so far into the Manhattan sky that I couldn't see their tops. On the other side of the street, I immediately recognized 30 Rock. The iconic Art Deco skyscraper overlooked a scene that had been familiar to me since childhood. All that was missing was the ten-story Christmas tree, which would arrive soon enough. I'd visited New York City numerous times before, but now I was living here—even if for only a short period of time.

When I finally made it to my apartment, I opened the door to a panoramic view of midtown Manhattan. It was a fully furnished two-bedroom near the top of a forty-eight-floor high-rise. I had the whole thing to myself, compliments of the campaign. I didn't find out until later that most staffers' accommodations weren't nearly as luxe, and I'm not entirely sure why I had it so good. I walked over to the window, and the neon glow of Times Square, just a block away, hit my face. I was a long, long way from home.

In the coming days, I wrote speech inserts for Mr. Trump's campaign rallies and strategized on ways to expand our social media reach by tapping into the large online following of our top surrogates. But my primary role was developing our messaging. Following Trump's lead by emulating the way he liked to talk about various issues, I'd draft talking points for senior campaign aides, coalition leaders, and TV surrogates. I'd get emails from people all over the country asking what the campaign's message was on just about every issue under the sun.

Occasionally Omarosa Manigault, who was traversing the country on a "Women for Trump" tour, would reach out for direction on how best to answer questions on issues related to women and minorities. I'd never met her, but I'd seen enough of *The Apprentice* to know that she'd earned her spot on *TV Guide*'s list of "The 60 Nastiest TV Villains of All Time." So let's just say I did my best to get her what she needed. I figured she was trouble I didn't need.

I realized quickly that the Trump campaign experience was dramatically different for two main groups of staffers: the small cohort who traveled on the plane, and the larger group who stayed behind at Trump Tower. The former spent most of their days traversing the country. They fed off the energy of the crowds and mood of the candidate. The latter rarely traveled farther than a few blocks' radius around Trump Tower. With rare exceptions, I was in the latter group. Most of us on the tiny communications team became fast friends. We ate lunch together almost every day, often riding down into the cafeteria on the same escalator made famous when Trump rode down it to announce his candidacy.

When Mr. Trump was preparing to take the stage at a rally, which I usually watched on television, I would sound a tornado-siren-style alarm on my computer and yell "Battle stations!" to the delight of our merry band of misfits. We were each doing the job of numerous Clinton staffers. The *New York Post* ran a report a month before Election Day revealing that the Clinton campaign had literally five times more staffers than we did. We couldn't care less. The way we saw it, they were the spoiled rich kids whose mommies and daddies bought them BMWs for their sixteenth birthday. We were still riding the bus to school and wearing last year's fashions. But if a fight broke out in the lunchroom, you'd much rather have us on your side. We came in early, stayed late, and heard the candidate's stump speech so many times that we could laughingly predict when the chants of "Build the wall," "CNN sucks," "Lock her up," and "Drain the swamp" were about to begin.

Bannon later described our war room team to *Politico* as "f—ing killers. . . . These are my psychos who do all this s—. They don't sleep. They don't care." We weren't entirely sure what to make of that. But he was spot-on about the lack of sleep, at least. It didn't take long, however, for me to realize we were playing with live ammo.

In September 2016, Alicia Machado, a former Miss Universe, accused

Trump of calling her "Miss Piggy." According to her allegations, Trump, who owned the Miss Universe pageant during Machado's reign in the mid-1990s, had been upset with her because she'd gained weight and decided to ridicule her for it. Pretending that it was suddenly news that Donald Trump said something offensive about someone, cable news channels covered this particular story nonstop for days, especially after Secretary Clinton brought it up during the first debate.

During that same debate, Trump had hinted at his own response—bringing up past accusations against the Clinton family, a subject that was decidedly not covered nonstop on the news. "I was going to say something extremely rough to Hillary, to her family," he said. "And I said to myself, 'I can't do it. I just can't do it. It's inappropriate. It's not nice.' But she's spent hundreds of millions of dollars on negative ads on me. . . . I will tell you this. . . . It's not nice."

Back at Trump Tower the next day, Jason Miller asked me to work up some talking points on what we might say if Trump were to change his mind and decide to go on the attack.

"How hot do we want these talking points to be?" I asked.

"Make them pretty spicy," Miller replied. "Not, like, nuclear, but let's start hot and then tone them down if we need to." It wasn't entirely clear what that meant, but it was as much direction as I was going to get, and I thought I had a decent idea of what he wanted.

Walking out of his office, I noticed Sarah Huckabee Sanders, the daughter of former Arkansas Governor Mike Huckabee, sitting in the back of the war room. Her family had been dealing with the Clinton machine in her home state since before any of them were household names. Sarah's job on the campaign was organizing pro-Trump coalitions in the faith community, and she went about it quietly in the midst of the war room chaos. When I introduced myself, she reminded me that her husband had been the top consultant on Robert Bentley's Alabama gubernatorial campaign. They'd closely followed my coverage of his scandals.

"I don't know what happened to him," she said. "He went from this sweet country doctor to . . . I don't even know what. It's sad."

I agreed, told her it was nice to have a fellow Southerner on the campaign with me, then went straight to work compiling information about all the times Hillary Clinton was said to have intimidated or sought to discredit Bill Clinton's past sexual accusers. It was a lengthy list. Then I drafted talking points that surrogates could use to go on the attack during interviews, such as: "Mr. Trump has never treated women the way Hillary Clinton and her husband did when they actively worked to destroy Bill Clinton's accusers." "Hillary Clinton bullied and smeared women like Paula Jones, Gennifer Flowers, and Monica Lewinsky," added another.

This was pretty controversial stuff. For many years, especially after the political fallout of impeachment, Republican candidates had refused to "go there" on Bill Clinton's women issues, including accusations of sexual assault and rape. Only those on the far right ever mentioned that Hillary Clinton had played a role in bullying accusers. Atypically for a man like Trump, who tended to say whatever was on his mind, he had largely stayed away from this, too. Perhaps this was because he'd faced his own accusations of sexual misconduct.

When I was done, I emailed the document around to our small team for review. It was more of a thought exercise than a work product that would ever be deployed. I didn't think much more about it for the next few hours.

It was business as usual in the war room, until Kaelan Dorr blurted out, "Oh, not good!" and pointed up at one of the TVs.

CNN's chyron at the bottom of the screen made my heart drop into my stomach.

TRUMP CAMPAIGN TALKING POINTS: BRING UP MONICA.

They spent the next several minutes discussing this shift in direction for the Trump campaign, quoting my draft talking points. An online story hit our in-boxes a few minutes later.

It's still unclear exactly how this happened, but someone in the group that received the draft document mistook it for a finished product that needed to go out. So it had been sent to every Trump surrogate in the country—hundreds of them, maybe thousands.

Moments later, deputy campaign manager David Bossie stormed into the war room with the CNN article printed out.

Bossie was a hard-nosed former firefighter. In the nineties he'd served as chief investigator for the House Oversight Committee that investigated then-

President Bill Clinton. He'd gone on to run Citizens United, a conservative activist group most famous for winning a Supreme Court case abolishing limits on how much companies and nonprofits could spend on political advertising. For two solid decades, nobody had been a bigger Clinton foe than Bossie, and even he wasn't sure what to think about these talking points.

"What. Is. This?" he demanded in a tone that verged on outrage.

I was mortified. In other campaigns, people got fired over things like this. Years before, Donna Brazile had been forced to resign from the Dukakis campaign for even mentioning accusations of adultery by George H. W. Bush. Was I next?

Bossie went into Jason Miller's office and shut the door, only to emerge minutes later.

"Hammer!" he yelled out, looking for me. "You wrote these? I mean, no one's going to accuse me of being soft, but dude."

"They weren't supposed to go out," I protested. "But everyone said they wanted to see some hot talking points, so there they are."

"Hot?" he said, his voice raising with his eyebrows. "Hot?! Ha." He crumpled up the printed-out CNN article and threw it in the garbage. "You know I was a firefighter, right? Okay. This isn't hot. This is arson."

Bossie was no-nonsense and extraordinarily loyal—to Mr. Trump and to anyone in the foxhole with him. He was giving me a hard time for being a part of the talking points fiasco, but he would have defended me to the death if anyone had actually tried to make it a real issue.

"Somebody supervise the arsonist," he said, walking out of the room.

Trump never mentioned the talking points himself—something tells me he probably liked them—and I quickly realized that such a misstep was light-years from a fireable offense in this campaign.

We didn't know it at the time, but if those talking points were hot, what would come later would be Chernobyl.

For most of the country, Fridays are the best day of the workweek. Everyone looks forward to heading home to start the weekend. But in Trump Tower, that day in particular was met with trepidation. Late in the campaign, it felt like a new, salacious story was dropped on us every Friday afternoon. "Leak 'em if you've got 'em!" Jason Miller would joke about how Clinton oppo researchers must have approached the day. The stories would then lead all of the Sunday talk shows, setting the tone for the following week.

On Friday, October 7, 2016, our comms team arrived at Trump Tower in time for our daily 7:30 A.M. conference call, then hunkered down in anticipation of what was to come. Sure enough, word slowly began to spread through the team that *The Washington Post* had obtained a video of Mr. Trump making lewd comments about women. We sat quietly for hours in the war room, anxiously anticipating the video's release.

"It's up," Surabian shouted. The short Armenian stood up out of his chair but continued hunching over his computer, sending an email alert to senior campaign staff and communications aides.

"Donald Trump bragged in vulgar terms about kissing, groping and trying to have sex with women during a 2005 conversation caught on a hot microphone," wrote the *Post*'s David Fahrenthold, "saying that 'when you're a star, they let you do it,' according to a video obtained by *The Washington Post*."

We'd endured plenty of hits that would have sunk most campaigns, but this was, even for Trump, a devastating blow. Americans have become numb to the constant flow of accusations and hit pieces during presidential campaigns. But video is a powerful medium. It displays nonverbal communication, so viewers can read body language. It includes audio so listeners can hear tone and discern the meaning beneath the words. Trump had mastered video as a communications medium, and now the same medium that had catapulted him to stardom was threatening to take him down. Within minutes the video was running simultaneously on every single one of the war room's eight TVs.

The entire atmosphere of the campaign immediately changed. On most days, our small communications team would be in nonstop contact with reporters and cable show anchors, working to correct stories, add our perspective, and shape the coverage of the day.

This was the first time that the coverage was so bad—and the backlash so severe—that there was essentially nothing we could do. The carnage was uncontrollable. Surabian was sending a nonstop torrent of emails to campaign staff. It was part of his job to "flag" important stories as they were breaking so everyone had situational awareness in real time. In this instance, he was sending email after email—it must have been hundreds in total—with statements of condemnation and withdrawals of support from prominent figures. "I feel like the prophet of doom, or something," he said ominously.

Many of our most loyal campaign surrogates refused to go on TV. Almost immediately, Republican National Committee staff stopped answering our phone calls, texts, and emails. At one point they even removed campaign staffers from their internal communications alerts, severing the operational ties that had bound the teams together since the convention. The drumbeat for Mr. Trump to exit the race began almost immediately.

RNC research director Raj Shah texted his counterpart on the campaign, Andy Hemming, summing up the attitude of many in the establishment wing of the GOP. "u wanna hear something a little f—ed up?" Shah asked. "I'm kinda enjoying this, some justice. I honestly don't think it's the worst thing he's done but he somehow got passes for the other acts."

"Trump is a deplorable," he concluded, echoing Hillary Clinton's controversial description of Trump supporters.

Campaign staffers' friends, family members, and acquaintances started peppering us with texts and phone calls asking if we were planning to abandon the sinking ship.

"You headed home yet?" one friend in Alabama texted me at the height of the fury.

I silenced my phone and walked down to the fifth floor of Trump Tower, which once housed the set of *The Apprentice*. It was now a large, open, warehouse-style room, with some tables and chairs and a portable basketball hoop in the center, which had been brought in by campaign aides as a way to blow off steam.

I grabbed a ball and shot by myself for a while—and thought. Had it been a mistake to come here? I had played a major role in exposing accusations of sexual misconduct by a Republican governor in Alabama. He never recovered. How could Trump come back from this? How would I?

Tired of shooting and not ready to return to the nonstop news coverage in the war room, I spent the next hour scrolling through Twitter and digesting the onslaught. Then I heard footsteps clicking on the concrete floor and glanced up from my phone.

To my surprise, Mr. Trump had walked into the room. To that point, I had not been around him very much. He was usually either crisscrossing the country, in his office twelve floors above the war room, or in his penthouse looking down on the world from above. Instinctively, I stood up. He was wearing a blue-and-white-striped tie and his usual dark suit with an American flag lapel pin. He clearly wasn't in a hurry to get anywhere. The fifth floor was home to the campaign's video recording studio. It was typically used for campaign aides to do satellite television hits, but tonight it was being used to record Trump's response to the *Access Hollywood* tape. Turns out, he had grown exasperated with the recording and walked into the cavernous room to take a break.

The thing I remember most about his demeanor was how remarkably calm he was. There may have been moments throughout the day when he was angry or frustrated or flew off the handle, but I wasn't there to see them. The Trump I saw was somewhat defiant, but more than that, relaxed—placid. The most embarrassed I ever remember feeling was when someone pulled my shorts down in front of my entire elementary school class at recess. I can still feel my face turning red decades later when I picture everyone laughing about it. Meanwhile, the entire country was coming unglued about Trump and he didn't even seem flustered. It was strange—but also inspired a sense of, well, *maybe we'll actually get through this.* Of course, Trump had been through major celebrity scandals for decades—two bitter and very public divorces, for example—and he was toughened by them in ways most of us weren't. (Or would ever want to be.)

Also sitting quietly in the room was a swimsuit model in her early twenties who had volunteered for the campaign. She had a large following on Instagram, but none of her fans were more committed to her than the unmarried campaign guys on the fourteenth floor.

Seeing her sitting alone at her laptop, Mr. Trump made a beeline for her, and she stood up to greet him.

"What do you think about all of this—the video and what everyone is saying?" he asked her with what seemed to be genuine curiosity.

"Oh, I don't understand why everyone is so upset," she said without hesitation.

He didn't seem to believe that.

"C'mon," he pressed. "Tell me what you really think about it. It's okay."

"I don't think people will care after a few days," she said confidently. "I was totally not offended—not offended at all, Mr. Trump."

With that, he smiled, shook her hand, turned around, and locked eyes with me on the other side of the room.

"Not offended," he said with a shrug. No big deal.

He walked by and tapped me on the chest with the back of his hand. Maybe he saw the doubt on my face. "Don't worry about it. We'll be fine, believe me."

He walked back into the tiny studio and finished the recording. "See you at the debate on Sunday," the video concluded, at his insistence.

Campaign staffers later came to call it "the hostage video" because we thought it resembled the terrorist videos where they force someone to read a prepared script. His face wasn't exactly in focus and the lighting wasn't great, but it got the job done.

With the video set to be released, we all assembled in the war room to watch the reaction. Our usual squad was joined by Bannon and campaign manager Kellyanne Conway. Now in her late forties, Kellyanne had spent the previous two decades building a public opinion research firm called The Polling Company. She had deep ties to conservative donors around the country and had run a pro-Cruz super PAC during the primary. She was initially brought onto Trump's campaign to advise the candidate on how to appeal to female voters, but she had been elevated to campaign manager in August 2016 upon the ouster of Paul Manafort. She was a Jersey girl, sometimes standoffish, but had thrived for decades in a business dominated by alpha males. She had earned a reputation on the campaign for being willing to go on any network at any moment and fight tooth and nail. Trump loved her for it.

Though she held the title of campaign manager—and was justifiably proud to be the first woman to manage a successful presidential campaign—Kellyanne functionally acted as the top spokesperson. Bannon, who held the title of CEO, was focused on preserving Trump as the vessel through which his populist nationalist ideas could hit the big time. He was also too ADD to manage much of anything. By my observation, if anyone besides Donald Trump was in charge of his presidential campaign, that person was Jared. He didn't need a title to be in charge.

But Kellyanne was a fighter, and a good one. When she arrived in the war room on *Access Hollywood* night, she looked exhausted, even frazzled. Her hair was slightly disheveled as she plopped down in a chair just behind Surabian and Cheung and put her cell phone down on a desk beside her. Her body language made it clear that she wasn't interested in making small talk, so everyone quietly went about their business as we waited for the video to post.

"None of our female surrogates will go out to defend us," Cheung whispered. "Except Scottie Nell Hughes. She's about to get her head kicked in on CNN."

The video began playing, and for ninety-five seconds the entire war room watched in total silence.

For reaction, CNN had assembled a panel on Don Lemon's show that included Hughes and André Bauer, a pro-Trump former Lieutenant Governor of South Carolina, and anti-Trump commentators Tara Setmayer, Bob Beckel, and Ana Navarro.

"This race is over," Beckel declared. "Tomorrow morning the money will dry up, the Republicans will start to hide. Trump has no place to go. This race effectively, as of tonight, is no longer a presidential race. . . . You might as well accept it."

Navarro was indignant. "Every single Republican is going to have to answer the question, 'What did you do the day you saw the tape of this man boasting about grabbing a woman's pussy?'"

When Hughes asked Navarro to stop saying the "p-word" because her daughter might be watching, the segment devolved into a screaming match.

The moment it ended, Bannon was the first to speak.

"Yes. Perfect. Let's go. Back in the game." I suppose that was the sort of thing you had to say at the moment. We were still standing. Move on. Keep fighting.

I still had my doubts.

I walked into one of the offices just off of the war room, closed the door behind me, and lay down on a couch. The statements Trump had made in the *Access Hollywood* video were abhorrent. Watching people defend them was a perfect example of why being a surrogate on TV never appealed to me— not for Trump or any other candidate. How could people go on TV, night after night, and defend things they knew in their heart were indefensible? But the question facing me in that moment was whether I should continue on the campaign at all.

As I thought about it, every argument I could come up with for why I should consider quitting was selfish: What would people say about *me*? What would my friends at church think about *me*? How will being attached to this debacle affect *me* in the future? Me, me, me. As I considered the bigger picture, I couldn't think of a single thing that would have been made better—for my country, my family, or myself—by Hillary Clinton being elected President.

I joined the campaign with no illusions about who Trump was—a deeply flawed man. But the balance of the Supreme Court was on the line, which mattered to me and so many others. In my view, this really was the Flight 93 Election: "charge the cockpit or you die."

I also thought about my Christian friends in Egypt, where I had enjoyed a lengthy visit earlier in the year. In 2013, they had taken to the streets by the millions to protest the Islamist government of Mohamed Morsi of the Muslim Brotherhood. They'd vocally supported the rise of military general Abdel Fattah el-Sisi. He wanted to crush ISIS in the Sinai and promised Christians—and other religious minorities—greater civic equality. El-Sisi wasn't George Washington. He wasn't going to rise to power, only to give it back to the people in an act of democratic heroism. He would still control a largely authoritarian, militarized state. And he was a devout Muslim. In short, he was far from everything Christians wanted. But he was far better than the alternative, so they campaigned hard for him.

Other sincere, well-meaning people of faith considered the same facts that I did, but came to a different conclusion with regard to supporting Trump. I respected them for refusing to violate their conscience. But in the coming weeks, when American Christians demeaned their Trump-supporting brothers and sisters for lacking moral courage, I often thought of Egypt. What about Egyptian Christians, whose churches were bombed and whose dead bodies were paraded through the streets while you flaunted your moral superiority on Twitter from the comfort of your couch? Did they lack moral courage, as well, for supporting a Muslim authoritarian over an Islamist who wanted the streets to run red with their blood?

That's a pretty hot take, obviously—probably hotter than the "arsonist" talking points I'd written about Clinton's accusers—so I never said this publicly. But these were the things I was thinking. They were the things I needed to tell myself in order to keep going on this campaign.

Lying in my bed that night, a scene from Harper Lee's novel *To Kill a Mockingbird* came to mind. This may seem random, but people from Alabama will understand. Lee's our most famous author, and the book is set in our home state. It's the pinnacle of our literary canon. At one point late in the book, one of the characters, Miss Maudie, consoles a crying girl and offers her some simple but profound advice: "Don't fret," she says. "Things are never as bad as they seem."

Donald Trump was the living embodiment of that statement. I know many of my friends on the left had a hard time understanding this, but it's why so many people stuck with him after that. No one questioned his toughness or his willingness to punch back. But one quality not often attributed to Trump was consistency. In fact, most often he was—and still is—characterized as the exact opposite: erratic, unpredictable, even unstable. There's no question that he displays each of those characteristics at times, but I thought there was something to be said for someone who just keeps going, no matter what. When it's a good day, he gets up and grinds it out. When it's a bad day, he gets up and grinds it out. Then he does it again. Then he does it again. And again.

It's a quality that seems to be more prevalent in Trump's generation than in my own. For decades, my grandfather, Lonnie Sims, worked at Trunkline Gas Company in the Delta of Mississippi. When he passed away, we found in one of his drawers a small box of lapel pins with different numbers on them—5, 10, 15, and 20. Turns out, the company had given each of them to him—one every five years—in a ceremony recognizing how long it had been since he missed a day of work.

Yes, Trump could be impulsive, even reckless. Sure, he operated almost entirely off of gut instinct. But he was also the most methodical, patient person I've ever seen in the midst of a crisis—the eye of the storm. And you could bet every penny you had that he was going to get up and go to work the next morning.

So that's what we did, too.

3

FIGHT OR FLIGHT

The morning after the *Access Hollywood* tape was released, a Saturday, the core of our communications team came to work early. When I arrived at the Tower, Cheung, Surabian, Kaelan, and Jason Miller were already there. But we quickly realized there were many others we would no longer be able to rely on—like, nearly the entire GOP establishment, which Trump would never forget.

I would come to find out later that, in a meeting upstairs on the twenty-fifth floor, RNC Chairman Reince Priebus urged Trump to drop out of the race. According to Steve Bannon, Reince told Trump, "You have two choices. You either drop out right now, or you lose by the biggest landslide in American political history." New Jersey Governor Chris Christie was there, too, and apparently didn't seem much more optimistic.

Campaign staff stopped receiving "comms alerts" from the RNC. This constant flow of emails helped us all stay up to the minute on the latest stories. It was a basic function for a comms operation that we had outsourced to the RNC's larger staff. Now in open revolt against its own nominee, the RNC had stopped providing that service to us.

In retrospect, the impact of that weekend continued to reverberate inside Trump World for years to come. During an interview on CBS's *60 Minutes* a year later, Bannon called it "a litmus test. . . . [It] showed who really had Donald Trump's back." In any team environment, bonds are forged in the darkest hours. Campaign aides who survived that weekend shoulder to shoulder were forever welded together. In contrast, we never forgot who quit when it was hard. That dynamic would later follow us into the White House, where survivors and quitters were forced back together. Some survivors were sub-ordinated to quitters, who scoffed at the media labeling us "loyalists," breed-ing even greater resentment. But from there on out, that was how Trump saw us, too.

Jason Miller gathered our small team together for a powwow.

"We can no longer trust anyone at the RNC," Miller said, which was a shocking declaration when you thought about it. The party's nominee could not trust its own party leadership. "Don't be hostile. Don't be rude. Don't say anything out of the ordinary to them. Just understand that we can't trust them anymore. At this point most of them would rather Hillary win than the boss."

Not all of them quit on us, though. Andy Hemming was another RNC staffer working out of Trump Tower. He was on a layover at Chicago's O'Hare Airport on his way to St. Louis, where the next debate was set to be held. While waiting for his next flight, he received a phone call from one of his superiors at the RNC telling him that no one would hold it against him if he bailed on the debate—and the campaign. He went to the debate anyway.

I walked to the other side of the fourteenth floor to poke my head in Brad Parscale's office. At six foot eight, Brad dwarfed everyone else on the cam-paign. He had a long beard that seemed more suited to a Navy SEAL than a tech guru, but in a way he was like our in-house spec ops for the digital world. He'd first come into Trump's orbit in 2011 by designing websites for his properties. In 2015, Trump hired Parscale's firm to create a website for his presidential exploratory committee. He then became the campaign's digital director, and now he was overseeing tens of millions of dollars in online advertising. He had a massive Apple desktop computer on his desk that was always scrolling through voter turnout models or mock digital ads. When I walked into his office, he was standing with his back to the door look-ing down at a crowd assembling on Fifth Avenue below. I walked over beside him to see what he was looking at.

"You know what we should do?" he asked. "We should get a crew together and go down there and hand out campaign signs to as many people as we can. Look at all the press—they'll eat it up."

"Great idea," I said. "Let's do it." I'd come this far, after all. Now that I'd made the decision to stay and weather the storm, I was in it all the way.

Fifteen minutes later we bounded out of Trump Tower's revolving front door and faced the competing mobs of pro- and anti-Trump activists. As predicted, the cameras swung in our direction and members of the press rushed to capture the campaign's symbolic display of defiance.

For now, the next major milestone we were facing was the second presidential debate, in St. Louis, Missouri, on Monday—two days away. I would be among the group flying out there to be on-site with the candidate for the big night.

Saturdays in the Trump Tower war room weren't much different from weekdays, at least for the communications team. We were a seven-days-a-week operation, although we tended to come in a little later and leave a little earlier on the weekends. For me, however, Saturdays were special. In the South, Saturdays in the fall are dominated by college football—SEC football, to be more specific. It's all-consuming. People plan their lives around it. Weddings are scheduled to avoid kickoff times, or sometimes to avoid football season altogether. In fact, #StopFallWeddings is one of the most popular Twitter hashtags for SEC fans during that time of year. In Trump Tower, it was well known that seven of the eight TVs in the war room could continue monitoring the news. But that eighth TV—the one farthest to the left, right in front of my desk—was reserved for Alabama football.

The morning would often start with ESPN's *College GameDay*, and October 8, 2016, was no exception. They were broadcasting live from College Station, Texas, where the Texas A&M Aggies were taking on the Tennessee Volunteers. The show is famous for the homemade signs that fans hold up in the background. On that day, the signs included anti-Tennessee classics like TENNESSEE CRIES LIKE A BUTCH because Coach Butch Jones had broken down in tears after they won the week before on a last-second touchdown. The best signs obviously don't need explaining, but college football fans got it.

As we tried to read all of the signs waving behind the commentators, we suddenly had a revelation. Every network produced live debate coverage in a similar format to ESPN's *College GameDay*. We should create our own signs and get volunteers to wave them behind the political commentators.

Most campaigns probably would have required at least a dozen people to sign off on such an idea, and lawyers would have vetted every one. In her memoir *Hacks,* Donna Brazile wrote that a guy in a duck costume who followed Mr. Trump around the country to mock him for supposedly "ducking" debates was approved by Hillary Clinton personally. We did it without asking anybody.

We came up with some basic signs like a giant locomotive with TRUMP TRAIN written above it, and a dark blue sign that simply said ONLY TRUMP WILL BEAT ISIS. But my personal favorites were more creative.

WikiLeaks had released over thirty thousand emails sent to and from Hillary Clinton's private email account, so one of our signs had a picture of WikiLeaks founder Julian Assange with the caption DEAR HILLARY, I MISS READING YOUR CLASSIFIED EMAILS.

We'd also been highlighting all of the foreign money that had poured into the Clinton Foundation while Hillary was serving as Secretary of State. So another one of our signs was a giant twenty-five-million-dollar check made out to the Clinton Foundation from "Foreign Donors." In the "For" line, it simply said "Access."

But the best of all, in my opinion, was an enormous light blue sign with just three words: HILLARY LIKES NICKELBACK.

When debate day came, the signs were everywhere on television. As MS-NBC's Stephanie Ruhle anchored pre-debate coverage outside the venue, the giant check waved just over her left shoulder. Over on CNN, the Nickelback sign hovered between Jake Tapper and various panelists sitting beside him.

As we spotted each of them—the Clinton campaign had nothing like this anywhere—our comms team watched and laughed together from a makeshift war room just down the hall from the debate stage.

"Well, no matter what happens tonight, at least that was fun," I said, reclining onto the back two legs of my chair and taking a sip from a can of Sprite.

Jason Miller eased out of his chair to walk toward the debate stage. "I think there's a lot more fun ahead of us tonight." The way he said it gave me an inkling that there was something unusual being planned, but he didn't say anything more, and I didn't ask.

Just before 3:30 P.M. Trump arrived in the debate hall at Washington University, with his entourage in tow. The stage was set up for a forum-style debate, with both candidates standing in the round, surrounded by questioners.

Trump, wearing a bright red silk tie and dark suit, perched himself on one of the stools and immediately started assessing his surroundings.

Ever the television producer, he wanted to know the camera angles. A member of the production team pointed out the cameras and explained at what times they would use each. Trump was told that he would be standing to

Secretary Clinton's right. He liked this piece of news, because the audience would be viewing the right side of his head, which he favored, more often than the left—something I'd learned from video recording sessions with him. He squinted up into the lights, which encircled the stage, washing out most of the shadows.

Campaign attorney Don McGahn was seated behind him to the right and chatting quietly with Rudy Giuliani. Both he and McGahn observed the scene with intimidating scowls. The former New York City Mayor had proven his mettle to Trump the day before by braving the Sunday show circuit at the height of the *Access Hollywood* scandal. His reward was to serve as a key member of the Trump entourage.

Various officials from the Commission on Presidential Debates looked on from the other side of the stage, including commission chairman Frank Fahrenkopf, a former chairman of the Republican National Committee. He had clearly never seen anything quite like our motley crew, and he had a hard time hiding it.

But most conspicuous of all was Bannon. True to form, he was the only man in the debate hall not wearing a suit, opting for his beloved khakis, a black shirt, and a dark tan leather jacket. His long hair fell over the top of his glasses, obscuring the view of his face. As Trump moved around the stage to get his bearings and did a sound check on his microphone, Bannon stood motionless, looking downward for long periods, lost inside his own mind.

"We good?" he finally asked Trump. "You feel comfortable with it?"

Trump signaled his approval with a nod and the group disappeared into a holding room.

As we walked the roughly twenty yards back to the makeshift war room at the debate hall, Jason Miller stopped several of us from the comms team and said he had something important to tell us confidentially. The look on his face suggested he wasn't joking around, so we leaned in.

"We've got several of Bill Clinton's accusers on the way here right now," he said. "Juanita Broaddrick, Paula Jones . . . I can't remember them all off the top of my head, but there are four of them."

I raised my eyebrows so high that they may have hit one of the klieg lights hanging above us.

I was no fan of Bill Clinton, to say the least, but he was going to be here, too. With the women who claimed he assaulted them only feet away. What would he do? What would his wife do? What would their daughter, Chelsea, do? *Wow. Just wow.*

As I stood there speechless, Cheung uttered what was the greatest understatement of the entire campaign. "Whoa. That's going to be nuts."

"Uhhh, yeah," Jason replied. "Keep it quiet for now, but there's no telling how this is going to play out."

Looking back, this should not have come entirely as a surprise. Hours before, Bannon's *Breitbart News*—which had become the all-but-official organ of the campaign—had published a video interview with Ms. Broaddrick, who sobbed while recalling her alleged rape by Bill Clinton forty years earlier. Another of Clinton's accusers, Kathleen Willey, consoled her during the interview, indicating that they were together—somewhere. *The Drudge Report* had made the interview the site's top banner headline.

After Jason told us what was happening, Cheung called Surabian, who was manning the war room back at Trump Tower.

"Something is going to happen thirty minutes from now and it's going to consume everything," he told him.

"What is it?" Surabian asked, expecting the worst.

Cheung made Surabian take him off speakerphone so the rest of the war room staff couldn't hear the details. "In about a half hour, the boss is going to do a press conference with Bill Clinton's accusers."

There was silence on the line.

"This should be the war room's only focus between now and then," Cheung concluded. "I'll call you after."

Shortly thereafter, members of the press who were on-site to cover the debate were ushered into a conference room with red carpet and a long table covered in an olive-colored cloth. It is very hard to surprise the jaded press corps—especially a press corps used to Trumpian theatrics—but this time was an exception. There were audible gasps from reporters when they came upon a scene so totally wild and unexpected.

Trump was already seated behind the table and flanked by Juanita Broaddrick, Kathleen Willey, Kathy Shelton, and Paula Jones. Trump introduced the four "very courageous women," and each of them made a brief statement. Bannon stood in the back left corner of the room, unable to hide a grin. The event lasted two minutes and fifty seconds—but that was long enough for cable media's collective head to explode.

Twitter melted down. Journalists were appalled. Democrats were indignant. Political operatives were stunned—I was stunned.

"This is the craziest thing I've ever seen in my entire life," I told Cheung as we watched the aftermath.

Bannon loved it all. "Everyone who ever ran against the Clintons wanted to do this!" he exulted, a proud father of the chaos he had birthed. "But nobody had the stones!"

"Yeah, or they thought it would be career suicide," Hemming said quietly, not yet sure what to make of the circus unfolding before our eyes.

Bannon wasn't done. He wanted the four women to be seated in the family section during the debate, which is typically reserved for only the candidates' immediate family members. That would place them right next to Bill and Chelsea Clinton. I'm sure he also had in his mind some dramatic confrontation between the women and Clinton that would totally overwhelm whatever happened on the debate stage. This, however, was a bridge too far for the debate organizers. An argument ensued between the campaign and representatives from the Commission on Presidential Debates. In the end, an aghast Fahrenkopf threatened to have security remove the women if they sat there, and Bannon acquiesced. The women ended up sitting in the general admission section, along with the rest of the debate crowd, but still close enough that members of the press snapped plenty of photos that added even more fuel to the online fire.

If the goal was to rattle the Clinton campaign, it definitely worked. But everyone was rattled. By the time the debate was set to begin, the general feeling throughout the building was that there was absolutely no telling what might end up happening. I shared that sentiment. And now here we were only minutes before the Clintons were set to arrive on-site.

When Bill Clinton walked into the debate hall for the first time that evening, he saw his accusers almost immediately. It was impossible to avoid them. Bannon had made sure of that. I don't believe I have ever witnessed a man look that shaken. Of all the things he'd seen and done as president—launched covert military action, endured relentless investigations, suffered through an impeachment, the list could go on and on—I'm not sure anything was more traumatizing than the moment he locked eyes with a woman who'd accused him of raping her almost forty years before. The man who was famous for maintaining his cool demeanor under even the brightest lights looked like he was melting. He kept glancing at them out of the corner of his eye. It was such a spectacle that even he couldn't entirely look away.

Back in the war room, Trump walked through on his way to the debate stage. The entire team stood up and cheered. Cool as a cucumber, Trump subtly pumped his fist in front of him and shook hands with aides as he slowly walked through.

Exactly one month earlier—to the day—Clinton had labeled "half of Trump's supporters" as "a basket of deplorables," a comment that even she later admitted was a mistake. The Trump campaign seized on it. Just before walking out on stage, Trump tweeted, "My team of deplorables will be taking over my Twitter account for tonight's #debate #MakeAmericaGreatAgain." That "team of deplorables" consisted of social media director Dan Scavino, digital director Brad Parscale, his deputy Ashton Adams, and me.

Being able to tweet directly from the @realDonaldTrump account—inarguably one of the most powerful communication instruments in modern political history—was a weighty responsibility. It had the power to bend entire news cycles to its will, making it one of Trump's most prized possessions. Nobody wanted to be the one who fired off a tweet he didn't like. I sure as heck didn't. So under the theory of "there is strength in numbers," the four of us sat side by side in the front row of the war room, right in front of the TVs. We constantly threw out tweet ideas to each other throughout the debate, trying our best to capitalize on key moments happening onstage. There were some real doozies, like when Clinton said, "It's just awfully good that someone with the temperament of Donald Trump is not in charge of the law in our country," and Trump shot back, "Because you'd be in jail." By the end of the night, *USA Today* speculated that it was "the nastiest debate ever."

When Trump came off the stage and walked back through the war room, the team once again erupted in applause. He seemed pleased—or at least relieved that it was over—but he was immediately drawn into the TV coverage. For about thirty seconds he stood in silence and watched CNN and MSNBC on the side-by-side flat-screens. "You know what?" he said, breaking his silence. "I'm not even going to watch this. They're awful. And really, what do they know anyway, right?"

He smiled and slapped me on the back as he turned to walk away. "Great job, everyone!"

In the thirty days between the St. Louis debate and Election Day, Trump would go on to do a stunning sixty-three campaign rallies. Clinton did just over half that number. He was relentless. Of all the character traits that Trump most liked to tout about himself, the boasts about his "energy" and "stamina" were the most undeniably true. While public speaking sucks the life out of most people, Trump's battery seemed to recharge itself on the energy of the crowds—twelve thousand in Ocala, ten thousand in Virginia Beach, eight thousand in Phoenix, fifteen thousand outside of Raleigh, nine thousand in Minneapolis, twelve thousand in rural Pennsylvania. And he would keep track of the numbers like they were a running tabulation of his wealth. They were a personal metric of his appeal and his success.

His own crowd estimates often tended to deviate wildly from official estimates. Why did Trump insist on inflating his crowd sizes when they clearly were dwarfing Clinton's, regardless of the actual number? Even those of us in Trump Tower didn't understand it at the time. But in retrospect I think there were three reasons.

The first one he described in his 1987 book *The Art of the Deal:*

The final key to the way I promote is bravado. I play to people's fantasies. People may not always think big themselves, but they can still get very excited by those who do. That's why a little hyperbole never hurts. People want to believe that something is the biggest and the greatest and the most spectacular. I call it truthful hyperbole. It's an innocent form of exaggeration—and a very effective form of promotion.

Second, this "truthful hyperbole" would compel members of the media to correct his crowd estimates, which, if you think about it, just forced them to spend even more time highlighting the size of his crowds.

And finally, it just drove people nuts. Trump is history's greatest troll. It either cracks you up or makes you so livid you have to close your Twitter app in disgust. Either way, he got you to react. We dismissed his fixation on crowd sizes at the time, but it would of course come back to haunt us in a memorable fashion.

While Trump was out on the road, the team back in the Tower scrambled to keep up with the frantic pace. There weren't enough hours in the day to complete every task. On the most difficult days—such as when a woman would come forward with a new allegation against Trump—it felt like our heads were just below the surface of the water, and we were breathing through a straw. Over time the understaffed war room grew numb to the constant anxiety of being overwhelmed. Trump's job was to stay out on the road, hammering away on the populist, nationalist themes that resonated with voters. It was the staff's job—especially Cheung, the director of rapid response—to fight back against the deluge. This led to yet another wild moment.

In mid-October, a seventy-four-year-old woman named Jessica Leeds claimed that Trump had made unwanted sexual advances at her during an airplane flight almost forty years earlier. In a visual that everyone could have done without, she claimed his "hands were everywhere . . . like an octopus." Jason Miller fired back in the press, calling the allegations "fiction" and politically motivated. "For this to only become public decades later in the final month of a campaign for president should say it all," he said.

In the midst of the media fallout, Kaelan Dorr from the war room team received an email from one of his former colleagues at Jamestown & Associates, the consultancy where he and Jason had worked prior to joining the campaign. The firm was contracted to produce ads for us, so when Kaelan saw the email, he assumed it was probably an invoice. Instead, it was a forwarded email, originally sent to Jamestown's general in-box, from a British man claiming he could debunk Ms. Leeds's allegations against Trump.

The man's name was Anthony Gilberthorpe. Campaigns get hundreds of wacky emails. This seemed to Kaelan like just another one to toss in the trash and move on, which is exactly what he did.

That evening, however, he mentioned the email in passing to Jason Miller, who perked up. Jason wanted to see the email—stat. Upon reading it, he immediately began trying to contact the man, who was likely asleep in England, where it was still the middle of the night.

At 3 A.M., Kaelan was startled awake by Jason, who had burst into his room in the apartment they shared. He'd gotten Gilberthorpe on the phone and wanted him flown to New York right away. Barely awake and bleary-eyed,

Kaelan dutifully booked the flight before falling back asleep with his laptop on the bed beside him and Miller crashing on the floor.

The following day, we arrived at Trump Tower for another early morning, when Kaelan rang Cheung's phone. He explained that they'd found someone who could "dispel the accuser's story," and asked if Cheung could do some background research on the guy. He agreed, hung up the phone, and typed Gilberthorpe's name into the Google search bar.

A British tabloid story was among the first results. In a 2014 exposé, Gilberthorpe claimed he was asked by a Tory Party leader in Scotland "to arrange for young rent boys to have sex with two high-profile cabinet members"—and that he actually did it. Another link claimed he had his apartment rigged with cameras, allowed a politician to have sex with a club hostess, recorded it, then sold the footage to a tabloid.

As Cheung read the stories out loud, I folded my arms in front of me, closed my eyes, and put my left hand on my face. "You've got to be kidding." The most generous reading of all of this was that our star defense witness was somewhere between a scumbag and a creep.

Cheung called Kaelan back to fill him in on our sobering discoveries.

"The guy's already on a flight now," Kaelan replied. "He'll be at the Tower in a few hours, so I guess just be ready for when he gets there."

A few hours later, Gilberthorpe arrived, as promised.

He stepped into the war room through the same wooden door I'd first walked through just weeks before, although by then it felt like years had passed. He was a short man, probably around five foot five, and almost completely bald. He was wearing a wrinkled dress shirt with the top three buttons undone.

He hesitated for several seconds at the entrance, his eyes surveying the war room and the sparse staff. He looked like the kind of guy who'd pull up to playgrounds with a basket full of candy. The room probably didn't darken once he arrived, but part of me wouldn't have been surprised if it had.

We acted like we didn't see him, until a young staffer greeted him and walked him into one of the corner offices to wait. A few minutes later, Miller and Bannon went in to meet him and closed the door behind them. They huddled with him for nearly two hours, presumably hearing his full story and prepping him to appear on Judge Jeanine Pirro's Fox News show later that night.

According to Gilberthorpe, he'd been on the flight with Trump and Ms. Leeds in the early 1980s, and because of his "photographic memory," he recalled everything that had and had not happened. It was Leeds, not Trump, he said, who had been flirtatious, and at no point did Trump do anything untoward. It was impossible to know whether he actually remembered this random flight or not. But as Donald Rumsfeld once put it, you went to war with the army you had. When they finished debriefing him, Bannon and Miller left the room. Normally Bannon would stop to talk to us, but not this time. His eyes were fixed on the floor as he walked toward his office in silence.

It was still several hours until Gilberthorpe was to appear on Fox. Though Jeanine Pirro was as reliably pro-Trump as anyone on cable news, Pirro's producers had refused to give him top billing on the show. Even they didn't know what to make of this guy. They ultimately agreed to do a short segment with him at the very end of the program, which left Gilberthorpe in our company until showtime.

As he waited to drive over to the TV studio, Gilberthorpe wandered around the war room, seeming to scrutinize everyone and to generally creep people out. He finally came to a stop by gorging himself on the pizza someone had ordered for the staff. No one said a word to him.

When it was finally time for him to leave, Miller and Bannon gave him one last pep talk before sending him on his way. When Gilberthorpe was finally gone and the door was closed and locked behind him, Bannon let out a loud sigh.

"We're so f—ed."

The Judge Jeanine interview was relatively anticlimactic, although she was visibly uncomfortable with Gilberthorpe sitting across from her. To this day, the "Pedo-Pimp" affair, as it became known, lives on in Trump lore and in the nightmares of those who experienced it.

In the aftermath of the campaign, one question seemed to get asked above all others. It would come in various forms, but it essentially boiled down to this: How, in spite of *everything,* did Trump win?

Doctoral dissertations could be written to answer that single question, but my view is that the election was the result of a handful of simple realities.

First, as a *Wall Street Journal* headline summed up perfectly in late 2014, AMERICANS OF ALL STRIPES AGREE: THE SYSTEM IS STACKED AGAINST THEM. The article laid out the results of an NBC-*WSJ* poll showing that 58 percent of Democrats; "51 percent of Republicans; 55 percent of whites; 60 percent of blacks; 53 percent of Hispanics; as well as decent majorities of every age and professional cluster, including blue-collar workers, white-collar workers and retirees," all held that belief that America's economic and political systems were stacked against them.

Trump hammered over and over again on his desire to blow up this "rigged system," while voters viewed "Crooked" Hillary Clinton as one of the key architects and beneficiaries of it.

Second, Trump ushered in a new era of authenticity in American politics. Over the decades, as campaigns became more "professionalized," candidates were packaged and sold to voters the same way ad agencies packaged and sold products to consumers. Consultants shaved down the edges to make sure their clients offended no one and appealed to the broadest possible group. Trump symbolized a broad cultural revolt against political correctness.

Third, as Trump was rising, the American media was facing a reckoning. Trust in the media as a whole was at a record low, and more and more Americans were gravitating toward ideological outlets that confirmed their worldview.

Finally, voters agreed with Trump on many of the issues, and that was what mattered to them the most. This was what the outrage machines in Washington, D.C., and New York City couldn't fathom. Were people offended by some of Trump's antics? Sure. We all were at one point or another. But Kellyanne Conway said it best: "There's a difference . . . between what offends you and what affects you."

As we headed toward the final stretch of the campaign, we were hoping that was true.

October 28 was a Friday, just eleven days before Election Day. Like all Fridays in the waning months of the campaign, every comms alert or "breaking news" chyron was met with the dread of yet another piece of opposition research being dumped on us.

Just after 8 A.M., we got some positive news, though, as a *Washington Post*–ABC tracking poll found Trump starting to close the gap on Clinton's lead, from six points to four in a single week. This loosely matched our internal data, which always saw a closer race than public polls suggested. But the Clinton campaign and some members of the media remained so confident that Hillary's victory was secure that, later that morning, word leaked out that Vice President Joe Biden was on her short list for Secretary of State.

At 12:57 P.M., Surabian stood up suddenly at his desk in the war room. His quick movement caught everyone's attention and caused us to look up from whatever we were working on.

"Jason Chaffetz tweet!" he exclaimed. "'FBI Director just informed me, "The FBI has learned of the existence of emails that appear to be pertinent to the investigation." Case reopened.'"

For the next ten minutes, the office buzzed with speculation from a room full of nonlawyers about what exactly this meant.

Then Surabian sprung to his feet again.

"Bradd Jaffy tweet!" he blurted out. "'FBI Director Comey, in letter to members of Congress, says FBI is investigating additional emails in Clinton private server case.'"

The tweet also included an image of the letter.

"In previous congressional testimony, I referred to the fact that the Federal Bureau of Investigation (FBI) had completed its investigation of former Secretary Clinton's personal email server," Comey wrote. "In connecting with an unrelated case, the FBI has learned of the existence of emails that appear to be pertinent to the investigation. I am writing to inform you that the investigative team briefed me on this yesterday, and I agreed that the FBI should take appropriate investigative steps designed to allow investigators to review these emails to determine whether they contain classified information, as well as to assess their importance to our investigation."

We all hunched over our computers reading the document and debating its significance. It felt like a big deal.

"CNN!" someone in the back of the room yelled. Looking up, I saw that CNN had a breaking news chyron on the bottom of their screen: FBI: NEW EMAILS FOUND RELATED TO CLINTON INVESTIGATION.

Surabian grabbed the remote and ran over to the TV to turn up the volume. CNN's Justice Department correspondent Evan Perez was breaking down the news. "This means that the investigation we thought was over with is now back open and the FBI is taking a look at whether there is something here for them to pursue," he said.

In the Trump Tower war room, staffers from other parts of the building were rushing in as word spread of this unexpected development. "This is what Republicans have been calling for," Perez continued. "Now this is a worry for the Clinton campaign as we come to the closing days of the election."

It didn't take long for Trump, on the campaign trail in New Hampshire, to find his way in front of the cameras to react. "I need to open with a very critical breaking news announcement," he told the raucous crowd. "The FBI has just sent a letter to Congress informing them that they have discovered new emails pertaining to the former Secretary of State Hillary Clinton's investigation." In a matter of moments, the crowd's voices rose in unison: "Lock her up! Lock her up! Lock her up!"

"Hillary Clinton's corruption is on a scale we have never seen before," Trump continued. "We must not let her take her criminal scheme into the Oval Office! . . . With that being said, the rest of my speech is going to be so boring!"

Back in Trump Tower, the atmosphere was euphoric. "This is what it must have felt to be them on all those other Fridays," I said.

"So what do we do now?" Kaelan asked.

"Nothing!" I said. "Absolutely nothing."

In the midst of the excitement, *The New York Times* tweeted out an updated probability of Hillary Clinton winning the presidency: 92 percent. "Clinton's chance of losing is about the same as the probability that an NFL kicker misses a 31-yard field goal," they wrote.

For the first time since *Access Hollywood,* we saw an opening that might actually lead us to victory. At the same time, I was also beginning to form a bond with the candidate I had sacrificed a lot to defend.

Video recording sessions were how Trump and I really first connected.

Having starred in a top-rated network television show—*The Apprentice*—for fourteen seasons, and after living decades of his life in the spotlight, he had developed a certain way he liked to do things. Watching him was like a master class in idiosyncrasies.

Walking in the room for a recording session, he said the same thing almost every time, at least when he was in a good mood: "Hello, everybody." When he wasn't in a good mood, it was either a sharp "Okay, let's go," or nothing at all.

Sitting down, he would look at the playback monitor to assess the shot. He almost always moved his chair immediately, regardless of how carefully it had been placed, so it was pointless to try to frame the shot precisely prior to his arrival.

He preferred to position his head in front of a darker backdrop, a lesson I wouldn't fully learn until we were in the White House. In many video recordings done direct-to-camera, his head is at least partially in front of the top of the presidential flag, which is dark blue. This is because he doesn't like the way his hair looks in front of a white backdrop. And if there's any hair out of place, somebody in the room better have the TRESemmé Tres Two hair spray, extra hold. I carried a travel-size can with me everywhere I went.

Once he was satisfied with his positioning, he placed his right hand on his cheek, a quick way to orient the brain to which side is right and left, since the playback monitor is like looking in a mirror. He often commented on the lighting, usually asking for it to be turned down.

He would then ask the person in the room he trusted the most what they thought. For months this was either Hope Hicks, his longtime PR aide, or Keith Schiller, his bodyguard, who had been at his side for two decades. But over time they no longer attended the recording sessions and it became me.

I learned when to press him for numerous takes and when to let small mistakes go, or when to encourage him to stick to the script and when to capitalize on his superhuman ability to ad-lib. For everything that has been said about his tendency to stray from the prepared text, what always impressed me the most was his ability to edit on the fly. He often rearranged sentence structure, chose alternative words, and added or deleted entire paragraphs in real time, as he delivered his remarks.

On Monday, November 7, 2016, the day before the election, Mr. Trump walked into the tiny Trump Tower recording studio in a hurry. He was already running a half hour behind schedule, and he was preparing for a furious final day of campaigning, with rallies planned in Florida, North Carolina, Pennsylvania, New Hampshire, Michigan, and Virginia.

Bannon was right behind him, along with Stephen Miller and Trump's oldest daughter, Ivanka.

"She's stunning" is a common phrase used to compliment a beautiful woman's appearance, but to use a Trumpism, it's usually "truthful hyperbole." With Ivanka, however, it wasn't. The first time I met her in Trump Tower I was genuinely stunned by what appeared to be a living, breathing Barbie doll.

I distinctly remember thinking her face didn't appear to have a single blemish—there was nothing being covered up by makeup. While her critics claim she has a plastic vibe, I didn't see her that way, though like anyone else, she could be scripted and find some topics and people more interesting than others. I was also struck by the fact that she was unfailingly polite. She laughed freely and had a breezy air of confidence about her. She could be assertive at times, but never rude. And if anyone could have gotten away with being rude, it would have been her.

"We've got a window of time here and we've got to own it," Bannon said the day before the election. "We've got six rallies today. Let's hurry up, we've got to get this done."

We just needed one video, about ninety seconds long, encouraging people all over the country to head to the polls and vote to Make America Great Again.

On this taping, Trump was anxious. The marathon he had been running for almost two years had led to this final dash, the public polling was almost universally bad, and he wasn't his usual gregarious self.

Still, with the air-conditioning turned off so it wouldn't be picked up in the microphones, the teleprompter ready, and the lighting set, Mr. Trump turned on the charisma and delivered flawless dialogue. For about sixty seconds, that is.

Suddenly the cameraman's cell phone ringer blared—loud enough to startle Miller, who was standing right next to him—and Trump abruptly stopped speaking. The cameraman fumbled with his phone for what seemed like forever, as Trump let out an irritated exhale and Bannon barked at the poor guy with some choice expletives and righteous indignation.

With the ringer muted and tempers cooled, Mr. Trump started over and delivered another sixty seconds of flawless dialogue.

Then, without warning, he was interrupted again, this time by a racket outside. "My God, is that a jackhammer?" Bannon blurted out.

It was. Somewhere in Trump Tower, a construction crew had started their work for the day, thinking Mr. Trump had already left the building for his final barnstorm around the country.

The distraction allowed Trump a chance to vent, and he seized it. He may have also welcomed the chance to release the nervous energy inside. "I bet it's Gucci!" Trump exploded, referencing his retail client on the ground floor.

"I guarantee you it's Gucci! I'm so sick of this s—; it's every day! Get Cala-mari on the phone right now."

As aides scrambled to contact Matthew Calamari, the Trump Organ-ization's chief operating officer, the jackhammering went on—for so long that Trump began to sweat under the lights.

"Let's get the air-conditioning back on," he said in complete exasperation. "There's no telling how long this is going to take."

Unfortunately, turning the air back on wasn't as easy as walking over to a thermostat. It required getting on the phone with the building superinten-dent, who apparently had to move heaven and earth.

Then, as suddenly as it began, the jackhammer went silent.

"Okay, let's just do it," said Bannon.

Trump again turned on the charisma and delivered about thirty seconds of pitch-perfect dialogue. Just then the air-conditioning rumbled loudly back to life.

Bannon launched into an expletive-filled tirade that seemed to catch Trump off guard and likely caused him not to lose his temper himself. But sensing a breaking point, Bannon kicked a handful of extra staffers out of the room who had come down to see the final taping.

I tried to be as inconspicuous as possible. I moved into a corner, surrounded on two sides by dark curtains, with a large-screen monitor blocking me from view, or at least I thought.

Collecting himself and making sure he was still satisfied with how every-thing looked in the shot, Mr. Trump suddenly unloaded again.

"Who is that behind the TV!" he exclaimed.

Standing up on my toes, I raised my head above the monitor just far enough that he could make out who I was.

"D— it, it's Cliff back there! I can't concentrate!"

With that, Ivanka burst out laughing, breaking the tension and causing the rest of the room—including Mr. Trump—to relax. She had a way of doing that. A unique way.

"We're going to win, Dad, don't worry about it." She smiled. "Let's get this done and go get on the plane." The future of their entire family, their brand, their place in history, was now only hours away.

4

SIZE MATTERS

I was startled awake by my alarm at 6 A.M. on Saturday morning, January 21, 2017, the morning after Trump was sworn in as the forty-fifth President of the United States. I'm a deep sleeper, but very few of my days in Washington, D.C., began serenely. More often than not, the first moments of each morning began with a suddenly racing heartbeat and a scramble for my phone to see if the President had fired off any tweets while I was asleep.

As I rolled out of bed, I stubbed my toe on one of the dozens of unpacked plastic boxes stacked throughout my apartment. Seeing Megan still sleeping soundly in the tiny, dimly lit room, I suppressed the urge to give voice to the pain and instead just hobbled to the bathroom. Megan was excited about our new adventure, although it was painful to leave behind our church and friends in Birmingham. She didn't enjoy the controversy that constantly swirled around Trump—and therefore around me, too—but when asked about it, she'd say, "Very few people get this opportunity, so if we don't take it and try to make a difference, then we can't complain that no one in D.C. is representing our beliefs."

We had leased our new apartment without even seeing it. After googling "apartments close to the White House," I had chosen the Woodward Building. It looked nice enough in the pictures online, and it had a serviceable gym, killer rooftop view of the city, and, perhaps most important, an outdoor terrace where we could let out our dog—a ten-pound shih tzu named Minnie—without having to walk to a nearby park.

Unfortunately, the apartment itself was only 687 square feet, roughly the size of the master bedroom suite in our 3,215-square-foot home in Alabama. Even worse, it cost more per month than our fifteen-year mortgage in Birmingham.

The cost of living in Washington, D.C., is one of the primary reasons that people who stay there for an extended period of time lose touch with much of the rest of the country. The costs are inflated. The salaries are inflated. The egos are inflated. But everyone carries on like everything is normal.

Shaking off the pain in my throbbing toe, I jumped in the shower, threw on a suit, and stepped outside into the quiet, empty streets of downtown Washington.

Looking to my left, the low-sitting fog was obscuring my view of the Washington Monument, about a half mile down Fifteenth Street. A block away, I could see that the short strip of Pennsylvania Avenue right in front of the White House was barricaded and still housing the temporary bleachers from which the First Family and their guests had watched the Inaugural Parade the day before.

The placid morning stood in stark contrast to the previous day's events. Just two blocks away, protesters had smashed the windows of Bank of America and Starbucks and destroyed a rented limousine while chanting, "Not my President!" Broken glass still littered nearby Franklin Square, where just hours before police had deployed flashbangs and tear gas to disperse the violent crowds.

Slipping on my white Apple earbuds, I began the 0.7-mile walk to the General Services Administration building, the headquarters of the Trump presidential transition. Augustana's "Twenty Years" provided the backing track as I walked past Lafayette Square in front of the White House, with the bronze statue of Andrew Jackson tipping his cap while riding his horse in the Battle of New Orleans at its center.

The song had long been one of my favorites. No lyrics have better captured the feeling of leaving home to chase a dream. But it took on particular significance for me when I left my wife in Alabama for several months to work on the Trump campaign in Manhattan.

"Just fall asleep with the TV, darling. I'll be back again."

The transition office was quiet when I arrived; most staff would not get in for another hour. While I didn't have anything particularly pressing on my agenda, I came in early in anxious anticipation of getting cleared into the White House for the first time.

My phone buzzed in my pocket, cutting off the music, and I pulled it out to see "Sean Spicer" on the screen.

To that point, my personal experiences with Sean had varied wildly. We had a tortured relationship with the RNC in general, but it was never that bad with Sean in particular.

During the campaign, he'd been a prankster in Trump Tower. If you left your computer unlocked and unattended, he'd send emails from your account and giddily await your reaction when you received a confused response from a colleague. He loved doing TV appearances and craved positive reviews from the staff. "How'd I do?" he'd ask after coming back upstairs from a satellite TV hit.

Then, just before Election Day, when the polls and pundits were all foreseeing a colossal Clinton victory, word got back to the campaign that Spicer had done off-the-record briefings with reporters, blaming our impending defeat on the campaign while defending the RNC's heroic efforts to keep the *Titanic* afloat.

Things got really crazy during the transition after we won.

At first Jason Miller was slated to be Communications Director, and Spicer was slated to be Press Secretary. During daily conference calls with members of the press, Spicer was clearly subordinated to Miller in the pecking order—in practice, if not in the org chart. But Miller suddenly backed out of the job after his adulterous relationship with a female campaign aide went public. That left Spicer to take on the dual role of both press and communications. This may seem like a natural fit, but while press and comms are inextricably linked, their day-to-day functions are dramatically different.

The press team deals with whatever is happening right this second. They're largely a reactive operation. Comms, on the other hand, is supposed to look up at the horizon and plan ahead. They're supposed to be proactive and not allow themselves to get sucked into the daily maelstrom of the news cycle. In addition to the differences in their tactical and strategic roles, combining the two jobs also created management issues that Spicer was clearly not interested in dealing with. This was an overwhelming amount of work for even the most confident and competent managers—and Sean was not known to be either. His personality went through a Dr. Jekyll and Mr. Hyde–like change almost immediately.

Spicer stopped answering phone calls from campaign aides trying to iron out the details of their White House job—or whether or not they would have one at all. At one point, when word was spreading that campaign aides were being frozen out, Reince Priebus, who by then had been named White House Chief of Staff, stopped by the comms area of Trump Tower and reassured everyone, "If you want a job in the White House, you've got one." The group sat in silence, not sure what to say or what was true.

For me, the uncertainty was becoming a problem. If I was going to take a job in the White House, I'd have to sell two houses, divest from my company, move halfway across the country, and help my wife find a job—and I had to do it all in two months.

Though we'd gotten along fine during the campaign, now that his job was assured, Spicer never answered a single one of my phone calls during the transition, and called me only once. He offered me the job of Special Assistant to the President and Director of White House Message Strategy, told me I'd be working in the West Wing, and laid out what my salary would be. I wouldn't find out until I'd moved to D.C. that my salary was actually thirty thousand dollars less than Spicer had promised in that phone call.

When I broached the subject with him, he told me, "You should be honored to even have a chance to work for the President" and I should "go work somewhere else" if I didn't like it. I dropped the issue. I didn't need the money, I just didn't think it was right he hadn't kept his word. And it wasn't just me; others were uprooting their lives based on his promises. It was unprofessional. And Spicer had seemingly turned into another person overnight.

When he called me the morning after Inauguration Day, he got right to the point.

"The attorneys are getting you set up this morning," he said, "so you need to get over here as fast as you can. It's a workday."

Most staffers would be on-boarded in waves over the next week, so I was excited to be among the first getting into the building.

I hurried down the wide hallway of the GSA building and into a conference room where several senior aides to the President and Vice President were sitting.

"Let's get started," a tall, slender man at the front of the room said. "I'm Stefan Passantino, Deputy Assistant to the President and Deputy White House Counsel."

He explained that he handled all compliance issues for the White House Counsel's Office, and he was giving us a crash course on adhering to the ethics rules of being a commissioned officer in the Executive Office of the President.

"I'm going to get this out of the way because I know you're not going to like it," he said. "You can no longer text each other about work-related issues. You're going to get a government phone. It won't have text messaging enabled because we haven't yet worked it out to comply with the Presidential Records Act."

There was an audible groan from several staffers, particular from the Advance Office, where they relied on the ease and quickness of text messages to coordinate their bosses' movements.

After an extensive discussion about the gift rules, Stefan deemed us fully briefed on the basics and cleared us to be driven into the White House complex for the first time by Secret Service. We piled into a fifteen-passenger van and made the two-block drive, pausing at two checkpoints and ultimately coming to a stop on West Executive Drive between the West Wing and the Eisenhower Executive Office Building (EEOB).

Once inside the EEOB, we plowed through a mountain of paperwork— health-care and retirement plans, bank account numbers, and every piece of personal information imaginable. We were then shuffled down the hall for IT training and received our government-issued laptops and cell phones.

"Can we pay out of our own pocket to get a Mac laptop instead of this thing?" someone asked, drawing a chuckle, followed by an apologetic "no" from the career White House IT staffer.

The final stop in the gauntlet was the Secret Service and Travel offices in the basement. They captured our fingerprints electronically, snapped head shots for our diplomatic passports, handed us our White House IDs, and sent us on our way.

"Now what?" I asked one of the career staffers who had guided us through the process.

"I don't know what you do here, man," he said with a smile. "You're free to go figure it out."

I walked out of the EEOB and back onto the driveway where we had been dropped off and saw a large white awning jutting out of the West Wing, emblazoned with the Seal of the President. I could feel my heartbeat in my chest as I walked under the awning, through two sets of double doors, and into the ground floor of the West Wing for the first time.

Just inside, I stopped at the desk of a uniformed Secret Service agent, who glanced up at me with a puzzled look.

"Do I, like, swipe in, or what?" I asked.

"No," he said. "You're wearing a blue badge. That's all you need." He looked back down at his computer and I slowly walked toward an open hallway with low ceilings and walls covered with large, empty black picture frames. All of the Obamas' pictures had been removed, and over the next twenty-four hours, every frame would be filled with pictures of the Trumps and various scenes from the inauguration.

Turning to the right, I walked hesitantly into a dimly lit corridor that quickly dead-ended at a soda machine. Glancing to my right, there was a white phone on the wall beside a dark wooden door, and what appeared to be a keyhole-style video camera.

SITUATION ROOM, read the plaque on the door.

I retraced my steps back out to the ground-floor hallway and walked past several tiny offices filled with people I had never seen before, through some double doors, and up a narrow stairwell.

Another uniformed Secret Service agent seated at the top of the stairs nodded in my direction and returned to reading a magazine. I walked past her as she pressed a button on her desk, automatically opening a set of double doors in front of me facing east toward the White House residence. I immediately recognized the White House Rose Garden, in spite of its lack of color in the winter cold.

Just up the colonnade I could see where Franklin D. Roosevelt had sat outside the Oval Office and contemplated how to defeat Hitler. John F. Kennedy had laughed while walking down this corridor with his young son, John Jr. President Ford and his wife, Betty, had traced these steps to the Oval Office immediately after the disgraced Richard Nixon had departed from the South Lawn on Marine One for the final time. President Reagan leaned against one of these columns for a portrait. George W. Bush and Afghan President Hamid Karzai had talked here in 2004, neither fully understanding just how intertwined our two countries would be in the coming decade. Barack Obama, the country's first black president, had walked this exact pathway with Pope Francis.

My senses were heightened by the weight of history all around me. I breathed in deeply, as if the very air were infused with the spirit of the great men and women who had walked here before. But I also couldn't help but notice every crack in the sidewalk, every nick on the white walls, and the overall plainness of so much of the West Wing.

I was reminded in that moment that Thomas Jefferson had greeted the British ambassador at the front door of the White House wearing bedroom slippers, sparking a diplomatic incident but sending the message loud and clear that we are not a monarchy. Our leaders are not demigods, clothed in majesty and working in a palace. The West Wing continues to be a powerful democratic symbol to every head of state who visits because of, not in spite of, its obvious flaws.

I walked back inside through the double doors, the Secret Service agent once again opening them for me automatically. Passing by her desk, I turned the corner and felt a slight chill shoot through my spine. About fifteen yards ahead I glimpsed for the first time the curved walls and distinctively bright lighting that make the Oval Office stand out in an otherwise nondescript and dim set of offices.

For some reason my first thought in that moment was of my grandfather Lonnie Sims, who had passed away less than two years before at the age of eighty-nine. He lived most of his life in Cleveland, Mississippi, a rural town in the state's impoverished Delta region. I recalled him marveling the first time we video-chatted on our phones.

"I remember picking cotton for a dollar in pennies for a hundred-pound bag," he said. "I never even imagined something like this would be possible."

I wish he could have seen this, I thought to myself, keeping my emotions from getting the best of me.

I then realized that I could hear muffled voices coming from a nearby office and walked toward it.

"I don't give a s—," I heard as I walked closer, recognizing Spicer's distinctive New England bite. "We need to figure something out in a hurry."

I pushed through the door into the Press Secretary's office, which by West Wing standards is a sprawling workspace, with giant windows, a sitting area, a small conference table, and a crescent-shaped desk.

Spicer was pacing behind the desk and furiously chomping on a wad of chewing gum. Seated around the office were several of Spicer's aides, including Principal Deputy Press Secretary Sarah Huckabee Sanders, Deputy Communications Director Raj Shah, and Sean Cairncross, a senior adviser to Chief of Staff Reince Priebus.

"What's going on?" I asked, sensing the tension in the room.

"The President's pissed," Shah said. "Like, really pissed."

"About what?" I followed up.

"It's the coverage," Spicer quipped. He looked riled up, too. "He's upstairs watching the TV and he's getting madder and madder about it—the inaugural address, the crowd size, this stupid MLK bust thing, all of it."

I had not followed the news closely that morning because I was so busy going through the on-boarding process, but the President's inaugural address, the group explained, was being widely panned for being "dark and angry."

"George Washington gave us the ambition of a quadrennial, peaceful, democratic transfer of power," wrote one *New York Times* columnist. "Abraham Lincoln appealed to our better natures and our charity in the midst of civil war. Franklin Roosevelt gave us the strength not to be afraid. John Kennedy inspired us to serve our nation. Ronald Reagan talked of a prosperous America as a beacon of democracy around the world. And Barack Obama talked about the hope of which he was the living embodiment. Donald Trump gave us 'American carnage.'"

Former President George W. Bush, who had been on the rostrum with Trump, was quoted as saying "that was some weird s—." The President never mentioned that remark to me, but considering his long-running feud with the Bushes, I can say with a high degree of confidence that he wasn't happy about it.

TV talking heads were lambasting the remarks, which was bad enough for a famously media-focused President, but he was actually angrier about two other story lines.

First, Zeke Miller, a reporter for *Time* magazine, had fired off a tweet claiming that a bust of Martin Luther King Jr. that had been in the Oval Office during the Obama administration had been removed. He also made this claim in a White House pool report that went out to news outlets and various other offices across D.C.

Trump's decision to remove the bust of an iconic civil rights activist from the Oval Office—as one of his first acts as President, no less—played right into the narrative that he was, at best, an enabler and tacit supporter of racists or, at worst, an outright racist himself. It was an irresistible story for eager journalists with itchy Twitter fingers. Except it wasn't true. Miller corrected his error in subsequent tweets, saying the bust was still there and had been obscured by an agent and a door. But the damage was already done. Stories based on Miller's initial false reporting were spreading all over Twitter and Facebook. In this instance, Trump was totally justified in his fury, and it ratcheted up the tension in our already frayed relationship with the press corps.

On the next one, however, Trump wasn't on nearly as sure footing, and the result was one of the most infamous moments of his entire presidency—a moment for which I share some of the blame.

Images emerged from *The New York Times* showing Trump's Inauguration Day crowd looking much smaller than President Obama's in 2009. On one hand, who really cared? Barack Obama had been the first African American president in our history. It was a seminal moment. Of course people would want to celebrate or commemorate that event, particularly African Americans who'd waited so long to see that day. It made sense that his crowd would be historic, too. On top of that, Obama's inauguration enjoyed clear skies, while Trump's was a rainy affair. You can always put on another layer and bundle up, but the prospect of spending hours trouncing through the mud and standing in the rain without an umbrella is too much for a lot of people.

But that's not how President Trump thought—particularly after, at least in his view, the media deliberately lied about the MLK bust and went out of its way to attack his inaugural address. To him, these were attempts to humiliate him and perhaps even delegitimize his electoral victory. As noted, the President loved to tout his crowd sizes on the campaign trail. It was the only metric he could reliably point to as evidence that the polls showing Hillary Clinton winning—all of them—were wrong.

On Election Night, once it was clear that he was going to win, Trump privately revealed what he had been thinking as massive crowds kept showing up at rallies even though he kept lagging in most polls.

"I kept thinking, 'Look at all these people. What am I missing? How could we be losing? It makes no sense.'"

So the current media effort to make him look less popular than Obama was the equivalent of a schoolyard argument escalating into a brawl after one kid brought the other's mom into the conversation. It was waving a red flag to a bull. It just couldn't stand.

But our argument about crowd size was much more difficult this time. The images being displayed side by side online and on television had been taken forty-five minutes before each President's swearing in. The comparisons didn't appear to be close. Not even remotely. President Obama's crowd was much larger, perhaps even twice as large. Anger and frustration can bring out the irrationality in all of us. Deputy campaign manager David Bossie used to compare the President to a teakettle. You need to just let him blow off some steam as a release valve. But sometimes he's more like a pressure cooker ready to explode. This was apparently one of those times.

"He wants me to say it was the largest crowd to ever witness an inauguration," Spicer deadpanned. The way he said it made it sound like he didn't believe it himself. He had eyes like the rest of us.

On top of that, he explained, the President wanted him to use the crowd picture and the erroneous reports about the MLK bust being removed as evidence that the media was bent on reporting "fake news" and delegitimizing his election and presidency.

Raj Shah said what most everyone was thinking in that moment. "How the f— are we going to find evidence to support the crowd thing?"

"The bigger issue is that this is going to be Sean's first time behind the podium," Cairncross responded. "Hell of a way to start."

That profoundly important insight didn't even seem to register with Spicer. In fairness, it didn't really impact the rest of us as much as it should have, either. But we were following Spicer's lead. He was laser focused on proving himself to the boss. The President liked Sean personally, but he had always eyed him, a lifelong member of the establishment that had desperately tried to prevent Trump from clinching the GOP nomination, with suspicion. He was never *really* one of his guys.

"We need to start writing this," Spicer interjected. "We don't have time to go round and round about it anymore." He looked at me. "Can you write it?"

I grabbed a spare laptop and started pecking out notes as other people threw out ideas.

Tom Barrack, a billionaire friend of Trump's who had chaired the Inaugural Committee, came in, having heard the President's frustrations first-hand. He laid out an idea, which we all assumed he had shared with Trump.

"Over one hundred thousand more people used the D.C. Metro transit system yesterday than they did on Obama's Inauguration Day," he explained. "I've got the statistics. It's a fact."

This, everyone agreed, was notable. It sure sounded notable, anyway. And authoritative. Nobody stopped to make certain it was true. Nobody had time. Spicer, in all his manic glory, had worked us all into a frenzy. And Mr. Barrack had more.

"You also have to understand that we had a great deal more fencing and magnetometers on the National Mall than Obama did. So even though they took those pictures at the same time, it's still not apples to apples. It took our people longer to get out onto the Mall."

I was typing as quickly as I could, following along as Mr. Barrack spouted off numbers and details, and taking notes on everything coming out of Sean's mouth—which was a torrent of expletives with a few salient points scattered in between. In the moments when he'd take a breath, I'd try to synthesize whatever I had into a coherent statement. We had no idea that nearly everything we were being told was wrong.

Meanwhile, the rest of the team was assembling visual aids that Sean would display on the large-screen televisions behind the podium in the Briefing Room.

To pull together those assets and additional facts, Raj was in constant communication with RNC research aides and incoming White House staffers who were still working out of the General Services Administration building. Raj was the prototypical anti-Trump establishment Republican. He'd jumped at the chance to work in the White House, even if it was for a president he loathed. But he had deep experience and a legit skill set. He was a talented operative. He exuded a calm confidence in the midst of a crisis. I viewed him as someone I could work with, past issues aside.

"All things considered," Cairncross said of Spicer's predicament, "this isn't *that* bad. You actually have some decent talking points here."

Spicer was standing in front of a mirror, applying makeup and inspecting his light gray suit jacket.

"Someone give the press a fifteen-minute warning," Spicer said. "Let's get this over with."

"How do we print?" I asked.

No one seemed to know, but Spicer's assistant went to find out from the White House IT staff.

Suddenly the computer made a loud beep. It'd been a long time since I had used a PC rather than a Mac, so I looked down to see if it was perhaps an audible signal that the battery power was getting low. Instead, to my great horror, the computer seemed to be going into some type of emergency shutdown. I scrambled to plug it in, thinking its battery might have run out of juice. Nothing. I frantically hit the space bar. Black screen.

Breathe.

Reboot.

Surely the document would still be in there, just waiting for me to hit "print."

It wasn't.

The draft remarks that we had collectively spent hours researching, compiling, writing, and editing had vanished forever.

Right on cue, an assistant came back into the room and announced, "We're set, we gave them the fifteen-minute warning."

Everyone froze in horror. Spicer had been on edge since the moment I walked in the room, and I thought this might be the tipping point for him. His face seemed to turn bloodred in an instant and his eyes narrowed on me. Would he spontaneously combust? Would he unleash a barrage of expletives and march off in rage? He took a deep breath and rallied.

"No, we're not set. But let's fix it. C'mon, let's go. Start writing."

Between Spicer, Cairncross, and myself, we pieced the prepared remarks back together as fast as we could. Meanwhile, the White House press corps had already packed themselves into the Briefing Room. The clock was ticking.

Chief of Staff Reince Priebus came into the room, saw the scramble taking place, and was confused. "I don't think you need to rush like this," he said. "I mean, the President isn't just sitting up there counting the seconds until this happens. You've got plenty of time to think it through and get it right."

Reince had worked closely with Sean at the RNC and knew him better than anybody. Maybe he sensed the disaster ahead. In any event, he offered advice only a fool would ignore. We were those fools.

"We already notified the press that I'm coming out in a few minutes," Spicer shot back.

In retrospect, of course, we were engaging in a senseless, unrecoverable act of self-sabotage. One that not only set the Press Secretary off on a bad note, but did enormous damage to the White House's credibility on day one. Here he was, moments away from engaging in a very public act that—if botched—could live with him forever, and he seemed to be mindlessly rushing into it as if the only thing to do was, to use his words, get it over with.

About twenty minutes after giving the fifteen-minute warning, Spicer dispatched his assistant to give a two-minute warning. The remarks were printed, Spicer took one last look at himself in the mirror, and our small team moved toward the Press Briefing Room.

In those last few minutes, as he prepared to throw away whatever credibility he'd built over decades in Washington, Spicer was quiet as a church mouse, almost like he was walking to his own execution. Realizing he was still nervously chewing on the ever-present stick of gum in his mouth, he quickly found a garbage can to throw it away.

As we filed into the staff seating area along the side wall, I was stunned at how packed the room was. In the couple of times I had come to the White House as a journalist during the Obama administration, there were always at least a couple of empty seats. Not this time. If it had been a Trump rally, the President would have touted the number of people waiting outside to get in.

I walked past the chairs along the side of the stage—there were only four of them and there were seven of us—and sat down on the floor. This earned me a quick scolding from a photographer anxiously awaiting Spicer's arrival. I was in his shot and needed to move. I walked back and crouched between the first chair and the doorway.

Moments later the door slid open and Sean walked in.

Camera lenses fluttered at a machine gun's pace as Spicer shuffled to the podium, printed remarks on loose-leaf paper in his right hand.

At 5:39 P.M., he began speaking—aggressively.

Good evening. Thank you, guys, for coming. I know our first official press briefing is going to be on Monday, but I wanted to give you a few updates on the President's activities. But before I get to the news of the day, I think I'd like to discuss a little bit of the coverage of the last twenty-four hours.

Yesterday, at a time when our nation and the world was watching the peaceful transition of power and, as the President said, the transition and the balance of power from Washington to the citizens of the United States, some members of the media were engaged in deliberately false reporting. For all the talk about the proper use of Twitter, two instances yesterday stand out.

One was a particularly egregious example in which a reporter falsely tweeted out that the bust of Martin Luther King Jr. had been removed from the Oval Office. After it was pointed out that this was just plain wrong, the reporter casually reported and tweeted out and tried to claim that a Secret Service agent must have just been standing in front of it. This was irresponsible and reckless.

Secondly, photographs of the inaugural proceedings were intentionally framed in a way, in one particular tweet, to minimize the enormous support that had gathered on the National Mall. This was the first time in our nation's history that floor coverings have been used to protect the grass on the Mall. That had the effect of highlighting any areas where people were not standing, while in years past the grass eliminated this visual. This was also the first time that fencing and magnetometers went as far back on the Mall, preventing hundreds of thousands of people from being able to access the Mall as quickly as they had in inaugurations past.

Inaccurate numbers involving crowd size were also tweeted. No one had numbers, because the National Park Service, which controls the National Mall, does not put any out. By the way, this applies to any attempts to try to count the number of protesters today in the same fashion.

We do know a few things, so let's go through the facts. We know that from the platform where the President was sworn in, to Fourth Street, it holds about 250,000 people. From Fourth Street to the media tent is about another 220,000. And from the media tent to the Washington Monument, another 250,000 people. All of this space was full when the President took the oath of office. We know that 420,000 people used the D.C. Metro public transit yesterday, which actually compares to 317,000 that used it for President Obama's last inaugural. This was the largest audience to ever witness an inauguration— period—both in person and around the globe. Even The New York

Times *printed a photograph showing a misrepresentation of the crowd in the original tweet in their paper, which showed the full extent of the support, depth in crowd, and intensity that existed.*

These attempts to lessen the enthusiasm of the inauguration are shameful and wrong. . . .

The President is committed to unifying our country, and that was the focus of his inaugural address. This kind of dishonesty in the media, the challenging—that bringing about our nation together is making it more difficult.

There's been a lot of talk in the media about the responsibility to hold Donald Trump accountable. And I'm here to tell you that it goes two ways. We're going to hold the press accountable, as well. The American people deserve better. And as long as he serves as the messenger for this incredible movement, he will take his message directly to the American people, where his focus will always be. . . .

At 5:44 P.M. he walked offstage. The whole thing had only lasted five and a half minutes, but sitting crouched in the corner motionless, trying not to become a meme on TV, had caused my legs to fall asleep. I stood with the help of the armrest of the chair beside me, and our group filed out of the Briefing Room and back to Spicer's office.

Spicer was sweating profusely as he took off his jacket and sat down behind his desk.

"Good job, Sean," one of Spicer's staff piped up.

"Yeah, difficult circumstances but I think that went about as well as could be hoped," added Shah.

The rest of the group added their congratulations and encouraged Sean, who was holding it together in spite of the palpable nervous energy still coursing through his veins.

"Turn the TV up," was all he could muster.

The Press Secretary's office has a bank of TVs in a wooden cabinet on the west side of the room, and every network was carrying reaction to Spicer's debut behind the podium.

He was being disemboweled.

The first thing I noticed in the replays was that his suit fit terribly. This was a point that the President would later make as well.

But even more disconcerting was that every argument he made was being shredded. The Metro ridership numbers were wrong. Spicer's point about additional magnetometers and fencing seemed dubious. Our comment about this inauguration being the first time floor coverings were used on the National Mall was quickly proven incorrect. Our touting of the worldwide viewing audience—almost certainly the largest ever by virtue of high-speed internet's global proliferation—was garnering eye rolls.

Many of the "facts" we had been given by various well-meaning individuals were just plain incorrect, and we hadn't fact-checked them. It was a devastating mistake. We were already on shaky footing trying to argue about the crowd's size to begin with, but this just made it all worse.

Ari Fleischer, who had served as Press Secretary for President George W. Bush, had the most spot-on tweet of the night: "This is called a statement you're told to make by the President. And you know the President is watching."

He indeed was watching. And he didn't like what he saw.

"I don't know what that was," the President would later tell me about Spicer's performance, "but it wasn't what I wanted, that I can tell you."

Months later, after he had left the White House, *The New York Times* asked Spicer if he regretted his first turn behind the podium, dubbing it "one of his most infamous moments as Press Secretary."

"Of course I do, absolutely," he replied.

But sincere regrets don't mend shattered credibility. From the very first moments of his tenure to the day he left the White House for the last time, Spicer's trustworthiness was a constant issue.

Quietly, without the glare of the lights, I was embarrassed, too. I would go on to write countless presidential statements and remarks, numerous @realDonaldTrump and @PressSec tweets, thousands of talking points, and dozens of op-eds in major publications. Nothing I wrote was a bigger disaster—and more damaging to the credibility of the White House—than the first piece of work I put my hands to.

Partly, I hoped, this could be attributed to typical first-day chaos. But the chaos never really went away.

5

EARLY DAYS IN THE "DUMP"

Donald Trump was a builder at heart. That was the business he grew up in, the business his father taught him. That was how he made, and remade, his fortune. Building, renovating, haggling over designs and costs, rebuilding—that was the world he knew best. So I guess it was no surprise that he fixated on his physical surroundings sometimes in minute detail. I found this intriguing, considering his general lack of interest in the minutiae of—well, pretty much everything else.

Among the first times he visited the campaign war room in Trump Tower, he became preoccupied with the renovations that had taken place since he'd last visited the fourteenth floor. No detail seemed to escape his discerning eye. He patted his black dress shoes on the new carpet. "This is quality stuff, very nice," he said admiringly. He ran his hands along the doorframes and inspected the trim.

His fascination with architecture and design came out in random conversations. From day one, the J. Edgar Hoover Building, the FBI's aging headquarters on Pennsylvania Avenue, was a particular focus of his ire. "Honestly, I think it's the ugliest building in the city," he said of the massive concrete structure. The building was like a giant tan blob—the size of a city block—with hundreds of tiny square portals for windows. It was built in an architectural style known as "brutalism," and the name was entirely fitting. You'd be hard-pressed to find anyone in D.C. who disagreed with Trump's assessment on this one.

Later, a Disney production team would come to the White House to record the President's voice and mannerisms for the animatronic Trump that would go in Disney World's Hall of Presidents. This was a presidential duty that filled the President with unusual boyish excitement. He was going to be up there onstage next to Lincoln, Reagan, FDR. An animatronic Trump would literally walk among giants.

I read through the draft script for him, which included Trump discussing "achievements of the American spirit," like inventing the lightbulb, the internet . . . "And the skyscraper," he interjected. "It should have the skyscraper in there." He smiled. "Then I could add a little, 'Which, of course, I know a thing or two about,' right?"

The Disney executives, unfortunately, didn't like that idea. "How can the President claim Americans invented the skyscraper?" one asked. "That's just a taller building." Americans didn't invent the concept of buildings—fine. So I agreed to keep that line out of the script and Trump never mentioned it. (For the record, the first steel-structured skyscraper appeared in Chicago.) The point is that building is never far from Trump's mind.

So, presented with the opportunity to remodel the most famous office in the world, the Oval one, it came as no surprise that Trump led the effort himself.

The President received a lot of criticism for press reports that he called the White House a dump—a charge he later denied. In this instance, both Trump and the media were telling the truth. He never denigrated the actual White House residence, the way most of the news reports were presented. But he did use that term, with some justification, about the working offices of the West Wing. He'd occasionally express disgust that, in his view, the Obamas had allowed the place to fall into disrepair.

When we arrived in the West Wing, the carpet was light brown and worn, and the walls were a dingy, yellowish color. There was no rhyme or reason to the decor. Sometimes a vase from the 1920s was placed next to a lamp from the 1970s, on top of a table from the late 1800s, next to a couch from the 1980s. It wasn't all from a lack of style or taste; in some instances it was simply the fact that the most highly trafficked workspace on earth hadn't been freshened up in eight years. Flies swooped down from the recessed lighting tucked along the walls, targeting my daily club sandwich like hawks attacking prey. Beside my desk, the light blue bulb of an "inside insect killer"—or "bug zapper" where I come from—buzzed 24/7.

Cosmetic updates happen with the transition of each new administration, of course, but I doubt any president has ever been as hands-on as The Donald.

Traditionally every new president, usually with the help of the First Lady, makes cosmetic changes to the Oval Office. In Trump's case, he personally selected the rug (Reagan era), curtains (gold, of course), couches (Bush 43 era), and wallpaper. He moved the most famous Thomas Jefferson portrait from the Blue Room in the residence to the Oval. He added a painting of Andrew Jackson, a fellow populist icon. One shift in artwork seemed to please him more than any other. Always looking to buck any precedent set by Obama, Trump moved Winston Churchill's bust back to the Oval after his predecessor exiled it to a hallway outside the Treaty Room.

"Did you see who we brought back?" he'd ask when guests would visit for the first time. "Churchill's back. We brought him back. Obama had sent him away—a disgrace. He's back now."

But then he went far beyond what a traditional President and First Lady would do, personally supervising, or even micromanaging, a redo of the rest of his Oval Office suite as well as the larger West Wing.

Trump never uses a computer himself, so instead he hovered over his executive assistant, Madeleine Westerhout, as she sat at her desk outside the Oval Office scrolling through decor options on her computer, while he pointed at items he liked. No item of decor was too small to pass his notice—from rugs to wallpaper.

When the White House called York Wallcoverings in Pennsylvania to tell them the President wanted an order for the Oval Office delivered by 7 P.M. that same day, they thought it was a prank at first. When they were assured that this was a personal request from the new commander in chief, they panicked. They'd stopped making the pattern that Trump personally selected three years before. So the good folks at York had to stop everything else they were working on, hand-mix the inks, print ninety-six double rolls of out-of-stock fabric, and make the two-hour drive to deliver the product, all before dinnertime. Which, miraculously, they did.

The President also, with great pride and concentration, selected the color palette for the rest of the West Wing and ensured that decorations in each room were from a corresponding time period. In those changes he was a little more patient.

Something else also caught his eye in the Roosevelt Room, a modest-sized conference room just across the hall from the Oval Office. Along the wall on the south side of the room stood eight flags: the U.S. flag, the presidential and vice presidential flags, and flags for each of the five branches of the military—Army, Air Force, Coast Guard, Marines, and Navy. The President especially liked the military flags, because they included streamers—long pieces of fabric—embroidered with the major campaigns in which each branch had fought.

Trump, who had never served in the military, held the armed forces in highest esteem. He famously referred to military leaders as "my generals" and was drawn to anyone in uniform. As President, he liked being chief executive—it was a role he'd been filling for decades—but he loved being commander in chief.

In the early days of the administration, aides would sometimes come into the Roosevelt Room and realize the flags were mysteriously missing. Invariably they would come to find out that Trump had requested they be moved into the Oval Office and placed along the walls behind his desk. So then they'd have to move them back into the Roosevelt Room for public events, once again prompting the President to ask for them to be returned to the Oval once he realized they were gone. Eventually they acquired a second set so the President could enjoy them encircling his office and the Roosevelt Room could be left in peace.

Once the renovations were completed, the President enjoyed giving tours of his private suite in the West Wing, including the rooms connected to the Oval Office that most Americans and staff members in previous administrations had rarely seen. He occasionally delighted in pointing out the history of one room in particular.

After being interviewed by Maria Bartiromo in the Roosevelt Room, the President invited the Fox Business Network host across the hall into the Oval for a quick tour. Turning right down the suite's hallway, he paused to turn on the light in the bathroom—the place where Lyndon Johnson famously used to give orders to his staff while sitting on the toilet. The flawless white marble glistened in the light and the President remarked on the craftsmanship. "Simply beautiful."

But that wasn't the room that interested him most.

A few steps farther on the other side of the hall, the President popped open the door to his private study. It's a small room, which his predecessors tended to use as a working office when the Oval felt too formal. Light poured into the study through the two floor-to-ceiling windows, and Trump had installed several plush, comfortable chairs. He didn't use the room very often, though as I would later experience, it was the ideal place to have private conversations that couldn't even be heard by the curious ears of executive assistants.

"I'm told this is where Bill and Monica—" Trump began, stopping himself before his sentence reached completion.

He shrugged and then moved on to the private dining room. "This place was a disaster when I got here," he said, "hole in the wall and many other problems." He'd had the room stripped down to its studs and refurbished in spectacular fashion. He purchased a giant crystal chandelier with his own money—which he called his "contribution to the history" of the White House—and had it hung above a table that was usually covered in crisp white linen. The carpet was deep red with golden stars every few feet. The seats of the wood-backed chairs were upholstered to match the stars. Large historical paintings were hung in gilded wooden frames. And suspended on the wall above the fireplace was his favorite toy: a sixty-plus-inch flat-screen television. "It's got, like, a super TiVo," he said as he grabbed the remote and scrolled through the day's clips that had been queued up for him. "I think it's one of the greatest inventions." He said this with a smirk, as if to acknowledge his reputation as a television addict.

He loved showing off the residence, too, and seemed genuinely awed by the sheer coolness of living at the world's most illustrious address.

The second week we were in the White House, Trump came out of the Oval late in the evening and, with raised eyebrows, said something that many of us never expected to hear, especially from him.

"This job is a lot harder than I thought it'd be."

It occurred to me pretty early on that the presidency is like an iceberg. The parts you see—the speeches, the ceremonial duties, the interviews, the walks out to Marine One, the photo ops before or after meetings—those are like the tip of the iceberg sticking out of the water. The other 90 percent of the job exists out of sight in the murky depths below. Intelligence briefings, policy briefings, legislative strategy briefings—briefings, briefings, and more briefings. And mountains of paperwork.

One afternoon after an event in the East Room, Staff Secretary Rob Porter was waiting for the President in the Green Room with a stack of official actions that needed to be signed right away.

"Here he is again," the President said, half joking but somewhat annoyed. "You've never seen somebody have to sign as many documents as me—big ones, little ones. It never ends." Porter laughed dutifully and explained why this particular stack couldn't wait.

Any decision that makes it to the President's desk is significant, otherwise it would have been handled by someone lower down the chain of command.

Though it may surprise people accustomed to Trump's "I'm a genius who can handle anything" public persona, in private, this new reality was not totally lost on him. Of course, I doubt anyone really knows what they're getting themselves into when they sign up to be Leader of the Free World.

During our early days in the West Wing, there was an entire genre of reporting devoted to Trump's "chaotic" management style. This was not "fake news." A lot of it, anyway. Press reports about it being the Wild West were somewhat overblown, but the underlying premise was generally accurate. We were all figuring it out as we went along.

In *The Art of the Deal,* Trump wrote that it's hard to be "imaginative or entrepreneurial if you have too much structure." Right away, his freewheeling approach collided with the presidency like an unstoppable force running into an immovable object. Anyone could see why it would pose such a challenge to someone in charge of managing the office—like Reince Priebus or, later, John Kelly.

His official schedule was more of a loose outline than a strict regimen. If the President was scheduled to come down from the residence first thing in the morning for a filming session, I'd wait for him on the ground floor outside his private elevator. It wouldn't be abnormal for him to be upstairs working the phones and ultimately come down a half hour, or even a full hour, later than anticipated. The same could be said of the evenings, when he'd linger in the Oval until after dusk, continuing to work long after his "official schedule" had concluded.

During the day, the Oval Office suite was a hub of activity.

In the "Outer Oval," the President's executive assistant, Madeleine Westerhout, shared a work space with Hope Hicks, whose title was Director of

Strategic Communications but who was, in reality, whatever Trump wanted her to be that day. Like pretty much everyone else.

Madeleine had previously been an executive assistant at the RNC. She'd first captured the public's attention—and Trump's attention as well—during the transition. Ever the showman, Trump paraded potential cabinet members in front of the cameras in the Trump Tower lobby and at his golf club in New Jersey. Ushering each one of them to meet the boss was a twenty-six-year-old brunette, smiling and making small talk along the way. That was Madeleine.

During the transition, campaign aides jokingly referred to her as "The Mockingjay," the young woman who came to symbolize a rebellion in the Hunger Games novels. In our case, she symbolized a broader push for RNC aides to swoop in and claim White House jobs that might have otherwise gone to campaign staffers. It was tongue in cheek—nothing personal against her. In fact, she was nothing but nice to me when we first arrived. But others who'd been with Trump much longer than me viewed her with deep suspicion. They believed Priebus and his top deputy, Katie Walsh, had installed Madeleine in such a sensitive role—within earshot and with full visibility of everything happening in the Oval—to act as their personal spy.

Hope's desk, sitting parallel to Madeleine's, was the closest to the Oval Office. The President would call out for "Hopey" to come in to see him count-less times each day. She'd assess the press coverage for him, give recommen-dations on which interviews to do and which to turn down, and advise him on how to respond to the media crisis of the moment. Trump has a reputation for surrounding himself with beautiful women. Hope was no exception to this rule. She was a twenty-eight-year-old former Ralph Lauren model, after all. But that shouldn't be taken to imply that she wasn't a pro. While Spicer was engaged in a blood feud with the entire Washington press corps and the Pres-ident was publicly calling them "the enemy of the people," Hope maintained strong relationships with almost all of them. Most important, the President trusted her completely. The reason was simple: unlike so many others in Trump's orbit, she'd proven time and again that she only acted in his best inter-est. She wasn't trying to build her brand or get famous. In fact, she longed for the anonymity she had enjoyed before politics. She was there to serve him.

She became one of my best friends in the White House. In my text con-versations, I didn't refer to her by her name, I'd just type the diamond emoji—a symbol inspired by the famous Hope Diamond on display in the Smithsonian. We'd later sit by the pool at Bedminster and talk at length about our jobs, the White House, and life in general, but in the early days of the administration we didn't have time to slow down.

In an even smaller office inside the Outer Oval, the President's personal aide, or "body man," Johnny McEntee, and his longtime bodyguard, Keith Schiller, shared a work space.

McEntee was a former University of Connecticut quarterback in his mid-twenties. His claim to fame was a YouTube video in which he showed off his accuracy and arm strength by performing tricks, like throwing a football into a basketball hoop from the upper deck of UConn's basketball arena. The video garnered almost eight million views. As an intern at Fox News, he'd watched Trump's freewheeling campaign announcement on TV and knew immediately he wanted to join his team. He sent messages to the campaign's public email address and eventually got a response inviting him to come on board. He became more than a political staffer; he was like an adopted family member. He was by the President's side sixteen hours a day. He'd later become a heart-throb throughout the Arab world when photos of him with the First Family went viral during the President's trip to Saudi Arabia. Arab newspapers didn't know his name, referring to him only as "the man in the red tie." "This man in the red tie shouldn't leave Saudi Arabia!" one woman said, according to *Arab News*. "Just give me the man in the red tie and throw me in the sea," another tweeted.

Though most outsiders didn't know it, Johnny's office mate, Keith Schiller, was the most important person on Trump's staff. His official title was Director of Oval Office Operations, but he may have been more accurately described as First Friend. In his late fifties, Keith's relationship with "the boss," as he always called him, went back further than anyone else's in the White House. He was tough as nails. As a New York City narcotics officer in the early 2000s, his job had been to kick in doors during drug raids. When a protester outside Trump Tower came after him from behind during the campaign, Schiller had turned around and smacked him so hard, he immediately cowered in fear. "He was reaching for my gun," Schiller later told me. He had served as Trump's head of security since 2004. He'd been at Trump's side through the good times and the bad, and he was one of the only nonbillionaires that Trump viewed as a peer.

Every president needs someone in whom they can confide, someone who will shoot straight with them—say things that other staffers could never get away with. That was Keith. He was always very respectful and deferential to the President, but he was an honest and trusted voice. He went up to get the President in the morning, then walked him back up at night, often making him the first and last staffer Trump would see. The two chiefs of staff that I worked with in the White House both resented his relationship with the President and tried to sideline him in any way they could.

Madeleine, Hope, Johnny, and Keith were the aides who kept the Oval Office humming and made sure the President always had what he needed. Participants in official meetings funneled through their office on the way in to meet with the President. In between meetings, aides who wanted to pop in for a second were often summoned when the President would notice them standing just outside. He fed off the energy of being around other people. He liked bouncing from issue to issue in quick bursts.

In the early days of the administration, my primary role in such meetings was something of a fact-checker for the press and communications team. Sometimes reporters would claim to have sources describing conversations that took place in the room. In those instances, I was able to quickly tell press aides, yes, that happened; or no, that did not happen; or well, there is a shred of truth there, but it is taken out of context. Then they could formulate a plan for how to respond.

There were very few people on the original Trump White House staff who had any experience in the West Wing. We would sometimes laugh about the differences between *The West Wing* television show and reality. Perhaps most notably, the halls of the real-life West Wing are nowhere near wide enough to accommodate the television series' famous walk-and-talk scenes, and in fact the entire place is much smaller and more cramped than it's often portrayed.

But as I tried to find my place in Trump's orbit, one *West Wing* episode—"20 Hours in America"—frequently came to mind.

In the episode, Deputy Chief of Staff Josh Lyman (Bradley Whitford) is left behind by the presidential motorcade after President Josiah Bartlet's (Martin Sheen) speech in Indiana. As a result, Deputy Communications Director Sam Seaborn (Rob Lowe) has to stand in for Lyman and staff the President once he returns to the White House.

Terrified, Sam explains, "There are going to be any number of areas on which I can't give him expert advice."

"Welcome to the club," Josh replies.

For the rest of the day, Sam desperately tries to staff the President from meeting to meeting, topic to topic. By the end of the episode, he's exasperated and reflecting back on what he has experienced.

"Until you sit in the room all day, you can't comprehend the chaos of the Oval Office," he says. "I had one good moment . . . but that was it. The rest of the day was just keeping up. And this was a pretty light day."

But in spite of being overwhelmed and feeling incredibly unprepared for the breadth of issues and the depth of each conversation with the President and his expert advisers, his one takeaway is "I've got to get back in there. That's where it's happening."

TV shows don't tend to get much right about what it's *really* like to work in the White House—at least in the Trump White House—but *The West Wing*'s writers were spot-on with this one. All of the action is in the room. Decisions are made in the room. If you want to matter—if you want to be a player—you've got to get in the room.

With that in mind, I attended presidential meetings on an insanely broad range of subjects and quietly took notes. I didn't say much for the first couple of weeks, but before long I was able to occasionally offer perspective that others didn't have. As a result, the President grew to know and trust me, and I never violated his trust.

This proximity also helped me in my official role as Director of White House Message Strategy. Unlike most politicians, who like staffers to bring them fully fleshed-out briefing papers and poll-tested talking points, Trump's communications strategy and messaging was all based on pure gut instinct. Being around him helped me get a sense of how he instinctively talked about various issues. And since there really isn't a "private" version of Trump, you could bet that anything he said behind the scenes was eventually going to find its way into his public comments.

The more time I spent around the President, the more I picked up on his quirks.

For one thing, I noticed that he had a strange habit of moving any item that was set in front of him. If a waiter placed a glass down beside him, he would immediately reposition it. If his name placard was directly in front of him, he would move it off to the side. If he was referencing notes in front of him, he would shift them from position to position while other people were talking. And if his silverware was not exactly perpendicular to his plate, he would carefully align it—an OCD habit that I subconsciously picked up myself, driving my wife insane. Sometimes he would actually do the same for his guests. When Wayne LaPierre of the NRA sat down beside him at the table in the Roosevelt Room, for example, Trump even slid LaPierre's own drink and coaster a few inches to the left. Maybe this was all subconscious, maybe it was a subtle power move. In any event, it happened all the time.

The staff often scheduled larger meetings with the President in the Roosevelt Room. He didn't like to venture far from his domain during the day, but just across the hall was acceptable. Regardless of who he was meeting with, or for how long, the President had a habit of ending the discussions the same way. When he became too bored and was ready to move on, he would interject, "Has anyone here ever heard of a place called the Oval Office?"

His guests would smile and nod. "Oh, of course, I'm sure you've all been to the Oval Office many times, right, as important as you all are?" he'd tease. With some exceptions, most had not.

"You know, the crazy thing is," he would continue, "President Obama didn't like to bring people into the Oval Office; he didn't want people to see it. I have no idea why, because it's just right through that door." It was unclear to us whether this was true or not, and I have no idea where the President heard that. But as I had noticed many times by then, he enjoyed making comparisons to Obama that made him look better in the telling.

The President would then look over his right shoulder and nod or point to the curved door on the southeast side of the room. "Would you like to see it? You know what? Let's go." And with that, the President would parade the group across the hall into the most famous office in the world. After all, was someone going to say, "No, thanks, Mr. President"? Of course not. It was a fail-proof, and clever, way to end any meeting early and on a good note.

His other recurring bit took place during meetings in the Oval Office itself, and it was by far my favorite.

The President liked to preside over small group meetings while sitting behind the Resolute desk. The desk itself was an extraordinary historical artifact. It was ornately carved out of English oak timbers from the HMS

Resolute and had been given by Queen Victoria to President Rutherford B. Hayes in 1880. Presidents Kennedy, Reagan, Clinton, Bush, and Obama all used the desk in the Oval Office, and it combined the two things Trump appreciated most in White House furniture: history and luxury.

Out in front of him, on the other side of the desk, four wooden chairs—historic, I'm sure, but fairly uncomfortable—would be set up in a semicircle. On many days, stacks of briefing papers, newspapers, and locked bags designed to carry classified documents would be stacked on the desk around the telephone. "I actually do work in here, unlike some of the ones before me," the President would say as an assistant would clear off the desk.

But always left behind, no matter what, would be a small wooden box, approximately nine inches long and three inches wide. A golden presidential seal was imprinted on top of it right in the middle, with a small red button right beside it, about the size of a penny.

The box with its bright red button would often catch the attention of guests, who would look at it silently as their minds raced.

What happens if he presses that red button? I'm sure many a first-time visitor wondered to themselves.

If Trump noticed someone glancing at the box—and sometimes completely unprompted—he would pick it up and move it farther away from himself. "Don't worry about that," he'd say. "No one wants me to push that button, so we'll just keep it over here. Now, what were you saying?"

Guests would laugh nervously and the conversation would continue, until several minutes later Trump would suddenly move it closer to him without actually saying anything about it. Then, later in the conversation, out of nowhere, he'd suddenly press the button. Not sure what to do, guests would look at one another with raised eyebrows. Moments later, a steward would enter the room carrying a glass filled with Diet Coke on a silver platter, and Trump would burst out laughing. "That red button!" he'd exclaim. "People never know what to think about the red button! Is he launching the nukes?!" Most guests would double over laughing at the prankster in chief. The prank also offered a subtle sense of self-awareness—there *were* people who thought Trump was volatile enough to start a nuclear war.

In addition to all the outside groups rolling through, cabinet secretaries also began sitting down with the President to discuss the vision for their agencies.

One of the most memorable exchanges I witnessed was with Dr. Ben Carson, Trump's former presidential rival turned supporter. He was now Secretary of Housing and Urban Development, despite having little to no experience running such a massive organization. That didn't matter to Trump; Carson was his guy. And he seemed to have genuine affection for him. Long gone were the days when Carson threatened him in the polls, when Trump had said he had a "pathological temper" that made him incurable, like a "child molester."

"My precious Ben," Trump said softly, swiveling his chair around to greet the Secretary.

During the 2016 campaign, Trump very famously diminished rival Jeb Bush by calling him "low energy." Next to Ben Carson, Bush was a rocket engine of excitement. Everything about his movements, his demeanor, even the somewhat sleepy look in his eyes seemed designed to lose your interest. In another life, he was an acclaimed neurosurgeon. Some people joked that was perhaps because he could put patients to sleep without the need for anesthesia.

Carson sat in front of the Resolute desk with a folder in his lap, feet neatly tucked under his chair, like an attentive student. I took a seat along the wall, figuring there might be a moment for me to slip out and return to my desk to catch up on the emails piling up in my in-box. There aren't many places I'd rather be than sitting in the Oval—in the middle of the action—but it was hard to imagine HUD policy capturing my attention for very long. Turns out I wasn't the only one in the room who felt that way.

The President leaned back in his chair, crossed his legs, and took a swig of his Diet Coke. Large cubes of ice clinked against the inside of the glass, which was running low on Trump's favorite dark brown liquid.

"So what're we going to do, my Ben?" Trump asked genially.

The Secretary's voice was so soft that I struggled to make out some sentences. Words left his mouth and seemed to evaporate once they hit the open air.

Referencing his notes, Carson began casting his vision for a department that would help lift people out of poverty through various programs that brought the public and private sectors together. Literacy was a focus. This came as no surprise to me. Carson's nonprofit had opened well over a hundred "reading rooms" around the country, a fact I'd learned when crafting the messaging around Carson's nomination.

I could see Trump starting to lose interest as Carson continued articulating the detailed plans inside his notebook. First, the President shifted in his chair and readjusted a small pillow he'd placed behind his back. Then, as Carson talked about different phases of his program and whatnot, Trump glanced around the room. At some point he noted his Diet Coke was nearly gone and went back to his button routine, but his heart wasn't quite in it this time. "People always wonder about this button," he told a confused Carson.

Finally, he pressed it again. Diet Coke arrived and Trump was done.

"That sounds wonderful, Ben," he interjected at one point. "I trust you to do it right." I had no idea what Trump had just approved, and I'm not sure he did, either. But he stood up, signaling the meeting was coming to an end. He shook Secretary Carson's delicate, valuable right hand, the one that had saved so many lives during his decades as a surgeon, and sent him on his way. The whole meeting lasted, maybe, ten minutes.

In other early strategy meetings, however, Trump was much more engaged.

"Get in here, Steven!" the President said, seeing Treasury Secretary Steven Mnuchin waiting just outside his office. "They said we'd never do it, but here we are in the Oval Office, raised more money than they ever thought. Saw the whole country—and they loved us, right, my man?"

"That's right, sir, we did," Mnuchin replied in his typical, low-key style. "I have some people that I want you to meet."

Behind Mnuchin filed in about a half-dozen men in expensive suits. "Holy crap," one of them said under his breath, pointing up at the eagle and stars intricately carved into the ceiling. It was the first time any of them had been in the Oval, an experience that gives pause to even kings, prime ministers, and presidents, much less the rest of us mere mortals.

"Welcome to the famous Oval Office," Trump said with a twinkle in his eye. "I'm sure you've all been here many times before."

With the Treasury Department's new senior aides now arrayed in front of the President, Mnuchin started introducing them one by one. Trump occasionally interjected with questions about their résumés and backgrounds, but mostly casually listened while sipping his Diet Coke.

After the introductions, Trump thanked the new staffers for joining the team and seemed like he was about to wrap it up. Then he suddenly stopped midsentence, sat up straight, and asked the group the first and only policy question of the meeting.

"Should I label China a currency manipulator?"

It was one of Trump's central foreign policy promises of the campaign. Now, in office, he took great pride in keeping his word to voters and was eager to check this one off his list.

"No, sir, you shouldn't," one of the aides said without hesitation as the rest of the group traded uncertain glances.

Surprised, Trump's head snapped around and he locked eyes with this new adviser, who was now probably worried this would be his first and last trip to the Oval.

"Really?" the President asked with great curiosity. "Why not?"

"We're developing a report for you that lays out in detail our economic relationship with China," the Treasury staffer said. "Using Treasury's criteria, China's worst offense is its massive trade surplus, but based on our research it does not appear to be actively manipulating its currency."

"Who the hell is this?" Trump asked with a laugh, looking over at Mnuchin.

"This is Dan Kowalski," the Secretary replied with trepidation. Kowalski had been a senior staffer on the campaign's policy team after working on the Hill for two decades. He was intimately familiar with Trump's history on this issue, and he was now one of the newly minted counselors to the Secretary.

"All right, Dan," the President said, leaning forward. "Talk to me about this. They're killing us—I mean absolutely killing us."

Mimicking his cadence on the campaign trail, Trump mock-yelled, "'China's beating the hell out of us! And I'm not going to let them do it anymore!' That's what I said, all the time, and the people would go crazy. Steven, you were there. You saw it. The people would go wild, I mean absolutely wild. And now you're telling me something different?"

"No, sir," Kowalski said. "There are a lot of tools at your disposal to push back on China, and you should use them. But our research shows that they are not currently manipulating their currency. We have a list of countries we watch closely—six of them, if I remember correctly—and China is one of them. They have a history of foreign exchange intervention. It's hurt us in the past, you are absolutely right. They undervalued their currency for a long time, so it did not appreciate even though its trade surplus soared. But that is no longer the case."

"I'm going to have to see this report," Trump replied, looking over at

Mnuchin. "I want to see it. We've got to do something about China, I'm just telling you. We have no choice. So I need to see this report."

In the coming weeks, the President held meetings with numerous officials throughout the executive branch, including senior members of the National Economic Council, National Trade Council, and National Security Council. Then, less than a month after the meeting in the Oval Office with Mnuchin's team, Trump announced he would not label China a currency manipulator.

This was my first memorable exposure to one of Trump's core operating principles, which could probably be best described as *strong opinions, weakly held*. He had strong opinions on pretty much everything under the sun, and he wasn't afraid to share them with the world. But the only two issues on which he seemed to have deeply ingrained, long-held beliefs were immigration and trade. On everything else he was willing to be convinced, with compelling evidence, that he should change his position. This was different from flip-flopping, which politicians do for political expediency. There's no doubt he changed his position, but from my vantage point he did it because he was presented with new information. And isn't that what we want from our leaders? Of course, we also needed China to ratchet up pressure on North Korea to abandon its nuclear weapons program. Navigating geopolitics is a lot more complex than campaigning, and I'm sure that played a role, too.

The West Wing adapted Trump's laissez-faire style, but there was sometimes uncertainty about who exactly was in charge and empowered to do what.

A traditional White House structure starts with the Chief of Staff at the top, followed by a couple of deputy chiefs, then the heads of departments (Communications, Legislative Affairs, Political Affairs, Intergovernmental Affairs, the National Economic Council, National Security Council, etc.), then their deputies, and so on.

But from the very beginning, Trump created something of a three-headed monster at the top with Reince Priebus holding the title of Chief of Staff, Steve Bannon as Chief Strategist, and Jared Kushner as Senior Adviser. Each of those individuals came in with staff who were loyal to them for various reasons, whether ideological or personal.

The selection of Priebus was puzzling to a lot of people—especially to anyone trying to reconcile his hiring with Trump's well-known obsession with loyalty. He knew, after all, that Reince had all but bailed on him after the *Access Hollywood* crisis. Maybe his selection of Priebus for the traditionally powerful post of Chief of Staff was meant to show that he was more open-minded and forgiving than the conventional wisdom suggested. Maybe it was a recognition that Trump needed an insider to help him govern, especially given Reince's close relationship with House Speaker Paul Ryan. Maybe it was done just so that Trump could torment Reince on a daily basis. Or maybe—and this tended to be my view—Trump didn't think much of titles. "Chief of Staff" meant little to him.

It quickly became obvious to everyone working with Trump that there was the official organizational chart, and the unofficial—also known as the *real*—organizational chart. The official org chart looked like a typical White House, perhaps just a little more top heavy. The *real* org chart, however, was basically Trump in the middle and everyone he personally knew connected to him—like a hub and its spokes. This exacerbated staff tensions when the official hierarchy was upended by the reality of how Trump operated.

As Director of Legislative Affairs, for instance, Marc Short was technically subordinated to Deputy Chief of Staff Rick Dearborn, whose portfolio included the White House's relationship with Capitol Hill. But in practice, Short was the President's go-to guy when dealing with lawmakers, and he operated mostly autonomously. This wasn't a big deal in Dearborn's case—he was comfortable enough in his own standing, and in his own skin, to not recoil at Short's spreading his wings a little bit.

Kellyanne was another one. As Counselor to the President, she managed to land a job with no fixed responsibilities. "What exactly does Kellyanne do?" was a question people asked all the time. So she was able to continue being the President's pit bull on TV—a job that never goes out of fashion in Trump World—and otherwise just dabble in areas that piqued her interest. She would later focus her efforts on the opioid crisis and veterans' issues, but early on she was content—very content—to sit back, go on TV, and let rivals eat one another alive.

And then there was Dan Scavino, one of Trump's longest-serving aides. Dan was the rare person in the White House who was universally liked by all the staff. He'd worked his way up from being Trump's golf caddy, to general manager of Trump National Golf Club in Westchester, to social media director on the campaign and then in the White House. He was glued to

Trump's side, capturing nearly every moment with his cell phone camera and blasting it out on social media for the world to see. He was the only person other than Trump himself who always maintained access to the @realDonaldTrump Twitter account. On his personal account, he was known as the unofficial conductor of the Trump train, and his online persona was a mirror image of Trump—bombastic, controversial, a hot-take machine. In person he was quiet, humble, and carried himself with a gentle spirit.

Any time Scavino's name would come up in conversations—which happened regularly; the guy was famous among Trump's followers—people would inevitably ask about "the tweets." *Is it really Trump? Does he give anyone advance notice what he's tweeting? Tell us how it works!*

This shouldn't come as a surprise to anyone: it's Trump. He'd fire off tweets from the residence at all hours and usually without any advance notice to staff. During the day, he would often call Dan into the Oval to dictate tweets, complete with punctuation instructions—dash, dash, "sad," exclamation point—and his own unique way of capitalizing seemingly random words for emphasis.

Early on, there wasn't an official channel to submit recommended tweets, but Dan would come in with a printout of various options. Trump would approve them, disapprove them, or make tweaks, but you can rest assured that he wasn't letting anything go out without his sign-off. In that regard he was like a publisher, fiercely protective of his brand and loyal to his audience—he only wanted to put out things they'd want to read. Over time I got really adept at tweeting in Trump's voice. Policy and communications aides would bring their topics to me and I'd craft the most Trumpian tweet I could, then submit it for approval, with a pretty good success rate.

In retrospect, I was both empowered and hurt by the unofficial org chart. Because of my relationship with Trump—and Hope, Keith, Jared, and Bannon, to name a few—and my status as a campaign "loyalist," I had wide latitude to be a part of meetings, to fly on Air Force One, to interact with the President, and later to play a leadership role in major efforts like tax reform. These were extraordinary, once-in-a-lifetime experiences, the kind you dream of when you think of what it must be like to work at the White House. Like the time I suddenly found myself organizing a videoconference call between the President and astronauts aboard the International Space Station.

In the first couple of months we were in the White House, NASA Communications Director Jen Rae Wang reached out to me and asked if the President might participate in some type of event celebrating astronaut Peggy Whitson's breaking the record for the most cumulative time in space. She was currently aboard the ISS and was set to break the record on April 24, 2017.

"I've seen past presidents call the Space Station before," I said. "Could he do that?"

"Oh, yes," she replied, clearly excited. "We could set up a videoconference anywhere you want and broadcast it live."

"The Oval Office?" I asked.

"Yes, of course, that would be amazing," she said.

The next day, standing on the patio just off the Oval Office, I asked the President if he was interested in doing the call. He was all in. "We don't capture people's imaginations anymore," he said, in a rare moment of wistfulness. "We used to do big things—incredible things. No one could do the things we could do. You have to inspire people. They went to the moon. But the call would be great. Honestly, how cool is NASA?"

Over the next few weeks, I brought in NASA engineers, who produced diagrams of the Oval Office with all the production equipment positioned where it would be. We went into the Oval and did a walk-through of exactly how it would play out. And we coordinated with NASA's spaceflight team to pinpoint the exact time the call would need to take place. This, as it turns out, was much more important than I initially realized. One of the engineers explained "orbital mechanics" to me, which boiled down to: *When the Space Station flies around the curvature of the planet, we lose touch with it.* That meant we had a very defined window of time—about twenty minutes—to make this happen. The President would have to be right on time, a rarity.

The day of the event, there was a buzz of excitement in the Oval suite. For staff, this was going to be one of those *How cool is this?* moments. With the production team setting up in the Oval, I pulled the President into the Private Dining Room for a final briefing on the sequence of events.

Also around the table with me were Secretary of Education Betsy DeVos (we had partnered with her to encourage teachers around the country to let their students watch the videoconference from their classrooms), astronaut Kate Rubins, and Acting NASA Administrator Robert Lightfoot Jr. We had about ten minutes before the broadcast, which I stressed to the President had to start and end exactly on time.

The President was sitting at the head of the table wearing a dark red tie, a small stack of newspapers and briefing folders sitting just to his right. I sat down in the chair just to his left. The giant flat-screen TV hanging on the wall was tuned to Fox News, on mute.

I started walking the President through the sequence of events as he scanned over his prepared remarks, crossing out some of the text with a Sharpie. He wanted to know the positioning of the cameras, which side of his head would be most prominently featured. I had made sure the press cameras would be positioned on the right side, his preference, and he nodded his approval. He also wanted to make sure the television audience would see both him and the astronauts in space, which I assured him they would.

As I continued working my way through the briefing sheet, he suddenly appeared distracted, distant. I could sense the gears inside of his head starting to turn. I was losing him. And he soon revealed why. With our small window of time for prep closing, the President suddenly turned toward the NASA Administrator.

"What's our plan for Mars?" he asked.

Mars? Where did that come from?

Mr. Lightfoot sat up straight, cleared his throat, and explained that NASA's plan was to send an unmanned rover to Mars in 2020, then to try for manned spaceflight to the red planet by the 2030s.

Trump bristled. "But is there any way we could do it by the end of my first term?" he asked.

Lightfoot shifted in his chair and placed his right hand on his chin. With hesitation, he politely told the President that he didn't believe that time frame was possible. A man on Mars in 2020 would be a logistical impossibility. He laid out all the challenges—distance, fuel capacity, etc. Also the fact that we hadn't landed an American anywhere remotely close to Mars ever.

I was getting antsy. All I could think about was that he had to be on camera in three minutes. We still hadn't yet discussed several key details, and yet we're in here casually chatting about shaving a full decade off NASA's timetable for sending a manned flight to Mars. And seemingly out of nowhere.

Trump dropped his briefing papers down in front of him. His head cocked to its side and he leaned forward. "But what if I gave you all the money you could ever need to do it?" Trump asked. "What if we sent NASA's budget through the roof, but focused entirely on that instead of whatever else you're doing now. Could it work then?"

With a subtle, uncomfortable laugh and a bewildered look, Lightfoot said, basically, "No." He was sorry, but he just didn't think it was technologically possible.

Trump was visibly disappointed, but I tried to refocus him on the task at hand. We were now about ninety seconds from going live.

The President and I walked down the narrow hallway connecting the dining room to the Oval, but just before we walked through the door, he decided to stop in his white-marbled bathroom for one final check in the mirror. *Optics.* "Thirty seconds, Mr. President," I said, now nearing full-on panic.

"Space Station, this is your President," he said to himself, smirking in the mirror. "Go ahead," he continued calmly, without even a hint of concern in his voice. "I'll be right in."

When he finally hit the door, camera shutters snapped in a flurry as I counted down "Five . . . four . . . three . . ." He sat down, perfectly positioned as the broadcast began. Nineteen minutes later I signaled for him to wrap it up, and we finished the broadcast just before the Space Station flew over the horizon and out of reach. If I'd ever doubted that his showbiz background actually brought any value to this job, I certainly never would again.

I wouldn't trade such experiences for anything, but this access also bred resentment, especially among people above me in the official org chart who weren't afforded the same opportunities, or thought I was too big for my britches, as they say in the South. This earned me extra enemies. And I didn't need any more of those, considering the tension that already existed between former campaign and RNC staffers. The list would grow longer over time, for various reasons.

On the press and communications teams, our official schedule was bookended by an all-staff morning meeting at seven thirty and an evening meeting at six, both of which almost always started well behind schedule. For a while we kept a running tally of the total man-hours wasted standing outside of Sean's office waiting for the meeting to begin. We quit a couple of weeks in when it reached into the hundreds and we gave up keeping track. Thirty people all waiting together adds up in a hurry. Once the meetings finally began, people would go around the room mentioning things they were working on, and their superiors—or anyone else, really—would play armchair quarterback, explaining why what they were doing was wrong.

I was often reminded in these meetings of a conversation I had with Secretary of Defense James Mattis while he was waiting to see the President. While he could go toe-to-toe with any warrior on the planet, it was his intellectual approach to his life and work that truly set him apart. In addition to "Mad Dog"—a nickname the President loved more than Mattis did—he was also known as the "Warrior Monk." Throughout his military career, he would bring his roughly seven-thousand-volume library with him as he traveled from post to post. So on the rare occasion there was an opportunity to pick his brain, I didn't miss it.

On one such occasion he launched into an explanation of "commander's intent." This is a well-known concept in the military that essentially boils down to everyone having a clear understanding of the team's goals and objectives. If the commander has made it clear what success looks like, no one needs to be micromanaged along the way. General Mattis recalled leading Marines into battle as they swept across Iraq on the way to Baghdad. To his memory, he only gave a handful of direct orders over the course of a few weeks. He'd made his intent clear, and his men were empowered to make the right decisions on how to achieve it as they went. He also explained that he preferred to spend time with his men in the field, seeing their challenges firsthand, rather than remaining far removed from them and being briefed after the fact.

Mattis's approach to leadership was diametrically opposed to what we experienced in the press and comms office. Roles, goals, and objectives weren't clearly defined. Spicer went weeks without interacting with the broader team "on the front lines," if you will. And every effort someone made was nitpicked and ridiculed in front of everyone else.

These meetings set the tone for the entire team, creating a culture of frustration and distrust, and ultimately leading to the entire operation being justifiably viewed internally—and, with time, externally as well—as a disaster. It was already a challenge for me going from being the CEO to working under someone else. Now I felt like I wasn't working in a meritocracy, or on a team, or with a press secretary who even cared about his people's well-being or success.

This is best illustrated by a story that started as an internal incident that made everyone just shake their head or roll their eyes, but ended up becoming the lead anecdote of a viral article in *The Wall Street Journal* and a major point of contention in Spicer's White House memoir.

The third week we were in the West Wing, Spicer came out of his office and complained to his secretary—whose desk was about five feet from my own—that he didn't have a mini fridge to keep his drinks cold. He had requested one, and I'm a little unclear on the backstory, but it sounded like he had been told by the staff who managed the facilities that they weren't allowed to give him one in the West Wing because of concerns about mold.

"I'm going to go across the street, because I know they have one over there," he said. This meant a visit to the Eisenhower Executive Office Building. The overwhelming majority of people who work at the White House actually work out of offices in the EEOB, located across West Executive Drive, a narrow private road. The research team worked there out of a large, open room with eight desks lined up in two rows. Real estate in the West Wing was highly coveted—proximity to the Oval was often an indication of stature. But the EEOB had its advantages as well, most notably the fact that the offices were massive by comparison. The furniture was old, the carpet was faded, but light cut through the rooms thanks to massive external windows, and there was a much calmer atmosphere overall.

In the back left corner of the research team's office sat Andy Hemming, the White House's Director of Rapid Response. "Hemm-dog," as he was known, had stuck with the Trump campaign even when many of his RNC compatriots had bailed. So he maintained a foot in both camps. He was quite a character, often blurting out jarring or inappropriate things during meetings—which we'd usually laugh about later—and he maintained something of a shrine to disgraced former Congressman Anthony Weiner on the wall beside his desk.

Weiner, who also happened to be married to Hillary Clinton's top aide Huma Abedin, had gotten himself embroiled in various scandals over the years. He'd sent explicit photos of himself on Twitter and via text message—photos that were later released publicly. He ended up being sentenced to almost two years in prison for sending obscene material to a minor, for which he also had to register as a sex offender. Every time Weiner found himself in trouble, the New York tabloids would run double entendre headlines on their front pages. Hemming had every one of them hanging on his wall, along with an accompanying @realDonaldTrump tweet.

Hemming was also keeper of the office mini fridge, where various junior staffers kept their Lean Cuisines and lunch-meat sandwiches. The West Wing had the Navy Mess. We could call down at almost any point during the day and order up a wide variety of made-to-order meals or snacks. The EEOB crew had a serviceable cafeteria that was open on a much more limited basis. But Spicer wanted their mini fridge for himself, nonetheless.

Hemming rebuffed him, and according to multiple people who witnessed it, Sean just kind of laughed and went on his way.

Then, a few days later, two other staffers approached Hemming and said that Sean had asked them to tell him to bring the mini fridge to his office. Again, multiple people who witnessed this conversation said that Hemming told them he wouldn't do it, and that if Spicer really wanted it then he could come get it himself.

One evening around 8 P.M. I got a call from a member of the comms team who worked in the EEOB. "Dude, I just saw the strangest thing," he said. "I walked out into the hallway and Sean was carrying a refrigerator out of the building with, like, the power cord dragging on the ground behind him."

The following day, Hemming returned to find their mini fridge missing. And upon attending the morning meeting in Spicer's office, he saw where it had gone.

The story became a symbol internally of Spicer's leadership style, but unlike most incidents in the building, it didn't find its way into the press. That is, until one night when a group of White House comms staffers went out for drinks with Mike Bender, a reporter for *The Wall Street Journal*. Although I wasn't there, I was told that the mini fridge story came up in the conversation— off the record. Bender pushed for them to let him write about it, but they refused. After a lengthy back-and-forth, they finally agreed to let him have the story, but not until after Spicer had left the White House.

In a twist of fate, Spicer resigned the very next day, and the lead anecdote in his resignation story was the mini fridge. It set the internet ablaze.

Spicer later wrote about the incident in his memoir, *The Briefing: Politics, the Press, and the President,* released a year after he left.

While expressing frustration with the media manufacturing "national moments of outrage or ridicule," Spicer wrote that "Mike Bender of *The Wall Street Journal* falsely accused me of taking a mini fridge from junior staffers."

I saw the press get a lot of things wrong during my time in the White House. That wasn't one of them.

6

TWENTY-ONE DAYS ON TOP
OF THE WORLD

On February 9, 2017, Andrew Jackson, the first disrupter-president, peered over the shoulders of two of his ideological descendants—Donald J. Trump and Jefferson B. Sessions—from inside a golden frame in the Oval Office. Trump, standing behind a blue podium beside the Resolute desk, was introducing Sessions as the country's new top cop.

"It is with great pride—very great pride—that I say these words to you right now," Trump said, beaming. "Attorney General Jeff Sessions, welcome to the White House."

The crowd of about thirty of us assembled in the Oval—Sessions's family members, former staffers, and friends—broke into wild applause, with someone whistling like we were at a college football game back home in Alabama. Trump leaned over and grabbed Sessions by his left shoulder, like Dumbledore gazing proudly at Harry for being sorted into Gryffindor. The new AG gave his President a swift pat on the back in response, then looked down at the floor smiling, embarrassed by the attention.

Steve Bannon was standing beside me, watching, with a contented grin crossing his face.

"Hell, yeah," he said to no one in particular. At one point, long before the 2016 election cycle got under way, Bannon had tried to coax Sessions into running for President. He sensed the growing power of illegal immigration and trade as issues that would energize a new, working-class Republican coalition. On this point, Bannon's foresight cannot be denied. Almost no one else saw it coming. Sessions, for his part, had for decades been the leading voice—albeit a lonely one—on those issues in the Senate. He was flattered by Bannon's overtures, but told him he thought a better vessel would come along to carry those issues to the forefront of the national debate. They had both been proven correct.

As Trump continued speaking, extolling his new AG's record of public service, Sessions glanced around the room, locking eyes with friendly faces, then smiling and nodding in acknowledgment that they were there at the proudest moment of his professional life. He had been a U.S. Attorney and Alabama Attorney General before serving in the U.S. Senate for twenty years—but Attorney General of the United States had always been his dream job.

"He's a man of integrity, a man of principle, and a man of total, utter resolve," Trump continued. "Jeff understands that the job of the Attorney General is to serve and protect the people of the United States, and that is exactly what he will do, and do better than anyone else can."

Sessions placed his hand on a Bible held by Mrs. Mary, his college sweetheart and wife of forty-seven years, as the Vice President administered the oath of office.

"So help me God," Sessions concluded with extra emphasis. As we applauded again, I looked to my left and saw tears welling up in the eyes of Deputy Chief of Staff Rick Dearborn. He'd been Sessions's Chief of Staff in the Senate for over a decade.

Bannon's joy was unbridled. "We got another patriot," he said, grabbing my hand and shaking it feverishly. "It's a win for the good guys, a win for the workingman. We're going to wreak total f—ing havoc on the elites, man—shock and awe. Can you believe this s—? It's f—ing Christmas."

As the event broke up, Mrs. Sessions saw me across the room and called out, "C'mere, sweet friend!" I wrapped her up in a bear hug as she got the President to sign the Bible that had been used for the swearing-in ceremony. It had been her father's, and as it continued to be passed down through generations to come, it would now take on even greater historical significance.

"Well, how're we doing so far?" a voice said from behind me. I could recognize that old Southern accent anywhere. I turned around, grabbed Sessions's hand, and told him, "We're doing great, Mr. Attorney General. This is a proud, proud day for all of us."

Just a week before, *The Washington Post* had labeled Sessions the "intellectual godfather" of Trumpism. "Sessions has installed close allies throughout the administration," wrote the *Post*'s Phil Rucker and Robert Costa. They listed me and Dearborn, along with top White House trade adviser Peter Navarro and Senior Policy Advisor Stephen Miller, who had been Sessions's communications director in the Senate. All of us were now at Trump's side on a daily basis. And because he helped install Dearborn as director of the transition, Sessions alumni were placed in jobs all throughout various agencies and departments. The *Post* went on to note that Jared Kushner "considers Sessions a savant." Newt Gingrich was quoted praising Trump for recognizing "how genuinely smart Sessions is." Everyone in Trump World paid deference to the man whose populist brand of conservatism had foreshadowed the rise of Trump before anyone even took him seriously as a presidential candidate.

On that crisp, cold Friday afternoon, Jefferson Beauregard Sessions III, from tiny Hybart, Alabama, began his twenty-one days on top of the world.

Late on the afternoon of February 14, 2017—Valentine's Day—I stood outside the Cabinet Room chatting with Attorney General Sessions, who was waiting for his first in-person meeting with the President since his confirmation. Standing off to the side was Secretary of Homeland Security John Kelly. He was an imposing four-star Marine general with deep wrinkles curving around his mouth and chin. His natural expression was a grimace, and when he smiled he looked like he was in pain. Ever the military guy, he wore a business suit like a dress uniform and walked through the place as if he were commanding a raid. I imagined him prepared at any moment to shout out, "You can't handle the truth!" if he was ever challenged.

"What do you think of him?" I asked Sessions quietly, nodding toward Kelly, who was chatting in the background and flashing that in-pain smile at everyone again.

"Well, I think he agrees with us on the border," he replied. "So that's good; that's what we needed."

Sessions and Kelly were waiting to meet with the President about coordinating the administration's immigration policies. Two weeks before, Trump had signed a controversial "travel ban" on individuals from seven countries: Iraq, Syria, Iran, Sudan, Libya, Somalia, and Yemen. The stated reasoning behind this order was that the U.S. government did not have confidence in our ability to properly vet travelers from those countries. Critics pointed out that the countries affected were all predominantly Muslim, a fair point considering Trump's campaign rhetoric, which at one point included a call to block all Muslims from entering the country "until our country's representatives can figure out what is going on." The haphazard implementation of the order—coordinated by Stephen Miller, who had gone from firing off quixotic emails from his desk in the Russell Senate Office Building to now activating sweeping policy for the federal leviathan—sparked intense backlash. Newly banned travelers were detained at airports because they were already en route to the United States when the surprise order went into effect. Protests swept the nation and dominated media coverage. Trump, Sessions, and Kelly were undeterred.

Two weeks later, Sessions sat in the front row of the House chamber as Trump delivered his first address to a Joint Session of Congress. The words were Trump's, but the ideas behind them had long been Sessions's. He railed against "drugs pouring into the country." He pledged to "restore integrity and the rule of law at our borders." And he called on the Department of Justice to crack down on violent crime and "criminal cartels."

It was like watching a midday C-SPAN broadcast of Sessions speaking on the Senate floor to an empty chamber, as he had done so many times, but now the entire world was paying attention.

During the speech, when Trump recognized the widow of Navy SEAL Ryan Owens—the first American warrior to give his life under Trump's command—the entire chamber stood for two minutes and eleven seconds of thunderous, sustained applause. I even stood up at my desk alone to feel like I was a part of it. For those of us sitting in the West Wing watching late into the night, it felt like we were living the real-life version of a film, just without the musical score swelling behind us.

Owens had been killed during a raid on al-Qaeda in Yemen that was personally ordered by the President. This event affected him deeply. When I heard that plans were quietly being made for him to partake in Owens's dignified transfer ceremony at Dover Air Force Base, I casually mentioned to him after a meeting in the Roosevelt Room how emotional an experience I thought that would be. Trump, who was wearing a silk tie in a lighter shade of blue than I was used to seeing, looked down. I immediately felt embarrassed for bringing it up. My entire body felt hot, and I'm quite certain my face turned bright red. *Who was I to be bringing this kind of stuff up to the commander in chief? Stupid, stupid, stupid.* The brief silence left me racking my brain for a way to change the subject, but as it turned out, Trump wasn't at all miffed that I'd brought it up. To the contrary, he felt inclined to say something about it. "I made the call and the next thing I hear he had died," he said softly. And that was it. I felt a lump in my throat and for the briefest moment grasped the incredible loneliness that must accompany the presidency's most difficult decisions—those of life and death.

This wasn't the only time I felt that way. Around that same time, Lieutenant General Keith Kellogg, Chief of Staff of the National Security Council, assembled a group of approximately two dozen newly minted special ops soldiers in the Roosevelt Room. The young men, who all appeared to be in their early twenties, sat around the large conference table and in chairs around the walls typically filled by ambitious political aides. They were just days or weeks away from deploying to the darkest corners of the earth. They were going to be the very tip of the spear. As I looked around the room, they were all physical specimens, their jaws chiseled out of granite and their uniforms barely concealing the fast-twitch muscle fibers underneath. Some were bulky and tall, others were trim and of average height or below. They were of every race. Some of them spoke with a familiar Southern twang that made me miss Alabama and reminded me of the World War II Victory Medal I'd seen sitting in a box at my grandfather's house in Mississippi. Others sounded like New Englanders, or California beach bros whose friends were probably back home enjoying the surf while they were enduring no telling what while preparing to defend their country. This was all of America in a single room.

As I looked at their faces—young, fearless, full of hope and vigor—I couldn't help but think that some of them would leave home one day and never return. Or if they did it would be to Dover in a flag-draped casket. I asked the man who, I think, had led their training what separated them from the rest of the pack. "I'd say a couple of things to that," he began. "These boys have a nearly inhuman ability to handle stress. Put them in the air, or under the water, or in the cold, or any place you want, really, and they're able to keep their emotions in check and focus. There are a lot of stoic philosophers in this room," he laughed, only half joking. "They suffer in silence. And then I'd say this is the most competitive bunch you'll ever meet. They don't like losing, and they won't." He paused and looked down, further considering his answer. "You know, so much of life is mental. Secretary Mattis said once that 'the most important six inches on the battlefield is between your ears.' These boys know that. They live it."

Just then, the door swung open, bringing the room to its feet and silencing the ongoing conversations.

"At ease, boys, at ease," the President said with a smile, stopping in the doorway with his arms open. "What are we, getting ready to shoot an action movie, or what? Look at all of you, straight out of central casting." The group laughed loudly and Trump worked his way around the room shaking hands with everyone before asking them to sit down so they could "have a little chat."

"Who's the toughest guy in here?" he asked. They looked around at one another for a few seconds and then seemed to simultaneously agree on one of their compatriots, who happened to be seated at the table right next to the President. "It's you, huh?" Trump said. "That's really saying something coming from this crowd. Good job, good job." They shook hands, with Trump adding his left hand for a couple of additional pats.

"They say the hardest decision a president makes is war and peace," Trump told the group. "I prefer peace, right? We prefer peace. But sometimes you have to be tough. We had to be tough just recently. I said, 'I wish I could wait, I just got here,' you know? But you can't wait. You've got to be tough, and I know you all understand that. You signed up for the hard job. Your President knows that. The whole country knows that. They may not know your names, but they know you're out there and you're protecting them. So I respect you and I respect what you do."

For the next twenty minutes, Trump talked and answered questions. He laughed with them and gave them serious advice. He seemed genuinely humbled by the weight of the presidency, but in a way more self-assured than ever that he was up to the task. He told them they'd never have to wonder, no matter to what murky corner of the earth they were deployed, whether their commander in chief had their back. "I'm with you," he said.

Thinking about it still gives me chills.

After Trump's speech to Congress, about twenty of us gathered in the Diplomatic Reception Room to surprise him when his motorcade returned to the White House. We cheered as he walked in. "We did all right, didn't we?" he said, adrenaline still coursing through his veins. Then he invited some of the staff upstairs to celebrate his triumph.

For once, the media coverage was almost universally laudatory. "Did you see what Van Jones said?" Trump beamed. "Every Democrat is worried sick—they can't believe it—they're not going to be able to get out of bed for a month! Zucker's going to close down CNN, he's going to have to close it down. Everyone's calling in sick!"

Jones, Obama's former green jobs czar, who was now a CNN commentator, called it "one of the most extraordinary moments you have ever seen in American politics, period. . . . For people who have been hoping that maybe he would remain a divisive cartoon . . . they should begin to become a little bit worried tonight, because that thing you just saw him do, if he finds a way to do that over and over again, he's going to be there for eight years."

The coverage was so positive that it was jarring. We had never experienced anything quite like this before. *This must be what it feels like to be a Democrat.* "No tweeting," everyone kept telling the President, dead serious, of course, but in a lighthearted tone. Trump begrudgingly agreed. Even he couldn't deny the benefit of being quiet in this moment. It would all be short-lived.

About thirty-six hours later I was bopping along Suitland Parkway in a column of blacked-out government vans on the way to Joint Base Andrews, where Air Force One was idling. The President was set to deliver remarks that afternoon to sailors aboard the soon-to-be commissioned USS *Gerald R. Ford.*

Staff boards Air Force One through a door near the tail of the plane, then climbs up two flights of stairs to the main deck. Stewards place quarter-page-size pieces of paper with names printed at the top—MR. SIMS, MS. HICKS, MR. BANNON—to mark where each passenger is seated. The entire inside of the plane is decked out in various shades of gray and brown. In the staff cabin, large leather seats face each other with a table between them. When the President leaves the White House on Marine One, an intercom message alerts the staff waiting on the plane to his ETA. As soon as he boards and sits down, the plane starts rolling. Every single movement is choreographed to ensure the President never waits for anything.

Traveling with the President was perhaps the most eye-opening experience of my early days in the White House. I had never considered the logistical achievement required to safely move him and his staff around the world. Every potential threat must be taken into account. Giant military cargo planes transported the presidential limousine—"The Beast"—everywhere we went. The well-dressed Secret Service agents wearing their shades were ever present at his side, but rarely seen were the counterassault teams decked out in tactical gear. The press had to be accounted for, too. They had a dedicated cabin aboard Air Force One at the back of the plane, and vans were provided to them as part of the presidential motorcade.

On this particular trip, we took off from Joint Base Andrews and made the half-hour flight to Langley Air Force Base in Hampton, Virginia. There, the President boarded Marine One, while the rest of us ran up the open bay doors of an Osprey, a hybrid helicopter-airplane. Once buckled in, we choppered five minutes to the shipyard and landed on the deck of the world's largest aircraft carrier. After assembling our group on the flight deck, a basketball court–size elevator—typically used for aircraft—lowered us down into the hangar bay. As soon as the President was visible, the thousands of sailors waiting below erupted in deafening applause as we descended. Once he finished his remarks, we reversed the process—up the giant elevator, Osprey to Langley, Air Force One to Andrews. Everyone was in good spirits, especially the President. He could be kind of a homebody and sometimes bristled at traveling during the week. But once in front of a crowd, he fed off their energy; it recharged his batteries. And on return flights he would often express a desire to "do this more often."

But the mood changed as the plane approached Andrews; cable news chyrons started teasing an upcoming press conference by Attorney General Sessions.

The day before, Sessions had come under fire over revelations that he had twice interacted with Russian Ambassador Sergey Kislyak during the campaign. This led to accusations that he had made false statements during his confirmation hearings.

During the hearings, Sessions had been asked by Senator Al Franken (D-MN) about whether "there was a continuing exchange of information during the campaign between Trump's surrogates and intermediaries for the Russian government."

Sessions replied, "I have been called a surrogate at a time or two in that campaign, and I . . . did not have communications with the Russians."

Sessions had, in fact, shaken hands with the Russian Ambassador—and dozens of other foreign officials—during a widely attended event at the Republican National Committee, and later met with him in his Senate office—along with his staff—in his official capacity on the Senate Armed Services Committee. Such a meeting was so routine that countless Democratic senators had met with him, too, including Senators Mary Landrieu (LA), Maria Cantwell (WA), Bob Casey (PA), Amy Klobuchar (MN), Jack Reed (RI), Sheldon Whitehouse (RI), and Claire McCaskill (MO). But none of that stopped Democrats from acting like they had caught Sessions inside the Kremlin with Putin himself, crafting a master plan to overthrow the United States government.

Jeff Sessions is a Boy Scout—figuratively and literally. The Scouts' motto, "Be Prepared," sat on his desk for decades. The Senators with whom he had served for years—including the Democrats—knew the kind of person he was. They had dined with him, traveled the world with him on congressional-delegation trips, saw the way he loved his wife, children, and grandchildren, and knew him to be a man of impeccable honor and integrity. And yet they still sought to destroy him. And members of the press—many of whom would scoff off the record about the absurdity of accusing Sessions of conspiring to rig an election—were complicit in the entire charade. I remain disgusted by it all.

But I also cannot deny how bad the optics were, especially in a political environment where nuance didn't exist.

"What's this about?" Johnny McEntee, the President's body man, said aboard Air Force One. My heart rate quickened. Members of the press had just asked Trump aboard the aircraft carrier if he thought Sessions should have to recuse himself from any investigations related to the campaign. He replied that he had "total" confidence in Sessions and saw no reason why he should have to recuse himself from that or any other potential investigation. Now, it appeared, we were going to see if Sessions agreed with the President. To my knowledge, he had not discussed this with anyone on staff, or with Trump himself.

As Sessions approached the podium, all of us in the staff cabin stopped talking and focused on the small TV nestled into the gray plastic wall paneling.

"I have been here just three weeks today," Sessions said with a smile and his patented aw-shucks demeanor. After his cordial introduction, it quickly became clear what he had come to discuss. He laid out a process by which he had solicited feedback from career DOJ officials about whether he should recuse himself from any investigations related to the campaign. He went on to explain that earlier that day, after considering the rules, his staff had "recommended recusal. They said since I had involvement with the campaign, I should not be involved in any campaign investigations."

Oh, no.

And then he said the words that would change everything.

"I have recused myself in the matters that deal with the Trump campaign."

When a reporter asked about his interactions with the Russian Ambassador, he dismissed the first one as trivial and said the second was done in his official capacity and alongside his senior staff. Neither, he said, was about the campaign, which was what he had been specifically asked about during his confirmation hearings.

Air Force One was now sitting idle on the tarmac at Joint Base Andrews. I'm not sure any of us fully appreciated the significance of what had just happened, but it didn't take a juris doctorate to know that it wasn't good. Most members of the staff stood in silence. A couple of others blurted out expletives directed at no one in particular. "The Obama people never would have done this," McEntee said.

He was right about that, we all agreed. After Obama's Attorney General Loretta Lynch held a clandestine meeting with Bill Clinton at the Phoenix airport, she never appeared to come remotely close to recusing herself from investigations related to Hillary. And not a single Democrat called for her to. Most conservatives viewed the Obama DOJ as a political operation. I knew Sessions. There was no question in my mind that he was trying to do the right thing—to avoid even the appearance of impropriety. He loved the Justice Department, its people, and its mission. He had devoted his entire life to the law. But I knew the President, too. And I figured he would view this as a personal betrayal—as if his friend had left him hanging.

Everything was personal to Trump—*everything*. In international affairs, he believed his personal relationship with foreign leaders was more important than shared interests or geopolitics. With his staff, having a personal rapport was more important to him than whether they shared his worldview, or whether they were even good at their jobs. In Sessions's case, I knew Trump wouldn't view this as the AG sending a message to the country that everything was going to be done aboveboard; he'd view it as the AG sending a message to *him* that he was being thrown to the wolves.

Normally, when traveling with the President, everything moved fast. You had to hustle from the plane to the motorcade unless you wanted to get left behind. This time no one was moving. The President was still holed up in his office, and as we waited, I decided to move toward the front of the plane to see what was going on. As I walked nonchalantly down the hallway connecting the staff cabin to the President's suite, I could hear muffled conversations. And then Trump's voice rising above the rest: "If he had told me he was going to do this," Trump exploded, "I never would have appointed him in the first place!"

I immediately turned around and made my way back to my seat. Press were beginning to make note of how long we were taking to disembark. When we finally made our way into the motorcade, it was an unusually quiet ride back to the White House. I put my earbuds in but didn't turn on any music; I just didn't feel like talking. I thought back to hugging Sessions and his wife sometime after 2 A.M. on Election Night, when we ran into each other at the Trump victory party and still could not entirely believe what was happening. I remembered sitting with him in Trump Tower during the transition, when famous politicians were coming out of the woodwork trying to land plum posts in the new administration, but Sessions refused to force himself on the President-Elect. He had been there for Trump when no one else was, and he believed Trump would do right by him, and he did. And I recalled his swearing-in ceremony, just twenty-one days before, when the entire scene felt like proof that sometimes the good guys actually do win.

Then I thought about Trump's anger. I heard his voice screaming in my head—"I never would have appointed him in the first place!" *How did we get here so quickly?* Later that night the President tweeted, "Jeff Sessions is an honest man. He did not say anything wrong. He could have stated his response more accurately, but it was clearly not intentional."

The following day, I was standing in the Outer Oval when Jared Kushner walked in to see the President. "I've got someone on the phone who wants to talk to you," he said. It was Senator Lindsey Graham, a South Carolina Republican who had served with Sessions for many years in the Senate. Jared put him on speakerphone.

"He had to do it, Mr. President," Graham argued of Sessions's decision to recuse. "The American people weren't going to allow him to oversee the investigation of a campaign in which he was involved. It just wasn't going to work. He had no choice."

The President calmly but vehemently disagreed.

"Lindsey, if Jeff couldn't handle this, he should have chosen a different job," he said. "I told him he could do some other things. We could have put him at Homeland and let him handle the border. General Kelly is doing a great job—I've got no complaints—but we could have put Sessions at the border."

I grabbed my overcoat, walked down the West Colonnade, and sat on a cast-iron bench beside the Rose Garden. I knew Sessions's relationship with Trump would never be the same.

"Get me the House and Senate leaders," the President called out from the Oval, "the Democrats and the Republicans."

It was the afternoon of May 9, 2017. I was sitting inside a small, almost closetlike office in the Outer Oval shared by Johnny McEntee and Keith Schiller. Johnny was popping in and out, as he usually did throughout the day. Keith wasn't around, but at the time I didn't really think anything of his absence. I was leaned back in a black mesh office chair, watching the television news coverage and waiting to talk to Hope.

Madeleine Westerhout, the President's executive assistant, jumped into action, queuing up the calls Trump had requested. There was nothing particularly abnormal or interesting about any of this. Trump worked the phones this way all day, every day. Tucked into the closet office, I couldn't really hear what he was saying, and I wasn't trying to. Just another day in the office.

After a few minutes, Hope came in, but she was in no mood to talk. Before I even broached the subject I wanted to discuss with her—which was so trivial that I can't even recall what it was—she told me, "Not now. We'll have to do this later."

"No worries," I said. "Nothing urgent." I got up and started to head back to my desk just in time to hear Senate Minority Leader Chuck Schumer tell Trump on the phone, "This is a mistake." I walked out before the President responded and once again didn't think much of the exchange. *Chuck Schumer's against something we're doing? Must be good.*

Once back at my desk around the corner, I went back to whatever I had been working on before.

Every TV network has audio cues that alert viewers to breaking news. I can't remember what network was on the TV in the press office, playing quietly in the background as I typed away, but the breaking news audio alert grabbed my attention: "Trump Fires FBI Director Comey."

Oh man, he did it. He really did it.

News had just emerged earlier in the day that the FBI had to correct the record regarding Comey's inaccurate congressional testimony the week before. As a result, Spicer had been asked during that afternoon's press briefing if the President still had "full confidence" in Comey. "I have no reason to believe—I haven't asked him, so I don't, I have not asked the President since the last time we spoke about this," Spicer said in his typical halting fashion. I don't know if he had been kept out of the loop, or if he was just buying time for the announcement to come.

The vast majority of the White House staff often learned about "breaking news" at the same time as the rest of the country. This is one of the main reasons why breathless reports about "the mood" in the White House should always be taken with a grain of salt; the experience is dramatically different for various aides. For instance, deliberations surrounding the Comey decision were a closely held secret in the West Wing. I learned about the firing at the same time as suburban moms picking up their kids from soccer practice. I was so clueless that I had been sitting thirty feet from Trump's desk and still had no idea what was going on. So you can imagine how the staff across the street in the EEOB experienced most breaking news events. Normal work continued on, with an eye on the TV screen, much like a typical corporate office.

I would learn in the coming hours—again, along with the rest of the country—that Attorney General Sessions and Deputy Attorney General Rod Rosenstein had both written letters to the President recommending Comey's dismissal. And Keith Schiller's unexplained absence earlier that afternoon? Turns out he had been dispatched to deliver the termination letter to FBI headquarters. Unfortunately, James Comey wasn't there. In fact, like so many of the rest of us, he learned about his dismissal through the television.

When I was trying to gauge the fallout from dramatic stories, my former campaign war room colleague Steven Cheung was always my first call. He monitored everything 24/7 as the White House Director of Strategic Response. "How's this Comey thing playing—it's getting pretty hot, isn't it?" I asked him. He chuckled. "Man, I haven't seen something consume the news like this since *Access Hollywood*," he said. "People are losing their minds—I mean, totally freaking out."

It's rare for all of Washington to be consumed by a single story line. The White House and Capitol Hill are often on different tracks. Every backbench congressman is firing off press releases touting their pet projects. House and Senate leadership push their agendas. There's nonstop prognosticating over certain bills making their way through the legislative process. Trump himself is usually pushing a few different things on any given day. But every now and then there's a story so all-consuming that nothing else has any chance of breaking through. TV networks bump all their scheduled guests and go for wall-to-wall coverage on the big story. Sometimes it's a tragedy—a national disaster, terrorist attack, or mass shooting. On the evening of May 9, 2017, the firing of James Comey took over everything. Even ABC, NBC, and CBS broke into their regular evening programming with special news alerts from the White House.

I stayed in my office and just watched it all unfold. Apparently Trump was doing the same thing I was, and he didn't like what he was seeing.

At some point, an exasperated Hope Hicks burst into the hallway between the press office and the Roosevelt Room, stumbling into a casual conversation between Sean Spicer, Sarah Huckabee Sanders, and Kellyanne Conway.

"He's in there watching TV and getting killed, and none of you are doing anything to defend him," Hicks said. "Where's the plan to line up surrogates and get people out there to back him up?"

She was right, of course. But while I'd normally be among the first to point out Spicer's inept leadership, in this particular instance, it's hard to plan for something you didn't know was coming. I was in charge of the messaging operation and even I had no idea how we were messaging this. On the flip side, once the story broke, there hadn't been a sense of urgency to jump into action, either. It was like we all started just watching the television show, forgetting that we were actually supposed to be supporting actors.

Sean, Sarah, and Kellyanne figured out who to send out on TV and I worked out a brief talking points document that could be sent out across the administration, to our allies on Capitol Hill, and to outside surrogates who needed to know how to defend the President on TV.

Two hours after the Comey firing hit the news, I sent out an email blast with the all-caps subject line: COMMUNICATIONS BRIEFING—COMEY EDITION.

The email included copies of three letters: the termination recommendations from both Sessions and Rosenstein, and the actual termination letter from Trump to Comey. And I added the following bullet points:

- Director Comey had lost the confidence and respect of the FBI rank and file; a large, bipartisan contingent of House and Senate members; and the American people.

- Deputy Attorney General Rod Rosenstein, who also served as a U.S. Attorney under the previous administration, recommended Director Comey's termination.
  - The FBI Director reports directly to Deputy AG Rosenstein.
  - He is a career Justice Department official who was confirmed by the Senate 94–6.
  - He assumed his new role just two weeks ago.
  - Upon his confirmation, Mr. Rosenstein assessed the situation and concluded he did not have confidence in the FBI Director.

- After receiving recommendations from Mr. Rosenstein and Attorney General Sessions, President Trump concluded that the only way to restore confidence in the FBI—the crown jewel of American law enforcement—was to end Director Comey's tenure atop the Bureau, effective immediately.

- The great men and women of the FBI deserve a leader in whom they have confidence—it is time for a fresh start. The search for a new director will begin immediately.

As we were walking over to the residence later that week, the President asked me what I thought about his decision, which had been met with outrage or distress, even among some Republicans. Democrats were nearly unanimous in calling for, as Senator Elizabeth Warren described it, "a real, independent prosecutor who Trump can't fire, Sessions can't intimidate, and Congress can't muzzle." Senator Schumer called for a "special prosecutor." Even Republican Senator John McCain, a frequent Trump critic, tweeted that Comey's removal confirmed the need for a select committee to investigate Russia's interference in the 2016 election.

"Was it the right move?" the President asked me. "What do you think?"

I had considered in advance that this question might come up at some point. First of all, I'm not an attorney and I couldn't even begin to fathom the legal ramifications of the decision. Secondly, I believed that accusations of so called "collusion" between Trump and Russia were farcical. I didn't doubt for a second that Russia sowed division and sought to influence the election through various disinformation campaigns. But we couldn't collude with ourselves, working in offices right next to each other, much less with a foreign government. So I understood Trump's frustration with what he viewed as an attempt to delegitimize his electoral victory. Third, Comey had made a series of high-profile mistakes in key moments. Even Democrats were furious with him over his handling of the Clinton email investigation. So, although I thought the optics were bad, I could also see legitimate cause to remove him. I also happened to agree with Trump's assessment of Comey as a "showboater." Finally, the decision was already made; Comey had been fired. What good would it do for me to raise doubts after the fact?

So I told the President, "I feel the same way about this decision that I did about most decisions during the campaign—trust your instincts. If your gut said he had to go, then you did the right thing."

I knew that Trump took great pride in his political instincts, so he would appreciate the sentiment. As we boarded the elevator on the ground floor of the residence, Johnny McEntee was more explicit.

"It was the right thing to do," he said emphatically. "Comey's a piece of s—."

The President looked at me with a grin, nodded at McEntee, and concluded, "He's right about that, believe me. I did the country a favor by getting rid of this guy."

7

THE PROFESSIONALS

It's nearly impossible to have a conversation while waiting on the President to make an appearance. Instead, everyone steals glances at the closed door, waiting for it to open, and converses in short, substance-free sentences that are all but forgotten as soon as they are uttered. Such was the case in February 2017 as I stood in the Roosevelt Room making small talk with House Speaker Paul Ryan and Senate Majority Whip John Cornyn, who, along with other Republican leaders, had arrived for their first legislative strategy session with the new President.

Compliments about neckties were exchanged, which led to a discussion about socks. I enjoyed wearing socks that matched my colorful ties, and lifted my pants leg to reveal University of Alabama crimson socks matching my tie of the same color. They seemed to prefer a more traditional approach. Before long we were talking about the weather, always a sure sign that a conversation is going nowhere. We were all looking toward the door.

Doors to the major rooms in the West Wing—such as the Oval Office, Cabinet Room, and Roosevelt Room—are all outfitted with sturdy, gold-plated hardware. When the knobs turn there's a loud *click,* followed by the quiet *whoosh* of a heavy door swinging smoothly on its gilded hinges.

Every presidential movement in the West Wing was preceded by an appearance by Johnny McEntee, the President's body man. Johnny would pop his head in to make sure everything was prepared in advance of the President, so Trump was never left waiting.

As he did—and that familiar *click, whoosh* sounded—conversation briefly stopped. When the men—they were almost all white, middle-aged men—saw that Johnny was alone, their faces dropped slightly and they returned to their chitchat. Johnny was becoming accustomed to appearing before crestfallen faces.

But the false alarm only added to the nervous energy that seemed to envelop the Roosevelt Room, where Republican leaders from both chambers of Congress were encircling the conference table. In addition to Ryan and Cornyn, Senate and House Majority Leaders Mitch McConnell and Kevin McCarthy were present, along with House Majority Whip Steve Scalise. After eight years of President Obama occupying the White House, the entire group was still growing accustomed to regular visits to the West Wing as the people fully in charge of the governance of the nation. After 2016, Republicans were in their best position in about a century, with control of a majority of state governorships, the United States Congress, the United States Senate, and now the White House. This was a once-in-a-generation opportunity for the GOP, and you could tell the members in the room sensed it. But they'd also have to work with a most unlikely President who had spent almost his entire campaign railing against them and seemed to them to have, at best, a glancing understanding of federal policy.

There were deep fissures between them and the President on certain issues. Perhaps most notably, Trump had won the presidency by bucking decades of Republican orthodoxy on free trade. He'd also shunned the business wing of the GOP—of which Ryan and McConnell were both card-carrying members—because he believed they preferred lax immigration laws that undercut the wages of American workers. Trump was malleable in many policy areas, but not on immigration and trade. On those two issues, he had been remarkably consistent for decades. He believed deep in his bones that he was right and viewed his election—with those two issues front and center—as his vindication.

There was also a personal concern, shared by many of the men in the room. They had all but left Trump for dead a few months earlier. And Trump didn't seem like the kind of guy who'd forget something like that. How was this going to work?

Click. Whoosh.

The President marched into the room like a man on a mission.

"My team," he said warmly, holding out his hand to begin greeting the lawmakers. "Hello, Paul . . . Mitch. Great to see everyone." They responded in kind, but their body language was stiff, uncomfortable, especially Paul Ryan's. If there was any Republican in Washington who looked to be Donald Trump's polar opposite—at least in personality, temperament, and background—it was the trim, earnest forty-seven-year-old from Janesville, Wisconsin. During the campaign, Ryan had made plain that he was not a Trump devotee. After *Access Hollywood,* Ryan broke with his party's nominee altogether, saying that he was "sickened" by Trump's comments, and declined to defend Trump or campaign with him from that point forward.

Chief of Staff Reince Priebus entered just behind the President. A much smaller figure than Trump—in both physical stature and personality—Priebus had billed himself as Trump's bridge to the GOP establishment in Congress. And he was clearly a bridge to at least one of them. Upon seeing his fellow Wisconsinite, Ryan's entire body seemed to loosen up. His shoulders relaxed, his face softened, and he greeted Priebus with a friendly handshake and a slap on his left shoulder.

"Take a seat, everyone," Trump said. "Let's talk."

The President, whose chair was a few inches taller than everyone else's, as is tradition, sat at the middle of the table. Following his lead, Ryan sat to his left and McConnell pulled up directly to his right. Priebus sat at the end of the table, and the rest of the lawmakers, along with a handful of additional White House aides, found their way into the remaining vacant chairs.

The purpose of the meeting was for all parties to agree on a timeline for delivering on one of the President's biggest campaign promises: to repeal President Obama's signature legislative achievement, commonly known as Obamacare, and to replace it with a Republican health-care plan to drive down costs and increase competition. Priebus opened the meeting, speaking confidently but glancing periodically at his notebook sitting on the table in front of him. Before long, the President cut him off with a look of impatience. This was a small but telling sign of how the Trump-Priebus relationship would work.

"We want to do Obamacare first, then tax cuts second, is that right?" he asked the room.

There was a moment of silence. The lawmakers exchanged glances, unsure about who should answer for them.

"Yes sir, Mr. President," Speaker Ryan finally said. "There are policy reasons for that, which we are happy to get into."

"But we can get it done, right?" the President asked. "We need to get this done. You guys have been promising for a long time—longer than I've been in politics, really. But I promised it, too, so we need no mistakes."

The President thought like a normal Washington outsider might think. House Republicans had made a great show out of voting more than sixty times to repeal Obamacare, a statistic they cited on the campaign trail all the time. How hard could repeal possibly be now that the GOP was in charge of everything?

I also saw his comment as a subtle indication that Trump was personally much more excited about cutting taxes. The prospect of eroding Obama's signature legacy was appealing, of course. But health-care policy was foreign to him. Taxes—now, that's a topic a billionaire businessman knows a thing or two about.

"We're going to get it done, Mr. President," Ryan said confidently. The rest of the men around the table seemed to be in agreement, so the conversation moved quickly into laying out a timeline.

In rapid succession, Priebus, Ryan, and McConnell threw out timetables for introducing bills and committee votes, and target dates for final passage. The conversation seemed choreographed. I was confident, based on the lack of pauses to consider what the others were saying, that they had orchestrated it all before this meeting. If they had, that was probably a smart approach. That all sounded fine to Trump. The President wasn't interested in getting down into the weeds. He just wanted Obamacare repealed. The commander's intent was clear. The details were left to the lieutenants. And they seemed to like that approach anyway. They were the professionals. They could take it from here. This was, in its way, astounding, since these same people, their consultants, their pollsters, and their aides had guided Congress to historic levels of unpopularity.

As the meeting was coming to an end, an offhand comment piqued the President's interest.

"We're going to have to keep everyone together, because we're going to be doing this without any Democratic votes," McConnell said.

"Really?" Trump replied, suddenly intrigued. "You don't think we'll get any?"

The owlish, placid Senate Majority Leader spoke quietly but firmly. "No, Mr. President," McConnell said. "Not one." Democrats had passed Obamacare without any Republican votes. If Republicans were going to repeal it, Mc-Connell believed they'd have to do it in the same way.

"What about Joe Manchin?" Trump asked, as if McConnell must have forgotten him. Manchin, a sixty-nine-year-old West Virginia Democrat who liked to position himself as above partisan politics and willing to work with the GOP, was coming up for reelection in 2018 in a state that Trump had won by forty-two points. On top of that, Trump viewed him as a personal friend. Surely his buddy Joe would play ball.

"Absolutely not, Mr. President," McConnell said in a tone that seemed designed to end the debate.

"Really?" the President asked. Often the contrarian, he seemed to view this as a personal challenge as well as a test of his persuasiveness. "I have a wonderful relationship with him; I think he might come around."

McConnell didn't flinch. He stayed sitting upright in his brown leather chair, elbows on the armrests and hands clasped underneath his chin.

"Mr. President," he began, "he'll never be with us when it counts. I've seen this time and time again. We're going to do everything in our power to beat him when he comes up for reelection in 2018."

Trump seemed taken aback. He cut his eyes at Priebus, as if to say, *Why did no one tell me this was an issue?* He didn't seem angry, just befuddled.

"Well, Joe's been a friend of mine, so we'll have to see," Trump said, turning his attention back to McConnell. "Do we have to go after him like that?"

"Absolutely, Mr. President," McConnell shot back without a moment's hesitation. "We're going to crush him like a grape." Outside the walls of the Roosevelt Room, the conventional wisdom was that men like McConnell would temper Trump's aggressive impulses. Just the opposite was happening right now.

There was a brief silence—maybe a half second—when the atmosphere in the room felt like the scene in *Goodfellas* when no one can tell how Joe Pesci is going to react to Ray Liotta calling him "funny." Would he freak out? Would he laugh it off? Finally Trump broke the tension.

"This guy's mean as a snake!" he said, pointing at McConnell and looking around the room. The entire group burst out laughing.

"I like it, though, Mitch," he continued, giving McConnell two quick pats on the back. "If that's what you think we need to do."

"I do," McConnell said, never breaking his steely-eyed character.

I saw a side of Mitch McConnell that day that I'd never appreciated as an outside observer. To many conservatives, myself included, McConnell had always been a symbol of what a loathsome place Washington is. He was too quick to compromise his principles, if he had any at all. He was a total squish with no ideological core. And he was first elected to the Senate the same year I was born, for heaven's sake. Wasn't it time to consider doing something else? When Trump supporters chanted "drain the swamp" during his campaign rallies, just as many of them—if not more—were picturing Mitch McConnell as they were Democrats like Nancy Pelosi or Chuck Schumer. The President also sometimes expressed frustration with his strict adherence to the Senate's antiquated rules. Most notably, McConnell refused to do away with the filibuster, which allowed Democrats to obstruct on almost every issue.

But his cold-blooded response to the President's Manchin questions revealed an underlying toughness that earned him a new respect and appreciation in the President's eyes, particularly compared to many of the more weak-willed, equivocating members of Congress he'd encounter. In 2016 his outright refusal to bring President Obama's Supreme Court nominee up for a vote had given Trump a chance to preserve the conservative court for a generation. In 2017 he would go on to ensure the confirmation of the most federal judges in history. I still don't believe anyone should stay in office for decades the way he has, but he wasn't soft like I'd always thought he was, that's for sure.

The President's relationship with Republicans in Congress developed through a series of fits and starts. In reality, the reasons they had trouble working together were deeper and more personal than differences in political ideology. They were cut from totally different cloth, not just as politicians, but as people.

In the 1950s, British philosopher Isaiah Berlin published a popular essay called "The Hedgehog and the Fox," designed to categorize writers and thinkers throughout history. The essay expanded on a sentence attributed to the Ancient Greek poet Archilochus: "A fox knows many things, but a hedgehog one important thing."

Hedgehogs, Berlin explained, "relate everything to a single, universal, organizing principle." They view the world through the lens of a single defining idea, which they apply to every problem they face. Foxes, on the other hand, seize "upon the essence of a vast variety of experiences and objects," and approach each new problem with a new idea. For a fox, every situation is viewed through a new lens.

I was first exposed to "The Hedgehog and the Fox" by former House Speaker Newt Gingrich as a way to understand Trump during the campaign.

"Clinton is a fox who knows many things you can fact check," he tweeted in September 2016. "Trump is a hedgehog who knows one very big thing: We need change."

The more time I spent with Trump, and the more I considered it, the more I believed this was correct: Trump is a hedgehog, viewing all of the world's problems through the lens that he is the agent who will deliver the needed change.

But to really understand how Trump sees the world, you have to layer multiple lenses on top of each other. Trump believes he alone, often through sheer force of will, can solve certain problems. That's one lens. Layered on top of that is his belief that all of life is a negotiation, and that every negotiation is a zero-sum game. There's no such thing as a "win-win"; someone will win and someone will lose. Layered on top of that is his belief that personal relationships are paramount, taking precedence in all negotiations, even over mutual interests. And layered on top of that is his belief that creating chaos gives him an advantage, because he's more comfortable in the mayhem than anyone else.

Remembering all of this helped me see the world as Trump must have, especially when his actions didn't seem to make sense.

Trump had a certain single-mindedness about him. The left derided this as ignorance, even stupidity. But in my experience it was, for lack of a better word, hedgehoggishness.

Members of Congress, on the other hand, were mostly foxes, bouncing from one topic—or bill, or election cycle—to the next, trying to cobble together a majority coalition of support based on shared interests.

Paul Ryan, for example. He was a brilliant guy, a serious policy wonk. He had an affinity for the granular details of complex issues and could go on—and on, and on—at length about the nuances of legislation. In contrast, Trump was a big-picture guy, the captain who charted the course and expected his sailors to navigate around the smaller obstacles. To shift the metaphor slightly, Trump was the guy who punched his ultimate destination into the

GPS, then sat back and turned up the radio. Paul Ryan was the computerized voice in the GPS, reciting every detail of every exit, turn, and lane change just loud enough to be heard and hopefully acknowledged.

This tendency in Ryan could come across as either earnest or condescending, and sometimes both. As a result, the relationship between the Speaker and the President would be awkward at best and, at times, overtly hostile.

Several weeks after the meeting with congressional leaders in the Roosevelt Room, Ryan was back at the White House for another conversation/tutorial on how things in Washington were done. I don't recall why I was even in this meeting. It might have been because I'd just finished filming something with the President and stuck around. It could have been because he saw me standing in the Outer Oval and waved me in. In a normal White House I probably wouldn't have been in there. Or there would have at least been others—like someone from the Legislative Affairs office or the Chief of Staff—in there as well. But this, of course, was not a normal White House, and my presence in this meeting could serve as Exhibit A of why some other—particularly more senior—White House aides came to resent me. But I didn't work for them.

"Mr. President," Ryan said, holding out his hand and walking ahead of Vice President Pence as the two of them entered the Oval Office.

The Resolute desk was piled high with newspapers and nylon courier bags of classified documents with locks holding their zippers shut. Trump motioned for an aide to clear them away as he rose to shake Ryan's hand, and the Speaker and Vice President sat down in front of the desk. I sat down in a chair against the wall, taking notes in case there were any notable developments to pass along to the legislative affairs, policy, or communications teams.

Trump seemed distracted. He wasn't rude, but his body language suggested he had other matters on his mind. Pence sensed this immediately. He was a master of reading the President's moods—an essential survival skill for anyone serving with Trump and wanting to stay in his good graces. He knew when to sit back and let Trump go on a storytelling tangent, which often included detailed recollections of his real estate conquests. But he could also sense when Trump was ready to get down to business.

Ryan, on the other hand, wasn't particularly interested in Trump's frequent asides—about real estate, or golf, or a recent TV segment he'd seen. Ryan didn't own commercial real estate and was more a gym rat than a golfer, fond of the P90X craze and in search of killer abs. The last TV program he'd seen was probably on C-SPAN.

Instead he launched into a detailed explanation of recent developments on the health-care bill. Impressively, he wasn't reading from any notes; he knew it all off the top of his head. Occasionally, after multiparagraph explanations, there would be a moment of silence. Then Pence would attentively jump in to nudge the conversation along.

As I sat there, I struggled not to shake my head in disbelief. It was hard to imagine a worse way to brief someone like Donald Trump. The President's short attention span was the stuff of legend. If he wasn't fully engrossed in what you were saying, you could lose his interest in a matter of seconds. Everyone, from the comms team preparing him for interviews to national security aides briefing him on the latest intelligence to trade advisers discussing ongoing negotiations, had to learn to keep the information tight, to the point, and engaging.

Welcome to the club, I thought to myself as Ryan droned on. Maybe he'd eventually figure this out.

For fifteen minutes, Ryan detailed the advantages of tackling health care before tax reform. His arguments were sound. Everything he was saying made perfect sense. The problem was that the President had already agreed to this approach. He was fully on board. There was no need to continue making the case.

The President's mind had started to wander—gallop, even—to something, anything, else in his line of view. Trump was leaning back casually, sipping on a glass of Diet Coke. He would occasionally glance up toward the Outer Oval, or out at the Rose Garden, or over at me sitting inconspicuously along the wall. I felt like I could see what he was thinking. *Jeez, can you believe this guy?*

Finally, in mid-Ryan-ramble, Trump set down his drink, placed his palms on the desk, and slowly stood up. His movements were leisurely enough that Ryan just continued on, turning his head toward Pence as he spoke. But it quickly became apparent that Trump was not just stretching his legs or repositioning himself. Instead, and without a word, he walked right past me, out of the Oval, and down the hall toward his private study.

I looked at the door and then at Ryan, who looked at Pence. *What just happened?*

But the VP just nodded, and the Speaker just kept on talking.

Just down the hall, I could hear that the President had turned on the giant flat-screen TV in his private dining room. He'd had enough of the ramble. He had agreed with the approach. He'd heard it all before. What was the point?

The quiet dialogue between Pence and Ryan waned after a few minutes, and even the Vice President was now facing the reality that this awkward moment would not resolve itself. Pence finally stood up and asked the Speaker to give him a second. Patting Ryan on the shoulder as he passed by, Pence walked into the dining room and briefly watched a TV news segment with the President. They mumbled in a low volume to each other, and I couldn't make out what they were saying. Meanwhile, the Speaker sat wordlessly in front of the Resolute desk, and I did the same in my chair along the wall, both of us ignoring the awkwardness.

It wasn't long, maybe ninety seconds or so, before Trump, looking somewhat rejuvenated, and Pence returned to the Oval. The President sat back down. With no explanation, apology, or acknowledgment of what had just happened, he resumed the conversation as if he hadn't just walked out of the room to catch up on TV. *What a power move.*

What was perhaps most telling was that Paul Ryan, the Speaker of the House, second in line to the presidency, a former vice presidential nominee of his party, just rolled with it, too. In fact, he didn't seem bothered or bewildered at all. It's hard to imagine that legendary pols like Sam Rayburn or Tip O'Neill would have just let it go down like that. Congress, after all, was intended to be a coequal branch of government. Only a few weeks in, it was clear Ryan had power that he seemed either uncomfortable with or incapable of wielding. That was a sign of weakness to a man like Donald Trump, and weakness was a quality he could never abide. In fact, it was clear that most of the "leaders" of Congress weren't really leaders at all. To them, courage was a risk. Which is why Trump dominated them all so easily.

The meeting came to an end shortly thereafter.

Days later, House leadership released their bill—the American Health Care Act—and it was a disaster.

Democrats screamed bloody murder that Republicans were trying to throw poor people off the health-care rolls, and conservatives slammed the bill for being "Obamacare in a different form." No one seemed happy, including the President, who was fielding angry phone calls from his hard-right allies in Congress.

Ryan's response was to hold a press conference and deliver a thirty-minute-long PowerPoint presentation explaining the bill. *If only they understood,* he seemed to be thinking, *everyone would agree that this is a reasonable proposal.*

The first several minutes of the presentation were devoted to laying out a "three-pronged approach" to "repealing and replacing Obamacare."

"Prong" number one meant the House approving a watered-down bill that the Senate could pass on a simple majority vote. It didn't include some of the major reforms Trump wanted—like allowing people to buy health insurance across state lines—because Senate rules would require sixty votes, and that would never happen with only fifty-two Republican senators.

Then, in the second "prong," Secretary of Health and Human Services Tom Price would use his power to roll back Obamacare's onerous "rules and regulations." Obamacare had granted wide powers to the HHS Secretary, which could now be turned against it.

And finally, the third "prong" would include new legislation that could garner Democratic support and reach the sixty-vote threshold in the Senate. These smaller bills would make narrow, popular reforms that would be tough for red-state Democrats to vote against.

Theoretically, it all kind of made sense, but it was hard to imagine that it could actually come to fruition.

The President was aghast. In true Trumpian fashion, his first criticisms weren't about the complicated, difficult-to-follow policy, but about the branding.

"'Prongs'—such a terrible word to use," he said in one moment of frustration after Ryan's press conference. "Is anyone listening to this stuff? Does anyone even think about what they're saying? 'Prongs'—it's just bad."

Ryan, the fox, knew many things—he was taking a complex approach to solving a complex problem. Trump, the hedgehog, knew one important thing—people need to understand the big idea you're selling, or they're not going to buy in.

A week after Ryan's ill-advised PowerPoint presentation, the Congressional Budget Office (CBO) released a report estimating that the Republican health-care bill would leave twenty-three million fewer people with insurance over the next decade. The headlines were devastating, regardless of the CBO's history of getting pretty much everything wrong, as the White House pointed out in a press release. As the saying goes, if you're explaining, you're losing.

The President fumed, privately and sometimes publicly, that he'd listened to these geniuses tell him this would all be done easily. After all, the Republicans had ostensibly been planning this for years. Surely they had some sort of plan. Now "repeal and replace" was blowing up in their faces. More to the point—it was blowing up in *his* face.

Annoyed and frustrated, the President horrified Republicans in Congress by seeking input from the unlikeliest of sources: Zeke Emanuel, one of the architects of Obamacare, who also happened to be the brother of one of Trump's favorite punching bags, Chicago Mayor Rahm Emanuel. I'm not sure if he took the meeting genuinely seeking new ideas, or if he just wanted to shock Republicans into getting their act together. But this was how Trump liked to do business: bring in people with opposing views and let them fight it out while he refereed. Although, much like the referees in professional wrestling—don't forget, Trump is in the WWE Hall of Fame—he would occasionally throw punches for one side or the other to either level the playing field or pile on.

Emanuel was an oncologist and bioethicist in his late fifties. His gray hair had almost completely thinned out on top, and one of the first things I noticed was that it had been a long time since the hair on the back of his neck had been cleaned up.

But Emanuel did have one thing going for him, at least as far as the President was concerned. He had advanced degrees from both Harvard and Oxford. Trump was an anti-elitist in his rhetoric and policies, but he was a hard-core credentialist. He loved to tout his own degree from the Wharton School of Business at the University of Pennsylvania. And he had privately raved about his Supreme Court nominee Neil Gorsuch's education. "He went to both Harvard *and* Oxford," Trump told a small group of us right after announcing his nomination. "Harvard's pretty good, right? But he says Oxford was actually harder, if you can believe it."

When Emanuel arrived in the West Wing, a large contingent of Trump officials was already waiting for him in the Oval. Vice President Pence, HHS Secretary Tom Price, Priebus, Bannon, Kushner, and Director of the Domestic Policy Council Andrew Bremberg were all there, along with Speaker Ryan. There was no way they would leave Trump and Emanuel to their own devices. Who knew what the President—who was always looking to make a deal—might agree to?

I stood along the wall with Kushner and Bannon, watching the drama unfold among the rest of the group seated around the Resolute desk.

Emanuel came to the meeting ready to make a simple argument.

"There are Democrats who want to improve Obamacare," he claimed. This prompted sarcastic laughter from Paul Ryan, who was sitting right next to him, and a smirk from Vice President Pence. "We can do this on a bipartisan basis," Emanuel continued, undeterred by the scoffing. "But they're not going to go along with repealing it. You have to quit saying 'repeal and replace.'"

"Stop saying 'repeal and replace'?" the President asked incredulously. "People hate it, doc. Honestly, you weren't out on the road in the campaign. People hate it—I mean *hate* it."

The President straightened his back and began imitating himself out on the campaign trail.

"We are going to *repeal* and *replace* the *disaster* known as Obamacare!" he said slowly, with his right index finger emphasizing each word. "And the people would scream like nothing you've ever heard."

Emanuel was unfazed. He spewed out a torrent of suggestions, assertions, ideas, and theories, leaving the President shrugging and not sure what to make of it all.

Bannon was now pacing along the wall and growing increasingly frustrated. He finally got the attention of Bremberg, the White House's health-care policy expert, and motioned for him to come over to him.

"He needs you right now," he told Bremberg sternly, pointing at Trump. Bremberg had been waiting patiently for the President to ask his opinion, as is the historical custom in such settings. We were still new in the White House, and aides who hadn't spent a lot of time around Trump were still getting used to brawling in front of him unprompted. But that is no doubt what he wanted.

"Yeah, you've got to get in there," Priebus urged. "You're his guy on this. Back him up."

Bremberg returned to his chair and asserted himself, teaming up with Ryan to push back on Emanuel's attempts to nudge Trump toward a more accommodating posture with Democrats. It quickly became clear that there was very little common ground from a policy perspective. And politically, Democrats had rammed Obamacare through without a single Republican vote. It was hard to imagine Republicans letting them have a seat at the table now that the GOP was in charge.

The entire episode foreshadowed a long-running challenge in the policy fights ahead. Trump was a dynamo as a pitchman. If you've got something to sell, there's no one on earth you'd rather have out there doing the selling. But he—being the one-big-idea hedgehog that he was—showed very little interest in the finer details of complex policies.

In the coming weeks, Republican members of Congress were brought in by the dozens so Trump could lock in their support for the Ryan plan. Some meetings included members of the staunchly conservative Freedom Caucus, who felt like the bill didn't go far enough to truly repeal Obamacare. Other meetings included the moderate Tuesday Group, as they were known, who thought the bill went too far. Other groups included waffling members who were somewhere in between the two.

Sometimes the meetings went off without a hitch. Many of the members couldn't wait to walk out and tell their constituents they had spent time with the larger-than-life President, whose influence among the conservative base could single-handedly swing primary elections. When he'd enter the room, they'd often burst into applause.

In one particular meeting in the Cabinet Room, Congressman Scalise pulled out his cell phone and asked the President to deliver a happy birthday message to his son.

"Your dad is a very powerful man," the President said into the tiny camera as the room erupted in laughter. It was a very Trumpian compliment. If there was anything this young man should know on his birthday, the President must have thought, it's that his dad was wielding enormous influence in the halls of power—so he should be proud and listen to him. Scalise captured a priceless moment that his family would watch for generations, and the entire room ate it up.

But many of the meetings also included some tense moments.

At one point, roughly thirty Republican members were brought into the Oval Office to express their concerns with the bill. The goal was for all of them to walk out having committed to vote "yes." It was the President's job to get them there, but he was going to have all the help he wanted from a diminutive Congressman from North Carolina named Patrick McHenry.

McHenry, who stood no taller than five foot five and almost always wore a bow tie, was House Republicans' Chief Deputy Whip. The whip team, led by Majority Whip Steve Scalise, was tasked with rounding up votes for bills being put forward by party leadership. As Scalise's top deputy, McHenry's job was to impose party discipline—to crack the whip, so to speak. And he clearly loved it. He had a note card in his hand with the names of lawmakers who hadn't yet committed to support the bill. He was geared up to put them on the spot in front of the President.

Trump was in a relaxed mood, seated in front of the Oval Office fireplace, a painting of George Washington hanging above the mantel just over his right shoulder. The members of Congress piled in around him like schoolchildren. Ten or twelve of them squeezed onto the two couches. The wooden chairs in front of the Resolute desk were scooped up and turned to face the other direction. Extra chairs from around the wall were dragged into the giant circle. It was a chaotic scene, which left the President's personal aide shaking his head, but Trump didn't seem to mind. After all, he was the one they were all scrambling to get closer to.

"Mr. President," McHenry interjected as the scrum died down. "If it's all right with you, why don't we go around the room and let people commit to you that they're going to support the bill?"

The President agreed, and one by one, members pledged their support. But to McHenry's enormous—and growing—frustration, most of them also wanted to take their rare moment in the Oval Office to add in personal anecdotes, or ask questions, or just about whatever else they could come up with that would give them a story to tell their constituents back home.

McHenry, knowing the group had a limited amount of time with the President, was desperately trying to move things along, until he finally reached his boiling point.

Congressman Robert Aderholt from my home state of Alabama remained noncommittal.

"Mr. President," he began when it was his turn to speak. "I have the privilege of serving the people of Alabama's Fourth Congressional District, who supported you by the widest margin of any district in the country. You won it with eighty percent of the vote, to just eighteen percent for Hillary."

He was speaking Trump's language. Reliving his glorious election victory remained a favorite pastime of his for the entire time I was in the White House.

"I like that!" the President said. "I love the people of Alabama—a truly great state. Go ahead, Robert."

"Thank you, Mr. President," Aderholt continued humbly. "But I have to say that I am hearing a lot of concerns about this bill. And these are your people, Mr. President. They are very worried about what this bill does to Medicare, and I'm just having a hard time."

"Robert," McHenry said tersely, "the President is asking you for your support."

"Are you, Mr. President?" Aderholt said, looking back at Trump. "Because if you are, it would be important for me to be able to go back and tell my constituents that you did that."

Trump nodded and leaned forward, placing his elbows on his knees.

"Look, we need everyone in here. I'm asking for all of your support for this. We're going to do such incredible things—we're going to do taxes and so much more. All of those things are going to be easy. But we've got to do this first."

Aderholt thanked the President, but McHenry wasn't leaving anything to chance.

"Robert, I need you to look your President in the eye and tell him that you're going to support him on this."

Aderholt looked back at the President.

"You have my support."

Finally getting what he wanted, McHenry buried his head back in his note card and placed a check mark beside Aderholt's name.

Trump was clearly amused, now sitting back with his arms folded and a half smile.

"Look at him," the President said, nodding toward McHenry. "Straight out of central casting."

The group laughed, and McHenry smiled sheepishly. This was high praise from Trump. Looking the part was every bit as important as doing a good job. McHenry was getting high marks from the Big Guy on both.

By the end of the meeting, every member in the room had committed to support the bill. Trump was thrilled, and his new friend Patrick McHenry could breathe a sigh of relief.

Unfortunately, things didn't go quite as well when another group of approximately thirty Republican lawmakers were brought into the Cabinet Room.

Trump's pitch on the Republican health-care plan boiled down to the two key points he'd made to Aderholt:

Number one, all of us said we were going to do this. You all have been promising to do it for years. You've already voted to repeal Obamacare dozens of times in "show votes." I promised to do it during the campaign. We've just got to do it.

Number two, we've got to stick together. This is the first of many big things we're going to do. Republicans control the White House, the Senate, and the House. If we don't band together and deliver what we promised, we're not going to have any excuses. Democrats always stick together; we'd better do the same.

They were both compelling arguments. But as the Zeke Emanuel meeting showed, things could go sideways when the debate turned to the finer details of the policy.

When Trump walked into the Cabinet Room, he was riding high from his previous success in getting lawmakers to commit to supporting the bill. As he went around the table, he continued to secure support, this time from the more moderate wing of the party.

Then he came to Charlie Dent of Pennsylvania.

Dent, who was first elected to the House in 2005 and had risen to Chair of the House Ethics Committee, was seated across the table from the President and several seats to his right. No one knew it yet, but Dent was planning to retire from Congress and would not be running for reelection. When it came his turn to talk, he leaned forward slightly but kept his hands in his lap, rather than placing them on the table.

"I'm a no, Mr. President," he said quietly, without elaborating.

Trump folded his arms in front of him, left over right, as he always did. His jacket sleeves rose slightly, exposing his diamond-encrusted cuff links. Such body language is universally read as defensive or negative. That's not always what it meant coming from Trump—sometimes he'd sit that way in even the most positive meetings. But in this case, it almost felt like he was hugging himself in hopes of holding in an explosion.

"You're hurting your party, Charlie," the President said like a disappointed father, launching into a lengthy recitation of his go-to arguments. *We've got to do this. We've got to stick together.*

Dent's eyes stayed steady on the President. He wasn't glaring. He was calm, his shoulders slumping slightly. And his slow, measured response once Trump stopped talking made it clear that he was hoping to avoid a big blow-up.

Leaning forward slightly, hands remaining in his lap, Dent calmly replied, "I'm still a no, Mr. President.

"I'm very concerned about the Medicaid changes in this bill," he continued, subtly raising his eyebrows as he spoke, causing three deep wrinkles in his forehead to become more pronounced. "I just feel like we need to slow down and make sure we get this right."

Trump's arms were still folded in front of him as he listened, but his frustration was becoming more evident. His lips were slightly pursed and he was no longer looking directly at Dent as he spoke.

"Charlie, I don't think you understand," Trump interrupted. "We need a win here, Charlie."

As Trump made his points, he was now gesturing with his right hand, although it was still tucked under his left elbow.

"We need to repeal Obamacare, okay?" he said. "Everyone here knows that. But you've got to think about this in a bigger way—it's so much bigger, there's a much bigger way of thinking about it. We're talking taxes, we're talking so many other bills that are going to come, but we need this first."

Trump was now leaning forward in Dent's direction, with his hands folded on the table in front of him. He emphasized his most important points by tapping his right index finger on the table or subtly pointing it toward Dent in sync with his words. Everyone else in the room was awkwardly silent.

Dent's jaw tightened.

"I just wish we could hear more from states like mine that have expanded Medicaid," he said. "If you'd be willing to consider some changes to the bill, Mr. President—"

"We can't," Trump stopped him. He then laid out the challenge of trying to negotiate major legislation through a Republican-controlled Congress.

"Charlie, you understand this," he said. "I give you something and I lose twenty votes from somewhere else."

Trump's hands were now out in front of him, palms up, like scales trying to balance.

"I met with conservatives earlier," he continued. "They all wanted something, and I told them—and look, you're getting more than they are—but I told them, 'Guys, we can't do it.'"

He flipped both of his hands over in a quick swipe.

"Because I knew I'd lose everyone in this room. Now, if I give you what you want, I'm going to go back to them and they're all going to say, 'Well, then, we need this,' and we start all over again."

All of this was true. House Republicans were an ideologically diverse group. A moderate like Dent had more in common with a lot of the Democrats than he did with the thirty to forty members of the staunchly conservative Freedom Caucus. Sometimes the only thing they seemed to have in common was the "R" beside their names, but that wasn't enough to keep them together.

Dent didn't respond, and there were a few seconds of quiet. His silence spoke louder than anything he could have said in the moment: he wasn't budging. Now Trump was mad. He'd successfully persuaded dozens of lawmakers in previous meetings, but he knew Dent's refusal to come on board would be a problem because it would lead to other defections.

"You're destroying your party," he said angrily. "We were going to do this, we were going to do taxes, we were going to do infrastructure—so many things. Big things. But we needed a win on this. And it's a very selfish thing to do. Very selfish. It's very selfish.

"I'm done with him," Trump said, turning his attention back to the rest of the room.

The next day, Trump had Speaker Ryan pull the health-care bill off the floor of the House, just moments before it was scheduled to receive a vote. It wasn't going to pass.

It was a devastating blow, capped by Ryan's public statement: "Obamacare is the law of the land."

Trump was enraged. This flop convinced him more than ever that he'd been right about GOP leaders all along. He had acquiesced to their approach—at least as much as he was capable of doing. Yet these guys were as ineffective as he'd been saying they were. From that point forward, he was driving the train, and they either needed to get on board or get out of the way.

8

KILLERS

On April 3, 2017, I sat quietly in the southwest corner of the Cabinet Room as senior national security and foreign policy officials filed in one by one for a bilateral meeting between Trump and Egyptian President Abdel Fattah el-Sisi.

Egypt was one of our most important Arab allies in the fight against ISIS, but this was the first time its head of state had been to the West Wing since 2009. Sisi and President Obama had endured a tense relationship, to say the least. Outside of Israel, no country received more military aid from the United States than Egypt, about $1.3 billion annually. But at one point, Obama sought to punish Sisi's government for human rights abuses—of which it was no doubt guilty—by halting the delivery of U.S. military hardware and cash. Obama ultimately relented, but he never invited Sisi to the White House.

Trump was determined to prioritize America's strategic interests over such humanitarian concerns. His intentions were never stated in quite those terms, but the shift was clear. This was a departure from recent iterations of U.S. foreign policy, which Trump believed focused too much on lecturing other countries about how they should conduct themselves. Trump's approach to geopolitics was still developing but was actually pretty well summed up by one of his campaign slogans: *America First*. He represented a return to real-politik: blunt, hard-charging, and transactional pragmatism on the world stage. Whatever the faults with his approach, he proudly owned them.

Of course, the fact that Sisi and Obama had not gotten along made Trump even more excited to meet with him. They were huddling one-on-one in the Oval while their top aides waited in the Cabinet Room next door.

One side of the table, with the Rose Garden visible through the windows behind them, was designated for the American delegation. On the other side a half-dozen Egyptian advisers, one of them in an ornate military uniform, stood behind their chairs. The small talk was minimal. The language barrier may have contributed to this, but neither side was really talking among themselves either. I was sitting alone along the wall, behind the rest of the American team, and thinking through the Arabic phrases I had picked up during my travels in the Middle East, including Egypt. I squinted to see the antique clock sitting on the mantel at the other end of the room. Was it afternoon yet? I figured I should know for sure, just in case I got brave and decided to greet anyone from the foreign delegation with *"Sabah al-khair"* (good morning) or *"Masaa al-khair"* (good afternoon/evening).

Click. Whoosh.

A Secret Service agent swung open the Cabinet Room door, bringing everyone to attention. Sisi entered, followed by Trump, and the two leaders took their places across from each other at the center of the table, flanked by their aides. Keith Schiller, the Director of Oval Office Operations, trailed the President into the room and took a seat right next to me along the wall. Charles Willson Peale's 1776 portrait of General George Washington, commissioned by John Hancock, hung just above our heads.

"Well, we just had a wonderful conversation," the President began. "There were some problems with the people who were here before us. But we're looking forward to no more problems, right, Mr. President? No more problems."

There was a bit of a delay in Sisi's reaction as the translator relayed Trump's words. But after a few seconds, a tight smile appeared on his face, and he gave the President a slow, downward head nod of approval.

"Now, I'd like to start by introducing everyone," Trump continued, "so you all know who you're dealing with." If this were a basketball game, the lights would have dimmed and the fog machines and dramatic music would have kicked in.

"This is General Mattis, my Secretary of Defense," Trump began, looking at Mattis, seated to his right. The general sat there expressionless. "They call him 'Mad Dog,' even though he doesn't really go by that name. Honestly,

I don't even think he likes that name, do you, General?" Trump didn't wait for a response. "But he's never lost a battle, and I'm sure you all know how much we love winning around here."

The group laughed, with a few seconds' delay for the Egyptians waiting on the translation. They had either seen Trump's campaign rallies, during which he would memorably declare, "We're gonna win so much, you may even get tired of winning," or they did a good job pretending they understood the reference.

All joking aside, Mattis's battlefield exploits genuinely were the stuff of legend—he was one of the few Trump Cabinet officials who garnered respect and acclaim across party lines—and I was confident that at least the gentleman sitting across the table in the military uniform was aware of his reputation.

"That's Gary Cohn," the President continued, pointing to his left toward the former Goldman Sachs president sitting near the end of the table. "He made a few hundred million dollars and had to pay a lot of taxes to come work here, but he did it. Thanks, Gary, the U.S. Treasury appreciates it." The President smiled, as Cohn laughed and nodded.

"There's Jared," the President said, looking toward his son-in-law and senior adviser. "We're very proud of him—a great talent. He did his first big deal while he was still in his twenties. We're very proud. And he's done not so bad for himself in the family department, I have to add."

Jared smiled politely, turning his head but never seeming to move his perfectly postured torso.

As Trump continued working his way around the room, I watched Sisi closely. He had a pleasant disposition, which I found interesting because of how it contrasted with his well-earned reputation as a strongman. There was something chilling to me about the apparent likability of a man who'd been known to have his enemies killed. Maybe it was the Arab version of walk softly but carry a big stick. Maybe it was deference in the presence of superior leverage and firepower. Or maybe it was just good diplomacy. Regardless, here he was, getting along swimmingly with the American President who had once said, "Islam hates us," and called for "a total and complete shutdown of Muslims entering the United States." This phrase shot to the front of my mind when I noticed the bump on Sisi's forehead. It was slightly darker than the rest of his skin. Known as a *zebibah* in Arabic, the mark was a point of pride among some Muslim men, who developed it through repeated contact with their prayer mat. Politically, it was a symbol to the 90 percent of Egypt's population who were Muslims that he was one of them.

Trump continued on making his introductions.

"This is Rex Tillerson," he said, nodding toward the Texan with his gray hair brushed back. "He ran a little company you've probably heard of . . ." Trump paused slightly and exaggerated the next two words. "*Exxon . . . Mobil*. Also known as the largest company in the world. Is it the largest, Rex? I think it probably is, or at least close, but it probably is. He knows everyone. If they've got oil in their country, he knows them, isn't that right, Rex? Now he's my Secretary of State."

After a couple more introductions, the President finally ended by reaching his hand over to the man beside him, patting his arm.

"And this is my Wilbur."

Having your name referenced in the first-person possessive by the President was a distinction for people with whom he felt a special connection. Commerce Secretary Wilbur Ross certainly fit into that category. Trump viewed him as a peer—a wealthy industrialist, approaching eighty years old, who had clawed his way to a fortune through grit and determination. He came across as mild-mannered and kind, and was "just the cutest old man," according to one of the young executive assistants in the West Wing. But he was also a tough-as-nails executive who had made his money through leveraged buyouts of distressed steel, textile, and coal corporations.

Trump was clearly proud this guy had joined his Cabinet. "He's so famous on Wall Street, all you have to say is 'Wilbur,' and everyone knows who you're talking about," the President raved. "No last name! You don't need it! Because everyone knows he's a total killer. He doesn't look like it, right? Look at him, he's a nice guy—one of the nicest. But he's a killer."

The President looked across the table at the foreign military leader who was smiling and nodding, with the translator in his earpiece trying to keep up. "And that's the only kind we deal with—killers. You understand what I'm saying, don't you, General?"

It's hard to say whether "killer" translated effectively into Arabic—*alqatil* could also be taken as "murderer" or "assassin," after all—but they seemed to at least understand that Trump was saying it all in good fun. Then again, I also couldn't help but wonder if there was a hidden subtext. *We're glad to reboot this relationship. But don't mess with us.*

Killer. This was the single highest compliment that Donald Trump—not the President, but the man—could pay another human being, and it had been for decades.

In 1980, a half decade before I was even born, Trump sat down with entertainment reporter Rona Barrett for his first-ever network television interview. "I think that the world is made up of people with either killer instincts or without killer instincts," Trump told her. "The people that seem to emerge all the time—it doesn't mean they're the best . . . are the people that are competitive and driven and with a certain instinct to win." In short, *killers.* And this was a mind-set that had been instilled in Trump since childhood.

In Harry Hurt III's Trump biography, *Lost Tycoon,* he wrote that Trump's father, Fred, used to tell his sons, "You are a killer . . . You are a king . . . You are a killer . . . You are a king." He'd gotten it honestly. It was deeply ingrained in his psyche since childhood. So if you're trying to make sense of almost any action he took as President, this is the prism through which everything should be viewed.

For instance, Trump would at one point publicly declare that if North Korea did not stop threatening the United States, they would be "met with fire, fury and, frankly, power the likes of which the world has never seen before." The entire planet—including many of us in the West Wing—were taken aback, uncertain of whether we were now lurching toward a potential nuclear conflict.

Trump, for his part, felt totally in control. Part of the Trumpian *killer* mentality was to negotiate by dragging an adversary into chaos and uncertainty and bet that they wouldn't be able to operate comfortably in that environment for as long as he could.

Sitting in the Oval one afternoon, he casually reflected on how he'd turned the tables after years of U.S. officials debating whether North Korea's leaders were rational actors.

"Now *they* don't know what to make of *me,*" he said of the North Koreans. "Maybe I'll do it, maybe I won't." *Will or won't what?* I definitely wasn't going to ask. "They don't have any idea. No one does. And that's a good thing. That's how it should be." *But what if there's a misunderstanding that leads to war?* I thought to myself, but Trump kept riffing. "It's negotiation, and you can't be any good at it if you're afraid. And why would you be when you have the upper hand? At some point they say, 'That's enough,' and you win. We're going to win this one, believe me."

Some months later, during a lull in the conversation as I walked with the President from the Oval Office over to the residence, I asked him what it took, in his view, to be a killer. He smirked, like Einstein being asked to explain the theory of relativity or da Vinci being asked to reveal the secret behind the *Mona Lisa*'s smile. But he didn't hesitate for a second with his answer.

"Extreme competence," he said, stopping for a moment to drive home his point. "And you've got to be relentless—totally relentless. You've got to be a winner. And, really, I think you've got to love the fight. You've got to have fun with it, in a way. I think that's important. Killers have a certain way about them where they're out there getting the hell knocked out of them and they still love the game. Now they'd rather be doing the knocking, but they can take it, too."

This was, in a nutshell, Donald Trump's theory of life. And throughout my time in the West Wing, there were plenty of killers rolling through.

One of the truly extraordinary things about working at the White House is the people you have an opportunity to meet. One day it's the wealthiest person in human history. The next day it's the king of an ancient country. The following week it's a world champion athlete, or Grammy-winning musician, or Medal of Honor recipient.

Early in the administration, the White House assembled several "advisory councils"—private-sector leaders who would lend their expertise to various pieces of Trump's agenda. The President loved these meetings, because it meant many of the world's wealthiest, most powerful—and often famous—businessmen would come together for an audience with him.

After one of these meetings, I walked from the State Dining Room back to the West Wing with legendary General Electric CEO Jack Welch. The octogenarian leadership icon was wearing a black overcoat with the collar flipped up to face the biting winter cold, but he had a spring in his step after meeting with the President.

"I've been coming to this place since 1980 and I've never seen anything like that," he said. "They can say what they want about him, but I don't know if any president has been more prepared to sit in that room and talk business. It was like talking to a peer, not a politician. Hell of a meeting." Maybe he was simply saying this for my benefit, hoping I'd tell Trump. But he seemed sincere.

In any event, I did tell Trump about the comments a few minutes later. He didn't even take time to fully absorb the information before saying, "Get Jack Welch booked on television to do as many interviews as he'll do." It wasn't technically my job to do this, but that didn't matter. And we made it happen.

On a different occasion, the President convened another of these types of meetings—this one an infrastructure advisory council—led by billionaire New York real estate tycoons (and stone-cold Trumpian killers) Richard LeFrak and Steven Roth.

We met in the Cabinet Room and I sat against the wall opposite Trump, toward the end of the room where the busts of Benjamin Franklin and George Washington sat silently, filling the niches on either side of the fireplace. I chose that seat, rather than my usual spot behind the President, because there was another guest in the meeting who had piqued my interest. I've noticed that when there's a gathering of powerful and important people, there's typically an individual or two in the group who are a big deal, even among people who are a big deal in their own right. Apple CEO Tim Cook, for instance, stood out among tech leaders, as did all-pro tight end Rob Gronkowski when the New England Patriots visited. Among the infrastructure group, however, one billionaire stood out among the others: Elon Musk.

He was worth about twenty billion dollars and had captured the public's imagination with his grand visions of human exploration and technological revolution. In the infrastructure meeting, Musk's presence was a point of fascination for several reasons. First, and perhaps most obviously, he was famous. Not famous, like, in the business community, but in pop culture. Second, he was doing massive things—humanity-changing things—like sending people into space and attempting to end our century-plus reliance on the internal combustion engine. And third, he was viewed as a bona fide genius, someone who was actually inventing and engineering this crazy stuff, not just marketing it or selling it.

As the infrastructure advisory council settled into their chairs, Trump kicked off the meeting.

"It's wonderful to have everyone here," he said. "Steve and Richard are the best in the world at this—real pros. We've been friends and competitors for a long time. We've done some big deals, right? But what we're doing now is a little bigger, wouldn't you say? We were dealing in billions, now it's trillions, right? So we're going to do something really special together."

Once the pleasantries were out of the way, Trump went around the room soliciting ideas and feedback from his guests. There were ideas for how to fund a giant infrastructure plan. There were thoughts on what and where to build. And Trump would periodically veer into rants about how U.S. leaders had allowed the country to fall into a state of disrepair, or how we didn't "do big things anymore."

Musk sat quietly—probably the only person in the room not wearing a tie—as other advisers shared their ideas for traditional building projects. When it was his turn to share, the President introduced him softly. "Elon, what do you have for us?" he asked, giving Musk the floor.

"Mr. President, I'd like to discuss a way to take people from Washington, D.C., to New York City in twenty-nine minutes by tunneling," Musk began. He spoke with a slight stutter, never in the middle of sentences, but occasionally at the beginning, as if his mouth couldn't quite form the words as quickly as his brain could transmit them. "Just imagine how much this would improve people's lives. There's no reason we should be okay with sitting in traffic all day, which is what people do, especially where I live in California. We can fix this."

He went on to explain that he had founded the Boring Company, which was developing technology to dig faster and more economically, and to transport people at up to seven hundred miles per hour in tubes known as hyperloops.

"It's a high-density area, so we'll want to remain underground the entire way," he concluded. "It will take right at twenty-nine minutes."

All eyes in the room swung back to the President to see how he would react to a proposal that was so wildly different from any other ideas that had been thrown out so far.

"Everyone else is talking about bridges and roads, and this guy comes in here talking about tunnels and this and that!" the President exclaimed, sitting back in his chair and drawing laughter from the group. He wasn't mocking Musk; he seemed to be both making a joke and acknowledging the fact that Musk was operating on an entirely different intellectual plane than most everyone else in the room.

"That's good, Elon," he concluded. "Do it. I wish you the best of luck. Do it."

And with that, Musk got the blessing of the President of the United States to build a tunnel from Washington, D.C., to New York City, or at least it seemed like he did.

In any event, while the President enjoyed surrounding himself with killers—whether they were military generals or titans of industry—the White House staff seemed to subconsciously adopt a certain killer instinct as well. But instead of focusing it on accomplishing policy goals or desired political outcomes, we far too often focused on devouring one another.

Cutthroat doesn't even begin to describe it. In *Washington Post* journalist Bob Woodward's book *Fear: Trump in the White House,* Reince Priebus was quoted as saying of the West Wing dynamic, "When you put a snake and a rat and a falcon and a rabbit and a shark and a seal in a zoo without walls, things start getting nasty and bloody. That's what happens."

This was sometimes a good thing. Pitting staffers with wildly divergent viewpoints against one another sometimes led to better policy outcomes. But more often than not the culture of ruthlessness—starting at the very top— was so all-consuming that survival became a full-time job unto itself.

In our first year in the White House, no group of people attracted more of the President's ire than "the leakers." Attending meetings in the West Wing was accompanied by the anxiety of feeling like everything that was said was likely to find its way into the press. Often the leaks were incomplete versions of the truth, one-sided and self-serving. Regardless, they made the President furious.

For instance, one unnamed White House official told *Politico,* "We are kind of helpless. And we are hoping the President doesn't tweet. Fingers crossed."

When *The Washington Post* declared working for Trump "the worst job in Washington," anonymous White House officials said, "The problem is not an incompetent communications shop, as the President sometimes gripes, or an ineffectual Chief of Staff, as friends and outside operatives repeatedly warn, but the man in the Oval Office." The *Post* reported that "impromptu support groups of friends, confidants and acquaintances [had] materialized" for Trump aides, who had also "started reaching out to consultants, shopping their résumé."

These are but two examples among the dozens of times White House officials were granted anonymity to trash their boss. I found these comments to be especially disgraceful. I understood the rationale of some people simply not wanting to work for Donald Trump. But what kind of person did it anyway, only to spend their entire time there taking anonymous shots at the President they were supposedly serving?

On April 10, 2017, *Politico* published a story by its chief White House correspondent, Shane Goldmacher, eviscerating the White House communications team.

The most brutal part of the story took aim at Mike Dubke, who had recently signed on as Communications Director, finally relieving Spicer from overseeing both press and comms. He had been a campaign consultant and an ad buyer, but he didn't have any high-level communications experience. No matter. He met the only discernible criterion: loyalty to Sean and Reince.

Dubke had assembled a large group strategy session on how to best promote the President's first hundred days in office. He

> *kicked off the discussion of how to package Trump's tumultuous first 100 days by pitching the need for a "rebranding" to get Trump back on track. . . .*
>
> *Staffers, including counselor Kellyanne Conway, were broken into three groups, complete with whiteboards, markers and giant butcher-block-type paper to brainstorm lists of early successes. . . .*
>
> *Dubke, who did not work on the campaign, told the assembled aides that international affairs would present a messaging challenge because the president lacks a coherent foreign policy. . . . "There is no Trump doctrine," Dubke declared. . . .*

Right after the story popped online, Dubke was torpedoed by a very unexpected source. Unexpected, at least, to those who didn't know her. The First Lady.

I know there are many outside the White House who have become invested in the mythology, often backed by anonymous sources, that Melania secretly hated her husband, or was planning to divorce him, or had some business arrangement that kept them together. As with every marriage, they had their good days and bad days, often centering around times when accusations of past infidelity were in the news. But from what I saw she never wavered in her support, and she was serious about her official role as First Lady and her self-appointed role as her husband's fiercest protector.

She obsessed over every detail of White House social events, such as the annual White House Easter Egg Roll, an event that attracts more external visitors than any other one-day event throughout the year. In 2017, twenty-one thousand people were invited to the event, which takes place on a packed South Lawn, with musical entertainment, refreshments, and games. Press coverage leading up to the event that year had noted that it was the East Wing's first big test, and ominously warned that they had gotten a late start on the planning.

On the day of the event, everything was in place—the staging, the decorations, the eighteen thousand colored Easter eggs, the band. Stephanie Grisham, her Communications Director, had mapped out all of the camera angles and movements. Mrs. Trump was wearing an elegant light pink silk dress. She looked at ease, as if the whole thing had come together without much effort. She and Barron were preparing to accompany the President out onto the balcony with a junior staffer dressed in an Easter Bunny costume when Melania froze. Her lips formed into a judgmental frown.

"That needs to be taken off," she said.

She wasn't talking to Barron or her husband, but the Easter Bunny. He was wearing a light blue vest, and for whatever reason the color or the fabric intruded on the First Lady's milieu. With seconds to go, staffers jumped into action, scrambling to undress the white bunny in full view of a slightly perplexed President.

"That's much better," she said. *Now everything was perfect.* And they walked together out of the Blue Room and onto the balcony to be received by the crowd below.

Mrs. Trump was also a savvy consumer of news, and her quiet work as the President's protector in chief was never fully appreciated by most people, either inside or outside the White House. She spent hours each day consuming the television coverage and tracking the palace intrigue inside the West Wing. That's how Dubke caught her attention.

Appalled by the *Politico* story, the First Lady rang the President in the Oval Office. He put her on speakerphone and listened with increasing alarm as she explained that he had serious issues within his communications team, particularly with this new guy Mike Dubke. She told him he needed to read the *Politico* story immediately. Hanging up the phone, he demanded for the story to be printed out and brought to him. Minutes later it was in his hands and he was stunned to see his communications director—whom he'd barely gotten to know—declaring to his staff that the President needed a "rebrand" and that he didn't have a coherent foreign policy.

Dubke told the President the article was false. Having been in the meeting and witnessed it myself, I thought it was pretty much accurate, although it did come across more dramatic in print than it had in person. Every detail wasn't presented in its precise context, but it certainly captured the sentiments Dubke had expressed to the team.

Instead of owning up to his comments, Dubke excoriated the "leakers" in our midst. It was a totally reasonable frustration, but not an excuse for what he said. With the article citing "six sources" who were in the room, we knew a crackdown was coming, we just weren't sure what it would look like.

When *Politico* had previously written a story critical of the press team, Spicer had brought all forty of us into his office, asked us to put both our government and personal phones on a table, then informed us that he was going to have lawyers from the White House Counsel's Office go through them to find out who had spoken to *Politico* reporter Alex Isenstadt.

They didn't find anything, and the entire absurd exercise promptly leaked to *Politico*. Spicer would later write in his memoir that the President had scolded him for employing such a bumbling tactic.

"Sean, what were you thinking?" he recalled the President saying.

"Of all my experiences with the President," he concluded, "that one was the worst."

This time, though, it felt like they were likely to go even further. Perhaps a lie detector test? I'm not sure what it says about our work environment that it seemed totally plausible that we might get polygraphed over a *Politico* story, but at that point it wouldn't have surprised anyone. This was a hot topic among communications aides, and everyone had their own opinion about how to handle such a situation. I figured I'd just tell the truth, and if they fired me for it, then so be it.

Sure enough, I got a cryptic phone call the next day from a lawyer in the White House Counsel's Office asking me to come upstairs. When I got there, Priebus, Dubke, and White House Counsel Don McGahn were all seated behind a conference table.

I didn't know McGahn well, but I liked the fact that he had long hair—falling over his ears and stopping just above his shoulders—and that he played the guitar in a rock band. As I walked into his office, McGahn was sitting back, one leg crossed over the other, with both hands holding up his top leg by the knee.

"Come on in," Priebus said. "Have a seat.

"Have you seen this story by Shane Goldmacher—the one about the 'One Hundred Days' communications meeting?" he asked.

I told him everyone in the building had seen it.

"Did you talk to the reporter? Were you one of his sources?"

I told him I had not given the story to Goldmacher, but that he had indeed called me about it.

I explained that Goldmacher had called and said he was writing the story based on the firsthand accounts of numerous other people who were in the room. But the part he wanted to talk to me about was that he'd heard the President was frustrated with Dubke and longing to bring back Jason Miller, the senior communications adviser from the campaign. He also said he'd heard Miller had been quietly advising Jared Kushner and Steve Bannon on communications strategy and had written a memo about how the White House should be communicating about the health-care bill, which had stalled in Congress.

Everything Goldmacher was laying out to me on the phone was true, but I knew it wouldn't be helpful for anyone. So I enlisted Miller's help and together we convinced Goldmacher to tone down that portion of the story. There was nothing I could do about everything else he had been told. He wasn't asking me to confirm it. He already had it from a half-dozen sources.

Fortunately, Miller had also called Priebus to give him a heads-up, so I assumed he knew that everything I was telling him was true. Priebus then moved on to asking who else might have leaked it.

"What about Kellyanne?" he asked. I told him that plenty of people viewed Kellyanne as a leaker, but then again plenty of people suspected their enemies in the White House of being leakers. No one had any hard evidence, so there was no way of really knowing. Plus, in this particular story *Politico* had six sources—*six*—so it was a bigger issue than just one person talking out of turn.

Priebus's one comment was that I should have called Dubke to alert him. Fair enough. I conceded that point. Then they let me go.

I considered it another example of Priebus and his allies being more concerned with bad press for themselves than they were about the fact that they'd hired a Communications Director who didn't believe in the President.

After leaving the Counsel's office, Dubke threatened me, saying that if word got out that I had been summoned to the Counsel's office for this, I would be fired. I told him he could rest assured that I'd come to him directly if I had a problem. But in retrospect it was that willingness to express my concerns directly that put me under suspicion in the first place. Because I was the only one openly expressing frustration, they assumed every negative story was a hit job planted by me. At the time I was sick of being suspected, but looking back I'm flattered they thought I was that prolific.

Keith Schiller, always a barometer of Trump's level of aggravation, talked to me about the leaking problem one day when we were gathered outside of the Oval Office. "Who do you think is doing it?" he asked, channeling the President's exasperation.

I told him there was really no way to know for sure but that everyone had theories, including me.

"We need to talk more about this," he said. "Let's catch up later."

That evening, Keith texted and asked me to come to his apartment, just off McPherson Square, about two blocks from the White House. When I came over, we walked to a nearby pharmacy so Keith could pick up some household items, and I laid out a simple theory.

When things got tough during the campaign—particularly after the release of the *Access Hollywood* tape—there were people who bailed and people who stuck it out. And even among those who stuck it out, there was a group from the RNC who seemed to spend their time talking to members of the press, trying to convince them that when Trump lost, it would not be their fault. And yet some of those same people somehow found their way into the White House.

The best-known example of this among former campaign staffers was Michael Short. Even before *Access Hollywood,* Short—on loan from the RNC—had left his computer sitting open on his desk in the Trump Tower war room, walked out of the building, and never returned. Once back at the RNC, he had cursed out campaign staffer Chris Byrne in a shouting match at one of the debates, berated Stephen Miller over email for insisting the RNC defend Trump against the *Washington Post* fact-checker, and was generally confrontational with every Trump aide he encountered. And yet Priebus and Spicer had tapped him to be an assistant press secretary in the White House, with a portfolio that included national security issues and foreign policy. Additionally, Raj Shah, whom Priebus and Spicer had named Deputy White House Communications Director, had been offered the research director job during the campaign, but turned it down to stay at the RNC. Several people close to him told campaign aides that he had decided not to let his reputation be tarnished by what was sure to be a crushing electoral defeat.

Keith was surprised by these stories, which had somehow never made it back to him and presumably never made it back to the President, either.

We were enduring another difficult period. The push to repeal Obamacare had turned into a debacle, and there was a nonstop torrent of damaging leaks. My theory was that the same people who had bailed and leaked during the campaign were probably doing the same thing again. When we made it back to Keith's apartment, he told me he wanted to share my thoughts—especially the Michael Short story—with the President.

He called an aide in the White House residence and told him he wanted to bring me up to see the boss first thing in the morning to talk about the leaking.

"Actually, he wants to talk to you right now," the aide replied. "Here's the President."

With Trump on the phone, at about eight o'clock at night, Keith quickly told him I had some insight into the staffing issues that he would want to hear.

I could tell the President was agitated and annoyed about all of this. He wanted answers from people he felt he could trust. This, of course, was not the first president to be concerned about leakers. Every president in recent history has been upset about anonymous sources within their team criticizing his leadership in the press. But few presidents were as immersed in the media as the current one. "Bring him to see me first thing tomorrow," he ordered.

The following morning, Keith called me and asked me to meet him in the hall between the Oval Office and the Roosevelt Room. This was unusual, since our desks were about twenty yards apart and he could just walk over and talk to me. This time, he didn't want to risk anyone overhearing what we were doing. It was pure palace intrigue. There was no one we could trust.

Thirty seconds later I was at our appointed rendezvous point. Unfortunately, so were Reince Priebus and several other members of the staff who were walking toward their offices just down the hall. Once they had cleared out of the hallway, Keith slipped me through the President's private dining room and into his private study. At this point I probably don't have to keep writing "in a normal White House, that's not how any of this would work." But normally staffers are not slipped in past the front office reception staff or without the approval of the Chief of Staff or their bosses in the chain of command.

A few moments later he brought the President into the famous "Bill and Monica" study.

"What do you have for me?" he asked.

"Tell him exactly what you told me," Keith said before closing the door and waiting outside.

I felt like this was an important moment in my relationship with the President. We spoke often, as I've noted, and he would frequently ask my thoughts on the news of the day as we walked between the residence and the West Wing before or after recording videos. He loved to ask about how other members of the staff were performing, especially Spicer. His assessments increasingly had turned sour.

"He couldn't even complete a sentence today without stuttering," Trump had complained during a recent conversation. "What do you think about Sarah Sanders? Would she be better?"

Those types of questions, which the President was known to ask of various staffers and friends, always put me in a tough spot. While anyone outside of Spicer's RNC loyalists conceded privately that it was probably time for a change behind the podium, I still had to work with Sean. Every day. I didn't love criticizing him behind his back. But when the President wanted my opinion I gave it to him.

"He's struggling out there every day, and sometimes it's tough to watch," I'd tell the President. "But he's probably got the toughest job in the building, other than yours."

Trump would generally agree whenever I said something like this and we would move on to other topics. But this time, this conversation, was different. The President was frustrated and wanted the unvarnished truth not only about Sean but about the never-ending problems in the press and communications shop.

Several months of events in the West Wing flooded into my mind.

Reince and Sean had marginalized almost every member of the campaign team who had come into the White House. I believed their staffers were the ones anonymously disparaging the President in the press. They occasionally mocked him in closed-door meetings. They had blocked former campaign aides from taking a leading role on any of the top projects or issues. And it wasn't like Reince and Sean were having success. They had botched nearly every major communications rollout or crisis management situation. And they had somehow made working at the White House—the honor of a lifetime—a miserable experience that left many of us dreading the walk into work each morning.

As I sat in front of the President of the United States, also exasperated with the state of play, I figured I didn't have anything to lose by just telling him the truth as I saw it. Besides, he was my boss, the ultimate boss, and my loyalty was, as it always had been, to him first.

"Mr. President," I began, "I remember what it felt like the night the *Access Hollywood* video came out. We all do. It was a gut-check moment for all of us. Everyone counted us out. But the next morning, I woke up at six A.M. and came into the Tower and went to work. We all did, except for a couple of people. One of them is named Michael Short. He quit even before *Access Hollywood,* and I didn't see him again for months. Until we showed up on our first day and he was here, too, because he's Sean and Reince's guy and they decided to bring him into your White House."

"Wait," the President interjected. "He quit on us, but they still brought him here?" That Trump didn't know this story—which had long since become a part of 2016 campaign lore—wasn't a surprise. During the campaign, he hardly interacted with most of the people working there, other than the top dogs like Bannon or Kellyanne.

"Yes, sir," I replied. "And that's just the tip of the iceberg."

Stunned, the President called out for Keith, who was standing just outside the door, and asked him to bring in a pen and a piece of paper. After returning with a Sharpie and White House note card, Keith stayed in the room. "I told you, sir," Keith said. "These are the kind of people we're dealing with."

"Give me their names," the President intoned. Only in retrospect did I see how remarkable this was. I was sitting there with the President of the United States basically compiling an enemies list—but these enemies were within his own administration. If it had been a horror movie, this would have been the moment when everyone suddenly realizes *the call is coming from inside the house.*

"Is there anyone in particular you're interested in?" I asked.

"Well, first, tell me who are our people from the campaign." I knew what he meant. People who weren't brought in by Priebus, Spicer, and the RNC.

I began listing campaign staffers from the fourteenth floor of Trump Tower, with whom I had spent countless hours in the trenches—people like Steven Cheung, Andy Surabian, and Kaelan Dorr, who had worked sixteen-hour days for months.

"Stephanie Grisham is another one," I said. I knew very well that the President loved Stephanie. While he didn't recognize some of the other names I was giving him, Stephanie was the traveling Press Secretary on the campaign and he loved her toughness. She had come into the White House as a Deputy Press Secretary under Spicer, but quickly left to join the First Lady's staff a couple of months in. "She's happy now," I said, "but Sean kept her out of everything because she wasn't one of his people from the RNC."

I knew this one would stick with the President because it directly impacted him. Stephanie used to hurry members of the media in and out of press gaggles. She had a good relationship with them—a mutual respect—but they tended not to break decorum when she was around. Since she'd left for the East Wing, the press seemed to cast etiquette aside more frequently. In one memorable example that would come later that summer, the press corps got so aggressive jockeying for position in the Oval that they knocked a golden lamp off an end table, sending Keith lunging to catch it before it hit the ground.

"Easy, fellas," Trump said, totally appalled. "Hey, fellas. Fellas, easy. Fellas—easy!"

"Guys, you're knocking the furniture down," Keith finally said in frustration.

They kept pushing.

"Stop it!" Johnny McEntee, the President's body man, demanded. "It's the Oval Office. Stop it."

These scrums drove Trump crazy and sometimes sent him into a rant about how "this never happened when Stephanie was here."

As I continued to tick off names, Trump would occasionally interject to ask about other members of the staff.

"Hope Hicks?"

"She's the best—rock solid."

"What about Keith?" he asked, both of us clearly aware of Keith standing right there.

I smiled. "Everyone knows Keith is with you one hundred percent."

He wasn't actually concerned about Hope or Keith. They'd long since proven themselves to be beyond reproach—certainly far more than I had. I assumed questions about them were more of a test of me. I wouldn't have been stupid enough to disparage either one of them anyway. But of course I meant what I told the President.

Then his tone changed.

"What about Mike Dubke?"

Already a dead man walking thanks to the First Lady, Dubke had spent the last several weeks spinning himself into a lather in a daily fit of incompetence, and he had inherited Spicer's animosity toward former campaign aides. In fairness to him, he had inherited our contempt as well. Neither side gave the other much of a chance.

"He has absolutely no idea what he's doing," I told the President.

"And Sean?"

"At this point he spends more time fighting for his job than he does fighting for you. I think it's really worth considering giving Sarah a shot behind the podium full-time."

"What about Reince?"

I paused.

"Just between you and me," the President said, leaning in. "I want to know exactly what you think."

"Mr. President, let me first say that I don't work closely with Reince, so I want to be fair to him. He's got a tough job and has to deal with a lot more than just problems with the communications team."

The President shifted in his chair. He didn't care to sit through people hedging before stating their opinions. *Just say it.*

"But I do remember when he told you that you should quit the campaign and allow Pence to take over," I continued. "When things got tough, his instinct was to tell you to quit. Your instinct was to fight. I don't have any reason to believe that Reince is a bad guy, but I do have reason to believe he's not a fighter, and he's filled your White House with an entire team of people who either aren't fighters or aren't loyal to you—or both. That's a recipe for disaster."

The President shot Keith a look that said, *It's hard to argue with that,* so I kept going.

"Ask any reporter in the White House press corps and they will tell you the same thing: If you want to get a response, write a story about Reince or Sean. The press shop will be all-hands-on-deck for the rest of the day pushing back. But if someone's working on a story about you, very few people over there even lift a finger.

"The reason for that," I concluded, "is that Reince and Sean have filled their staffs with people who are loyal to them, not you."

By that point the President was indignant.

"Keith, I want these people out of here," he said, "starting with"—he looked down at his note card—"Michael Short. Go fire him right now and throw him out of here. We'll take care of the rest later."

Keith agreed, but wanted to "do it by the book."

"There's Secret Service protocol for this type of thing," he said. "They walk them out. I'll go ask about the process."

The President stood up and shook my hand.

"I'm going to take care of this," he said. "We're going to get rid of all the snakes, even the bottom-feeders."

The President walked out of the private study and back into the Oval Office, and Keith shuttled me out into the back hallway. I went back to my desk on the other side of the Roosevelt Room and exhaled.

I felt relieved, but I also felt—I don't know—something very close to guilt. I had told the President the truth. I wasn't making up lies about anyone. He had asked and I had given my sincere opinions. But in doing this I sensed that I was losing myself in what I had rationalized as a necessary struggle for survival.

I missed Alabama. I missed my friends from church. The ones who couldn't care less about politics or where I worked. The ones who would come over to our house every Tuesday night for Bible study. We still went to church faithfully every Sunday. But I had lost the support of a community that made sure I wasn't finding my identity in a job. After all, to paraphrase the Gospel of Mark, *What does it profit a man to survive in Trump's White House but forfeit his soul?*

The whole Dubke/*Politico* episode had put me on Priebus's radar, and several subsequent run-ins with Dubke only heightened their desire to push me out. So when Trump confronted Priebus with a list of his allies who the President was suddenly wanting to get rid of, I immediately came to mind.

The President agreed to hold off on making any moves with regard to staff until he came back from his first foreign trip, about a week and a half later, but the wheels had been set in motion. Something was going to change.

Sure enough, just two weeks after the President invited me into his private study to give my thoughts on the communications operation, news broke in *Axios* that Dubke was resigning. This stoked speculation that more changes were on the way.

"Bring in the killers," *Axios*'s Mike Allen wrote. "Trump is considering much broader changes."

Priebus and Spicer were on the defensive, and I witnessed this firsthand. The day after Dubke's resignation, I was sitting at my desk when I noticed Reince flagging down *Time* magazine reporter Zeke Miller in the hallway. I stepped into the hallway, just close enough to overhear Reince around the corner telling him that no more changes were imminent; everyone was safe. He then told him he should tweet it out.

When I returned to my desk, I waited a few minutes and then pulled up Miller's twitter account.

"Snr White House official to me a few min ago," he'd written. "'There's no shake-up coming. You should tweet that. It's also true.'"

A few short weeks later, that tweet would be proven wrong.

9

THE MOOCH IS LOOSE

"I heard poorly rated @Morning_Joe speaks badly of me (don't watch any-more). Then how come low I.Q. Crazy Mika, along with Psycho Joe, came to Mar-a-Lago 3 nights in a row around New Year's Eve, and insisted on joining me. She was bleeding badly from a face-lift. I said no!"

With that tweet, fired off from the residence at 7:52 A.M. on June 29, 2017, the President kicked off our workday in the White House by going after Joe Scarborough and Mika Brzezinski of MSNBC's *Morning Joe.*

The tweet set the internet ablaze and caused serious backlash across party lines, and it marked a major escalation in the growing feud between Trump and his two former friends.

Late in the campaign, comms staffers had been surprised one day to look up and realize Joe and Mika were walking through the war room with Trump. The candidate paused to show off the giant wall full of televisions. When he saw one of them was airing CNN, he dismissed it. "We have to see every-thing, but we don't want to watch that, believe me." The two morning show hosts chuckled, then continued on their tour.

They had occasionally been Trump's guests at Mar-a-Lago, and I'd seen them at least one other time in the lobby of Trump Tower during the transition. But somewhere along the way their relationship with Trump turned sour. And the drama played out daily on MSNBC's flagship morning show, which re-ceived poor ratings nationally but was the go-to wake-up show inside the Beltway.

I met the President on the ground floor of the White House residence about an hour after the tweet went out.

"Good morning, sir," I said as he stepped off the elevator. I then directed him toward the Diplomatic Reception Room, where we had a camera crew waiting to record his weekly address to the nation.

At that point in the administration, I was typically the only West Wing staffer there for the recording—the President preferred recording with as few people in the room as possible—but on this particular morning, Spicer had decided to come over from the West Wing as well.

Seeing Sean, Trump stopped in the grand hallway on the ground floor. Unwitting White House tourists were standing about fifteen yards away on the other side of partitions, which blocked them from being able to see us.

"Did you see the tweet?" he asked. His tone was serious, but there was a hopeful glint in his eye, as if he were a new father asking us if we'd seen his newborn child.

"Oh, I'm pretty sure the whole world has seen the tweet," I replied, drawing a laugh from Keith Schiller, who had come down from the residence with the President. He was almost always the first to see the President in the morning, and he was carrying the President's stack of newspapers.

"Well, what did you think?" the President continued. He was looking at Spicer.

"It was . . . aggressive," Spicer said, hesitating. Trump pondered this for a moment before responding.

"They're going to say it's not presidential," he said. "But you know what? It's modern-day presidential. I'm not going to stop telling the American people what I think because it makes some people uncomfortable. And by the way, it's true—one hundred percent true."

Spicer's face betrayed no emotion. He didn't have time to respond anyway.

"Don't you dare say I watch that show," the President snapped. "I wouldn't have any idea what happens on there, but people call me about it." This may or may not have been accurate. He certainly preferred *Fox & Friends* in the morning, but who among us doesn't find ourselves hate-watching something from time to time?

He continued to rage on about Mika and Joe.

"They're pathetic. They were desperate for access. They came to Mar-a-Lago and I promise you she was bleeding. I saw the bandages. And when the cameras weren't around they were like groupies. So don't say I watch them, because I don't."

Whether or not the President of the United States should get so worked up over two talk show hosts was a question we had long since stopped asking. It didn't matter; it was a fact of life.

Then things got awkward. Or more awkward.

"You're not briefing today, are you?" the President asked Sean. Spicer shook his head and said Sarah Huckabee Sanders, his deputy, would be briefing the media in his stead. She had been doing this more and more often.

"Good," the President responded. This seemed to please him, but his tone of satisfaction quickly shifted to something between tough love and heartfelt disappointment. "You just can't go out there, Sean. I've been talking to a lot of people about it, and your credibility is shot. It's just bad—really bad. You just can't go out there. Sarah needs to be the one out there. You can't right now—you just can't, okay?"

It was true, of course, but brutal nonetheless. Spicer knew he was having a hard time with the press. He was constantly coming up with new reasons to either not hold a press briefing or to let Sarah do it. Yet he clearly did not want to relinquish the job.

He seemed enamored with the fame—or infamy, depending on your perspective—and would occasionally boast about the hordes of people who wanted to take selfies with him out in public. It wasn't clear that he had absorbed just how badly his credibility had been damaged. But worse than that, in Trump's eyes, was that he looked inept at parrying reporters' questions and offering nonresponses. Every White House Press Secretary has moments when they can't or won't answer reporters' questions, but they usually manage to maintain some respectability in the process.

Sean mustered a little "Yes, sir" in response.

It took a lot to make Spicer a sympathetic figure in my eyes.

The main difference between him and Sarah was basic human decency. If Sean had ever heard the old saying "Be kind to everyone on the way up; you'll meet the same people on the way down," he definitely didn't act like it.

At one point we met one-on-one in his office to discuss my role and the overall organizational structure of the press and communications teams.

"You've got thirty people sitting across the street in EEOB who don't have any direction, don't have any purpose, and don't feel like they are a part of the team," I told him, communicating a frustration many of the EEOB staff had relayed to me.

"I don't have time to walk around and give everyone a f—ing hug," Spicer snapped.

"They don't need hugs," I replied. "They need a leader."

Our mutual friends told me that he blamed nearly every negative story written about him on me. And I usually left work at night feeling like he would do just about whatever he could to push me out.

But he occasionally endured such indignities that I almost felt bad for him—*almost*. Now Spicer was about to suffer the biggest indignity yet.

Trump was going to bring in another "killer."

In mid-July 2017, I did some late-afternoon socializing with the First Lady's staff in the East Wing. I liked to go over there for a change of scenery, to decompress, and sometimes to vent. The atmosphere was much more pleasant and inviting than that of the West Wing, like floating in a rooftop infinity pool instead of swimming with piranhas in the Amazon.

As I came back through the Palm Room, I ran into the President and his dinner companion for the night. He immediately introduced us—not that his guest needed an introduction. It was Bob Kraft, owner of the New England Patriots.

"I'm surrounded by a lot of winning right now," I said.

"You're a wise man," Kraft said. "Where are you from?"

"Alabama. Roll Tide."

"Oh, so you know a lot about winning, too, then. We have one of your best guys on our defense," Kraft bragged. "Dont'a Hightower—but the guys call him 'The Stripper.'"

A quizzical look came across Trump's face.

"The Stripper?" he said, laughing. "What kind of nickname is that for a football player?"

"Oh, they call him that because he stripped the ball from the Falcons' quarterback in the Super Bowl," Kraft replied. "It was a big turning point in the game. So he's been 'The Stripper' ever since then."

As the conversation turned to my role in the White House, the President interjected with what at the time seemed like a random question.

"Hey, what do you think about Anthony Scaramucci?"

Scaramucci, a wealthy hedge fund manager, had been one of the President's best television surrogates during the campaign. This was admittedly a pretty low bar. I had gotten to know him because, since I was a communications adviser with a focus on messaging, he would call me before going on TV to ask how the campaign wanted him to answer certain questions or talk about specific issues. But more memorably for me, he would call back after his appearances to ask how he could improve. That seemed to be a rare quality in the mega-ego world of television talking heads: some semblance of humility and self-awareness. Whether by calculation or just because that's who he was—I tended to think the latter—the Mooch oozed earnestness.

"Oh, I think he's great," I told the President, launching into a brief explanation of my experience with his coachability and desire to constantly improve. That left Mr. Kraft nodding his head.

"That's good to hear," the President said. "Let's talk about him more in the morning. I think you're going to be very excited. Big plans!" With that, the two titans retreated to the residence for dinner.

A few hours later, I got a phone call that brought clarity to the President's cryptic reference to Scaramucci.

"No one knows this yet," a close friend of Scaramucci's told me, "but the President is probably about to make Mooch the new White House Communications Director." The problem, the friend explained, was that Reince Priebus and Steve Bannon were going to do whatever it took to keep him out.

Bannon and Priebus. The West Wing's odd couple. By all accounts they were strange bedfellows.

Bannon had built *Breitbart*'s media empire into a platform that eviscerated establishment weaklings like Priebus. One of Bannon's young deputies in the White House, Julia Hahn, had earned her hard-nosed reputation at *Breitbart* for going after Priebus's best friend in Congress, Paul Ryan. She'd driven up to his gated home in Wisconsin, at Bannon's direction, just to snap a photo to go along with the headline PAUL RYAN BUILDS BORDER FENCE AROUND HIS MANSION, DOESN'T FUND BORDER FENCE (for the country).

Priebus, on the other hand, almost certainly viewed Bannon as someone better suited for a psych ward than the West Wing (although you could argue it was sometimes hard to tell the difference). In the moments when chaos reigned supreme, Priebus was visibly uncomfortable, probably longing for what a more peaceful existence might have been like inside Jeb Bush's White House. In those same moments Bannon seemed like a hog who had unexpectedly found himself a mud puddle to wallow in on a hot day—he lived for it.

They put their differences aside—in terms of both policy and style—to keep other White House enemies in check.

Priebus was fighting enough battles and simply preferred for Bannon to not be one of them. Bannon viewed Priebus as the weakest Chief of Staff imaginable, which he was, allowing Bannon relatively free reign. But even more important to Steve was that keeping Reince in place and on his side made it more difficult for Jared Kushner—and the rest of "the globalists," as Steve derisively called them—to push him out. If Scaramucci came in, however, that could immediately destabilize Reince's already tenuous hold on power.

Bannon had scolded me before about openly expressing my frustrations with the RNC regime. "You've got to cut this s— out," he snapped. "These guys are fine, dude. We've got a good thing going here. F— this up and we're going to be dealing with some s— you can't even imagine. They'll be trying to have us all frog-marched out of here. The country's at stake. You've gotta understand that."

The whole thing felt like *Game of Thrones,* but with the characters from *Veep.*

Scaramucci was looking for advice on how to handle the entire situation, and our mutual friend thought I was in a good position to help him out, especially since I was so frustrated with Spicer.

Within minutes, I was on the phone with Scaramucci.

I didn't know him that well, but he began our call by confessing his deepest fears. That was how he talked—stream of consciousness and filter-free. No wonder he and Trump got along.

"This is my last shot at coming in, you understand what I'm telling you?" Scaramucci said.

He had initially sought to join the White House as Director of the Office of Public Liaison. This would have made him the conduit for outside groups—companies, trade associations, and coalitions—to interact with the White House. Priebus, viewing him as a direct threat, blocked him from landing the job. Since then, Scaramucci's name had come up in rumors about various White House roles, but nothing had materialized.

"Reince and Bannon don't know what the President's doing yet, okay? But his plan is to bring me in Friday morning and surprise them by announcing me as Comms Director. They're going to do everything they can to block me. They've been successful so far, right? So what I need to know is, how can we make sure this time is different?"

I guess it should have concerned me more than it did that I was now involved in a plot to undermine the White House Chief of Staff. But it didn't even cross my mind. This was the Trump White House and this sort of thing happened every day. And I rationalized it all by convincing myself it was all an effort to help the President. And I suppose it was. But I was trying to help myself, too, and in retrospect that was probably my primary concern.

Priebus's opposition to Mooch was nothing new. I had not previously been aware that Bannon was so vehemently opposed to him, too, but it made sense. Bannon's nemeses—Kushner, Ivanka Trump, and several other New Yorkers in the President's inner circle—were advocating hard for Scaramucci.

Bannon was a survivor. He had weathered being on the outs with the President before, such as when he seemed to be taking too much credit for Trump's election victory. But he'd then return to his good graces by keeping his head down and falling back on his most valuable asset: the fact that he and the President had an ideological mind-meld on Trump's favorite issues—immigration, trade, and foreign affairs.

Throughout the summer, a months-long internal battle over troop levels in Afghanistan had been raging. The President was uncertain that the presence of American troops in the tribal nation was serving the vital national security interests of the United States. This debate led to a broader discussion about the value of America's troop deployments around the globe. He wanted his top national security officials to justify the entire premise of projecting hard power all over the world.

To address these issues, Secretary of Defense James Mattis organized a meeting of the top military brass, national security officials, and the President in a windowless room called the Tank, deep inside the Pentagon. The day before the meeting, Trump was already spun up. "Somebody's going to have to answer a very simple question for me," he said, standing just outside the Oval. He stretched out his arms as he spoke, seeming to compare the length of his suit-coat sleeves. Perhaps it was newly tailored. "It really is quite simple," he said. "We've been in Afghanistan for seventeen years. What has it gotten us and why are we staying? It's like this all over the world. We go in—bing, bing, bing, our people get killed—we never leave, then at some point nobody can remember what we were doing there in the first place." This was music to Bannon's ears, but I knew it would not sit well with Mattis and others in the national security establishment.

I didn't accompany the President to the Pentagon the next day, July 20, but the meeting later became infamous for Secretary of State Rex Tillerson reportedly calling Trump a "f—ing moron" after it was over. All parties involved denied he ever said that, so we'll likely never know what actually happened. But when the President returned to the White House, I was waiting for him in the Oval and witnessed the aftermath firsthand.

He entered through the external door with Bannon just steps behind, and they were both exuberant. "Steve, Steve, that was spectacular," the President said. They both stopped in the middle of the room and recounted the meeting in the same way my former high school or college basketball teammates relive the victories of our youth. "We had them on the ropes," the President continued. "Rex didn't have any idea what to say. He was totally unsure of himself."

"He'll never get it, Mr. President," Bannon said of Tillerson. "He's totally establishment in his thinking."

"Totally establishment," the President echoed. "That's the perfect way to put it: completely and totally establishment. Everyone in the room was completely and totally establishment."

This was Bannon at the height of his power: ideologically aligned with the President and encouraging him to go with his gut, disrupt the status quo, and demand "the establishment" get on board or get out of the way.

With Bannon riding high after the Pentagon meeting, I was worried he would have the extra juice he'd need to keep Mooch out. And in this instance, I thought he was putting his interests ahead of the President's.

Priebus and Spicer were hurting Trump's ability to accomplish his agenda—the President had lost trust in them—and they either needed to shape up or ship out. I believed Scaramucci's entrance into the West Wing was likely to ensure one of those two things would happen, and I told Mooch I was going to do whatever I could to help make it happen.

Scaramucci told me the President was bringing him into the White House at 10 A.M. for a meeting in the Oval Office. I decided the best course of action was to meet Trump on the ground floor of the residence the following morning, catching him right when he stepped off the elevator. So that's what I did.

I quickly told him what I was hearing from the Mooch. And I shared my fears about Priebus and Spicer.

"Mr. President, they're going to do anything they can to dissuade you from hiring Scaramucci this morning," I said. "For what it's worth, I think anyone who is arguing against this and in favor of the status quo has their best interest—not yours—in mind."

The President flashed a wry smile. "They can argue all they want." He seemed very secure and confident about what he was doing.

With that, I knew it was a done deal, and we casually walked down the West Colonnade discussing O. J. Simpson, who had just been paroled after serving nine years for armed robbery. "The Juice is loose," I said as he turned left toward the Oval and I kept walking straight into the press office. I wish I could remember what the President said to that. He loved talking about celebrities, especially disgraced ones. What I didn't fully understand yet, though, was that the Mooch was about to be loose as well—in one of the weirdest weeks ever recorded in the history of the American presidency.

About an hour later, Scaramucci walked into the communications office flashing a toothy grin.

"It's a done deal," he said. "And Spicer is out—resigned in protest."

I was stunned. *Spicer quit? Wow.*

He shook my hand. Not satisfied with that, he then pulled me in for a big hug.

Ours was a unique White House, to say the least, with reality television stars and famous First Family members as senior staffers, billionaire industrial titans as Cabinet members, a multilingual supermodel for a First Lady, and a celebrity CEO as the President. The Mooch was an Ivy League–educated, former Goldman Sachs investment banker turned private financier who had amassed a nine-figure fortune. But, more than anything, he was perfect for Trump World because he was born to be in front of the camera—and there was no bigger stage than this White House.

This guy's going to fit right in.

The communications and press teams were quickly assembled in the Press Secretary's office. Spicer, Priebus, and Scaramucci stood shoulder to shoulder behind the large, crescent-shaped desk that has been the White House Press Secretary's workstation for decades, and about forty staffers crowded into the office. It was a tight fit. Most were totally unaware of what was taking place.

Spicer was gracious in announcing his departure. He thanked the team for their hard work and promised to help with the transition. He looked relieved. Though he loved being in the spotlight, the constant fight for survival must have been exhausting. Finally, his agony was over. He leaned comfortably against his standing workstation, his right leg casually crossed over his left. Priebus, on the other hand, was wound up so tight he looked like he might spontaneously combust. His position was now more precarious than ever. He raved about how close he and Scaramucci were—which seemed dubious—and how good a team they were going to make, which seemed preposterous. Junior aides—particularly former RNC staffers—looked down at their shoes, pondering what the sudden changes might mean for their own jobs.

The truth, of course, was that Reince was fuming. Not only had the Mooch made him look like more of a joke than ever, he had also persuaded the President to add a line into the press release announcing his appointment explicitly stating that he reported directly to the President. The media was feasting on the spectacle.

Hours later, the President saw me standing just outside the Oval and waved me in. Mike Pence was already inside.

"I heard you were the happiest son of a b—— in the entire building today!" Trump howled. The Vice President laughed along conspiratorially, though he was not exactly sure what Trump was talking about. "Mike, this is the happiest guy in Washington—I guarantee it."

"Yes, sir," I said sheepishly. "I think this is going to be a great thing for us all, especially you."

Three days later, on a Monday, Scaramucci came into the building to start his first day of work. He declared that his first order of business was to stop the leaking. This was his mandate from the President. His plan to accomplish this was simple: he was going to scare everyone to death. After an uneventful weekend, the combined press and communications teams packed into the Roosevelt Room with nervous anticipation for the Mooch's first full day at the helm.

As the group was waiting, Scaramucci and I stood in his new corner office. The floor-to-ceiling window made it one of the West Wing's most coveted spaces. My desk was about ten feet from his, where it had been since my disastrous first day with Spicer. Mooch was standing with his back to me, shifting his weight from one foot to another and shaking his arms like a baseball pitcher warming up. As he looked out at the North Lawn, the kinetic energy pulsing through his body was starting to make me nervous. I couldn't tell if it was semi-controlled anger, or just first-day jitters. But he was amped.

"They're going to remember this day for the rest of their lives," Scaramucci said, turning around to face me with a subtle head nod and a sly grin. "They've messed with this President for too long and I'm not going to stand for it anymore." *They* referred to his new staff. Some of them, most of them, all of them? It wasn't clear.

"What's your plan?" I asked, trying to sound more curious than concerned. I was both.

"Just watch, Cliffy," he said, moving toward the door. He marched through the upper press office and stopped in the hallway. He still didn't know his way around. "We in here?" he asked, pointing to the Roosevelt Room door just a few feet away.

"Yeah, everyone's in there waiting for you," I said.

Click. Whoosh.

He calmly walked through the room toward the head of the table. It felt like everyone—including the paintings on the wall—was tracking his every move with their eyes. He came to a stop just under Rough Rider Teddy Roosevelt on horseback. Present were the entire comms team and Kellyanne Conway, who wasn't actually in the communications division but floated in and out when she felt it was warranted. Mooch seemed to view Kellyanne, who disliked Reince, as an ally, albeit with some skepticism. But as far as I knew she hadn't weighed in heavily with the President for or against Mooch. She may have been conflicted between wanting to get rid of Reince and Sean, which she obviously did, but also wanting more control over White House comms herself. She was content to observe and see what happened. She was in for quite a show. We all were.

"There are some people in this room who are leakers," he began. "And guess what? I know who you are."

People glanced around uncomfortably.

"I've been watching you. I've been reading the stories that you put out there. I've been paying attention to which reporters write which stories. I've been keeping track of everything."

More awkward side glances.

"I know who you go to when it's a really important leak. I know who you go to when you want to attack your colleagues. I know who you go to when you want to attack the President. And I know who tells you to do it. I know it all—I know everything."

The room sat in stunned silence. Senior press aides sat at the long conference trying not to show their growing anxiety. Junior staffers stood around the walls looking down. No one dared even shift in their chair for fear that the sound of crinkling leather might attract Mooch's attention. Even Teddy Roosevelt looked taken aback.

"I'm going to fire every last one of you until the leaking stops," Scaramucci said. "I'm going to make it where you're left selling postcards out on Pennsylvania Avenue, and that's the closest you'll ever be to getting back inside the White House."

It was like an iconic scene from *The Office,* after Dwight Schrute takes over as manager of the paper company and threatens his friends and coworkers in a bizarre motivational exercise: "I love you guys, but don't cross me, but you're the best." Except Dwight's speech lasts about five minutes. The Mooch ranted, largely uninterrupted, for a solid hour.

He alternated between righteous indignation and fatherly disappointment as he berated his new staff, most of them strangers to him, for hurting the President, disrespecting the office of the presidency, and not being sufficiently patriotic.

At one point he seemed to reverse course. "I don't want to fire everybody," he declared, with seemingly sincere emotion. "But you guys are just not going to give me a choice, are you?

"I don't want to do it, guys. I don't—but I'm just going to have to.

"Or am I?"

Then came the dramatic finish. "I guess it's up to you."

Scaramucci finally walked out of the room, leaving the team shaken in his wake. I followed him back across the hall to his office and closed the door behind me.

Whoa. I had been the biggest booster of the Mooch in this entire building, as the President gleefully noted. *I owned this, for better or worse.* Most other staff had sat it out.

I didn't articulate any of these thoughts, of course. I smiled and encouraged the fire-breathing dragon that had just returned from laying waste to the unsuspecting peasants in the village. His was certainly an unorthodox approach, there was no doubt about that. But he was right about the leaks. I kept telling myself that.

"That was great, wasn't it?" he said with a wry grin, jumping right back in before I could answer. "They're scared to death! Did you see the looks on their faces?! No more leaks. I'm telling you, no more leaks."

If that were true, maybe it would be worth it.

The following morning the full staff meeting followed a similar trajectory. But this time Scaramucci declared that he was offering "amnesty" to the entire staff, allowing them to keep their jobs as long as they didn't leak anymore.

He motioned toward Deputy Press Secretary Lindsay Walters, a former RNC staffer who was very close to Spicer and Priebus. The day before, after his first staff meeting, he and Walters had engaged in an animated discussion, after which she had stormed out of the room red-faced.

Now he was focusing in on her again.

"Right, Lindsay?" he said, walking over behind her and gripping the back of her chair. "No one's getting fired, right, Lindsay?" She gave a subtle nod but looked like she might melt.

As Scaramucci's diatribe continued, his phone buzzed in his pocket and he finally pulled it out to see who kept calling.

"Give me a second," he said, smirking, then answered the phone.

"Mom, I'm trying to work here!" he told her, winking to the group. She must have jumped right into what she needed to tell him, because soon he was trying to cut her off.

"Mom, Mom, Mom, okay, Mom," he pleaded. She kept going. "Mom, give me a second, okay? Here, talk to Kellyanne."

Mooch handed the phone to an amused Kellyanne, who spoke politely with Mrs. Scaramucci, allowing Mooch to return to his speech. A couple of minutes later, Kellyanne handed the phone back to him, but he didn't let himself get sidetracked again for long.

"Love you, Mom, but I'm just in the middle of this thing, okay? Call you right after."

He finally hung up, flashed a big grin, declared Mrs. Scaramucci "the greatest," and for a few moments the entire room seemed to actually be entertained.

Then he jumped back in with a brand-new, horrifying motivational technique: role-playing.

He would pretend to be a senior White House staffer trying to convince someone on the comms team to leak something against one of their colleagues. Mooch was convinced this was how it often worked, so that senior aides could "keep their hands clean" by having subordinates "do their dirty work."

"Here's what I want you to say to anyone who tries to get you to do that," Mooch said, holding his hands out in front of him like he was trying to stop traffic. "'I cannot do that. I only report to Anthony Scaramucci and he reports directly to the President of the United States.' Okay, we got it?" He looked across a sea of bemused faces. "Let's give it a try."

Every single person in the room labored to avoid making eye contact with him. For one poor sap, the task proved fruitless.

"What's your name?" Mooch asked a young staffer on the regional media team.

"Tyler Ross," he replied. Tyler was a hardworking guy in his mid-twenties who tended to keep his head down and plug away. He was probably the last person in the room who would ever leak anything.

"Okay, Tyler. I'll be Reince Priebus and you be you."

Reince Priebus? I thought. *The White House Chief of Staff is going to be the villain in this exercise? By name? Amazing.*

"Tyler," he continued, "I need you to leak something for me."

There was a brief silence, as we all looked at poor Tyler. What in the heck was he supposed to do? Finally, Tyler did what we all would have done in his position.

"I cannot do that," he said. Like a conductor leading a promising violinist, Mooch twirled his finger in a circle, prompting Tyler to continue.

"I cannot do that," Tyler reiterated. "I report to Anthony Scaramucci and he reports directly to the President of the United States."

"Perfect," the Mooch replied, clapping his hands together. "See, this isn't so hard, folks. I'm your shield, okay? I'm taking all the arrows for you, okay? Don't worry about it."

But a lot of staffers were definitely worried about it. The Mooch was coming in too hot—way too hot. And the heat was overwhelming some of the staff.

As the meeting inched along, Jessica Ditto, a Deputy Communications Director and close Spicer ally, at one point broke down in tears. She tried to explain to Scaramucci that "there are some really good people" on the team that Scaramucci was misjudging.

The sudden flood of emotions seemed to take Mooch by surprise, so he softened his tone and shifted gears—again.

"Let me tell you all a story," he said.

Okay, at this point I have to admit I was interested to hear where this was going.

"You guys probably don't know this about me, but I used to own an ice cream shop," he said. I was certain absolutely no one in the room was aware of this.

"The ice cream was incredible—I'd go in there and order every flavor and you wouldn't even believe how good it was. But for some reason the place wasn't making any money. We were going broke. It didn't make any sense. Great ice cream, great location, but no money. How does that happen? Well, guess what? I know how that happens, I just had to prove it."

He smiled knowingly, a detective about to reveal how he cracked a tough case. Kellyanne sat listening to all this, just like everyone else. I don't recall her saying a word. What was there to say?

"So what I did was, I went in there and told the manager, 'Hey, go grab me something from the back.' And while he was gone, I'd stuff a hundred fifty dollars in the cash register. The next day I'd do it again and stuff sixty-five dollars in the cash register. The next day I'd do ninety dollars. I did it all week. And every day, at the end of the day, I'd say, 'How was your count?' And every day the manager would say, 'Oh, we were under by a dollar twenty-five, but I'll take that out of my pay,' or, 'We were over by three dollars because I think I forgot to give Mrs. So-and-so her change on that ten,' or whatever. It doesn't take a genius to understand that he was stealing from me, okay?"

His eyes narrowed. "And no one steals from the Mooch, okay?

"Now, you're probably sitting there asking yourself, 'Why's he telling me this?'

"That's a good question. The moral of this story is this: I always find out. I always, *always,* ALWAYS find out."

The room was so silent you could have heard an ant crawling on the carpet. Then someone broke the tension with the question on everyone's minds. "What happened to the guy who was stealing?"

"Oh, he's fine, don't worry about him," Scaramucci answered. "He was married to someone in my family, so I fired him but let him off the hook for being a thief. I even helped him get another job."

Then we finally came to the real lesson. The Mooch was a great guy. "You see, guys, I've got a big heart, just like our President. It's kind of like here, if you think about it. I may end up firing all of you, but I'll help you find the best job you've ever had somewhere else."

Scaramucci left the room again, triumphant. He really felt he had won over the crowd, had taught them a lesson, had made them feel loved, had felt love back in return. In some cases, he was actually right. Some staffers, particularly those from the campaign, were enjoying watching the Spicer allies— their longtime oppressors—squirm. But others were petrified.

Lower-level staff members started begging their superiors to let them stay out of the morning meetings. "If I'm not there, there's no way someone can think I'm a leaker," one staffer from the digital team reasoned. Others probably feared this guy might fire someone at random just to prove he could.

The paranoia reached its peak the Wednesday morning of Scaramucci's first—and ultimately only—full week on the job. The evening before, Scaramucci had called me into his office and declared, "I have to fire this kid Michael Short—how do I do it?"

The President, Scaramucci explained, had given him explicit orders to fire Short because Priebus had not done it when he'd ordered him to months before. I told Mooch that I assumed the process would involve Deputy Chief of Staff for Operations Joe Hagin and the White House Counsel's Office, and he dispatched me to find out what had to be done.

I walked through the Roosevelt Room and into the back hallway where Hagin's office was. I wasn't particularly thrilled about being anybody's executioner, but it was too late now. The die was cast. I had mounted the dragon and there was no jumping off.

Hagin, a longtime senior aide to President George W. Bush, had been brought into the Trump White House because of his vast institutional knowledge. He was soft-spoken and had a reputation for doing things by the book. So when I walked into his office explaining the Michael Short saga, he was confused, to say the least. We walked together back to Scaramucci's office, and Mooch launched into a lengthy explanation of what he was needing to do, and why.

Picking up a piece of paper and a black Sharpie marker, Scaramucci began drawing a diagram.

At the top of the paper he wrote "POTUS," and drew a circle around it. In the middle of the paper on the left side, he wrote "REINCE." On the bottom of the paper he wrote "SHORT," and drew a circle around it. Holding the paper in front of him, he turned back to Hagin.

"This guy told this guy to fire this guy," he said, pointing in order from "POTUS" to "REINCE" to "SHORT."

"He didn't do it, Joe. I'm just telling you, he didn't do it, okay?"

He returned to the diagram, wrote "MOOCH" in the middle of the page across from "REINCE," and drew one final circle around it.

"Now," he continued, repeating the process, but this time pointing to his name instead of Reince's. "When this guy tells this guy to fire this guy, you better believe it's going to happen." He drew an "X" through Short's name over and over.

"Here's something you need to understand about me, Joe," Scaramucci said. "When the President tells me to do something, I'm just going to do it and that's all there is to it."

Hagin, who was sitting on the arm of Mooch's couch with a bemused look on his face, laughed. At least he didn't have to participate in a role-playing exercise. Hagin said he understood, but that it was the White House Counsel who was going to need to initiate the process.

Scaramucci again dispatched me, this time to the Counsel's office. But it was late in the day, and they asked if the dismissal process could start the following morning. I reported back to Scaramucci, who relented, but was insistent that it had to happen first thing. "I want to show the President that when he makes a call, I execute immediately," he told me.

The following morning I began the day in the Counsel's office, even though I was growing increasingly uncomfortable. They started the process of putting together the paperwork, but as I waited in their lobby on the top floor of the West Wing, a frantic Scaramucci called my cell phone.

"Have you read *Politico* this morning?" he exclaimed.

I hadn't.

"Go pull it up right now."

Putting Mooch on hold, I pulled up *Politico* on my phone's browser, and saw the headline: SCARAMUCCI THREATENS "TO FIRE EVERYBODY" TO STOP WHITE HOUSE LEAKS.

"Headline sounds accurate," I laughed as I clicked on the article. But the first few sentences revealed a problem. The story's lead was all about the firing of Michael Short, which obviously had not yet happened.

"I don't know why they're reporting this!" Scaramucci snapped. I wasn't sure if he was blaming me for the leak. As I read down through the story, however, it was Scaramucci himself who had confirmed to the reporter, Tara Palmeri, that Short had been fired.

"I don't know why she would do this," he complained. "I told her not to post it until nine A.M.!"

I glanced at my watch.

"Mooch, it's nine-fifteen."

I walked back downstairs to find Michael Short sitting beside my desk.

"Did you do this?" he asked me, angrily. "Because everyone thinks you did this, and I think so, too."

"I didn't have anything to do with this story," I replied. "And you got yourself into this mess."

Short and I weren't friends—far from it. But I also thought he was a talented operative, and no matter what, no one deserved the public humiliation he was starting to experience.

As press inquiries came streaming in, Short said on the record, "No one has told me anything and the entire premise is false." Several hours of confusion went by, with Scaramucci nowhere to be found. Around 12:45 P.M., Short began calling reporters to tell them that he had resigned. Shortly thereafter, Mooch went on another tirade, vowing to rid the White House of leakers.

"This is actually a terrible thing. Let's say I'm firing Michael Short today. The fact that you guys know about it before he does really upsets me as a human being and as a Roman Catholic," he told reporters. "I should have the opportunity if I have to let somebody go to let the person go in a very humane, dignified way, and then the next thing . . . is help the person get a job somewhere, okay, because he probably has a family, right? So now you guys are talking about it, it's not fair. . . . Here's the problem with the leaking, why I have to figure out a way to get the leaking to stop, because it hurts people." Asked again how he was going to get rid of the leakers, Scaramucci had a simple answer: "I'm going to fire everybody, that's how I'm going to do it."

During an interview on CNN's morning show *New Day,* with Chris Cuomo, Mooch explained that he had "interviewed most of the people on the communications team in the White House, and what the President and I would like to tell everybody, we have a very, very good idea of who the leakers are, who the senior leakers are in the White House. . . . As the President would say in his own words, the White House leakers are small potatoes. I'll talk to you about a few leaks that happened last night that I find reprehensible. But the White House leaks are small potatoes, relative to things that are going on, with leaking things about Syria, North Korea, or leaking things about Iraq. Those are the types of leaks that are so treasonous that a hundred fifty years ago people would have actually been hung for those types of leaks."

In interview after interview, Scaramucci lambasted the leakers and vowed to expel them all from the White House—and generally had a grand ol' time in the process.

Similar to other senior White House aides, Scaramucci would frequently record television interviews at "Pebble Beach," the area on the North Lawn of the White House—which acquired its name because it was at one time covered by gravel—where news organizations set up their cameras for 24/7 coverage. But unlike with most other interviewees, who record their interviews and walk back into the West Wing without much fanfare, a crowd of reporters would assemble on the driveway and wait for Mooch, knowing that he would be more than willing to deliver a viral sound bite.

One morning, the White House regional media team organized a "radio row" in front of the West Wing, inviting various local and regional broadcasters to interview top administration officials. In a lineup of Cabinet officials and household names, Scaramucci was the biggest attraction. As he moved from tent to tent, a cloud of reporters, producers, and photographers tracked his every movement.

Secretary of the Treasury Steven Mnuchin was taken aback. Mnuchin was no stranger to red carpets, having produced Hollywood blockbusters including *American Sniper, Mad Max: Fury Road, Batman v Superman, Suicide Squad, Wonder Woman,* and *The Lego Movie.* But even he had never experienced anything quite like The Mooch Show.

"That's what a star looks like," he said as Mooch—in his patented shades—moved with the press in tow, the way the sun effortlessly holds the planets in its orbit.

On another occasion, Scaramucci finished up an interview at Pebble Beach and, as he walked back down the West Wing driveway, was approached by several cameramen from one of the networks, each of whom wanted to take a photo with him. This was not normal—rarely do cable network staffers ask for pictures with political aides. But Mooch was becoming a rock star—the subject of fascination, consternation, and conversation at dinner tables around the country—so even seasoned staffers turned into tourists when he came around.

"Guys, gather around, we've got to get a picture," he said to the four cameramen. "I hear you're the best in the business, so you're going to be my guys. We're going to have a blast."

I snapped the photo on one of the cameramen's phone and handed it back to him as Mooch shook their hands, hugged several of them, and predicted great times to come.

Then he put both hands on his belt buckle, leaned in close to the cameramen—each of whom happened to be African American—and said, "Can I tell you guys something? We've already hit it off, and I think I know one of the reasons why."

Mooch paused for a few moments to build the anticipation.

"It's 'cause I'm black from the waist down."

The cameramen fell over laughing hysterically.

"He's crazy!" one of them howled as Mooch swaggered down the driveway and back into the West Wing.

"This is fun, right?" he asked as we walked back into the West Wing, not hesitating for an answer before moving on to greet the receptionist, Secret Service officer, and various guests waiting in the lobby. It was Mooch's world, and all of us were living in it.

His media appearances were becoming must-watch television and, his initial management style aside, in most cases they were also incredibly effective. This stood in stark contrast to Spicer's work, which had been must-watch for much different reasons.

Mooch's first—and ultimately only—press conference behind the podium in the Press Briefing Room was a master class in how to give and take with a hostile press corps. And similar to the President, he possessed an inherent likability that left people smiling, even when they disagreed with his points. Perhaps most important, he displayed an intense loyalty to the President and his agenda. Prior to joining the Trump campaign he had been a vocal critic, and after leaving the White House it was clear that he did not agree with many of the President's policies. But during his tenure in the West Wing, he understood something that many others never did: when you work for the President, you subordinate your views to his. That does not mean you shy away from making your case behind closed doors, but once he makes a decision, it is your job to execute it with the same vigor you would if it had been your idea all along. Scaramucci understood this, and he also realized that some other senior aides did not.

"There are people inside the administration that think it is their job to save America from this president," he said, with great insight, on CNN. "Okay, that is not their job. Their job is to inject this President into America so that he can explain his views properly and his policies so that we can transform America and drain the swamp and make this system fairer for the middle- and lower-income people."

But in spite of his virtuoso early performances, it soon became apparent that Mooch was drunk on the attention and adulation. Most normal human beings would be, but he was guzzling it in a way that I had never seen before.

"I'm going to lower my profile a little bit," he told me in his office after one tough interview that had not gone quite as well as he had hoped.

"That's probably not a bad idea," I replied. "Let's let it calm down some, get the palace intrigue stuff off of the front page, then roll you back out once you're settled in and can sell the President's agenda."

"Exactly," he said. "That's what we're going to do."

A half hour later I looked out of our West Wing office window and he was holding a gaggle with two dozen reporters. He was about to crash, and there was nothing anyone could do to stop it.

Media attention in Trump World is a double-edged sword. There is nothing the President values more than a loyal, effective surrogate who will go toe to toe with an aggressive interviewer and not give an inch. During an appearance on *Face the Nation,* Senior Policy Advisor Stephen Miller was pressed by host John Dickerson to defend the President's executive order banning individuals from certain countries from entering the United States. Miller had been largely responsible for the order's drafting and rollout, which had resulted in widespread protests and confusion.

"Our opponents, the media, and the whole world will soon see as we begin to take further actions that the powers of the President to protect our country are very substantial and will not be questioned," Miller responded.

The Washington Post called it an "authoritarian declaration."

Later that morning he went on ABC's *This Week* and defended the President's claim that millions of people had likely voted illegally in the 2016 election.

"I'm prepared to go on any show, anywhere, any time . . . and say the President of the United States is correct, one hundred percent," Miller said without blinking an eye. *The Huffington Post* proclaimed the appearances "a disaster," but the President loved every second of it.

"Congratulations Stephen Miller—on representing me this morning on the various Sunday morning shows," Trump tweeted. "Great job!"

However, when a staffer's media coverage detracted from the Boss, it could prove disastrous.

In author Robert Greene's modern take on Machiavellianism, *The 48 Laws of Power,* the number-one law is to "never outshine the master":

Everyone has insecurities. When you show yourself in the world and display your talents, you naturally stir up all kinds of resentment, envy, and other manifestations of insecurity. This is to be expected. You cannot spend your life worrying about the petty feelings of others. With those above you, however, you must take a different approach: when it comes to power, outshining the master is perhaps the worst mistake of all.

Steve Bannon learned this "law" the hard way. Just three months after the President's inauguration, *Time* magazine made Bannon its cover story, dubbing him "The Great Manipulator" and adding the tagline, "How Steve Bannon became the second most powerful man in the world." I had been told that *Time* originally planned to declare him "the most powerful man in the world," but realizing how the President would react, Bannon and his allies pressed them to change the line. *Time* acquiesced, but the damage was done. *Saturday Night Live* had already begun portraying Bannon as the Grim Reaper, bending the President to his will, and the President's patience was growing thin.

"I like Steve, but you have to remember he was not involved in my campaign until very late," Trump told his favorite hometown paper, the *New York Post,* the same week Bannon's *Time* cover debuted. "I'm my own strategist and it wasn't like I was going to change strategies because I was facing Crooked Hillary."

In October 2017, Press Secretary Sarah Sanders walked into the Roosevelt Room, where the President was hosting prominent business leaders to discuss tax reform. As she quietly walked across the room, the President said, "There's my Sarah—my star." After the meeting we walked back to Sarah's office as she joked that, after seeing the rise and fall of others in the President's orbit, she figured his remark signaled the beginning of the end for her. "When he says you're his big star, you know your time is almost up." She laughed.

But for Scaramucci, the rise and fall that took some other high-profile aides months or even years to experience took place in a matter of days.

On Wednesday, July 26, five days after Scaramucci accepted the job as White House Communications Director, Mooch and I finished off the workday by walking over to the White House residence. He was excited because he had organized a dinner for the President that evening with Fox News personality Sean Hannity, a Trump favorite, and former Fox executive Bill Shine. Scaramucci's master plan included bringing Shine onto the staff to build out a revolutionary broadcast component to the White House communications operation.

"A-level talent attracts A-level talent," Scaramucci said as we walked down the West Colonnade connecting the West Wing to the residence. "They're going to be shocked when they realize the people we're going to be bringing in to replace Spicer's hacks."

As we walked into the Palm Room on the bottom floor, we ran into Reince Priebus, who was walking toward us.

"Can I talk to you a minute?" Priebus asked Scaramucci.

"Go ahead upstairs, Cliffy," Mooch said. "I'll be up in a minute."

As much as I wanted to hear what those two could possibly have to discuss, I went ahead and walked up the stairs to the State Floor. I turned the corner just as the President stepped off the private elevator.

Trump saw me and nodded. "How're we doing?" he asked. Usually when he asked this, which was often, he was referring to the day's media coverage, which was usually terrible. We quickly went over a couple of stories that were dominating the media coverage, which naturally brought us to the topic of Scaramucci.

"Is it going how we hoped it would?" he inquired.

I didn't have any time to reflect on that question. I mean, where to even begin? So I stuck to the basics.

"We've got a lot of work to do to professionalize the operation, but we're headed in a better direction," I replied (and hoped). "And at least you know the comms team is going to have your back now." That, for sure, was true. The Mooch was a lot of things, but disloyal to the President was not one of them.

"It's about time," the President said as Scaramucci topped the stairs and joined the conversation.

"There he is," Trump said, smiling. "Let's go have dinner."

I wasn't at the dinner, and I don't know what was on the menu. But what happened afterward was something everyone in Washington, D.C., would feast on. It was precipitated, as so many things in the Trump White House were, by a tweet. At some point that evening, Ryan Lizza, a writer for *The New Yorker,* tweeted that a senior White House official had informed him that the First Lady, Hannity, and Shine were at dinner with the President.

The Mooch was enraged by this. *Another leak!*

After having just run into Priebus on the way over to the dinner, Scaramucci was convinced this "senior White House official" was Reince. He had no proof of this, but he was probably right. I could not quite understand why it was such a big deal. Nobody would really be surprised that the President was meeting with either of these guys. Maybe I was too conditioned to everything leaking.

Backstage right after what *USA Today* called "the nastiest debate ever." Steve Bannon had invited several of Bill Clinton's accusers to the event. Trump thought it was a home run. "I'm not even going to watch this," he said of the post-debate coverage. "They're awful. And really, what do they know anyway, right?" (*Photo courtesy of Cliff Sims*)

Our Trump Tower war room team the day before the election. (*Photo courtesy of Cliff Sims*)

The President looks at me as he talks on the phone with Rupert Murdoch on Election Night. "Not yet, Rupy," he said. "We have a three-stroke lead with one hole left. We can't celebrate until we're in the clubhouse." (*Photo courtesy of Cliff Sims*)

Because we had eight TVs hanging on the wall, Trump decided to watch election returns in the war room. So I planted myself beside him all night. (*Photo courtesy of Cliff Sims*)

Prepping the President for an interview on his tax reform plan, which the brander-in-chief wanted to name "The Cut Cut Cut Act," to the great frustration of Congress. (*Official White House Photo by Shealah Craighead*)

Ever the producer, the President was meticulous about what he wanted in our recording sessions. And I always kept a can of his TRESemmé hairspray in my pocket, just in case. (*Official White House Photo by Shealah Craighead*)

Who's up and who's down? Here the President pulled me aside to ask about how Reince Priebus and Anthony Scaramucci were getting along, with both of them standing five feet away. (*Official White House Photo by Shealah Craighead*)

The Mooch, the myth, the legend. We were all smiles for a few crazy days. But the "Reince-seeking missile," as Jared called him, ultimately hit his target, only to blow himself up in the process. (*Official White House Photo by Shealah Craighead*)

Briefing the President for his call with astronauts aboard the International Space Station. He quickly got sidetracked by the possibility of sending an American to Mars by the end of his term. (*Official White House Photo by Shealah Craighead*)

Briefing the President before an event almost exactly one year into his term in office. He was riding high after the passage of tax reform and starting to feel more comfortable in the job. (*Official White House Photo by Shealah Craighead*)

Left: My wife, Megan, and me as French President Emmanuel Macron arrived at the White House for his State Visit. (*Photo courtesy of Cliff Sims*)

Below: One of the Syrian refugee families Megan and I met in northern Jordan. My experience in the Middle East sometimes left me personally at odds with the White House's posture toward refugees. (*Photo courtesy of Cliff Sims*)

My granddaddy James Breland after a tour of the West Wing. Once I figured out how to use the phones on Air Force One, he was the first person I called. (*Photo courtesy of Cliff Sims*)

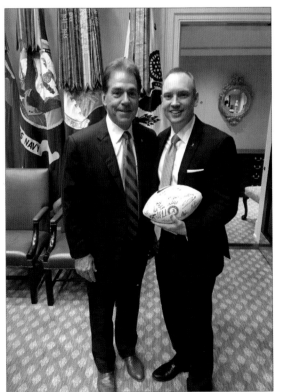

With the greatest coach in college football history, Nick Saban, and the infamous football that set in motion a bizarre series of events that ended up in a *Politico* hit piece on me. (*Photo courtesy of Cliff Sims*)

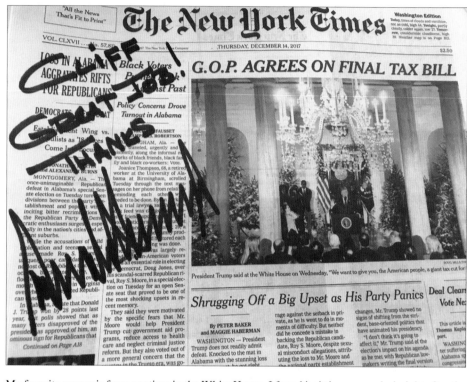

My favorite souvenir from my time in the White House. I found it sitting on my desk right after the President signed the largest tax cut in recent history. (*Photo courtesy of Cliff Sims*)

"He's always going to try to ruin anything I try to do here," he growled about Priebus. "That's okay, watch what I do. I'm going to take care of this." What happened next became so infamous that it survived as a topic of conversation for months, even in the Trump White House, where story lines changed by the hour.

Here's how it was told by Ryan Lizza in *The New Yorker.*

> *On Wednesday night, I received a phone call from Anthony Scaramucci. . . . He wasn't happy. . . .*
>
> *In Scaramucci's view, the fact that word of the dinner had reached a reporter was evidence that his rivals in the West Wing, particularly Reince Priebus, the White House Chief of Staff, were plotting against him. . . .*
>
> *"They'll all be fired by me," he said. "I fired one guy the other day. I have three to four people I'll fire tomorrow. I'll get to the person who leaked that to you. Reince Priebus—if you want to leak something—he'll be asked to resign very shortly. . . .*
>
> *"The swamp will not defeat him," he said, breaking into the third person. "They're trying to resist me, but it's not going to work. . . ."*
>
> *Scaramucci also told me that, unlike other senior officials, he had no interest in media attention. "I'm not Steve Bannon, I'm not trying to suck my own c—," he said, speaking of Trump's chief strategist. "I'm not trying to build my own brand off the f—ing strength of the President. I'm here to serve the country."*

The story went live just before 2 P.M. on Thursday, July 27, the day after the dinner. It melted the internet, then completely took over cable television. Scaramucci, who had returned to New York, called me, defiant.

"Don't sweat it," he said dismissively. "I talked to the President. He thinks it's hilarious. But can you believe this guy Lizza? I've known his family for years and he still set me up. There's no loyalty. That's changing, though, starting with the White House. Reince is going to be gone soon. They're going to try to use this against me, but it's going to backfire because the President is behind me 100 percent."

I caught the President before he went up to the residence that evening. He was less dismissive of the media coverage than Scaramucci had let on. But he seemed less angry than he was befuddled.

"Can you believe this guy? I've never seen anything like it." Said the guy who hosted a reality show with Dennis Rodman, Omarosa, and Gary Busey.

I still believed the Mooch could be a great asset to the President—if he could survive the initial craziness and bring himself under control. Trump didn't seem so sure anymore.

"He's completely out of his mind—like, on drugs or something—totally out of his mind," the President continued. "We'll figure it out, but the guy is crazy." I didn't think Mooch was on drugs, and I don't think Trump really meant that, either. He was just trying to say that there had to be *some* explanation for this guy, who seemed totally competent and in control in one moment, only to run completely off the rails the next. Regardless, on a rainy Friday evening, the President began "figuring it out."

I have no idea how Reince Priebus reacted to Mooch's tirade with Ryan Lizza. He couldn't possibly have been happy about it. But in a flash, that—or anything else at the White House—was no longer his concern.

"I am pleased to inform you," Trump tweeted not twenty-four hours after the story hit, "that I have just named General/Secretary John F Kelly as White House Chief of Staff. He is a Great American and a Great Leader. John has also done a spectacular job at Homeland Security. He has been a true star of my Administration.

"I would like to thank Reince Priebus for his service and dedication to his country," he added. "We accomplished a lot together and I am proud of him!" Reince effectively lasted a week longer than his closest ally in the White House, Sean Spicer, although Sean stuck around "on the payroll" for a while, but was no longer involved in the day-to-day operations. It was a devastating blow to the RNC faction of the Trump White House.

The following morning, I poked my head into Jared Kushner's office— along with me, he had been another Scaramucci booster and Priebus nemesis. I silently raised my eyebrows.

"Mooch was like a Reince-seeking missile," Jared said with a laugh. "We'll see if he blew himself up in the process." Looking back, I wondered. Was this Jared's plan all along? He was as smooth as they came—sharp, low-key, always dressed immaculately in well-tailored attire. But maybe what the

President liked most about his son-in-law was that he was a "killer," too. Silent, but deadly. Did he see this all coming? Did he know what was going to come next?

Scaramucci was elated that he had finally taken out his longtime nemesis, but General Kelly's no-nonsense reputation immediately concerned him. Understandably so. Kelly had been a four-star Marine general, and in the few times I'd seen him in the West Wing, he didn't seem like the most pleasant guy to be around. But I was also optimistic that his approach might be able to unite a fractious West Wing that couldn't seem to get its act together.

"What do you think this means?" Scaramucci asked me on the phone. "Have you talked to the President about me or heard anything?"

I had not spoken to the President since that announcement and did not share with the Mooch what Trump had said the night before. But the fact that Scaramucci had gone from dismissive about his prospects to worried was a telling sign.

In reality, the backlash over Mooch's meltdown was still the main story on the news. The President had watched this with growing irritation.

The following Monday morning, Scaramucci came into the West Wing ready to get back to work. He seemed like he had finally committed himself to keeping his head down and trying to stay out of the news. Maybe, just maybe, I hoped, he could survive this and focus on his duties. Then he gave me another reason to keep having his back.

"First things first," he said. "You're officially getting named my number two—Deputy Communications Director and Chief of Staff for the Communications Department. We'll announce it in the team meeting this morning. Second, I've got the first draft of a plan that is going to be our starting point for restructuring everything. Let's start going over this, and after General Kelly is sworn in this morning, we'll get his buy-in and start getting it done."

With Priebus and Spicer both out, he wanted to enter a new phase. "We tore it down," he quipped. "Now we've got to build it back up." These were comforting words. I only hoped he meant them.

A few minutes later, Madeleine Westerhout, the President's executive assistant, knocked on the door and told Scaramucci that the newly sworn-in Chief of Staff wanted to see him. He hopped up, gave me a hopeful smile, and followed her to his office. I stayed behind and began glancing over the ideas he had sketched out.

Wow, this is actually really good.

He was planning for a slimmed-down operation with everyone having clearly defined responsibilities, lines of communication, and accountability. At this moment I was reminded that Mooch, prior to becoming an unlikely media star, had been a wildly successful CEO. I hadn't even gotten through the first couples of pages, however, when Mooch walked back in, sat down, and leaned back in his chair.

"How'd it go?" I asked.

He sat completely still, looking at a blank space on the wall.

"I got fired," he said calmly.

"Shut up," I said with a chuckle.

He turned and looked straight into my eyes. "No, I'm serious. He fired me. The Lizza piece did me in. They killed me. It's over." He had just entered his eleventh day on the job—and it came to the most humiliating, if self-inflicted, end. I couldn't help but feel bad for him.

He returned to staring blankly at the wall for a few moments, then looked back at me. "I'm sorry I let you down," he said, reaching out to shake my hand. "You stuck your neck out for me and I'll never forget it."

I didn't know what to say. I tucked the plans back inside a purple folder and set it on the floor beside me.

"Dude, don't worry about me," I said. "I'll be fine. But what're you going to do now?"

I watched him for a moment sink deeper into despair, and then just as quickly, saw a new spark slowly taking flame in his eyes. This was not going to destroy him. He was going to get back up again.

"I've been up and I've been down." He shrugged, slumping down in his chair. "This is the White House, man. This is the top of the mountain. I made it. But I've been low, too. I know what that's like, but I always come back. Always." The transformation took place in milliseconds.

He wasn't quite done yet. He hatched a plan to try to get Kushner to make an end run around the new Chief of Staff and make an appeal directly to the President to save his job. Jared might have had the power to pull this off, if he really wanted to. But why? The Mooch had done his task—he blew up Reince. If he had to blow up himself in the process—hey, this is the big leagues, baby.

Still, for the next several hours, Mooch gave it a try. But the decision had been made, and General Kelly had been given the authority that Priebus never earned. Still, it's hard to imagine Kelly would have done this, on his first day, without at least Trump's tacit approval. Tellingly, the firing did not leak and only made its way to the press hours later, after Mooch had quietly left the White House of his own volition.

In a matter of eleven days, Scaramucci had gone from being little known outside the rarefied society of Wall Street tycoons to being a household name in Middle America. A pollster friend told me that his name recognition had gone from basically zero to over 50 percent nationally in the span of a week. "I've never seen anything like it," he said with genuine amazement.

Walking home from the White House the night that Mooch was fired, I passed by two homeless gentlemen. One was leaned over, resting his arms on the handle of his shopping cart. The other was seated on the ground, looking up at his friend, pounding his fist into his other hand and speaking passionately. As I got closer, the topic of discussion quickly became clear.

"Mooch is my dude!" the man on the ground proclaimed. The two men didn't own TVs, but they not only knew who Mooch was, they had fully formed opinions about him. And amid this reality was the key to Mooch's future. Trump had made him a star.

The Mooch affair demonstrated many of the flaws—serious flaws—in the Trump White House operation. There were too many factions, too many people interested in hurting others rather than carrying out their duties, and a lack of leadership in making sure this was all managed. But I also saw in retrospect the flaws in myself. The Scaramucci affair encapsulated every human flaw that I embodied during my time in the White House.

I was selfish. I viciously criticized Priebus, Bannon, and Spicer—all of whom outranked me—for their self-serving desire to keep Mooch out. But I let myself off the hook for my self-serving desire to have him come in. I was nakedly ambitious. I clawed, schemed, and maneuvered to secure a better position for myself, and saw Mooch as the ideal vehicle to help make that happen. I was ruthless. Spicer had a lovely family—a beautiful wife and precious children—whom I had met. I had even taken a family photo of them together in the Press Secretary's office. But they never crossed my mind when I was laboring to push Sean out. I was a coward. I wasn't as aggressive as I should have been in pushing back on Mooch's early tactics, mainly because that could have hurt me (selfish once again). I lacked compassion. I relished the horror of former RNC aides who were suddenly terrified for their livelihoods and careers. Most of all, I saw how the White House, the need to stay in and cling to your access, can become more important than the values that you brought with you. This was a fate that would befall other good people I knew there.

Eight months after Scaramucci's unceremonious departure from the West Wing, he came back to D.C. for the annual White House Correspondents' Association Dinner. Prior to the event, we met for lunch at the Four Seasons Hotel in Georgetown. Dressed in tan cargo pants and a black, long-sleeve pullover, he appeared to be in high spirits.

"I kiss the ground every single morning I wake up," he said, smiling. Over a massive plate of shrimp cocktail and crab cakes, Scaramucci explained that his White House experience—as short as it was—had been transformative.

Since early in the administration, when Scaramucci and Priebus first locked horns over Mooch's potential White House job, Scaramucci had been in the process of selling his company, SkyBridge Capital, to a Chinese conglomerate for $180 million. The move required a lengthy review and regulatory approval that was not certain to come. Additionally, while his business was in limbo, Scaramucci's relationship with his pregnant wife was deteriorating. In fact, she would later reveal that Mooch took the White House job without even discussing it with her.

"We actually never really talked about it," she said in a televised interview. "So, obviously, he was campaigning with him. And then one thing led to another [and] kind of like spiraled out of control."

She eventually filed for divorce, but after he left the White House they reconciled before their separation was finalized.

Sitting in the dining room of the Four Seasons, Mooch explained that his desire for revenge against Priebus, combined with his ambition to work in the White House, was so strong that it caused him to lose sight of what was truly important in his life, namely his family and the company he had spent over a decade of his life building.

"I got my priorities out of order," he said, biting into a shrimp before wiping his mouth with a cloth napkin. "And I want you to never forget what I'm telling you right now, because you need to learn from me instead of having to learn it for yourself. I got sucked into this political stuff. The President wanted me to run OPL but Reince stopped it. I got angry. I let my pride get in the way. So when people came along and wanted to use me to take him out, I did it. I got him back and I made it into the White House. But you know what? It wasn't worth it, and I almost lost everything in the process.

"But now I'm like Ebenezer Scrooge on Christmas morning. I woke up. I realized that I'd almost lost my wife, I'd almost lost my family, and I'd almost lost my business, and the good Lord gave me a second chance. I got visited by the three ghosts and I'll never be the same."

Mooch walked me to the lobby of the Four Seasons and finished up by giving me one last word of wisdom: "None of this matters if it costs you what *really* matters."

This was the best advice I received from anyone during my entire time in the Trump White House. I wish I'd taken it more often.

10

BETTER ANGELS

On March 22, 2017, the leaders of the Congressional Black Caucus (CBC) came to the White House to meet with the President for the first time since he'd taken office. There were seven members of Congress present, all of them Democrats, none of them Trump supporters, including CBC Chairman Cedric Richmond of Louisiana, Gwen Moore of Wisconsin, Karen Bass of California, and André Carson, a former law enforcement officer from Indiana and the second Muslim elected to Congress.

The weather outside was beautiful, and I had lingered by the Rose Garden a little longer than usual on my way into work that morning. Waiting in the Cabinet Room for the meeting to begin, I took my usual position behind the President's chair to his left.

At some point, I said hello to one of my friends at the White House, who made sure she was in the middle of this action.

No matter what else she had going on, you could be sure of one thing: if there was any meeting, event, or policy specifically relating to the African American community, Omarosa would make sure she was right in the middle of it. She prided herself on being the President's only African American senior adviser. That was her calling card, her legitimacy in the White House.

Omarosa was wearing a deep blue dress with black accents.

"Nice dress, O," I said with a smile.

"Trump doesn't like frumpy, honey," she said, smiling as she gave me a hug. A thin silver necklace with a tiny cross dangled around her neck. Affixed to her dress, just below her right shoulder, was a white Secret Service "hard pin." Such pins were designed to help agents quickly identify staff who could enter the President's protective bubble while traveling outside of the White House. They also became something of a status symbol in the West Wing. If you were "hard-pinned," as I was, too, that typically meant you were someone who had direct access to the Boss.

Dan Scavino, the White House Social Media Director and one of Trump's longest serving aides, sat down to my right. "What's up, brother?" he whispered. "It's quiet in here."

Dan was right; it was very quiet. There was a nervous tension in the air. On the other side of the room, the seven CBC members were speaking to one another in hushed tones, and the handful of Trump aides weren't talking at all. We were all a little nervous and a little uncomfortable. A meeting between the CBC and a Republican president is probably never without its tensions. But in this case, some of Trump's comments on the campaign trail—some clumsy, some hostile, and some insensitive—bore a lot of the blame for the atmosphere.

In the summer of 2016, Trump had traveled to Michigan for a campaign stop in Dimondale, just outside of Lansing. Speaking directly to black voters, Trump unloaded on what he described as the failed policies of Democratic politicians. "You're living in poverty, your schools are no good, you have no jobs, fifty-eight percent of your youth [are] unemployed." And then he delivered the line that became most associated with his pitch to African Americans: "What the hell do you have to lose?" Democrats were incensed by the suggestion that they didn't care about African American voters, a core constituency. "This is so ignorant it's staggering," Hillary Clinton tweeted.

The CBC didn't forget those comments, even seven months later. When the members showed up at the White House, they were carrying thick binders prominently titled "We Have a Lot to Lose." The stage seemed to be set for a contentious meeting.

The President was running about ten minutes behind schedule, per the usual, but when he arrived he seemed to be in a good mood. Trump prided himself on his ability to charm visitors, any visitors. And in some ways, he had an advantage with the CBC. Almost certainly its leaders expected him to be hostile, ignorant, even stupid. That was, after all, how he was often portrayed in various media reports.

"Hello, everybody," he said as he breezed into the room, along with Vice President Pence, whose Zen-like expression of total support for what Trump was saying was once again affixed to his face.

"Good afternoon, Mr. President," replied CBC Chairman Cedric Richmond. Richmond was a four-term Congressman from Louisiana's Second Congressional District. A New Orleans native, in addition to being a seasoned legislator, he was a former college baseball player and a polished communicator.

As the President sat down, the rest of the group followed his lead. Joyce Meyer, a top legislative affairs aide, and Ja'Ron Smith, who led urban affairs and revitalization policy for the White House, sat to his left. The Vice President and Deputy Chief of Staff Rick Dearborn sat to Trump's right, and in between Pence and Dearborn sat Omarosa.

With everyone now seated, Congressman Richmond presented the President with the CBC's "130-page policy document" meant to educate him and his administration "on the difficult history of black people in this country, the history of the CBC, and solutions to advance black families in the twenty-first century." The President accepted it and promised his staff would dig through it. The group discussed ways to bring down the costs of prescription drugs. They chatted about the importance of historically black colleges and universities. They expressed mutual support for rebuilding the country's crumbling infrastructure and revitalizing urban communities.

Trump was Trump. He was open and direct, and rambled in a way that made it clear he had no filter between the thoughts in his head and the words coming out of his mouth. I can't imagine that the CBC members had ever experienced an encounter with any head of government remotely close to this. They may have found it strange, but I'd also guess it was refreshing. Before long they came to the same realization I had seen so many others come to before: it's dang near impossible to spend one-on-one time with Donald Trump and not end up liking him.

In about twenty minutes, the atmosphere had completely shifted from anxious to relaxed. They talked, shared ideas, and laughed together.

At one point in the meeting, Congressman Richmond said something to the President directly that appeared totally sincere.

"Mr. President," he began slowly, "I believe you have the ability to be one of the best presidents this nation has ever had."

That's the kind of thing Trump always liked to hear, even if the source was a surprise.

"I mean that," Richmond continued. "I don't always agree with the things you say. In fact, sometimes I think you say things that you don't even realize are offensive. But I also think there's something special about you. And I want to work with you to make your presidency a success."

It was the kind of earnestness that is rarely heard across party lines in Washington, D.C. I had no idea if he meant that, or if he said something like that to every president. But he looked like he meant it. Trump certainly thought so.

"I'd love that, Cedric," the President said as he stood up, extended his arm across the table, and shook Richmond's hand. Trump had a triumphant look—he'd talked again and again about how he wanted to meet with the CBC and now it looked like it was paying off. He believed he shared policy views with African Americans, if only they'd give him a chance. Of course, he hadn't made it easy for them. These were, after all, some of the Democrats he'd slammed on the campaign trail for taking black votes for granted while not helping to improve their lives.

As the meeting broke up, a CBC staffer told me they wanted to hold a press gaggle outside the West Wing to discuss what happened in the meeting. This was a routine request, one we'd allowed for other groups, and we agreed to help facilitate it. As a White House press aide alerted the media and gathered them outside, I continued to chat with the CBC members and their staff in the West Wing lobby. Everyone was in good spirits, and they seemed hopeful that this was the beginning of a positive working relationship with the President and his staff. After all, there were a number of issues on which the CBC and Trump could find agreement—repairing roads and bridges among them. If the members would just say that—that this was a good start— that would be a huge win for the Trump White House. That would go a long way to repairing some of the damage Trump's rhetoric had done over the past year. I, for one, was pleasantly surprised by how it all seemed to be coming together.

One of the young White House press aides poked her head in and told me the press was ready for them outside.

"All right, are you guys ready to go out?" I asked. A few other White House staffers were standing alongside me, including Omarosa.

"Actually, would it be possible for us to have a few moments in private before we go out?" one of the CBC members asked.

That seemed fine to me. I assumed they wanted to plan out who would talk and agree on what they would say. But before I could respond, Omarosa—who had been mostly silent during the meeting while Trump was still present—spoke up. I had always heard she was like a hand grenade without a pin—able to blow up at any moment—and now the Omarosa I'd long feared had rolled into the room. You could see the transformation in seconds—her composed, almost regal bearing gave way to a narrowed glare and a menacing scowl.

"Privacy?!" she exclaimed. "You think you can come up in our house and demand f—ing privacy? Hell, no! You must be outta your d— mind."

Uh-oh.

I was so stunned by this out-of-nowhere response that I'm still surprised my eyes didn't pop out of my head and roll onto the floor.

Equally stunned by the outburst, one of the female CBC members shot back, "See, this is why we can't deal with you."

"Whoa, whoa, whoa," I interjected as calmly as I could. I turned to my colleague and tried to soothe her. "O, it's all right, no biggie. Let's just give them a second to get on the same page before they go out."

"I just don't think they should be coming in here making demands," she said, flipping her hair back over her right shoulder. "The President of the United States met with them in *his* house and they're still making demands!"

I hurriedly corralled the CBC members and their press staffer into a small foyer and walked back into the lobby, closing the double doors behind me.

Omarosa was still fuming.

"We're the ones in f—ing power now," she said as I walked toward her. "They've gotta learn to deal with it." She sounded like she was reliving a scene from *Celebrity Apprentice,* screaming at Gary Busey, or whoever else was in her way to the top.

"Eh, it's all right," I said, laughing, trying to lighten the mood. "I think you've scared them enough for one day." She had scared me, too.

A few minutes later, a CBC staffer told me they were ready, and a now clearly offended Congressman Richmond led their group outside, where about a dozen reporters were waiting on the driveway. I followed them out the door, along with their press aide, and walked around behind the media to ensure we were out of the camera shot.

Omarosa, on the other hand, walked out of the West Wing's front doors and positioned herself about twenty feet directly behind the CBC members, ensuring that she would be clearly visible, lording over them like she was queen of the manor. She displayed a villainous grin from ear to ear.

Had she been plotting to sabotage this event all along? Was this some sort of psychological power play? Who knew what the heck was going on.

Congressman Richmond expressed his appreciation to the President for taking the time to meet, calling it "a meeting where both sides listened." He called the President "receptive" and said "the surprising part was that when we talked about the goals, there were more similarities than there were differences." He also said he looked forward to "further engagement on a consistent basis." So far, so good. But then he departed from that script. He claimed to have confronted the President about his past comments alleging President Obama wasn't born in the United States. I looked over at the CBC's press aide. To my recollection, that topic had never come up during the meeting. And I had taken notes.

Then came the question everyone had been waiting for.

"[The President's] been accused of being a racist, a bigot, encouraging white supremacists," a reporter said. "Coming out of this meeting with him, do you believe those things to be true?"

The meeting had gone so well, and Congressman Richmond had been so sincere and complimentary of him behind closed doors, I thought he might at least be willing to say he didn't personally believe Trump was racist. But he didn't.

"You'd have to talk to the people who made those allegations and ask them what they would say about it," he said. "I will tell you that he's the forty-fifth President of the United States . . ."

I looked over at the CBC press aide who was standing right beside me. The subtle smirk on his face reminded me of a card shark at the moment he revealed his winning hand to a befuddled mark.

I whispered to him. "After everything he said in that meeting when no cameras were around, he's still going to stand in front of the White House and suggest the President might be a racist?"

He shrugged. "Tell Omarosa to keep up the great work."

I walked back into the West Wing. There was no need to watch the rest of the press conference. It's impossible to know whether they were actually getting back at Omarosa, or if the entire thing had been some kind of setup from the beginning.

Three months later, Omarosa invited the CBC leadership back to the White House "to continue the discussion of issues presented in our previous meeting."

In a letter released publicly, Congressman Richmond declined. "Based on actions taken by you and your administration since that meeting," he wrote, "it appears that our concerns, and your stated receptiveness to them, fell on deaf ears."

With that, what started as a hopeful effort to improve race relations was officially crushed under the weight of hard feelings, pettiness, mistrust, and the cynicism of Washington, D.C. The whole episode was a metaphor for the Trump administration on race. Even when the intentions were good, the end result was almost always a mess. And then, of course, sometimes the wounds were needlessly self-inflicted.

On June 3, 2017, my wife, Megan, and I were sitting in McLean Bible Church in northern Virginia, attending the Saturday-evening service. The preacher, Dr. David Platt, had been our pastor back in Alabama. He had gone on to become president of the International Mission Board, the largest Christian mission organization in the world, and was now the pastor at McLean, where he counted the Vice President and numerous White House aides among his regular congregants.

Platt's sermon that evening encouraged us to approach the world's growing migration crises from a biblical perspective. It wasn't a political statement; he wasn't advocating for specific policies. In fact, he went out of his way not to. "We know that there is much debate in our country today surrounding these issues, so we pray for wisdom in the leaders of our government, many of whom are in this church," he said. "My aim is to help us see that far before we listen to what the world says about refugees, or even immigrants, we must listen to what the Word says."

At the precise moment I was listening to this thoughtful approach to a complicated issue, my Apple Watch buzzed with an alert—a tweet by @realDonaldTrump. "We need the Travel Ban as an extra level of safety!" he tweeted. The President was referring, of course, to his famous "Muslim ban," just the latest White House controversy that brought to the fore difficult racial and cultural issues—and caused me to yet again struggle to reconcile the President's statements with Christian teachings.

As I felt this tension, my mind was transported six thousand miles away to a village in northern Jordan, a forty-five-mile drive down Damascus Highway from the Syrian border. That's where I was in the summer of 2015, sitting on the floor of a 550-square-foot apartment. The concrete walls were painted a dingy off-white. The floors were covered in thin, cracking gray tiles, and rust was beginning to corrode the apartment's heavy metal door around its edges. A thin silver tray sat on the ground in the middle of the room holding miniature cups of coffee. An early-2000s black TV sat in the corner on a wooden stand—the only piece of furniture in the entire apartment—airing Al Jazeera news reports on mute.

That tiny apartment was home to a family of seven. Two sisters—both in their thirties and wearing hijabs—lived together with five children between them: four boys, ages fourteen, twelve, seven, and two, and a three-year-old little girl. My wife, Megan, played with the younger kids, blowing bubbles and bouncing an inflatable ball as we talked. Until recently, they had been living in the Syrian city of Daraa, just north of the Jordanian border. They were all, of course, Muslims and their story was far more complicated, and tragic, than America's future president—or most of the rest of us—seemed to believe.

In 2010, as the so-called Arab Spring swept the Middle East, forcing Egyptian President Hosni Mubarak and Tunisian leader Zine al-Abidine Ben Ali from office, many Syrians hoped their president—ophthalmologist turned dictator Bashar al-Assad—might be next. In early 2011, a group of boys in Daraa graffitied three words on the wall of their school: YOUR TURN DOCTOR. The "doctor," of course, was Assad. At the time, the teenage prank hardly seemed like the type of event that could spark a revolution, but Assad wasn't taking any chances. The regime arrested, imprisoned, and tortured twenty-three boys who were believed to have been involved in the graffiti incident. This prompted local protests, which led to a government crackdown and killings, which only spurred more protests. Eventually the government released the boys in an attempt to ease tensions. This worked, but only briefly. In the coming months, as the Syrian people revolted against their oppressors in greater and greater numbers, Daraa became a rebel stronghold, commonly known as "the cradle of the revolution."

One of the sisters, named Qamar, explained to me through a translator that even as the fighting grew more intense, they remained in their homes. "Our family had lived there for generations," she said. "It's our home. We didn't want to leave."

In April and May 2011, the Assad regime laid siege to Daraa. At one point, Qamar explained to me, tanks rolled through their neighborhood and the battalion commander demanded that every fighting-age male renounce the revolution and join them, or face death. Her husband and other men in the neighborhood refused, prompting the Assad forces to bind them and lay them in the middle of the street in the path of the tanks. "We were pleading with the soldiers to let them live," she said, fighting back tears. "By the grace of God, the commander realized that my husband was his cousin, so he let him get up." The others were not so fortunate. The tanks slowly rolled over them all, one by one, leaving their lifeless bodies sunk into the gravel and mud below. The siege of Daraa ultimately left hundreds of protesters dead and as many as a thousand more in prison. Dozens of defected soldiers, who could not bring themselves to carry out such atrocities, were slaughtered as well.

In the coming years, Daraa would remain a rebel stronghold during the ever-expanding Syrian civil war. ISIS overtook roughly half the country. Proxy battles broke out between Russian-, Iranian-, and American-backed forces, but the sisters and their families remained in Daraa. That is, until they just couldn't anymore.

"We stayed right up until the bombs reached our neighborhood," Qamar told me. The day they decided to leave, they rushed to pack whatever belongings they could carry. They hoped to catch a ride that evening on a flatbed truck bound for a refugee camp on the other side of the Jordanian border. They didn't make it in time, but this turned out to be a blessing in disguise.

"A bomb hit the truck," Qamar said, stone-faced. "Everyone was killed." Nearly the entire population of their neighborhood—all of their friends, and many of their family members—was lost in an instant.

They did catch a ride the following day, though, and made it to the Zaatari refugee camp. At the time, they were a group of ten. In addition to the seven I had met, the sisters were accompanied by their husbands and Qamar's elderly mother. Living conditions were deplorable. They were piled on top of one another in white tents without air-conditioning, at a time of year when daytime temperatures could hover as high as 113 degrees. Tragically, Qamar's mother succumbed to heatstroke just days after they had escaped the bombs.

Realizing they could no longer withstand the camp, they fled into Zarqa, a city of roughly a half-million people, where displaced Syrian refugees were pouring into urban neighborhoods by the thousands. Qamar's husband, Ali, found work as a cook in a local restaurant, being paid under the table as an illegal. This type of arrangement bred intense resentment among the local population, whose jobs and wages were being undercut by the growing population of refugees desperate for work. I was immediately conscious of the parallels between this situation and the debate over illegal immigrant labor in the United States.

But Qamar was struggling to stretch her husband's income into even one meal a day for her family; they were withering away. Desperate and unable to find formula for their baby, Ali approached an imam at the neighborhood mosque and asked for help. That evening, Ali came home with a hopeful message for his wife: "The imam is going to help us find food." With their children sleeping on makeshift pallets across the room, empty stomachs growling with hunger, Qamar and Ali hugged each other a little closer that night, clinging to the hope that help was on the way. It wasn't. The following day, as Ali arrived for work at the restaurant, Jordanian security forces arrested him. As it turns out, the imam had not only decided he wouldn't help, he had turned Ali in to the police as an illegal worker, getting him deported back to Syria. The only reason his family had been able to stay was that Ali lied to the police, telling them he had no family in the country.

"What about your sister's husband?" I asked.

"He left the apartment one day and never came back," she said through the translator, rolling her eyes. *"Jaban,"* she added with greater feeling. *Coward.*

At that point, my translator, Hasan, a Christian Jordanian national in his early thirties, interjected, first in Arabic and then in English. "And this is when we met," he said.

Qamar smiled and nodded, then explained that she had asked one of her neighbors—there were hundreds of Syrian refugees in their apartment complex—how they were making ends meet. They somehow always seemed to have food, and their kids even had a soccer ball to play with. With a mixture of bewilderment and awe, the neighbor explained that Hasan had been regularly bringing them enough food to get by. She offered to give Qamar his number, and later that afternoon, she skeptically reached out to him.

The following day, Hasan arrived on their doorstep with enough food and baby formula to last them for two weeks. And for the first time since she'd left her Syrian home behind, she broke down in tears. She'd always wanted to stay strong for their children, she explained, so she refused to let herself cry—even as they lost their home and her mother, were betrayed by their imam and separated from her husband. But the kindness of a total stranger, with whom she didn't share a nationality or religion, overwhelmed her emotions.

In the following months, she explained, Hasan and a small group of Jordanian Christians had taken care of them. They had spent countless hours talking about their families, their governments, and their dreams. Yes, even in the depths of despair, Qamar still had dreams. She dreamed of returning to her home. She dreamed of her children going back to school and playing soccer in the streets with their friends. She dreamed of going to sleep in a real bed, beside the husband she had not seen in over a year. They talked about their different faiths, and why a Christian was doing so much to help Muslims. And at some point, Qamar said, she had a revelation.

"My government failed me, my religion failed me," she said, "and when my family had no one else to turn to, the Christians were the only ones who didn't let us down." As a result of this entire experience, she asked Hasan how she could become a Christian. He told her, and now, months later, her entire family—including her husband back home in Syria—had converted.

This story—and others like it—was the reason that Megan and I, and a small group of others from our church in Alabama, had traveled to the Middle East. We wanted to support the work that Hasan and his team were doing in Jordan. We wanted to help meet their physical needs, and hoped that by doing that, doors would be opened to meet their deeper, spiritual needs as well.

In the year between that first trip to Jordan and joining the Trump campaign, I traveled to various countries in the Middle East—sometimes with a group, sometimes alone. There's nothing quite like stepping out of a Middle

Eastern airport by yourself as a lily-white, blond-haired, blue-eyed American, knowing just enough Arabic to get by. Those experiences changed my life. And I didn't realize it at the time, but they would later make me one of the few people in the West Wing with a firsthand perspective on the refugee and migration crises that would so often be the focus of an intense and often painful political, cultural, and national security debate.

In the first week of April 2017, innocent Syrian citizens were bombed with toxic gas, including sarin, killing dozens and injuring hundreds more. The U.S. government, along with many of our allies and humanitarian organizations, attributed the attack to the Assad regime. The regime, however, claimed it was a "fabrication," and its Russian allies said the whole attack was staged.

As images of dead and wounded children flooded our TV screens and newspapers, I thought about my Syrian friends, and the President grew increasingly angry.

"This guy is a sick son of a b——," he said as I entered the Oval after his national security team had briefed him and left. He tossed a *New York Times* newspaper on the corner of the Resolute desk and pointed his finger at the headline CHEMICAL ATTACK ON SYRIANS IGNITES WORLD'S OUTRAGE. As I walked closer, I could see the image of a child clinging to life with an oxygen mask covering his mouth and nose.

"What do you even do when you've got animals like this running a country?" Trump wondered aloud.

"I don't know, Mr. President," I said, not knowing what more to add. The unusual grimace on his face told me he was deeply affected by what he was seeing. And while I didn't know what his national security team was telling him, it was clearly weighing on his mind.

Shortly thereafter, the USS *Ross* and USS *Porter* unleashed Tomahawk missile strikes on a Syrian air base, with fifty-eight out of fifty-nine missiles hitting their intended target.

Trump was pleased with the military precision. "Congratulations to our great military men and women for representing the United States, and the world, so well in the Syria attack," he tweeted. But privately he also kept reiterating his belief that President Obama had in 2012 set the stage for the Syrian mess we were dealing with almost five years later.

"I'm having to enforce 'red lines' he drew and then wouldn't enforce himself," he would say, seemingly frustrated at the need to put aside his noninterventionist instincts.

He had a point. In August 2012, Obama told reporters assembled in the Press Briefing Room that "a red line for us is we start seeing a whole bunch of chemical weapons moving around or being utilized. . . . We have communicated in no uncertain terms with every player in the region that that's a red line for us and that there would be enormous consequences if we start seeing movement on the chemical weapons front or the use of chemical weapons."

A year later, almost to the day, the Syrian government unleashed a gruesome chemical weapons attack that killed fourteen hundred civilians and caused thousands more to endure paralysis and violent convulsions.

In spite of the clear threat, the Obama administration did nothing militarily, choosing instead months later to cut a deal with the Russians and Syrians to remove or destroy six hundred metric tons of Syria's chemical weapons stockpile.

One of the Syrian men I had met in Jordan remembered this vividly. He was in his mid-forties and had lost his home and much of his family in the war. "Bashar killed us," he said through a translator. "Obama abandoned us."

I shared the President's aversion to military adventurism in the Middle East. But for all of Obama's nonstop moralizing, it was Trump, not he, who took a stand against the evil the Syrian people were enduring. For this, I was proud of the President for having the courage to do the right thing. But when it came to refugees, I was more conflicted.

My firsthand experience led me to believe that Trump had a valid point from an abstract policy perspective, which many on the left seemed incapable of acknowledging. The President's first duty is to protect the American people. Refugees are often impossible to vet. Many of the refugees I met had no identification other than what they received when being processed into a camp. They openly discussed their fears that ISIS had infiltrated the camps, and bristled at the violence and drug use that had become so prevalent. Some of them also talked about how they did not want to be relocated to the West. They hoped to one day return to their homes, and they wanted to maintain their culture, rather than assimilate somewhere else. All of these realities seemed to support Trump's stated desire to relocate refugees as close to their homes as possible. I sometimes cringed at the rhetoric he used to make his case, which totally lacked nuance. But more than that, I felt like we were not keeping our commitment to persecuted Christians.

A week after his inauguration, Trump sat down for an interview in the Blue Room with Christian Broadcasting Network reporter David Brody. Brody specifically asked Trump if persecuted Christians would receive priority status in the refugee program. "Yes," Trump replied. "They've been horribly treated. . . . So we are going to help them." Yet statistics in 2018 showed that the number of Christian refugees admitted to the United States had fallen more than 40 percent under Trump. And as I write this, the State Department's Refugee Processing Center says that the U.S. is only admitting an average of about one Christian refugee from Syria per month.

At the same time, some members of the administration downplayed the successes of immigrants who came to America, assimilated, and made remarkable contributions to society, while going out of their way to vilify all immigrants with the stories of the bad apples. Any time a refugee or immigrant committed a gruesome crime in the United States, for example, Stephen Miller would come down to the comms office demanding a press release about it. Normally I would help make that happen. I was and am a hard-liner on the issue of illegal immigration. I wholeheartedly supported the President's proposals to crack down on illegal border crossings and to ratchet up internal enforcement. I viewed it as an issue of both national security and of basic fairness. I supported moving to a merit-based system, rather than a random visa lottery, and I pushed as hard as anyone to deliver on Trump's promise to build a border wall. I wanted the President to keep all of his promises, and usually he did. But not the ones he made to persecuted Christians.

I once took this concern to Stephen Miller, who was in the middle of every immigration or refugee debate. Sitting outside of his office upstairs in the West Wing, I kept the conversation casual so as not to push myself too aggressively into an area outside of my purview. It was a fool's errand. "I would be happy if not a single refugee foot ever again touched American soil," Miller said dismissively. I didn't press the issue with him; there was no use.

Unfortunately, while the plight of Christian refugees got a lot of traction in faith-based news outlets, I never heard any of the faith leaders who actually had access to the President mention the issue to him. Trump's evangelical advisory board was an eclectic mix of characters. There were Christian pastors with impeccable credentials built over a lifetime of faithful service, and televangelists frequently accused of being charlatans while raking in millions of dollars, flying around in private jets and living in luxurious mansions. The latter group made me uncomfortable, but I knew exactly why Trump had brought them on board. In his mind, people on television were at the pinnacle of their field, so the same must be true for pastors, right? Maybe he didn't know about the reputations of many televangelists. Maybe he didn't care, as long as they supported him and had a platform to exert their influence.

In fairness to members of the board, I don't want to paint them all with a broad brush. Some of them were humbly willing to offer biblical advice if asked. Eric Metaxas, for example, is a brilliant Christian author whose books have had a great deal of influence on my life, and I was impressed by him in our interactions at the White House; he seemed like the real deal. While I was there for many of the advisory board's interactions with the President, I wasn't there for all of them. But based on what I did see, I would be surprised if most of them pressed him on, well, anything.

One particular experience illustrates why I grew skeptical of some of their motives and doubted their ability to be a positive moral and spiritual influence on the President.

Not long after Trump's inauguration, Sarah Sanders and I started working on continuing the tradition of hosting an Easter Prayer Breakfast at the White House. This wasn't a long tradition; it had actually been started in 2010 by President Obama. But it seemed like the perfect opportunity for the President to assemble, early in his administration, the evangelical leaders who had been integral to his electoral victory. Christians had voted for Trump in record numbers. We wanted to send a message that they had a seat at the table in a big way, and I had an idea for a keynote speaker: Dr. David Platt, our pastor from McLean Bible Church.

Platt was the *New York Times* bestselling author of a book titled *Radical: Taking Back Your Faith from the American Dream*. The book is an indictment of materialism and encourages readers to use the resources God has given them to spread the Gospel message. It's not a guilt trip for the wealthy and successful; it's a challenge to fulfill God's purpose, rather than just buy more/bigger/better stuff. And it's not just talking about how to allocate money, but also time. This concept is what initially compelled my wife and me to organize mission trips in Latin America and the Middle East.

Platt was the most gifted preacher I had ever heard, so I knew he would do an outstanding job at the prayer breakfast. Sarah liked this idea, so I started working to set it up, while we both worked our contacts to line up some well-known Christian musicians to be a part of the event.

Unfortunately, Platt's approach was the polar opposite to that of Paula White, the de facto leader of Trump's evangelical advisory board. White was among the country's most famous purveyors of the so-called "prosperity gospel," which can be summed up by the frequent TV pitches to *send me your money and God will bless you with your own health and wealth because of it.* Prosperity gospel preachers tend to use the false premise that wealth is the surest sign of God's blessing to justify their own lavish lifestyles. White's teachings frequently got her labeled as a "charlatan" and "heretic" by mainstream evangelical leaders, but she had her hooks set in Trump, and she wasn't going to let anyone threaten her position.

As preparations for the Easter Prayer Breakfast continued, she came to the EEOB to meet with Jenny Korn, who was the administration's liaison to faith groups. As usual, White dressed in a form-fitting dress that accentuated her curvy figure, and designer leather pumps. I didn't go into the meeting. This was politics, not theology class, and I didn't want to let my personal feelings about White interfere with anything. So after the meeting, Jenny came over to the West Wing to recount what had happened.

"Pastor Paula said inviting Dr. Platt would be a big mistake because he's too controversial," Jenny told me. I was immediately annoyed. *Controversial? The thrice-married televangelist who refused to cooperate with a Senate investigation into her moneymaking operation is worried about controversy?* But I kept that to myself. "She said he believes the American dream is evil," Jenny continued. "Then she asked, 'Would the President really want to associate with someone who thinks it's bad for people to be prosperous and provide better lives for their families?'"

I rolled my eyes. "Give me a break," I said. In hindsight I shouldn't have been surprised. White made a living convincing mostly lower-income people to send in money in exchange for a blessing, so of course she would be willing to disingenuously go after another pastor.

As it turned out, Platt was planning to decline my invitation anyway, hoping to stay more behind the scenes and quietly offer input if asked—again, in contrast to White and others who nudged their way as close to Trump as possible during photo ops.

The Easter Prayer Breakfast fizzled. But in early May, we did manage to host a private dinner for evangelical leaders in the Blue Room. Standing in the back of the room as Trump spoke, I could feel the mutual affection in the room. "I just want you to know this," Trump said. "I'm with you. You were with me during the election. And I'm with you now."

The alliance between Trump and evangelicals was powerful, and both sides reaped the political benefits. Trump was propelled into the world's most powerful office. Evangelicals immediately got a dream Supreme Court nominee in Neil Gorsuch. But when the President occasionally struggled to lead with moral clarity, to unify the country on divisive cultural issues, the silence of his "spiritual advisers" was deafening. What is the point of having moral authority, as all of these pastors claimed to, if you don't stand up for morality? But as is so often the case, when I point my accusatory finger at someone else, I have three more pointing back at me. My greatest regret from my time in the White House is that I wasn't a better picture of my faith to the President and my colleagues. I'm haunted by the late author Brennan Manning's quote, "The greatest single cause of atheism in the world today is Christians who acknowledge Jesus with their lips and walk out the door and deny Him by their lifestyle. That is what an unbelieving world simply finds unbelievable."

Donald Trump is not a religious man—that's no secret to anyone. He viewed the faith community as a political constituency. In that regard, he was as committed as any church member. He delivered massive political results. I'd argue that no president has done more to advance the policy agenda of evangelicals than Donald Trump. For that, I—and millions of Christians around the country—will be eternally grateful. But I still wonder what could have been. With unprecedented access to the Oval Office, what if these pastors had provided private counsel, as men like Billy Graham reportedly did for other commanders in chief? At no time was their absence felt more than in the summer of 2017.

In George Stephanopoulos's White House memoir, he referred to his rival political consultant Dick Morris as "the dark buddha whose belly Clinton rubbed in desperate times." For the first six months of Trump's presidency, Steve Bannon filled that role, but he was more like a nesting doll. Even after the President had put him on the shelf for a while, a moment of uncertainty would find Trump reaching for him again—opening him up, with each layer revealing a familiar message: double down, triple down, quadruple down.

In early August 2017, the President was pretty much fed up with Bannon. Trump thought he was a leaker and an attention hound. Bannon increasingly felt like the last remnant of a bygone era—the chaos before the Kelly crackdown. Kelly was kind of like the good girl that your mom wants you to settle down with, while Bannon was the edgy, wild one that drove you crazy but could also be a heck of a lot of fun. Trump knew in his mind that he needed the former, but his heart couldn't quite let the latter go.

Friday, August 11, 2017, was as quiet as any day in the Trump White House had ever been. The President was enjoying a working vacation (never just a vacation; he insisted on trying to maintain the public perception that he was always working) at his golf club in Bedminster, New Jersey. There was a dramatic difference in the atmosphere on campus when the President was gone. The entire operation slowed down and much more closely resembled the nine-to-five jobs that were familiar to many in corporate America. Some of the staff had even taken advantage of the President's absence to go on vacations of their own.

The laid-back mood was enhanced by the fact that the remaining staff had all been moved over to the EEOB while the West Wing underwent renovations. This meant rather than being stacked on top of one another in the White House, we were all spread out across the EEOB's roughly ten acres of floor space. I was taking advantage of the rare absence of urgency to plan ahead for the fall, when the President was hoping to overhaul the tax code. But I also looked for reasons to take breaks throughout the day and catch up with friends in the building. I left campus for a long lunch and went out of my way to stroll under the trees in Lafayette Square on the walk back. That afternoon the press and communications teams huddled briefly for our usual evening "wrap-up" meeting. It was totally uneventful. I walked home in the rarest of all moods: relaxed.

That evening after dinner, I scrolled through my Twitter feed and watched in horror as pictures and videos showed what appeared to be a torch-wielding mob of white supremacists marching through the University of Virginia. *This is what lynch mobs must have looked like,* I thought to myself as I kept scrolling. I went to bed that night feeling relieved that I wasn't staffing the President in Bedminster. Any planned response to the madness taking place in Charlottesville was someone else's problem.

The following day was one of the few Saturdays when I didn't go into the office. That afternoon I jogged from my apartment a block from the White House down to the Jefferson Memorial and around the Tidal Basin, and stopped for a break along the water, about fifty yards from the Martin Luther King Jr. Memorial. Pulling out my phone as I sat on a bench underneath the low-hanging branches of a cherry tree, I opened Twitter to see that the situation in Charlottesville had escalated. There were Nazi flags being paraded through the streets. White supremacists with homemade wooden shields and clubs were brawling with black-clad counterprotesters with masks over their faces. Some guy proudly proclaiming his allegiance to the Confederate White Knights of the Ku Klux Klan was brandishing a pistol, and others in Confederate flag T-shirts were walking around with assault rifles. Most tragically, some lunatic had driven his car into a crowd, sending bodies flying into the air, killing a young woman and injuring nineteen others. The City of Charlottesville and the State of Virginia had both declared a state of emergency.

I came to find out that the mayhem began with a group of white nationalists planning to protest the removal of a Robert E. Lee statue from a local park. Hearing about the event, militant left-wing activists known as "antifa" (short for "antifascist") had organized to physically resist the protesters. The entire city of Charlottesville—one of the country's most idyllic communities— had descended into chaos that looked more like the streets of Gaza than Virginia.

No one in the White House had anticipated any of this. In fact, my former campaign colleague Steven Cheung, who was now the White House's Director of Strategic Response, was the only staffer I saw being proactive in any way. The night before, he had sent around some recommended talking points and a draft tweet to go out on the @PressSec Twitter account. No one else responded or acknowledged what he had sent.

There was no doubt the President was going to have to weigh in now. I tucked my phone back into my pocket and began the jog back home. I made it back to my apartment just in time to see the President speak live from Bedminster. Backed by a row of perfectly aligned American flags, Trump stepped behind a microphone wearing a black suit and bright red tie. There looked to be pent-up stress in his shoulders as he lifted them slightly and gripped the edges of the podium with both hands.

"We condemn in the strongest possible terms this egregious display of hatred, bigotry, and violence—on many sides, on many sides," the President said. I had written enough remarks for him, and been in enough video recording sessions, to recognize when he was reading the prepared text and when he was ad-libbing. He tended to end sentences by throwing in Trumpian expressions, the unique phrases that gave him one of the world's most recognizable speaking styles. "On many sides, on many sides" was obviously an ad-lib, but I'd be lying if I said it stuck out to me in the moment. He went on to say that hatred, bigotry, and violence had "no place in America. . . . The hate and the division must stop. . . . We have to come together as Americans with love for our nation, and true affection—and really, I say this so strongly— true affection for each other."

In the coming hours, Republicans and Democrats alike condemned the President's remarks and harshly criticized him for not calling out Nazis, white supremacists, and the KKK by name. The following day, talking heads on the Sunday-morning political shows were in a full-on meltdown. What had started as a bunch of idiots causing problems for local law enforcement had turned into a nationwide outcry causing problems for the White House.

I wasn't in Bedminster to see the President's reaction to the backlash, but I'd spent enough time with him to know how he generally approached such situations. He never said it in quite these terms, but it goes something like this:

Don't give an inch. If I give in and give my critics what they're demanding, the media won't give me credit for it anyway. So what's the point? Better to power through it, show no weakness. I might even throw out something new and irresistible for the media beast to feed on—change the subject. Regardless, everyone will move on.

For Trump, the general effectiveness of this approach was hard to deny. After all, during the campaign it had propelled him through countless mini scandals, any one of which could have ruined most candidates. So why change now? By this point, most aides had accepted this as standard operating procedure, but not the new Chief of Staff. General Kelly wanted Trump to deliver a second statement, and he wanted it to happen at the White House. So he got the President on Air Force One, returned to D.C., and sent him out in front of the press pool assembled in the Diplomatic Reception Room.

"To anyone who acted criminally in this weekend's racist violence, you will be held fully accountable," Trump declared. "Justice will be delivered. . . . Racism is evil. And those who cause violence in its name are criminals and thugs, including the KKK, neo-Nazis, white supremacists, and other hate groups that are repugnant to everything we hold dear as Americans."

The *Los Angeles Times* editorial board summed up the prevailing reaction to the second statement: "Trump's first response to Charlottesville was tepid and mealymouthed. His second was too late." *I told you so,* he was no doubt thinking as other outlets echoed the same sentiment.

"Made additional remarks on Charlottesville and realize once again that the #Fake News Media will never be satisfied," he tweeted. "Truly bad people!"

I called Bannon to see what he thought and found him maniacally insisting that this was "a moment" that had to be seized upon. "They have no idea what they've just done," he said. I wasn't exactly sure who "they" were, other than *the enemy.* "This is a winning issue for us."

"What do you mean?" I asked, genuinely curious.

Bannon, who grew up in southern Virginia, replied, "Our heritage, our statues—I told the President to stand up for who we are. *They* want to take it all away. That's what this is about. The freaks running around with torches are a sideshow, they're irrelevant, they're losers. We can own the real issue. We've got to take control of the narrative. This is a winner."

He got off the phone suddenly with another call coming in. I wasn't clear on exactly what he was planning. Was he sensing "a moment" for the President, or a moment for himself? By this point I'm fairly certain those two things were indistinguishable in Bannon's mind.

After a few days spent bottling up his frustration—and apparently being nudged by Bannon—Trump let it all out at once during a press conference in the Trump Tower lobby. He defended his original statement, claiming there was "blame on both sides," and then went a step further, saying there were also "very fine people on both sides." As he spoke, Transportation Secretary Elaine Chao dutifully maintained a pleasant smile and Treasury Secretary Steve Mnuchin stood motionless and stone-faced. But NEC Director Gary Cohn was visibly uncomfortable. Usually the most self-assured person in the room, Cohn delicately clasped his hands in front of him at his waist. He shifted his weight back and forth and seemed to be subconsciously moving farther and farther out of the camera shot.

"Not all of those people were neo-Nazis, believe me," Trump continued. "Not all of those people were white supremacists by any stretch." He went on to decry the push to tear down historical monuments, saying it was an effort to "change history."

As the Charlottesville fallout continued, there was deep anxiety among Trump's staff, unlike anything I had felt since *Access Hollywood*. I overheard some younger staffers discussing whether they should take this "off-ramp" to protect themselves from damaging their future careers.

"None of us are going to be able to get a job in this town after all this," one former RNC aide in the EEOB said fatalistically.

"I'm going to try to go to an agency," said another. "I talked to a friend from the Bush White House and they said that's the way you exit—go to an agency for a while, then leave for whatever part of the private sector your agency dealt with."

A third staffer laughed and said, "Sounds good, but you're forgetting that everyone thinks we're racists."

These conversations became even more widespread as business leaders began resigning one by one from the President's American Manufacturing Council, and reached their peak when Cohn—a corporate titan in his own right—publicly distanced himself from Trump.

"This administration can and must do better in consistently and unequivocally condemning these groups and do everything we can to heal the deep divisions that exist in our communities," Cohn told the *Financial Times*. "I have come under enormous pressure both to resign and to remain in my current position. As a patriotic American, I am reluctant to leave my post. . . . But I also feel compelled to voice my distress over the events of the last two weeks. . . . Citizens standing up for equality and freedom can never be equated with white supremacists, neo-Nazis, and the KKK."

This was the dance that many prominent staffers did, although usually behind closed doors, off the record to reporters or friends. *I'm repulsed by what's happening here, but if good people like me don't stay, just imagine who will replace me.* It was an irresistible mix of moral superiority and personal ego-stroking all wrapped into one.

Months later, when Gary left over policy differences with the President on trade, some White House staff joked that the neo-Nazis made Gary uncomfortable, but it was the tariffs that were truly a bridge too far. Like many jokes, it was funny because it exposed an underlying truth, and not just for Gary, but for most of us. We were willing to pay a steep price to get what we really wanted: proximity to power, and maybe a little of it for ourselves.

The only person who seemed entirely comfortable—thrilled, really—with the Charlottesville debacle was Bannon. "That press conference was a defining moment," he declared. "Our guy refused to back down to the mob. The opposition party," the media, "doesn't know what to do with themselves. A total win for the good guys." He gleefully added in for good measure that Cohn, his sworn enemy, had "pissed himself."

But of all the things Bannon said, one stuck out to me more than any other. A couple of weeks after Charlottesville, he sat down with journalist Charlie Rose to discuss his tenure in the White House. But as it so often did, the conversation turned to the defining moment for anyone in Trump's orbit: *Access Hollywood.* "[That] Saturday showed me who really had Donald Trump's back," Bannon said, "to play to his better angels." It seemed like a strange, almost warped comment in that context. But I recognized the reference immediately, as I'm sure Bannon, an avid student of history, did as well. It was from Lincoln's first inaugural address.

"We are not enemies but friends," Lincoln said, laboring to keep his nation from plunging into civil war. "Though passion may have strained, it must not break our bonds of affection. The mystic chords of memory, stretching from every battlefield and patriot grave to every living heart and hearthstone all over this broad land, will yet swell the chorus of the Union, when again touched, as surely they will be, by the better angels of our nature."

It's little remembered now, but this is exactly the tone that Trump struck at 3 A.M. on Election Night, when he finally took the stage to announce that Clinton had conceded and he was victorious. He threw out the original remarks that had been prepared for him; he knew what he wanted to say. His instinct was to bring the country together.

"Now it's time for America to bind the wounds of division," he said. "To all Republicans and Democrats and Independents across this nation, I say it is time for us to come together as one united people. . . . I pledge to every citizen of our land that I will be President for all Americans. . . . For those who have chosen not to support me in the past . . . I'm reaching out to you for your guidance and your help so that we can work together and unify our great country. . . . Working together, we will begin the urgent task of rebuilding our nation and renewing the American dream. . . . The forgotten men and women of our country will be forgotten no longer."

For someone whose reputation was built on viciously tearing down his opponents, his instinct in victory was to be a uniting figure. But for reasons I cannot fully understand, when the most perilous moments came in the White House, the better angels—the impulse toward unity, harmony, positivity—rarely prevailed over the demons of division, discord, and negativity.

Nonetheless, the Charlottesville response did not cause me to reconsider working in the White House, the way it seemed to with others. Part of it may have been that I was battle hardened after a year in the foxhole. But I also just flat-out did not think he was racist. I know many people reading this book think otherwise, but I personally never witnessed a single thing behind closed doors that gave me any reason to believe Trump was consciously, overtly racist. If I had, I could not have possibly worked for him. Of course, it's easy for me to say that now.

As the media firestorm continued, Trump's frustrations kept growing. And eleven days after the Charlottesville protests began, I finally saw him come unglued.

As noted, the President and House Speaker Paul Ryan had always maintained a tenuous relationship, one based largely on political necessity and mutual disdain. Even after Trump walked out on him in the middle of one of their first Oval Office meetings, they at least held on to some cordiality. They occasionally joked with each other and had come to something of an understanding. Unlike McConnell, who Trump eventually seemed to like, he still thought Ryan a weak man.

Ryan, for his part, was under constant pressure to hold together his slender GOP majority in Congress and to respond to endless questions from Capitol Hill reporters about the latest Trump tweet or statement that had outraged them. The Speaker walked that tightrope with something less than a gymnast's finesse, although he clearly tried. In Ryan's initial statement about Charlottes-ville, he didn't even mention Trump by name, but under criticism, the Speaker later conceded that the President had "messed up" in his comments and needed to communicate with greater "moral clarity." As criticism of Trump went, this was rather mild.

But Ryan's comments only kept the Charlottesville story alive—a story that, despite all of the President's efforts to push past it, clearly upset him on a personal level. I happened to have just walked into the President's private dining room off the Oval when he first saw Ryan's comments on television. You could see fall across Trump's face every frustration he'd ever had with the Speaker, and with the Charlottesville crisis in general. His eyes narrowed. His jaw clenched.

"Get me Paul Ryan on the phone right now," he barked out loud enough for his secretary, who was sitting down the hall, all the way on the other side of the Oval Office, to hear clearly.

He was now standing. The remote control for the television was in his left hand, like a pistol. On the table in front of him rested a stack of newspapers. On top of that pile sat a landline phone. His right hand hovered just above it.

Within seconds a shout came back from his secretary. "I have the Speaker for you." Ryan had just made his statement about Trump, so it couldn't pos-sibly be a mystery as to why the President was calling him. I imagined Ryan somewhere in the U.S. Capitol taking a deep breath with his eyes closed while he waited for Trump to get on the line.

The President pressed the flashing button, snatched up the phone, and put it to his ear. There was no opening greeting, no small talk, no prelude.

"Paul, do you know why Democrats have been kicking your a— for de-cades?" He didn't wait for a reply.

"Because they know a little word called 'loyalty.' Why do you think Nancy has held on this long? Have you seen her? She's a disaster. Every time she opens her mouth another Republican gets elected. But they stick with her. She got them to vote for Obamacare and half of them thought it was the dumbest bill ever written." His voice was loud and getting louder. "But they're loyal. They stick together. Why can't you be loyal to your President, Paul? I even went along with your 'Repeal and Replace' plan."

As he spoke, I slowly stepped back from the table and stood in the entry-way to the dining room. I kept my eyes fixed on the TV to avoid distracting him or inadvertently becoming the target of his ire myself. I couldn't make out anything the Speaker was saying on the other end of the phone. It was like a much quieter version of the adults on the old Charlie Brown "Peanuts" cartoons. Whatever it was, though, it was brief and unpersuasive, because the President jumped right back into it.

"You know what else I remember?" he snapped at the Speaker of the House of Representatives, next in line to the presidency after the Vice President. "I remember being in Wisconsin and your own people were booing you. You were out there dying like a dog, Paul. Like a dog! And what'd I do? I saved your a—. I said, 'Oh, c'mon, Paul's going to be with us.' Maybe they were right, though, who knows? But I'll tell you this, Republicans better figure out loyalty or we're not going to get anything done."

At that point I felt like it was best to exit, so I gave the President a nod and took my leave. He was still yelling as I walked down the hall and out of earshot.

11

A TALE OF TWO GENERALS

A half-dozen White House staffers—most of them from the National Security Council—and a handful of think-tank academics crowded around a table in the Ward Room in the basement of the West Wing. This private dining room was right next door to the larger White House Mess and had become a favorite meeting place for senior aides who wanted a secure spot to chat, but didn't want to reserve the larger Roosevelt Room upstairs or the more formal Situation Room across the hall. There were glasses of water sitting on top of an off-white tablecloth. Gold-framed pictures of large ships on the walls were an ever-present reminder that the Navy handled all of the food service in the West Wing.

The names of these aides would not be familiar to the public, but they were the deputy assistants and special assistants to the President who did a lot of the heavy lifting for their more well-known bosses. The one exception was Steve Bannon, who had positioned himself at the head of the table.

Interactions with Bannon often had an almost cinematic quality to them, as if he were playing out a part for a camera in the corner capturing his every utterance and movement. The Ward Room's tight quarters and dark-stained wood paneling accentuated that feeling. This was the proverbial smoke-filled back room where the world's problems are hashed out, and the type of place that often left me feeling self-conscious, out of place, maybe even in over my head.

Bannon had asked me to attend the meeting of this group, which he had put together to discuss countering the rise of China, which Bannon viewed as the nation's most pressing geopolitical threat, perhaps even an existential one. When I asked him what I would bring to such a discussion, he sold it to me as only he could, "Somebody's gotta figure out how we're going to talk about this s—. Sit there, shut the f— up, soak it in, and then come up with a way to sell it."

Fair enough.

I didn't have the guts at the time to ask the logical follow-up questions, which were things like, "Is the National Security Advisor aware of this meeting?" General H. R. McMaster most certainly was not. Nor, I could only assume, were the folks at State, or CIA or DoD, or a half-dozen other acronymed agencies that had staffers devoting their entire lives to the issue. Bannon was running his own op here, and who was I to question the White House Chief Strategist? General Kelly's arrival clearly wasn't going to change his MO.

Like most Bannon meetings, it was a freewheeling affair, filled with bold assertions, multiple tangents, and a generous sprinkling of expletives. Most of it was a blur.

"You've got to respect these SOBs," he said of the Chinese at one point. "They're out for themselves and they don't give a f— what anyone thinks. They're playing hardball. They're lying, cheating, and stealing." He loathed them, despised them for daring to challenge the United States for global supremacy. But there was also something in him that had a deep appreciation for how they went about their business.

"They've got spies in our universities," he continued. "They own our think tanks, present company excluded, I hope. They're spending more on infrastructure in a year than we will in a decade. It's a beautiful thing to behold, man. Xi's a motherf—ing nationalist and he's still going to be President after half this room is dead. They're gonna kill us, man. They're just gonna kill us."

I sat there blinking, shoveling spoonfuls of vanilla ice cream from the Mess into my mouth, as he envisioned our inevitable doom.

The public perception, often cultivated by Bannon himself, was that he was an evil mastermind of the Trump White House—a maniacal courtier from the Renaissance period, lifted off the pages of Machiavelli's *The Prince* and dropped into the modern world's most powerful court. As with most legends, this one took a thread of truth and wove it into a larger tapestry that seamlessly mixed fact and fiction.

Looking back, this random meeting on China—off the books, somewhat cloak-and-dagger, with no clear purpose and no apparent plan to execute on anything discussed—was a microcosm of Bannon's tenure in the White House. It was fueled by visions of grandeur; he alone was leading a tiny band of misfits to take on a rising communist power that had bested the elite minds of multiple past administrations. And somehow he would win.

In the Great Man Theory of history, the course of human events is largely determined by the impact of highly influential individuals who, by sheer force of will, personality, or talent, reshape the world in their image. There's an argument to be made that Trump is such a man, whether people like it or not. But Bannon seemed to view himself as the true Great Man of the partnership, on whose fulcrum the course of history pivoted.

Bannon's office on the main floor of the West Wing was ground zero for a revolution that other parts of the building probably weren't even aware was going on. Even the revolutionaries he enlisted, myself included on occasion, didn't quite understand.

As reporters started using various terms to describe what Bannon believed, such as nationalist, populist, and alt-right, he had his deputy Andy Surabian— my old campaign war room colleague—put together a packet that included definitions and background research on how accurate those terms were.

"I'm an economic nationalist," he said after reviewing the documents. "Love it."

He advocated forcefully for policies that advanced his views, especially on immigration, trade, and infrastructure, and he wasn't afraid to lose internal debates. Many operatives spent most of their time holding their finger up in the air trying to figure out which way the political winds were blowing. They just want to be on the "winning" side in the end. Not Bannon. He'd go down fighting for what he believed, which I'd say is a respectable quality in any man. And his office was prepared for war—with charts and maps and screens everywhere, as the great general surveyed battlefield conditions all over the world.

The centerpiece of the office was the "promises made, promises kept" list, tracking every Trump campaign promise, which ones he'd already delivered on, and which ones were works in progress. On one of his walls hung two giant flat-screen TVs, each displaying four panels tuned to eight different news channels: Fox News, Fox Business, CNN, CNN International, MSNBC,

CNBC, Bloomberg, and C-SPAN. He stood in front of the TVs almost all day, absorbing all of it and none of it, pacing back and forth, pecking out a non-stop stream of texts and emails as ideas popped into his head. Opposite the TVs was a standing desk—really more of a podium—where he would scribble notes, or read books on grand strategy or history, along with the news of the day. There were a handful of wooden chairs positioned around the perimeter of the room. This was where I and other aides would sit as Bannon berated us for not pushing back forcefully enough on negative stories, or when he strategized out loud on how to take back a congressional seat or dissected the ulterior motives of foreign leaders. Or sometimes all three.

To be sure, he had his successes. Perhaps most memorably, Bannon won a fight between the "nationalists" and the "globalists" over whether Trump should withdraw the United States from the so-called Paris Accord, a multi-nation agreement to address climate change.

With Trump set to pull out, a small group of senior aides, led by Ivanka, launched a gambit to convince him to change his mind. Knowing the President's views could occasionally be influenced by titans of industry, just about the only people whose opinions he actually respected, they urged business leaders to call Trump directly and make the case for staying in the deal. At one point it looked like the President might actually change his mind.

Bannon, sensing the tide turning against him, called Surabian and told him he had an important task that needed his immediate attention. "Surabian, drop everything you're doing right now," he demanded. It was the Saturday afternoon of Memorial Day weekend, but that didn't matter. "I need you to find every time that Trump ever promised to pull out of the Paris deal. Put it all in a document and send it to me ASAP. Okay? Go." He hung up without waiting for a response.

Surabian grabbed his laptop and spent the next four hours scouring the internet for everything Trump had ever said about the Paris Accord. We would later laugh that those few hours of work may have changed the course of history. The following week, Bannon walked into the Oval Office and plopped a stack of papers down on the Resolute desk. The President pulled it toward him and flipped through page after page of his public comments eviscerating the Paris deal and promising to pull out.

Checkmate.

Three days later he delivered on his promise in a Rose Garden speech in which he declared, "I was elected by voters of Pittsburgh, not Paris." When Bannon was focused and under control, this was his true value to the Trump presidency: being an ever-present reminder of the promises and agenda that propelled Donald Trump into the Oval Office to begin with. Unfortunately, neither focus nor control was Steve's strong suit.

A disproportionate amount of General Bannon's war-fighting capability was focused not against Trump's political opposition, or the media, or China, or any of his other external enemies. It was instead used to prosecute his fruit-less war with Jared and Ivanka—or Javanka, as he called them. The core principle of Trump World, as even outside observers could glean after five minutes, was never pit yourself against the family. Anyone with "Strategist" in their job title should have seen how foolish this was. Even Bannon's per-ceived allies, like Stephen Miller, recognized it was counterproductive. Bannon seemed to think of Miller as a sort of right-wing protégé. But if surviving—much less thriving—was the goal, Miller proved himself to be a more skilled strategist than his mentor. He was an ideological clone of Bannon—a hard-liner on immigration and trade who believed we should always maintain a confrontational posture with the press. But contrary to public perception—and I'm pretty sure contrary to Bannon's own perception—Miller was not Bannon's ally against the so-called globalists inside the White House, Kushner in particular.

In our early days in the White House, Miller had made his way over to the ground floor of the residence to witness one of our first-ever recording sessions for the President's weekly address to the nation. On the walk back to the West Wing, Miller and the President walked ahead of me. Miller glanced back over his shoulder, as if to see who might be listening, but I'm not sure if he noticed I was behind him, rather than a Secret Service agent. Of course, the person who should have been most worried about his back was Steve Bannon, as Miller plunged in the knife and, to borrow from Richard Nixon, twisted it with relish.

"Your polling numbers are actually very strong considering Steve won't stop leaking to the press and trying to undermine Jared," Miller told the Pres-ident as we walked up the West Colonnade.

"So you think that's really hurting me, huh?" the President asked.

"It's getting nonstop coverage. If Steve wasn't doing that, I bet you'd be ten points higher," Miller replied.

I knew Miller and Kushner had a good relationship, which they had forged on the campaign. I just wouldn't have guessed he'd be an active combatant against Steve, with whom he'd enjoyed a close alliance for years. But maybe he just knew that any fight against the family wouldn't end well, and he wanted to be on the winning team. There's a reason Miller outlasted so many others in the West Wing.

By April 2017, only four months into the administration, a shockingly short amount of time, the Chief Strategist of the White House had no clear strategy for his own survival. The President had grown frustrated with the incessant infighting and the media's Bannon-fueled portrayal of Steve as some kind of Svengali, constantly bending the President to his will.

Responding to reports that Steve had been using the media—*Breitbart News* in particular—to go after Kushner and the rest of his West Wing enemies, the President said, "Steve is a good guy, but I told them to straighten it out or I will."

From that point forward it felt like his days were numbered. To me. To the President. To every single person in the West Wing. To everyone, it seemed, but Steve Bannon. Once Trump replaced Priebus with Kelly and gave him the authority to put the entire staff under his thumb, I figured Bannon was finished. Kelly was bent on installing a more defined staff hierarchy, with himself at the top, and it was hard to imagine Bannon subordinating himself to another staffer, even a four-star Marine general. After all, he was still organizing off-the-books meetings on China and who knows what else. It was only a matter of time before it came to a head.

"How much do you think that bird's worth?"

The forty-person White House communications team was huddled together in the Roosevelt Room late in the afternoon, and I was listening to a small group of junior aides debate how much the golden eagle statue in the corner might cost. The sculptures—there were actually two of them, one on each side of a large cabinet that hid a giant flat-screen TV behind its antique doors—stood about two feet tall. They had been added to the decor as part of the latest round of renovations. The eagles were perched atop a rock with their wings extended high above their heads, like they were forever stuck on the first letter of the "YMCA" dance.

"Gotta be, like, twenty thousand dollars, or something like that," one of the young aides estimated.

"I'm pretty sure it's bronze, not gold," argued another. "Probably knock it down some. I'd guess ten thousand."

"What's up with certain parts looking darker than others, though?" a third chimed in.

"It's called patina, dude," the second one shot back incredulously.

I chuckled to myself as they walked across the room together to get a closer look. I already knew what they were about to find out: the eagles were actually made of wood. The statues were intricately carved and beautifully painted. But they weren't quite what my colleagues thought they were going to be.

That isn't a perfect metaphor for the experience of working in the White House, but it's a serviceable one nonetheless. I could vividly recall what it felt like to stand on Pennsylvania Avenue and wonder what must be happening behind those white walls and curtained windows. It had now been six months since I learned the answer to that question. And much like the experience of getting a close-up look at the bird statues in the Roosevelt Room, it was somehow nothing like I thought it'd be—more wooden than gold—but still beautiful and interesting, nonetheless.

When friends or acquaintances would ask what it was like, I had a standard, three-phrase response: Always interesting. Sometimes amazing. Usually exasperating. The past few weeks had fallen firmly into the exasperating category. And now here I was, back in the Roosevelt Room, where just days before the Mooch had reigned supreme. The entire comms and press staff had been called in for an all-hands staff meeting, but we hadn't yet been told why.

With that familiar *click, whoosh,* the answer immediately became clear.

Everyone's eyes darted toward the door just as General Kelly marched in. He had a certain presence about him. He was physically imposing, probably about six foot two and weighing around 230 pounds. His New England accent hit my Southern ears like a pick breaking through a block of ice, but his tone wasn't abrasive. He didn't have to yell. The four stars he used to wear on his shoulder weren't there, but the respect they demanded still remained.

The entire room stood up, like privates first class reporting for duty. This already marked a dramatic departure from Priebus's time in the White House. He would occasionally float in and out of our meetings without most staffers lifting their heads out of their phones, much less their entire bodies out of their seats.

Kelly, whom aides had already taken to calling "The Chief," another respectful nod that Priebus never received, motioned subtly for everyone to sit down. He didn't make small talk. "How many of you here have prior government experience?" he asked straightaway. Out of the forty people in the room, only one or two hands shot up.

For reasons that were unclear, he cut his eyes at one of his personal aides, who had come into the room with him. "Let me give you some advice, okay? You're going to be dealing with the press. Tell the truth. That's important. I know what you all do. You know, other generals would get mad at me sometimes because I got such good press. But that's because I knew how to talk to the press. I knew how to work with them, and they didn't." The words flew out of his mouth like perfectly fired salvos from a cannon. As he continued to speak, I thought to myself, *This is a man who's used to commanding people.*

"I want you to know I understand how valuable what you do is," he said, wrapping up his brief remarks. "And so does the President."

After he'd left, several press aides joked that the new Chief had already exposed himself as a leaker by talking about what great press he used to get. The only people who attract positive stories in this town, they noted, are the ones who reporters can't take shots at because they're scared to lose them as a source. I'm not sure if that's true, exactly, but it was certainly the way most senior aides operated in the Trump White House. To me, it was more interesting that he had zeroed in on whether we had prior government experience. This was a relevant question, of course. There was certainly something to be said for institutional knowledge. But as someone who had come out of the private sector, it worried me that he might be drawn to the couple of aides with prior experience in government, whom I coincidentally—or perhaps not—viewed as some of the least capable staffers on the team. At this point there was no way to know. In any event, those comments proved to be far less concerning than what I heard him say next.

Shortly after that, Kelly assembled all of the staff working in the EEOB to deliver his introductory remarks. He stood at a podium at the intersection of two large hallways, black-and-white-checkered floors stretching the length of a city block. Several hundred staffers crowded around him. Some of us from the West Wing walked across the driveway as well, curious to hear what he would say.

"Nice to meet you, I'm from Boston," he said right off the bat. I smirked and nodded my head. We were from dramatically different places, but I was proud of where I came from, too. I felt like it said something about who I was. Kelly clearly felt the same way about his blue-collar roots. I liked that about him right away.

But then things got a little weird.

The primary theme of his speech was that he planned to approach his new job by serving the country, then the President, in that order, and that we should do the same. At first blush, this didn't seem like a particularly profound statement, much less a controversial one. But the more he spoke, the more he seemed to really be hammering on this construct: country, then President, country, then President. And the more I let it soak in, the more I thought that what Kelly was saying—country first, POTUS second—was, at best, a bit curious, and at worst, potentially hostile.

We believed that the way we served our country was by serving the President. Kelly, on the other hand, seemed to be intimating that those two goals might be at odds, perhaps even mutually exclusive at times. And you know what? Maybe they would be. But if they ever were, the honorable response would be to resign. Maybe we were being paranoid after being in the Trump bunker for so long, but Kelly seemed to be saying that, in such a scenario, it might be necessary to subvert the President's wishes in service of some amorphous higher calling.

Most of us had met his arrival with optimism after enduring six months of staff upheaval. Now I was watching some of the President's most ardent supporters shuffling back to their offices, hanging their heads in concern.

"What a letdown," one of them said. "He comes across like he doesn't even like the President, much less want to work for him."

I am still not certain what motivated Kelly to use his first interaction with the majority of the White House staff to say what he did. We might have completely misread him. Indeed, he would go on to make other bizarre comments in the press—and behind the scenes—that suggested he might just be a poor communicator at times. But right off the bat his remarks hurt his standing among loyal aides who were hoping he could unify the fractious staff behind a singular mission: advancing the President's agenda.

That was about to be more important than ever. After the failure on health care, a push to overhaul the tax code—a major component of Trump's economic agenda—was now looming. But before Kelly could even begin to approach that challenge, the battle-hardened Marine was going to get a taste of a different type of warfare.

During Kelly's first week on the job, the senior members of the President's trade and economic teams clustered together in the Outer Oval, waiting to go in for their first presidential-level policy meeting of Kelly's tenure. At the time trade issues were in my comms portfolio, so I was waiting as well. This was my first glimpse at Kelly in action, and Kelly's first glimpse at a White House paralyzed by inaction—at least when it came to a coherent position on trade.

Trade was one of the White House's most contentious issues. The ideological diversity among the President's senior economic aides swung wildly, from avid free traders to hard-core protectionists. This made for some of the most interesting debates, but also some pretty hard feelings.

On the protectionist—or economic nationalist—side of the debate were Bannon, Stephen Miller, U.S. Trade Representative Robert Lighthizer, and Director of the National Trade Council Peter Navarro. Lighthizer, pushing seventy years old, had been Deputy U.S. Trade Representative—the first to ever hold that title—under President Ronald Reagan. He was a fierce advocate for bilateral trade deals, in which two countries would hash out an agreement directly, rather than multilateral deals that involved numerous countries. Trump often denounced multilateral agreements, saying they were "bad deals" that eroded U.S. sovereignty and often put American workers and companies at a disadvantage. That was music to Lighthizer's ears.

Navarro, in his late sixties, was a former college professor who had joined the campaign as an economic adviser after Jared Kushner stumbled across one of his books, *Death by China*, online. Needless to say, he was a China hawk, but really I'm not sure there was a single country on earth on which Navarro didn't want to slap tariffs. He was a prickly character, probably the least diplomatic senior aide in the White House. But he was a true believer in both his economic beliefs and in the President. And much to the chagrin of his internal enemies—of whom there were many—Trump viewed him as a loyalist who should be empowered.

Together, the nationalists were a formidable group, mainly because they had one really big thing going for them: Trump agreed with them. Trade was one of the few issues on which the President walked in the door with a fully formed opinion, and he'd been consistent on it for decades.

The free traders were led by Gary Cohn, Director of the National Economic Council. Cohn was a Wall Street tycoon worth about a half-billion dollars, giving him the credentials needed to be one of the few people in the building Trump actually respected as a peer. He had struggled his way through school as a middle-class kid with dyslexia, at a time when educators were still figuring out how to best serve such students. He went on, through sheer tenacity, to graduate from American University, and got a job selling aluminum siding for U.S. Steel. Then, after a chance meeting with a Wall Street executive in a taxicab, he landed a job as a runner on the trading floor. He caught the attention of Goldman Sachs in 1990 and jumped at the opportunity to work for the investment juggernaut. Twenty-six years later he was named the firm's president, making him one of the most powerful executives in the finance world. In his mid-fifties, Gary was bald-headed and physically imposing, standing about six foot three and weighing around 220 pounds. He had a well-earned reputation for being "one tough cookie," as the President put it. The best-known Cohn anecdote from his time at Goldman Sachs was that "he would sometimes hike up one leg, plant his foot on a trader's desk, his thigh close to the employee's face, and ask how markets were doing."

In a White House full of both real and imagined enemies, Bannon had Cohn right at the top of his list. He dubbed Cohn "Globalist Gary" and derided him as the leader of the "Wall Street Wing" of the administration. Together with Treasury Secretary Steven Mnuchin and a handful of other advisers with business backgrounds, they were often able to slow down the nationalists' (i.e., the President's) agenda, even if they couldn't stop it altogether. Their go-to argument against tariffs or withdrawing from multilateral deals was that doing so might blunt the stock market boom. The Dow Jones Industrial Average had hit numerous record highs since Trump took office, a fact the President loved to tout.

Often siding with the free traders in these debates—albeit somewhat more quietly—was Rob Porter, the Staff Secretary. At forty years old, Porter's pedigree was that of a pre-Trump-era White House aide. Harvard undergrad. Rhodes Scholar. Oxford master's degree. Harvard Law. He had served as Senator Orrin Hatch's Chief of Staff prior to joining the administration. The Staff Secretary title may give the impression that he served in some type of clerical role, but every single piece of paper going to the President had to first flow through the Staff Secretary's office. That's a powerful job in any administration, but his constant interaction with Trump made him even more influential than usual. On top of that, General Kelly had made it clear from his first day on the job that Porter was being given additional power that he never had under Priebus. He would totally control the paper flow to POTUS—no more sticking *Breitbart* articles in his evening briefing book to get him riled up—and he would also coordinate internal policy debates.

By August 2017, Bannon's star was clearly fading. Even he could see that, though he tried to mask it, like an aging movie star hoping for one more chance to find a hit. Kelly was establishing himself as the alpha dog, and both Cohn and Porter were ascendant. But as we all waited patiently in the Outer Oval, it quickly became clear that Kelly's arrival had not softened the tension between the warring factions.

Porter walked over behind the desk of Madeleine Westerhout, the President's executive assistant, and picked up a large foam-core board showcasing a complicated chart. I don't know much about making charts, but I do know that the point of them is to present complicated data in a simple way. And yet there was so much information packed onto this poster-sized chart that it should have been accompanied by a copy of Adam Smith's *The Wealth of Nations*.

"What is this?" Porter asked in disgust.

"Don't worry about it, Rob," snapped Navarro. "It's for the President. He'll want to see it."

Porter rolled his eyes.

"Okay, but all of the paper that goes to the President—including charts like this—has to go through the Staff Secretary's office for vetting," he said. "That's the process, Peter, and you know it. That's what the Chief wants. No one's even seen this or had a chance to fact-check it, and you're just going to take it in to the President."

Navarro snatched the chart out of Porter's hands and walked off a few yards, over by the closed Oval Office door. Propping up the chart against the wall, he folded his arms and kept his back turned to the rest of the group. "You guys just don't want him to see the whole story," he said under his breath. "You want him to hear *your* facts, not *the* facts." Judging by the look in Navarro's eyes, this chart must be a killer. When the moment came, it would shut up everyone else in the room.

A TV mounted on the wall was tuned to Fox News, and I pretended to be interested in what was on the screen to avoid making eye contact with the two aides who clearly hated each other's guts. Cohn shook his head and chuckled quietly. Bannon's head was buried in his phone, as usual. Was he listening? No one was ever quite sure.

Moments later the door swung open and the Chief invited the group to come in.

"We're on the clock, gentlemen," Kelly snapped. "We've got twenty minutes blocked off for this."

Now that's new, I thought to myself. Up until that point the schedule had been kind of a suggestion, more of a loose outline than something to which everyone paid close attention. *Maybe this is how it's supposed to work.*

Lighthizer, Navarro, Miller, and Cohn sat down in the wooden chairs in front of the Resolute desk, with Bannon standing right behind them. Porter stood off to the left, and I sat down on one of the couches. Kelly, who wouldn't move from his position standing at Trump's left hand the entire meeting, was clearly in control. The President seemed to enjoy this—his handpicked general running the show, shaping things up. I wondered how long that would last.

The topic of discussion was potential actions the administration could take to crack down on Chinese theft of American intellectual property and the forced transfer of our companies' technology. Both issues were posing serious problems for American enterprises, and in some cases jeopardizing U.S. national security. Kelly expected everyone to stick to the topic.

Trump set the tone right away. "It's the geniuses again," he said mockingly, leaning back in his chair and looking up at Kelly. "These same geniuses come in here every week, with the same problems, and I tell them the same thing: 'Let's do some tariffs, bring me some tariffs.' But here we are again and I bet nothing has happened."

Kelly's deadpan expression never changed.

"So go ahead," the President said, looking back at the group. "Let's hear it."

Lighthizer laid out various options for how to deal with the China problem, but Trump was clearly right, tariffs were not currently on the table. He looked up at General Kelly as if to say, *I told you so.*

With a brief lull in the conversation, Navarro picked up his precious giant chart and presented it to the President with great pride. Trumpets may have sounded in Navarro's head. Trump held it out in front of himself, cocking his head to the side as he tried to understand what he was looking at. He was a visual learner, so usually charts and graphs were a smart way to present information to him. Except this one. A few seconds later, Trump dropped it back on top of the desk and looked back to Navarro in confusion.

"I have no idea what I'm even looking at here," he said. "No one on earth could make sense of this thing. What is this, Peter? C'mon, Peter, what is this? Makes no sense."

Navarro looked frustrated and started to explain, but it was pointless; the President had already moved on. Porter was now standing with his arms crossed, rubbing his forehead with his left hand, and also staring at Kelly with his own *I told you so* look.

Sensing an opening from this blunder, Cohn took the opportunity to make his own case for a path that did not include tariffs, which he believed could start a "trade war" that would slow growth at a time when the economy was revving up. Trump raised his eyebrows and took a sip of Diet Coke. He seemed receptive to Cohn's arguments, which prompted Bannon to jump in.

"The Trump program is about working people," he snapped. "Some people here want to derail the Trump program. They've got their reasons, I suppose." This of course was classic Bannon. With a whiff of conspiracy, he yet again framed himself as the defender of the Trump agenda and others as nefariously trying to stop its implementation. It drove his adversaries nuts, mainly because it was effective.

Kelly, who I assumed didn't know much about trade policy, was still standing there quietly grasping a folder in his hands. But I could see the frustration growing on his face. *Is this how this always plays out?* he seemed to be wondering.

I almost wanted to catch his attention and silently nod my head. *Yes, General, this is about par for the course.*

"I don't understand why this is so difficult," the President continued. "I want tariffs—tariffs! Can anyone in this room of geniuses bring me some tariffs?"

Glancing from person to person, the President finally locked eyes with Cohn, sending him into a mini tirade. "Oh, now of course I know there are some globalists in the room!" Trump said, elongating the "o" in "glooobalists." "They don't want to do it, but they didn't get elected. This is what I ran on. This is what we're going to do."

Bannon, who was pacing behind the rest of the debating aides, gleefully turned away, almost as if not to gloat too openly. This moment was another reminder to me of the ideological bond Trump and Bannon shared. On the other hand, the fact that Cohn & Co. had largely held off Trump's nationalist instincts for the first seven months of his presidency was impressive in its own right. For the next few minutes, the aides waged a rhetorical war in the Oval Office, with Bannon, Navarro, and Lighthizer advocating for tariffs and Cohn—and to a lesser extent Porter—predicting economic doom if the administration pursued such "protectionist" policies.

Bannon and Navarro were relentless, urging the President to economically crush America's enemies under the weight of punitive tariffs. Bannon stood up and sat down, paced, then paused to punctuate a point, lowered then raised his voice to draw in his audience before hammering home an argument. Navarro angrily growled that "some other people in the room" were refusing to execute the President's orders, although it was still unclear to me what specific actions were being proposed.

Cohn, who had survived his fair share of boardroom squabbles as president of Goldman Sachs, was equally relentless in laying out the impact that retaliatory tariffs would have on American workers and consumers, particularly in the Middle American states that had put him in office. He tended to stay seated in his chair in front of the Resolute desk to Trump's left, presenting himself as a measured check on Bannon and Navarro's nationalist fervor.

General Kelly tried to referee the discussion, with limited success, and at some point it became clear that this wasn't a policy debate that could end with the President making a decision. Instead it was—once again—a free-for-all argument between people who couldn't stand one another. It was basically a Twitter fight in real life—in the Oval Office, in front of the President of the United States. The President interjected one last time.

"John, this is your first time here for this," he said to Kelly, "so I want you to understand my position. I want tariffs. Someone better bring me some d— tariffs."

"Yes, sir, Mr. President," the Chief said. "We're going to break up this meeting for now and come back when we have some clearer options for you." Kelly motioned for the group to head for the exit, another new technique after six months of everyone hanging around and chatting with the President at the end of meetings for seemingly as long as they wanted.

Porter, trying to assert himself in front of the new boss, had an idea.

"Guys, let's convene in the Roosevelt Room for a few minutes for a de-brief," he said. Bannon didn't seem interested in participating, and didn't. Lighthizer stayed behind to talk to Kelly. The rest of the group silently walked across the hall into the conference room.

With everyone inside, Cohn shut the door and unleashed all of the frus-trations he had coolly masked while in front of the President.

"You're a liar, Peter!" he roared.

Oh, boy, I thought, *Peter's gonna have to take this all by himself in Bannon's absence.*

"You can't keep going in there and telling the President lies. Nothing you said in there was true," Cohn raged. "This isn't college anymore," he contin-ued, a nod to Navarro's lengthy tenure as a college professor. "This isn't the-oretical. You're going to tank the global economy and it's all going to be based on lies."

Cohn was right, of course. Navarro should not have plopped a Rube Goldberg–esque chart in front of the President without anyone having a chance to see it. And some of the facts he threw out did seem a bit dicey.

Navarro, a much more diminutive physical presence than Cohn, nonethe-less did not back down.

"I'm a liar?" he shot back. "You guys are the ones who walk out of the Oval all the time and refuse to do what the President asks. I know exactly what you all do: You go back to your offices and you come up with a way to slow everything down. You hatch all these reasons to slow-walk everything. That's why he's so mad in there, because you all refuse to do what the Presi-dent asks you to do—he's the President of the United States!"

Navarro was right on this point. When it came to trade actions, everyone knew that was exactly what they did.

The back-and-forth continued along those same lines for several minutes, leaving Porter standing there in silence, totally vexed. *So much for this great idea.*

In the end, the entire group dispersed to their various corners of the White House complex—Cohn upstairs to the NEC Director's wood-paneled office, Porter downstairs to the Staff Secretary's low-ceilinged suite, and Navarro across the street to his palatial digs in the EEOB.

I walked across the hall to my desk, at the time in the corner office that had recently been vacated by Scaramucci, looked out the window onto the White House North Lawn, and took a deep breath. *Well, that was something.* This was the Wild West Wing John Kelly was brought in to tame. I silently wished him luck. But it wasn't going to be easy. Even Wyatt Earp had to first survive the gunfight at the O.K. Corral before he could bring Tombstone to heel.

A couple of weeks after the trade meeting blow-up, a tiny desk clock ticked the seconds away in a sprawling office on the main floor of the Eisenhower Executive Office Building. In contrast to the cramped confines of the West Wing, the EEOB, across the road, offered spacious accommodations. The furniture was aging and mismatched, and didn't look like it had ever been particularly nice. But the high ceilings and large windows made even the smaller offices feel open and airy. The overhead lights were turned off, as I sat patiently on an uncomfortable couch, listening to the barely audible clock marking each second. But I could see dust particles moving slowly through the air, thanks to two giant windows allowing shards of light to stab through the thin shroud of darkness.

I was doing what nearly anyone trying to talk to Steve Bannon had to do: wait for him to finish sending a text message.

Bannon was working out of the EEOB while the West Wing had its decades-old air-conditioning unit replaced. The President, the Chief, and a handful of the President's closest aides had decamped to Trump's retreat in Bedminster, New Jersey. I was going to join them in the next few days. Bannon, tellingly, was not. He was fully on the outside looking in for the first time since he signed on to be CEO of Trump's campaign. Since he had raged to the point of panic at me over what he saw as my efforts to undermine Priebus, I'd asked to come by to hear how he was feeling about the new regime. He was seated behind a desk—something I wasn't used to seeing—and he was in good spirits, at least in his own way.

"Okay, done," he barked, standing up from his desk after firing off his text. He walked over toward me. "Listen, me and the General are great," he said, getting right to the point.

Steve seemed genuinely enthusiastic. "This is the best thing that could have happened. We're on the same page. He knows the border is f—ed. He dealt with it [as Secretary of Homeland Security]. It's going to be good."

I told him I was glad to hear that, but that things were going to be dramatically different from how they were under Reince—probably in both good ways and bad.

"Look, dude," he said. "I'm a Navy guy, he's a Marine. It's going to work out fine."

Steve was putting on a brave face, but surely, I thought, he must feel the walls closing in around him. He had all but run out of friends in senior roles by this point. He couldn't possibly be that out of it. Sure enough, I found out later that he had slipped out of town for a day to meet with the Mercer family, major financial backers of *Breitbart* and longtime Bannon benefactors. He was exploring what it was going to look like for him to return to the private sector. Just in case.

As Steve and I continued discussing the new Chief, I heard the door handle jiggling, but knew whoever it was wouldn't be able to get in. Some of the EEOB offices had electronic locks. To enter, you either needed to punch in a pass code or someone on the inside needed to press a button to unlock it. This was one of those offices. A few moments later, I could hear a female voice apologizing and nervous fingers frantically punching in the pass code. This was followed by the loud *snap* of a lock disengaging and the slow creaking of a heavy wooden door easing open to reveal the man who Steve, unbeknownst to me, had been waiting for—the Attorney General of the United States.

I hopped up to greet Sessions, whose expression made me feel like he was pleasantly surprised to see a fellow Alabamian. We hadn't seen each other much since we both joined the administration, outside of an occasional dinner with our wives or a quick catch-up by phone. We were both weathering storms, although mine were more like scattered showers compared to the hurricane he often found himself enduring.

I'm not sure who had requested to meet with whom, but Bannon and Sessions were longtime allies, and now they were both Trump administration outsiders. Sessions joined Steve and me in the sitting area of his temporary office, and the conversation quickly turned to a familiar topic: leaks. But these leaks—the ones that were concerning Sessions—weren't the kind that so often consumed the West Wing. The leaks that had made it onto Sessions's radar were the ones that jeopardized U.S. national security.

A few days earlier, transcripts of classified conversations between Trump and the leaders of Mexico and Australia had been published in *The Washington Post*. During the calls, Trump had urged the President of Mexico to pay for the construction of a border wall and sought to walk back an agreement President Obama had struck with the Prime Minister of Australia to accept two thousand refugees currently detained in his country. The leaks were universally condemned, even by the fiercest Trump critics. Foreign leaders and diplomats around the world were shaken to think that conversations at the highest level of the U.S. government were no longer secure.

The day after the calls leaked, Sessions announced that the Trump administration had tripled the number of criminal investigations into illegal disclosures of classified information. He decried the "staggering number of leaks" that were undermining "the ability of our government to protect this country." The FBI, Sessions explained, had created an entirely new unit devoted to handling leak cases, which totaled more in the first six months of the Trump administration than in the previous three years combined.

"I have this warning for would-be leakers," he concluded. "Don't do it."

As Sessions sat down to talk to Steve and me, his frustration had only increased. "We've got to do something about it," he intoned.

"It's despicable," Bannon agreed. I noticed throughout the conversation that Bannon didn't seem to curse in his conversations with Sessions, a rare—and welcome—display of deference to someone he saw as an elder statesman and consummate Southern gentleman.

The term "deep state" had risen in popularity online among conservatives who believed that bureaucrats within the national security establishment were purposefully undermining Trump's presidency. Critics scoffed at these "conspiracy theorists." Sessions didn't use those words, but it quickly became apparent that he did believe there were an unusually high number of leakers—at least some of them holdovers from the Obama administration—who were releasing classified information. And they weren't doing it to "blow the whistle" on corruption. In fact, most of the leaks only revealed that Trump said the same things in private that he did in public. But the leakers still did their best to time their releases to inflict political damage on the President.

At his wit's end, Sessions had an idea. Transcripts of the foreign-leader calls were only accessible to a relatively small number of aides, most of them on the National Security Council staff. This small universe offered a potential opportunity to root out the leakers, or at least scare them into hiding for the foreseeable future.

"Some people have suggested a single-issue polygraph," Sessions said, pausing for a moment, perhaps to gauge Bannon's reaction.

Bannon leaned forward in his chair, wanting to hear more. The way it would work, Sessions briefly explained, was that each person who had access to those transcripts would be brought in and only asked about that one issue. The results might not be conclusive, much less actionable. Even if they showed deception, the DOJ historically didn't seem to favor using polygraphs in court proceedings. But when word got around that national security aides were sitting for lie detector tests, leakers would presumably crawl back into their holes, hopefully never to be heard from again.

"We're dealing with a bunch of spooks who know how to cover their tracks," Bannon said cynically. "They need a shot across the bow. One way or another they've gotta know we're serious." I didn't get the impression that Sessions was actually close to implementing the polygraph idea, but the fact that it was even within the realm of discussion indicated just how dire the situation had become.

"All right, Hammer—out," Bannon said finally. "The Attorney General and I gotta talk."

I stood up and shook Sessions's hand. "It was great to see you," he said, smiling. The lines around his eyes seemed to have deepened ever so slightly since his dream job had turned into something more closely resembling a nightmare. But he was hanging in there. "Tell Mrs. Mary I said hello," I replied, then found my way to the door.

It could have all gone so differently. After one of the presidential debates, I had sat next to Sessions on the campaign plane and listened to him and Bannon debate everything from Middle East strategy to budget policy. Together, along with Stephen Miller, they had built the intellectual framework that turned Trump's raw, gut instincts into actual policy positions. But Sessions's recusal on Russia—a principled decision that nonetheless destroyed his relationship with the President—and Bannon's self-destructive streak would likely prevent their vision from ever being fully implemented the way it could have been.

That meeting was the last time I ever saw Steve on the White House's seventeen-acre complex.

Days later, Bannon inexplicably called up a left-wing, vehemently anti-Trump writer at an obscure publication called *The American Prospect* and gave him a random, albeit extraordinary, on-the-record interview.

He talked about "fight[ing] every day" with Gary Cohn and various other adversaries who were "wetting themselves" over his ideas to confront China on trade. He named a senior State Department official he was in the process of pushing out so that he could "get hawks in." And most outrageous of all, he declared that there was "no military solution [to North Korea's nuclear threats], forget it. . . . They got us."

It was strangely reminiscent of the meltdown that did Scaramucci in, except this time there were national security implications, and there was no way General Kelly was going to abide that.

Three days later, and about three weeks after the President tweeted Kelly's arrival, Trump tweeted Bannon's departure.

"I want to thank Steve Bannon for his service," he typed. "He came to the campaign during my run against Crooked Hillary Clinton—it was great! Thanks S." It felt like the end of an era. He and Trump had ridden a tornado together, and now it was dissipating back into the clouds.

I was weirdly saddened by how it all ended. There was a part of Steve Bannon that I loved, but in a disturbed kind of way. There are people, myself included at times, who can be painfully self-aware, always wrestling with whether we're good enough and obsessing over our shortcomings. And then there are people like him, people who genuinely believe they are giants of history. Bannon thought he was an action figure who had been stuck in a hermetically sealed package for decades until Trump finally freed him and brought him to life. I couldn't help but appreciate anyone who had the stones to be that grandiose.

Steve's perception of his departure was, predictably, Bannonesque. He viewed it less as a blow to him personally than as a pivotal moment in history. "The Trump presidency that we fought for, and won, is over," he declared in an interview with *The Weekly Standard.*

But not to worry, he was still going to find a way to complete his mission to save the country, maybe even the world. No longer burdened by the restraints of being a government employee, he had grand visions of leading a nationalist movement that would sweep across the globe.

"I can do whatever I need to do," he told me over the phone. "It's going to be epic, brother."

Kushner was the last man standing in the original Priebus-Bannon-Kushner triumvirate—which was wholly predictable from the start. But from my vantage point it looked increasingly like the Kelly and Cohn show.

Every once in a while over the previous year I would see a bald, bespectacled man in his sixties sitting in the West Wing lobby. He didn't seem to have any reason to be there. One day, after seeing him several times, I asked the receptionist who he was. "I think he's a journalist, or a writer, or something like that," she replied.

I thought that was strange; journalists weren't usually allowed outside of clearly defined press areas to just mill about. But I didn't think much of it.

I, along with the rest of the world, would later learn his name—Michael Wolff—and in January 2018, excerpts from his book *Fire and Fury* set the internet ablaze. Bannon was all over the book, on the record. Wolff quoted Bannon as saying that Donald Trump Jr.'s decision to meet with a Kremlin-connected lawyer during the campaign amounted to "treason." He went on to say that Special Counsel Robert Mueller's prosecution team would "crack Don Jr. like an egg on national TV."

There were other parts of the book that didn't ring true to me. Some of them were second- or thirdhand rumors. For example, he claimed Trump was displaying signs of deteriorating mental health; that none of the Trumps actually wanted to win the presidency, and when he did Melania broke down into tears of horror; and that Trump treated female staffers with "casual misogyny and constant sexual subtext." The inaccuracies in Wolff's book were too numerous to debunk them all. But his supposed insider's account confirmed what some people wanted to believe it must be like. However, it also included sporadic nuggets of truth, like the Bannon quotes, which he never denied making.

The President was understandably furious at Bannon—and confused by this epic self-immolation. Bannon, after all, had been trying very hard to stay in Trump's good graces; it was the key to his livelihood and continued relevance. Why, we all wondered, would Bannon act so recklessly by giving quotes to his guy, apparently while he still worked in the White House? I could only guess that he was seduced by the idea that this book would show his great contribution to history, and that overcame his judgment.

The President was as livid as anyone had ever seen him over this betrayal. Trump allies and surrogates were calling and texting senior members of the White House communications staff, asking how they should respond to the salacious quotes. Standing just outside the Oval Office, I asked Hope Hicks what she wanted me to do. Sitting behind the Resolute desk, Trump overheard my question.

"Cliff!" he yelled from his desk. "Tell them this: they're either with me or they're with Steve. That's it."

I looked back at Hope and raised my eyebrows. "It's time for choosing," she said. "And no one can have it both ways."

12

CUT CUT CUT

In mid-August 2017, I jumped through the open doors of an Acela passenger train moments before it left Washington's Union Station bound for New Jersey. It was summertime in the swamp. The heat was sweltering, and my rush to make the train had left me drenched in sweat underneath my dark blue suit.

Growing up in the South, I saw trains as more of a novelty than a legitimate mode of transportation. Some of my friends enjoyed a tradition of riding an Amtrak train from Birmingham to New Orleans to watch the Alabama Crimson Tide football team play in the Sugar Bowl, but that's about it. I'd completely avoided the subway in New York during the campaign, and had rarely ridden the Metro since moving to D.C. But if the President was at his private club in Bedminster, New Jersey, and you didn't catch a ride on Air Force One, the train was the next-best option.

The Acela train jolted to a start before I'd found my seat, briefly knocking me off balance. But I couldn't sit down yet. I was looking for Tony Sayegh, the former Fox News personality who'd been named Assistant Secretary of the Treasury. Tony, a New York native with a dark tan and perfectly coiffed hair, ran the Treasury Department's comms operation. Although we didn't yet know each other, a mutual friend had connected us upon finding out we'd be on the same train—and as fate would have it, with the same mission.

When I finally found Tony, I sat down across a table from him, plopped my bag down beside me, and shook his hand. We immediately hit it off. We both were on the way to Bedminster to meet with Hope Hicks for a communications strategy meeting. The President and congressional leaders were discussing a massive overhaul of the tax code. Everyone knew the stakes, and

Tony and I had both put together plans that would put us in the middle of the action.

A buzz was building in the press that in spite of Republicans controlling the entire government, Trump might end his first year as President with no major legislative accomplishments. Passing major legislation is a herculean task. The wildly unpredictable—and sometimes violent—swings of democracy had scared the Founders as much as monarchy, so they'd designed our republican system of government to make sweeping changes nearly impossible. This is a good thing for stability. But in the summer of 2017 I wanted to grab James Madison by his tiny shoulders, shake him as hard as I could, and yell at him for making our lives so difficult. *We really needed to pass this dang bill.*

By the time we arrived at the train station in New Jersey, Tony and I had combined our plans. We were going to pitch the idea of us partnering up to design and implement a communications strategy that would culminate with Congress overhauling the tax code for the first time since Ronald Reagan was President.

The plan was almost derailed before it even had a chance, though. When we got off the train, Tony asked me where the proposal was. I'd left it in the overhead storage compartment. I sprinted back into the train car and found it sitting right where I'd left it. Mini disaster averted.

As a staffer drove us slowly around the Bedminster golf course toward the President's villa, it was easy to see why Trump loved the property. The trees lining the driveway were swaying in the light breeze, with the immaculate grass on one of the fairways visible through their leafy branches. The rolling New Jersey countryside served as the perfect backdrop for the Georgian-style clubhouse, which was once the home of John DeLorean, whose namesake car was made famous by the *Back to the Future* movies. A few hundred yards past the clubhouse, we arrived at Trump's luxury cottage, a white brick home with a steep pitched roof. The backside of the house included a two-story, cylindrical tower overlooking a large swimming pool. That's where Hope was waiting for us.

She was seated under an awning outside of the snack shop by the pool, and much more relaxed than I was accustomed to seeing her. She was wearing a skirt and a white blouse with her hair pulled back.

Hope was a little bit of a conundrum. She could be vulnerable, down-home, a Southerner in spirit. She listened to country music. But she could also be aggressive—even cold—sophisticated and elusive. Her mom was from the South and her dad was a Northerner. She'd attended college at Southern Methodist University, but she'd lived most of her life in the Northeast. Her personality was part New York City and part front porch of a country farmhouse—all mixed into one.

No one I knew hated living in D.C. more than Hope. In a city where the most highly anticipated annual event is literally nicknamed "Nerd Prom," she, Ivanka, and the First Lady had burst onto the scene looking like they'd been torn out of the pages of *Vogue*. But while FLOTUS was living in the world's most secure building and Ivanka seemed to generally enjoy the attention, Hope longed for Manhattan, where, as she put it to me, "no one cares who you are."

After we finished up our tax reform planning, Hope and I stuck around and talked awhile longer. Scaramucci's implosion had left the comms team with a lot of uncertainty. To that point, Hope's job—Director of Strategic Communications—had given her unfettered access to the President without the day-to-day responsibilities of managing a large staff. But Trump was nudging her to take over the entire department. She was apprehensive about it. In truth, there wasn't much upside for her, just more headaches. But she also seemed anxious to take on a new challenge that might prepare her for whatever she'd go on to do next. She was still only twenty-eight years old.

As we talked, Jared Kushner walked through the pool area and spotted us. Normally in a perfectly tailored suit, Kushner was now wearing lightweight dark pants, a gray T-shirt, and sunglasses.

"Take your tie off, Cliff!" he called out to me. "This is Bedminster—you can relax here!"

I smiled, flashed a thumbs-up, and loosened up my Carolina blue tie.

Jared and Ivanka shared a cottage right across from Trump's, and it looked very similar, although it did not have the two-story tower on the back side. Jared walked into the snack shop and sat down at a table with Jason Greenblatt, a former Trump Organization attorney turned White House Special Representative for International Negotiations. I assumed they were huddling about the administration's Middle East peace efforts, in which they were both integrally involved.

General Kelly, settling into his new job, walked through not long after that, wearing a T-shirt and jeans, ever-present scowl still on his face. He didn't seem to notice us.

"You have to take this job," I finally told Hope. "First, it's the best thing for the President. He's not going to trust anyone to do that job like he trusts you. Second, it's a good thing for you—a new experience. And third, and I know this is selfish, but it'd make the campaign folks feel a lot better about everything. A lot of them have been completely screwed to this point."

She didn't seem to disagree with any of those points.

"Do you know who Mercedes Schlapp is?" she asked toward the end of the conversation. I had to google her, but when her picture came up I recognized her from Fox News. She and her husband, Matt, were both former Bush administration officials. He had been Bush's political director and she had served as a spokesperson to Spanish-language media.

"There's some discussion about her coming into the White House, too," Hope explained. "What do you think?"

What did I think? The guy who pushed the President to hire the Mooch? Let's just say that I didn't feel inclined to get involved in any more staffing decisions for the time being. Still, I liked Hope a lot and wanted to be of help to her.

I noted that it could be helpful to have another experienced spokesperson who could go on TV and defend the President. Hope was uninterested in brawling in the rough-and-tumble world of television punditry. That wasn't the value she brought to the table anyway; she was comfortable enough in her own skin to acknowledge that she was a novice when it came to policy and politics. And there were other people—like Kellyanne—to toss into the shark tank. Hope's value was that she knew Trump, all of his likes, dislikes, quirks, and eccentricities. In planning meetings she was the authority on what events, interviews, or settings he would and wouldn't feel comfortable with. A single word from Hope could squash weeks of planning if she felt like it wasn't up to snuff or sufficiently on brand. However, there was always room in Trump World for a telegenic female surrogate willing to fight it out on the airwaves, and maybe Mercedes fit that bill. I didn't know. On the flip side, if she wasn't a team player, she'd be yet another senior comms official elbowing around, trying to carve out space for herself.

We would soon learn there was a deeper motive behind this selection.

Factionalism didn't end just because there was a new Chief of Staff in charge. In some ways, it only got worse.

Several weeks later, Tony Sayegh and I were sitting among staff assistants on the top floor of the West Wing. The ceilings were low and the wood paneling in some of the rooms made it feel a little bit like the executive suite of a 1960s law firm. But this was prime real estate, because the offices were generally larger than ours down on the main floor below.

The National Economic Council was given internal supremacy over all other White House departments when it came to getting the tax bill passed. Gary Cohn, the Director, was leading the charge, along with Treasury Secretary Steven Mnuchin, another Goldman Sachs alumnus. Cohn and Mnuchin shared a friendly rivalry. This sometimes put Tony Sayegh in an awkward position. As Assistant Secretary of the Treasury, he worked directly for Mnuchin. But when it came to the tax push, Cohn wasn't going to subordinate himself to anyone other than Donald J. Trump.

The door to Cohn's office swung open and a handful of aides streamed out. Peering in, I could see Gary sitting at the head of his conference table. He was leaning back, with his chair on two legs, and glancing at CNBC airing on a small flat-screen TV set up in the corner beside him.

"You guys can go on in," his assistant, Kaitlyn Eisner-Poor, said.

In the weeks since we had hatched our plan with Hope at Bedminster, Tony had become known as "Tax Man" to most of the staff. But to Gary, he was always "Taxing Tony."

"Get in here, Taxing Tony," Cohn said as we walked in the door.

I took a seat at the end of the table opposite from Cohn, and Tony sat midway down the table, closer to him. I glanced at the opposite corner of the room and saw the gray Ohio State University football helmet sitting on the shelf. We'd often go back and forth about which college football program was better, his Buckeyes or my Tide. But not today.

"Tony, let me ask you a question," Cohn began. Tony nodded his head, put his pen down on the table, and leaned back in his chair.

"Am I a co-principal in tax reform?" he asked.

"Of course," Tony replied. "You and the Secretary are co-principals leading the team."

"Is that right?" Cohn replied sarcastically. "Because I've got to tell you, Tony, I'm not feeling like a co-principal right now."

I laughed quietly at the other end of the table. I genuinely thought he was joking. He wasn't, and Tony knew it. As it turns out, Mnuchin had released a statement about one of the negotiating points on the tax bill, but Cohn's statement had somehow not gone out from the White House. As a result, Gary felt like he was being given second billing.

"I take responsibility for that," Tony said, taking the heat like a pro. "I approved the release of the Secretary's statement. I'll make sure everything is perfectly coordinated going forward so these types of things happen simultaneously."

Gary had a habit of pushing his tongue into the side of his mouth as he listened, causing his cheek to bulge out on one side. That, combined with his furrowed brow, created an even more intimidating persona, on top of his imposing size. He finally sat forward, bringing his chair back down onto all four feet, and leaned across the table.

"You work for me, too, now, Tony, and so do you," he said, looking down at me. "So I just want to make sure everyone's clear on that."

We were. In truth, this was a conversation that probably would have happened at some point anyway, so it was better to get it out of the way early on.

Every other interaction I ever had with Gary was positive. All he really cared about was performance, and you can bet we wouldn't have lasted if we weren't at the top of our game. But he made it clear from that point forward that he and Mnuchin were going to be on equal footing in every way. He'd left one of the top jobs in the finance world because he saw a chance to overhaul the tax code, which could impact the economy for decades. He hadn't done that to take a backseat to anyone.

If you want to identify a White House's priorities, look no further than the President's schedule. Who's he meeting with? Where's he traveling? His time is the single most valuable asset any administration has, and everyone wants a piece of it. So whatever—or whoever—actually makes it onto his calendar must be important. And anything that pops up on a recurring basis must be *really* important.

Word went out across the entire White House that our tax team had top billing on the President's schedule for the rest of the year. We worked closely with the NEC and the political and legislative affairs teams to map out a schedule that included consistent travel to targeted districts and states. This meant a lot of traversing the country on Air Force One.

Most of these flights were relatively uneventful. The President typically stayed up front in his office, rolling through phone calls and chatting with senior aides popping in and out. Otherwise we were in the staff cabin working, chatting, watching TV, or taking full advantage of the top-notch food service (we had to pay for it individually). The best recurring prank, though, was compliments of Johnny McEntee. During his countless hours of downtime waiting for the President to finish up meetings, he'd become a master at forging Trump's signature. He'd come rushing back to the staff cabin with a "message from the President" scrawled on a piece of paper folded in half. The unsuspecting victim would open it up to find a note—usually angry, occasionally laudatory—in Trump's recognizable, all-caps penmanship.

I was the target of one of Johnny's best schemes. He passed me a note during one flight that said, "Cliff—Print out today's top Breitbart stories and bring them to me. Do not tell Gen. Kelly." Upon his arrival in the West Wing, Kelly had famously choked off the information flow to the President. No articles, proposals, or ideas were supposed to reach Trump without first going through the Staff Secretary's office and then receiving final sign-off from the Chief. The last thing I wanted to do was run afoul of Kelly's explicit directive, but what was I supposed to do if the President of the United States was giving me a direct order? My heart rate was rising, and the look of horror on my face made Johnny crack. He burst out laughing, and to my great relief I realized I was his latest victim. The funniest and most brilliant part of it all was how realistic it was. Of course, issuing such an order was exactly something Trump would do.

Long flights also offered great opportunities to get to know people, from colleagues and Cabinet secretaries to members of Congress. Much as Tony had to get acquainted with the White House staff when he first came over from the Treasury Department, I wanted to get to know the Treasury team, including Secretary Mnuchin. And I thought I had come up with a pretty good icebreaker for him whenever the time came for us to get to know each other— a reference to one of his movies.

From the staff cabin on one tax reform trip, Tony saw Mnuchin standing in the hallway just outside the conference room and motioned for me to follow him. The Secretary was making small talk with his Chief of Staff, Eli Miller, and Tony interjected, "Mr. Secretary, this is Cliff Sims. He's running the messaging for tax reform and I wanted you guys to get better acquainted." We exchanged pleasantries, and when there was a brief lull, my icebreaker idea popped into my head.

"Mr. Secretary," I began, "there was a small group of us on the campaign in Trump Tower who basically spent all day fighting with the press over their coverage. It was such a ragtag group of characters and our mission was so impossible that we jokingly started calling ourselves 'The Suicide Squad' . . . I figured you might get a kick out of that."

He didn't.

After a moment of awkward silence, Mnuchin looked at Tony and said, "Mmm, Tony, let's get together in a few minutes to talk about this event." He walked away without acknowledging what I'd said. Maybe he didn't like the movie? Maybe he thought I was making fun of his work? Maybe he hadn't even been listening to what I was saying? Regardless of the reason for his reaction, Tony and I were left walking back to the staff cabin, laughing so hysterically at my epic embarrassment that we were gasping for air.

Back at the White House, Tony developed a "playbook"—managed by my old campaign war room colleague Kaelan Dorr—that acted as a checklist for every event and ensured every member of the team was engaged, knew their role, and was held accountable for executing it. I sat down with three of the President's top speechwriters—Vince Haley, Ross Worthington, and Ted Royer—and built what we called the "messaging architecture" for tax reform. These were the words everyone used to sell the plan to the public. Meanwhile, Cohn and Mnuchin—along with their top tax policy aides, Shahira Knight and Justin Muzinich—hammered out the details of the legislation with their counterparts on Capitol Hill.

For the first time since I'd been at the White House, it felt like the staff machine was actually working, even humming. And we were having fun. Well, some of us were. In other parts of the White House, resentment was growing.

Along with Hope's elevation to comms director, Mercedes Schlapp joined the staff, at General Kelly's behest, with the title of Senior Adviser for Strategic Communications. Kelly clearly viewed Hope as an inexperienced, naïve young girl who could not be fully trusted to oversee the embattled comms team. He also knew that there was no way on earth that he could push Hope out; the President loved her too much. Instead Schlapp was brought in to be his eyes and ears. The Schlapp hire seemed to contradict the Chief's goal of eliminating overlapping and ill-defined jobs, but it was totally in keeping with existing White House modus operandi—surround yourself with allies.

It wasn't entirely clear to anyone what was included in Schlapp's portfolio, but what was clear to everyone was that being left out of tax reform—the administration's number-one priority—was driving her up the wall. She would constantly insert herself into the process of planning tax events around the country or at the White House, often setting various departments in motion, only to have to tell them "never mind" once it became clear that what she was doing was not part of the tax team's plan.

In an effort to diffuse the growing tension, Tony and I invited Mercedes to the Treasury Department's dining room for lunch. The dining room was a small but well-appointed space on the west side of the building, with an outdoor balcony overlooking the East Wing of the White House. The waitstaff was hospitable, and Tony and I ate there so much that they knew our names and regular orders by heart. We got a kick out of the fact that they would place nameplates atop the white-linened tables to signify who from the Treasury Department's senior staff was dining there that day. Tony would jokingly turn his nameplate toward me when we'd sit down, lest I forgot how big a deal he was.

When we sat down to dine with Mercedes, the conversation began cordially. Like a large number of Trump appointees, Tony and Mercedes had both been Fox News contributors. As a result, they had been friendly for years. But Mercedes wasn't even halfway through her salad when her anger boiled over.

As I sat there awkwardly, her face reddened and she launched in at Tony. Who did he think he was to come in and take over tax reform? He was arrogant, a bull in a china shop, not a team player. For a minute I forgot whether I was having lunch with the affable Tony Sayegh that I knew—the guy who literally made it a game to greet every single person as he walked back in the EEOB, whether he knew them or not—or the maniacal Mr. Burns from *The Simpsons*. Tony took it all in stride, much as he had when Gary lit into him before.

During a rare moment when Mercedes took a breath, in an admittedly lame attempt to ease tensions, I commented on the food. "I think this is the best salmon I've had since we started coming here," I said earnestly. "The glaze is perfect."

Tony looked at me across the table in utter disbelief. He was getting accused of all kinds of nonsense, and the best I could muster was a compliment on the salmon glaze? In every subsequent retelling of that story, Tony would refer to me as "Foxhole Sims," the last guy you wanted to be in a foxhole with when the bullets started flying. We'd laugh, genuinely befuddled by Mercedes's outburst. But it would later become a serious problem.

The fact of the matter was that the tax team was operating outside of the formal White House structure. This was a mandate from the Chief. He called us the "tiger team," a military term for a small group of handpicked specialists brought together to plan and execute a specific mission. Regardless, good staff work wasn't going to be nearly enough to pass the largest tax reform package in thirty years. Pulling that off was going to require the President to put himself out there in a way he had not needed to up until that point. He was going to have to risk something.

After a messaging briefing with some of the White House's top outside allies, Newt Gingrich cornered me. The seventy-four-year-old former Speaker of the House was a fascinating character. I'd found his reputation as an idea machine to be generally accurate—a lot of them were genuinely brilliant, a fair number of them were borderline crazy, but no matter what, they were always interesting. As he approached me, his chin was tucked and his facial expression suggested he was in a serious mood. If he'd been wearing glasses, he would have been looking at me over the top of them.

"We're about to have a serious problem on our hands," he said right away.

"What's going on?" I asked intently.

"You guys have got to start pushing Congress to get this tax bill done this year—it *has* to be this year. You should start publicly calling for them to do it by Thanksgiving in hopes that it forces them to finish by the end of the year. Otherwise they're going to try to slow the momentum down and ask for more time."

Gingrich had served in Congress for twenty years, including four years as Speaker of the House. If anyone could forecast the whims of 435 politicians whose only sense of urgency seemed to revolve around the date of their next election, it was Newt. And his prediction proved prescient. Days later I got a phone call from one of Paul Ryan's top aides. "Our members are expressing some concerns about setting expectations too high in terms of timeline on the tax bill," he said. "We're going to go as fast as we can, but realistically it's going to be tough to get it done this year."

I exhaled in a long, quiet sigh. Gingrich had called it, but I was still annoyed. In fairness, though, I had been there when they'd set the timelines for the health-care bill, only to watch them all get blown up. Perhaps their concerns were well founded. "Is there any way you could talk to the President about not being too vocal about timing?" Ryan's aide asked. "It'd obviously look bad for him—for all of us—if Congress wasn't able to meet an arbitrary deadline."

Walking from the West Wing toward the residence, I broached the subject with the President. I told him the Speaker's office had expressed concerns with him publicly putting a hard deadline on passing tax reform. He wasn't even slightly interested in what some staff member in Ryan's office was suggesting. Before I'd even finished my explanation—in which I planned to lay out their reasoning, then say I thought he should actually push harder—he had an idea.

"Tax cuts for Christmas," he said. "That's what it's going to be."

Not long after that conversation, Trump hosted Republican congressional leaders for a lunch in the Cabinet Room. With Paul Ryan sitting to his right and Kevin Brady, chairman of the tax-writing House Ways and Means Committee, sitting to his left, Trump declared, "We'll have it done before Christmas, and that will be one of the great Christmas presents."

I jumped into hyperdrive making sure news outlets latched on to this comment. TRUMP PROMISES "BIG, BEAUTIFUL" TAX CUTS FOR CHRISTMAS, read the *Washington Examiner* headline later that day. TRUMP: TAX CUT IS MY GIFT TO YOU and TRUMP SEES TAX PLAN AS CHRISTMAS GIFT added CNN and *The Wall Street Journal*. Expectations were set. The Speaker's office never mentioned delaying the date again.

Meanwhile, I was continuously huddling with the President's speechwriting team to keep the messaging fresh. As we all know, no two Trump speeches were the same—not even close. But in terms of the prepared remarks, the outline was the same. So we tried to add a new element each time, whether it was a specific policy announcement or a new headline-grabbing quip—and hoped that Trump would decide to use it.

I spent a weekend watching every speech Ronald Reagan gave selling his tax overhaul in the early 1980s. While Reagan and Trump were stylistically far apart, the way they spoke directly to blue-collar workers and families in Middle America was remarkably similar. A phrase popped into my head, "middle-class miracle"—that's what we believed this tax cut was going to produce. During a speech in Indiana, Trump rolled it out.

"Democrats and Republicans in Congress should come together finally," he said, "and deliver this giant win for the American people, and begin the middle-class miracle—it's called a middle-class miracle—once again."

I made another round of phone calls and fired off texts and emails encouraging news outlets to pick up on this new phrase. ABC, NBC, CNBC, *Roll Call,* the *Washington Examiner,* and numerous others all used it in their headlines. But it didn't always work exactly as planned, as we found out with our next messaging creation—that the tax cuts would be "rocket fuel for the economy."

We'd had so much success with securing glowing headlines before, I was hoping to repeat the process again: Trump delivers the remark, I highlight it to reporters, positive headlines come flowing in.

During an event in St. Charles, Missouri, I was scrolling through the prepared remarks on my phone as Trump delivered them. "The tax cut will mean more companies moving to America, staying in America, and hiring American workers right here. So that's so important, right?"

The crowd applauded. *Okay, here we go . . .* "Because these massive tax cuts will be rocket fuel . . ." The President paused midsentence for no apparent reason. I looked up from my phone to see if something had gone wrong with the teleprompter. It hadn't. But now the crowd had begun to chuckle. They could sense what was coming, and suddenly so could I. Days before, Trump had dubbed North Korean dictator Kim Jong-un "Little Rocket Man," sending the foreign policy world—well, the whole world, really—into a frenzy. Our decision to include the word "rocket" in his remarks had triggered this memory and brought a mischievous smile to his face.

"Little Rocket Man!" he declared, giving the crowd exactly what they wanted and sending them into hysterics, before finishing the original sentence. "Rocket fuel for the American economy." The crowd cheered, before Trump added one more barb at Kim. "He is a sick puppy." Thankfully, plenty of news outlets—the Associated Press and *The New York Times* among them—still put "rocket fuel for the economy" in their headlines. Our good run continued.

Back at the White House, Trump worked the phones constantly. If someone mentioned in a meeting that a lawmaker was waffling or didn't like a part of the tax plan, the President would call out for his assistant Madeleine to call them up. If a policy briefing alerted him to something he wanted the bill writers to take a look at, he'd have her get them on the line right away. The same for television hosts or guests, if he saw something that piqued his interest. In one memorable instance, I was with him in the private dining room when an obscure economist came on Fox News to talk about how Trump was right, the tax bill would spur economic growth. He paused our conversation and watched the segment intently.

"This guy's great!" he said, jotting down the man's name with a black Sharpie. "Who is he?"

I didn't know; neither of us had ever heard of him. The President shouted for Madeleine to come in, and she didn't let her stilettos slow her down as she speed-walked through the Oval Office and down the hall to where the President was sitting. "I want to talk to this gentleman as soon as possible," he said, handing her the note with his name on it. I didn't hang around long enough to hear the call, but I assume a relatively unknown economist—whose name I still can't remember—received a very unexpected call that day from the President of the United States.

In mid-October, as our tax reform push was in full swing, the White House was suddenly pulled into another unexpected media firestorm. Earlier in the month, four American service members had been killed during an ambush in Niger. The death of U.S. military personnel always hit the President hard, going back to the first one, Navy SEAL Ryan Owens, who was killed during a firefight with al-Qaeda militants in Yemen about a week after he took office.

Trump was one of the least sentimental individuals I had ever met. But when it came to military service members and their families, he had a soft spot. When people serving under him as commander in chief gave their lives, he seemed to feel a sense of duty to make sure their families knew he personally cared about them, that their loved one's sacrifice was not in vain.

So on a Monday afternoon, he picked up the phone in the Oval Office and called family members of the four American soldiers killed in Niger, including Myeshia Johnson, the widow of Sergeant La David T. Johnson, a twenty-five-year-old African American war hero from Miami. Unbeknownst to the President, Democratic Congresswoman Frederica Wilson was also listening in on the call. And within a matter of hours, she was publicly slamming the President for being insensitive, claiming he had callously told the Gold Star widow that her husband—whom he only referred to as "your guy"—"knew what he signed up for."

As I stood watching the drama unfold on TV in the West Wing press office, I couldn't think of anything to say about it other than, "This is messed up." Trump was not always innocent in such dust-ups. He was, after all, the same man who'd questioned former POW John McCain's military service during the campaign and attacked a Gold Star family during the Democratic National Convention. But in this particular instance, I had no doubt in my mind that Trump had done his best, undoubtedly in his own awkward way, to console a grieving widow, and a Democratic Congresswoman was cynically twisting it for political gain.

This was the kind of public spectacle that made my stomach churn. "Imagine what's going through the Chief's mind right now," Tony said, as we continued watching the fallout on TV. *Whoa, I hadn't thought about that.*

The Chief's son, Second Lieutenant Robert Kelly, had been killed in action in 2010 in Afghanistan, giving Kelly the tragic distinction of being the highest-ranking American military officer to lose a child in the conflict. I could only imagine how he must be feeling as mean-spirited politicians stirred up some of his most heartbreaking memories.

But as was often the case in the White House, we had to just put our heads down and keep working. We were preparing for a "radio row" event the following day, during which dozens of local, regional, and national radio hosts would descend on the White House for a chance to interview senior officials, including the President himself. The purpose of the event was to promote the President's tax plan, but when Trump arrived and sat down for an interview with Fox News host Brian Kilmeade, it didn't take long for the topic to turn to the controversy surrounding his phone call with the Gold Star widow.

"I mean, you could ask General Kelly did he get a call from Obama,"

Trump quipped. "You could ask other people, I don't know what Obama's policy was. I write letters and I also call."

I was standing right behind the President, tasked with guiding him from interview to interview, when he made the comment. And I immediately knew this was going to bring the most sensitive time of General Kelly's life into the world's most glaring spotlight—the last place he wanted it to be.

The following day, however, he tackled the issue head-on, and accomplished something I had not experienced before: he brought the entire White House to a standstill.

He wanted to speak out publicly, and decided to do it from the White House's biggest stage: the Press Briefing Room.

As he stepped behind the podium, even the usually rambunctious press corps took on a more somber mood. White House aides throughout the building stopped what they were doing, gathered around the nearest TV and turned up the volume. In the press office, we stood spellbound as Kelly explained in excruciating detail "what happens when we lose one of our soldiers, sailors, airmen, Marines, or Coast Guardsmen in combat.

"Their buddies wrap them up in whatever passes as a shroud, put them on a helicopter . . . and send them home," he explained. "Their first stop along the way is when they're packed in ice, typically at the airhead. And then they're flown to, usually, Europe, where they're then packed in ice again and flown to Dover Air Force Base, where Dover takes care of the remains, embalms them, meticulously dresses them in their uniform with the medals that they've earned, the emblems of their service, and then puts them on another airplane, linked up with a casualty officer escort, that takes them home."

Staffers were already fighting back tears as Kelly, the Gold Star father, continued his clinical description, trying to keep himself emotionally detached from his words.

"While that's happening, a casualty officer typically goes to the home very early in the morning and waits for the first lights to come on. And then he knocks on the door; typically a mom and dad will answer, a wife. . . . And the casualty officer proceeds to break the heart of a family member, then stays with that family until—well, for a long, long time, even after the interment."

I stepped out into the West Wing lobby for a moment to grab anyone who might not be aware of what was taking place, only to find uniformed Secret

Service agents, staffers, and even a handful of guests huddled around a tiny TV facing out to the lobby from a coat closet.

It was beginning to feel like a moment everyone would remember about their time in the White House. From there, Kelly turned to the topic of the day—the phone calls.

"I said to [the President], 'Sir, there's nothing you can do to lighten the burden on these families. . . . Let me tell you what my best friend, Joe Dunford, told me."

Kelly's voice cracked softly. The corners of his mouth dipped, and for the briefest moment it felt like the battle-hardened Marine might break down. He quickly composed himself, biting his bottom lip and looking down for a half second before continuing on.

"He said, 'Kel, he was doing exactly what he wanted to do when he was killed. He knew what he was getting into by joining that one percent [who serve in the military]. He knew what the possibilities were because we're at war. And when he died,' in the four cases we're talking about in Niger, and my son's case in Afghanistan, 'when he died, he was surrounded by the best men on this earth: his friends.'

"That's what the President tried to say to four families the other day."

Numerous White House aides were now in tears, and for perhaps the first time since we'd been there, it felt like an unexplainable sense of camaraderie was engulfing the building.

I emailed the Chief later that day—the only time I ever sent him a one-on-one email—and told him that, for many of us, it had been our proudest moment in the White House.

This is what it's supposed to feel like, I thought.

He never replied, and I never expected him to on such a busy and emotional day. Still, I was glad I told him that and I hoped he had a chance to read it.

As the tax push continued, and the House Ways and Means Committee inched closer to rolling out their version of the tax bill, Tony Sayegh called and mentioned that the Speaker's office wanted the President's input on naming the bill.

"What do you think about getting the brander-in-chief involved in coming up with the name?" Sayegh asked.

"Oh, I think he'd love that," I replied with a laugh. "I'll talk to him about it tomorrow."

The next day I walked with the President from the Oval Office to the State Dining Room to film the weekly address, which we were planning to film unscripted for the first time.

The President had grown frustrated reading from the teleprompter each week, and he felt the videos lacked the energy and improvisation that made him such a compelling figure to watch. We discussed various topics he could riff on and ultimately landed on teasing out his soon-to-be-announced decision on who he would appoint to be the new Chairman of the Federal Reserve.

After the recording sessions, we walked out of the State Dining Room into the Cross Hall and I mentioned to him that the Speaker's office wanted help naming the tax bill.

"They wanted to see if you'd like to put your branding genius to use," I told him.

His eyes lit up and a subtle smile appeared on his face. "They say I might be the world's greatest brander. I don't say that necessarily, but some people have said that."

The President gripped his belt buckle with both hands, leaned back on his heels, tilted his head back slightly, closed his eyes, and drew in a deep breath. For a few brief moments he stood silently, then his eyes opened and he drew his right hand up to shoulder height and held it in his patented "okay" sign.

"I've got it," he said, releasing his index finger and thumb. "We're going to call it 'the Cutting Cutting Cutting Bill.'"

I paused for a moment and considered. "Well, it definitely gets the point across," I said with a subtle laugh.

"People have got to quit calling it 'tax reform,'" he continued. "No one knows what that even means—'reform.' People think that's not going to help them. It might even be a tax increase. We've got to call it a tax 'cut' instead. And that's exactly what it is, it's a tax cut. Yeah, we are reforming, but mainly we're cutting. Make sure everyone knows that."

Having fully explained his view, the President decided he wanted to record a video announcing the name of the bill immediately. So we walked back into the State Dining Room, where the video crew was still set up, and explained that we were going to record one more message.

"My fellow Americans," the President began. "Many members of Congress have been asking me, 'Mr. President, what are we going to name the tax bill?' And I'm proud to announce today that we are naming it the Cutting Cutting Cutting Bill!"

As I looked around the room, every cameraman, teleprompter operator, lighting tech, photographer, and Secret Service agent had a giant smile on their face. They knew what a bizarre idea it was. *However,* I thought to myself, *it might also have a grain of genius in it.*

Ultimately, Trump seemed pleased, and that's all that really mattered, so we walked back over to the Oval Office, where I left the President to continue his work and went about informing our team about his bill-naming epiphany. As I recounted the story, the reactions varied from hysterical laughter, to confusion, to full-throated support, to vehement opposition.

"Wow, it sounds kind of violent," Sarah Huckabee Sanders told Tony and me in the Outer Oval as Hope sat laughing behind her desk.

But the President wasn't done. After sleeping on it, he came back with an updated version.

"I've given it some more thought," he said, smiling ear to ear. "It's too long. It's going to be 'the Cuts Cuts Cuts Bill.'"

I told him I'd found out that the bill's name actually needed to have "Act" at the end of it, and he came back one final time.

"Actually, it's still too long," he concluded. "This is it, make note of this: it's the Cut Cut Cut Act—no 's' at the end of 'cut.'" I told him I would let everyone know, and immediately started making phone calls, first to our team, and then to our counterparts on Capitol Hill.

Over the next several days, it became clear that Republican congressional leaders—or perhaps more accurately their staffs—were very much opposed to the President's recommendation. "We just can't do that," one Hill aide told me. "It's got to be more serious. You guys understand that, right?"

The more they pushed back, the more I grew to like the name. And they were the ones who had asked for his help in the first place. What'd they think they were going to get? This is the "Make America Great Again," "Drain the Swamp," and "Build the Wall" guy, after all.

When it became clear that Hill staffers would not relent, we set up a call with House Speaker Paul Ryan, Ways and Means Committee Chairman Kevin Brady, and the President. Hope Hicks, Tony Sayegh, Joyce Meyer from Legislative Affairs, and I sat around the Resolute desk as the President discussed the bill name with the two lawmakers.

"I'm surrounded right now by my marketing geniuses," the President said, winking to the group. "And I've got to tell you, I think I've got a great name for this bill—it's going to be really cool. We need to call it 'The Cut Cut Cut Act,' because this is a tax cut. When people hear the name, that's what we want people to know. And that's what they're going to know."

He paused. There was silence on the other end of the line.

"Now, I know what you guys like to do," he continued. "You like to name these bills something like 'The Economic Revitalization and Reforming . . .'" The President slumped in his chair and let out a giant snore. "Guys, people fall asleep before you can even get to the end of your bill names."

By that point, as Trump ridiculed senior Republican members of Congress, we were just trying not to be heard laughing in the background.

"So I really think if we name this thing 'The Cut Cut Cut Act,' people will love it and everyone will be talking about it. And best of all, everyone will remember what we're doing here—we're cutting taxes."

There was another brief moment of silence on the phone and then Brady spoke up. "You know, I think that's fine, Mr. President," he said. "Plus, people are always going to remember this as the Trump tax cuts when it's all over with, so I don't see a problem with us doing something a little different with the name."

The Speaker didn't interject, at least not then, so the issue seemed to be resolved, and the President hung up.

"These guys are going to learn one day," he told us. "Everyone's going to love it. They've really got to lighten up."

But at the staff level, the issue was most certainly not resolved. The Speaker's staff in particular was indignant that such an *unserious* name would be attached to such a *serious* bill. Their boss presumably agreed, although he did not have it in him to tell the President directly.

Within a matter of days the disagreements over the name leaked to the press and "Cut Cut Cut" immediately became the top trending topic on Twitter. Plenty of people derided the name and made fun of it. Of course, these were many of the same people who scoffed at "Make America Great Again." But others immediately got it. "Let's be real," tweeted conservative commentator and frequent Trump critic Ben Shapiro, "The Cut Cut Cut Act is better branding than anything the GOP has come up with in 20 years." Even the liberal publication *The Atlantic* declared it "effective branding," adding that "Congress is manifestly awful at naming its own bills."

But in the end the House rolled out a bill officially named The Tax Cuts and Jobs Act—the kind of snoozefest the President warned about. "They don't get it," the President later told me aboard Air Force One on the way to our next tax event. "Then again, maybe they were right on this one, who knows. We'll get it done anyway."

On December 6, 2017—as the tax push was entering the home stretch—I stood in the back of the Diplomatic Reception Room as Trump delivered remarks that sent shock waves around the world, particularly in the Middle East.

"I have determined that it is time to officially recognize Jerusalem as the capital of Israel. While previous presidents have made this a major campaign promise, they failed to deliver. Today, I am delivering."

The day after the announcement was made, the President walked out of the Oval Office into the Outer Oval, where I was waiting to walk him into the Cabinet Room to record a video. His attention immediately went to the muted television hanging on the wall. Images of Palestinians protesting the Jerusalem decision were flashing across the screen.

"How widespread is it?" Trump asked.

"It's hard to tell," I replied. "They always just show footage from the hot spots."

Some protesters screamed "Down with America!" and "Down with Israel!" while others chanted in rhythm, "Trump, Trump, you will see— Palestine will be free."

They torched American flags and burned posters of the President's face. Angry mobs stomped on his picture and others hanged him in effigy. As we continued to watch, I felt an urge to look away. It reminded me of the feeling I get when I see someone trip and stumble in public. Their instinct is to immediately look around to see if anyone noticed; my instinct is to look away so they won't feel embarrassed.

The President had done nothing wrong. He had taken a stand and made good on a promise that Clinton, Bush, and Obama had all bailed on. I was proud of what he had done—we all were. But I could not help but feel uncomfortable as he calmly watched a mob carry a stuffed Trump through the streets hanging on a cross.

I find it difficult to explain what it feels like to watch that level of hatred being displayed on TV screens all over the world while standing right next to the person at whom the hatred is being directed. And yet the President was the calm in the eye of the storm. He watched the segment casually but intently, without his usual running commentary. And when it concluded, he turned to me without seeming to have been affected negatively in any way and asked—à la President Jed Bartlet in *The West Wing*—"What's next?"

I learned something important from the President that day—something that I have tried to make a core operating principle in my life: you have to make peace with being misunderstood.

Disruption always brings out critics. Some of them will be well-meaning critics who have a different perspective or opinion. Others will be not-so-well-meaning critics with ulterior, selfish motives. Either way, the longer you're willing to be misunderstood, the bigger, more disruptive change you can deliver. I often feel an insatiable desire to be understood, to explain myself. Even as I write these words, I cringe at the thought of people misjudging my motives. I marveled at Trump's willingness to endure a seemingly limitless amount of criticism and never waver. He was fearless—the rarest of traits among politicians. If he believed he was doing the right thing, he was willing to weather any storm.

And yet Trump always remained a walking contradiction. He was the bravest person I'd ever seen in the face of public scrutiny, but resented relatively mild critiques from his aides. He was arguably the toughest political combatant in modern American history, but often shied away from making much-needed staff changes that would cause conflict in private. He was an idealist—a true believer in his populist, nationalist worldview—but pragmatically cut deals with anyone willing to make an interesting offer. He was less afraid to do the right thing—the difficult thing—than anyone I'd ever met, but sometimes seemed to lack the guiding principles that could lead him to what exactly the "right thing" was.

As winter descended on Washington, the President's self-imposed Christmas deadline was fast approaching and our operation had a lot of moving pieces. Among the most important of those moving pieces was Ivanka.

The press emptied countless barrels of ink analyzing the role of the First Daughter—and she was the first in every sense of the word, even though the President had other children and a second female child. To many, her appointment to the White House staff reeked of nepotism. *What does she know about running a country?* When she briefly filled the President's seat among world leaders at the G-20 summit, the internet outrage machine kicked into high gear. UNELECTED, UNQUALIFIED, a *Washington Post* headline noted. Her ceremonial duties and their family's occasional vacations also earned them some additional critics inside the West Wing who accused them of "playing government." Kellyanne was predictably resentful of both Ivanka's and Jared's immovable status in Trump's orbit. And Bannon used to occasionally rant about her "going into Daddy's office and putting her head down on his desk" to try to get what she wanted.

In fairness, as she would herself acknowledge, Ivanka had very little experience in politics and government. And at times I sensed a fair amount of naïveté, which, on the other hand, could have been explained away as an absence of D.C. cynicism. After all, in many instances I could easily be accused of being naïve, too. An unprecedented number of us, in fact, had come into government from the private sector, having experienced success at various scales, and we were applying our skills to new challenges, in a new setting.

The Washington establishment from both parties wants the country to think "governing" is some kind of superhuman skill that the rest of us mere mortals could never understand. During my time in D.C., I met kings, conversed with princes, dined with diplomats, and shook hands with some of the wealthiest people in human history. In every one of those experiences, even when I walked away impressed, I harbored the same nagging feeling: they're not any smarter than me—or you, or most people that I hang out with or work alongside. This experience is both horrifying and liberating—realizing that, as Apple founder Steve Jobs once said, "Everything around you that you call life was made up by people who were no smarter than you."

Ivanka was and is a valuable asset to the President for a simple reason: he trusts her. This was the kind of trust John F. Kennedy had in his brother, Bobby, when he was nominated for Attorney General. Or Bill and Hillary had in Chelsea when they let her run a two-hundred-million-dollar enterprise, the Clinton Foundation. He wasn't acquiescing to her every wish, especially on policy issues. Quite the opposite, in fact. But at the very least she eased his moods and made him happy. And for a mercurial leader like Trump, that's not nothing. No one wants the alternative.

In my experience, Ivanka also happened to be one of the most persuasive surrogates the President had, both in terms of selling his agenda to the public and in twisting the arms of wavering members of Congress. On tax reform, both of those talents proved valuable.

The main issue we were facing at the time was that the President was preparing to spend almost two weeks in Asia. There was nothing we could do about the fact that this long-scheduled trip was happening right in the middle of the biggest legislative push of his young presidency. We had to be able to juggle both foreign and domestic affairs. While he was gone, we knew that Ivanka was one of the few people we could deploy to targeted districts and states around the country and generate enough news coverage that it would have a real impact. So we mapped out an aggressive travel schedule that would send her into the suburban areas where she was extraordinarily popular.

Tony and I then went into the Chief's office to get his sign-off on the plan, which included extensive travel for both Cabinet secretaries and Ivanka. "Fine," he said. "But Ivanka needs to understand that this isn't just one of her pet projects. And she needs to stay in her lane and not start talking about whatever else it is that she likes to say in these interviews."

Ummmm, okay?

We didn't react to this comment—we both considered Ivanka a friend, in addition to being our colleague—but it told us all we needed to know about how Kelly regarded her and viewed her role in the West Wing. The look he had on his face while talking about her made it seem like there was a dead skunk somewhere in the room. His tone was dripping with contempt. And we weren't even close with the Chief; there's no telling what he was saying to his confidants.

In any event, Ivanka was all-in and traversed the country on commercial flights and trains, surrounded by her Secret Service detail, selling the tax bill in any venue she could. She and Secretary Mnuchin also traveled together to an event at the Reagan Library in California, invoking the memory of the last time a Republican-led tax cut triggered an economic boom.

In addition to her public sales role, Ivanka worked behind the scenes to leverage the personal relationships she had developed with some of the Republican senators who were the most at odds with her father. This group included moderate Susan Collins of Maine and Bob Corker of Tennessee, a prickly senator who had called the Trump White House an "adult day-care center."

Ivanka and Jared hosted them and other senators for dinner at their opulent eighty-two-hundred-square-foot home in Kalorama, and she spoke to them frequently, both in their Capitol Hill offices and on the phone. She also deployed to high-tax states—mostly in the Northeast—where the tax bill was particularly controversial because it eliminated federal deductions for state and local taxes.

In early December, we experienced a major setback when Corker announced he would not support the bill. This set off a mad scramble to address his concerns, with Ivanka as the tip of the spear. We might be able to pass the bill without him, but in a Senate that had only fifty-two Republicans, that would be cutting it way too close.

In the second week of December, while he was walking up the West Wing driveway, Tony Sayegh's phone rang. It was Ivanka.

Tony stopped walking, leaned up against the fence in front of the West Wing, and answered the call. This was a somewhat risky move. The driveway on the North Lawn is one of the few areas of the White House where press are allowed to roam freely, back and forth between the press room and the tents where they record their TV hits with the White House residence in the background. But he was immediately engrossed in whatever Ivanka was saying and oblivious to whatever might be happening around him.

Suddenly, Tony bit his bottom lip and pumped his right fist in the air. Covering the phone with one hand, he said the words that very likely meant we were going to get the bill across the finish line: "Corker's a yes." Ivanka—along with Secretary Mnuchin spending a great deal of time walking him through the numbers—had won him over.

Hanging up the phone with Ivanka, Tony rushed across the street to the Treasury Department, where Mnuchin was taking pictures with staff at their annual holiday party. He whispered the news in his ear, and Mnuchin slowly pulled back to look him in the eye. He knew victory was within reach. In the end, lawmakers in every district Ivanka targeted voted in favor of the bill, a fact that contradicted blanket criticisms of her time in the White House as being substance free.

On December 13, with less than two weeks to go before the Christmas deadline, we were on the one-yard line and Trump was about to deliver his final speech on tax reform—his "closing argument," as we were framing it to reporters.

It was a cold, crisp Wednesday afternoon, and Tony and I were waiting for Trump in the State Dining Room. This was the second-largest room on the State Floor of the White House and one of my personal favorites because it had been Thomas Jefferson's primary office. As we waited, I looked over to the southwest corner of the room, where Jefferson's desk once sat. I could almost picture my favorite Founder reading dispatches from the Lewis and Clark Expedition, or weighing whether to approve Napoleon's offer to sell the Louisiana Territory. After being in the White House for ten months, it wasn't often anymore that I was cognizant of the history I was living. This was different. The Reagan tax cuts, and the subsequent economic explosion, were the stuff of legend in Republican circles. I couldn't help but wonder if the Trump tax cuts would be that for the next generation.

My phone vibrated in my pocket—"Unknown," the screen said. This almost always meant a White House number; some senior staff maintained the caller ID screening function for their outgoing calls. Sure enough, it was Marc Short, the Director of Legislative Affairs.

"Are you briefing the President for this event?" he asked. I was. "Okay, you should consider updating the remarks, because we've got a deal. The bill is going to pass. He should announce it first, before anyone on the Hill can."

Short and his team had spent every waking moment for the past five months trying to get this bill passed, and they'd just had the final breakthrough they had been working toward.

I hung up and looked over at Tony, who was pacing nervously while reading a copy of the President's prepared remarks. Through an open door I heard three buzzes, signaling that the President was about to get on his private elevator and come up to where we were. My heart rate picked up slightly.

In the thirty seconds between that moment and the President's walking in the room, I filled Tony in and he identified the key line in the speech that needed tweaking: "As we speak, Congress is putting the finishing touches on a plan" needed to be changed to "Congress has reached an agreement on tax legislation. . . ."

The President glided into the room as Tony marked through the old line and scribbled in the updated language. He was wearing a cobalt-blue tie with tiny circle accents that created a subtle, textured look. I noticed his hair right away. Maybe it was because of all the filming sessions I had been in with him, or the handful of times I had helped tame stray hairs trying to fly away, but I noticed he was having a good hair day. The left-to-right swoop was hugging close to his head. On top of that, he was in a cheerful mood. He shook my hand—which wasn't typical for these briefings—and gave me a swift smack on my left arm with his other hand.

"What've we got, guys?" he said, looking back and forth between Tony and me.

"Mr. President, this is going to be the speech everyone remembers about the tax bill," I began. "There are two things you will be saying for the first time today. Number one, the IRS has confirmed that if this bill is enacted before Christmas, people will start seeing a change in their paychecks beginning in February."

The President nodded his head. This was something the Treasury team had pushed hard for, and he was pleased.

"That's going to come late in your remarks," I continued. "But before that, right near the top, you're going to be the first to announce that Congress has reached an agreement on the final bill. It's going to pass."

Tony handed him his copy of the remarks with the updated language, and Trump squinted to read Tony's chicken-scratch handwriting.

"You okay with this?" I asked.

He nodded his approval, and I ran off to have the sentence updated in the teleprompter.

Minutes later, Trump stepped up to the podium centered between four towering white marble columns. To his left and right were a dozen perfectly triangular Christmas trees, covered in silver tinsel and faux white snow. Directly behind him, the door leading into the Blue Room was left open so the official White House Christmas tree could be seen inside.

As he began speaking, I ducked into the White House Usher's office to see what it looked like on their small flat-screen television monitor. People all over the country must have thought the President was delivering his remarks from some kind of winter wonderland. *Tax cuts for Christmas.* It was perfect. General Kelly, who was watching as well, agreed. "This is great staging," he said. "Very well done."

I walked back out to the Cross Hall to watch from the President's left, just out of sight of the cameras. It was the most exciting moment of my entire time in the White House, but it was accompanied by an unexpected—and frankly, unexplainable—air of melancholy.

Looking back, I still can't exactly put my finger on it. I slowly surveyed the scene I was standing in—one that very few kids from Alabama will ever get to witness—and I distinctly remember thinking to myself that I might never be a part of something of this magnitude ever again. It's a strange thing to ponder the very real possibility that your professional career has peaked in your early thirties.

And just that quickly it was over. The event was finished and the President was about to walk by me. As he stepped back onto the elevator, he flashed a thumbs-up at me before the doors slid shut.

The following day, *The New York Times*'s front page was a work of art. The picture above the fold was of the President delivering remarks from our makeshift winter wonderland, with the all-caps headline G.O.P. AGREES ON FINAL TAX BILL.

The President loved it.

"This is spectacular," he said. "We need to get this framed. Put it in a nice gold one." Then he had another thought. "In fact, any good articles you see— on anything, not just the taxes, on anything—go ahead and get them framed and we'll put them here and there. People like that."

By people, I'm pretty sure he meant himself.

On December 22, three days before our deadline, Trump signed into law one of the largest tax cuts in American history. After he signed the bill, I walked back to my desk and noticed there was a newspaper sitting on top of my computer keyboard. It was the iconic *New York Times* front page the

President loved so much. And just to the left of the picture, written in all-caps with a black Sharpie, was the following inscription:

CLIFF, GREAT JOB! THANKS - DONALD J. TRUMP

If this was indeed the pinnacle, I'd take it.

"Is Melania already here?" Those were the first words out of the President's mouth when he stepped off the elevator on the State Floor of the White House. "Yes, sir," I replied as we walked out of the elevator vestibule into the Cross Hall. "She's waiting for you in the Blue Room."

The atmosphere in the White House at Christmastime is kind of like Buddy the Elf being at the North Pole—the magic of the holidays is magnified tenfold. On the ground floor, decorators had positioned dozens of pots full of leafless tree branches, all painted stark white. It created an effect I referred to as "Jack Frost's Tunnel," which I traversed every day walking to and from work. Just down the hall on the ground floor of the residence, President Reagan's china was set up as if for a family Christmas dinner in the China Room. Franklin D. Roosevelt's 1866 edition of *A Christmas Carol* was displayed in the Library. Upstairs on the State Floor, a 350-pound gingerbread house was sitting in the State Dining Room. A giant nativity scene was displayed in the East Room below the famous painting of George Washington, the one Dolley Madison saved when the British burned down the house during the War of 1812. Lining the Cross Hall were about a dozen frosted Christmas trees, all decked out in thousands of white lights and gleaming silver tinsel. In total, fifty-three Christmas trees throughout the executive residence were adorned with twelve thousand ornaments. Seventy-one wreaths were positioned throughout the White House complex. The whole place radiated with the soft glow of over eighteen thousand feet of Christmas lights.

President Trump was feeling the spirit—humming bits of Christmas carols and remarking on the decorations—although there were days when his ceremonial duties almost sucked it out of him. A few days before, my wife, Megan, and I had stood in line to have our picture taken with him and the

First Lady at the staff Christmas party. When one of the First Lady's aides saw us, she warned that his mood had turned sour about an hour before. "Watch out," she said with a smirk. "He's had about all he can stand, but the line just keeps going and going." Thankfully, his eyes lit up when he saw me. "Oh, honey, it's my Cliff," he said to the First Lady. "Oh, my," he said as his eyes shifted to Megan. It was the first time they had met. "Cliff, I knew there was a reason I respected you so much!" We all laughed and the President flashed his famous thumbs-up as the photographer snapped our picture.

Today he had walked over from the West Wing to perform another one of his ceremonial duties: recording a Christmas video message to the nation. Such recording sessions were far from his favorite task, but he was looking forward to this one because he and Mrs. Trump were doing it together.

As we breezed through the Red Room, he straightened his tie and looked down to make sure his flag lapel pin was perfectly positioned. Walking into the Blue Room, directly in front of us stood the centerpiece of all the immaculate decorations: the official White House Christmas tree. The enormous evergreen from Wisconsin stretched all the way to the ceiling and was decorated with glass ornaments depicting the seal of each U.S. state. But none of that mattered to the President, because the only thing he cared to see at that moment was his wife.

"Hey, baby," he said as he walked over and kissed her on the cheek. "Are we ready to do some recording?" She looked stunning in a red lace dress that couldn't have fit better if she had been born wearing it. "No one's even going to be paying attention to me in this video!" the President said to the crew. "Do we agree, guys, no one's even going to know that I'm here!" He leaned over and nudged the First Lady with his shoulder and she smiled shyly.

She was a bit nervous ahead of video recordings and public appearances in which she would speak. She occasionally expressed concerns that her accent was too strong and made her hard to understand. So she practiced relentlessly for any speaking role she needed to play. This stood in stark contrast to her gregarious husband, of course, who never met a crowd he didn't want to entertain and loved nothing more than shooting from the hip. But when the First Lady was around, she was always the focus of his attention.

As the recording session began, he was clearly trying to impress her. He was focused. He wanted to nail his lines on the first take. When it was her turn to speak and she'd make a mistake, he'd encourage her. "You sound like you're from New York, honey," he said. "Can't even tell you have an accent."

Her Secret Service code name was "Muse," which fit with the way the President viewed her.

The President was affectionate with all of his family. He'd beam with pride in Ivanka any time he'd introduce her to guests at the White House. "She gets so much better coverage than I do," he'd laugh. He'd praise Don Jr.'s skills as a retail politician—"The base loves him"—even though practically speaking he was rarely involved in the governing decisions like Ivanka was. And one day, in a scramble through the ground floor of the residence on the way to board Marine One on the South Lawn, the entire entourage screeched to a halt when the President spotted one of his grandchildren. He rushed over, swept him up in his arms, and kissed him on the forehead, just like any doting grandfather would, before rushing off to the chopper.

These were helpful reminders that as abnormal as the Trump administration—and the President himself—often seemed, he could be normal, too. At least relatively normal. And he had a reason for his festive mood. Just as the President had vowed, he got his tax cuts for Christmas.

As our first year in the White House came to an end, I thought back over everything that had happened. In addition to slashing taxes for most American families and businesses, the tax bill repealed Obamacare's individual mandate, delivering on a key Republican promise even though members of Congress couldn't get it done earlier in the year. The bill also opened up the Arctic National Wildlife Refuge for energy exploration, something Republicans had tried and failed to accomplish for nearly forty years. After pledging to roll back two government regulations for every new one created, the actual ratio ended up being about 22–1. As a result, unemployment plummeted among every demographic and the Dow Jones Industrial Average hit record highs nearly seventy times, creating over six trillion dollars in new wealth.

Justice Neil Gorsuch was confirmed to a lifetime seat on the Supreme Court and Trump set a record for first-year judicial appointments to federal appellate courts, moving the federal judiciary to the right for a generation.

ISIS's once-expanding caliphate was almost completely eradicated after Trump approved Mattis's plan to move from "attrition tactics to annihilation tactics." He enforced the "red line" in Syria that Obama hadn't. He moved the U.S. embassy in Israel to Jerusalem, making good on a pledge that Clinton, Bush, and Obama had each abandoned.

He kept promise after promise, from withdrawing from the Paris Climate Accord, to cracking down on illegal immigration, to leading a resurgence of the U.S. economy. But the greatest accomplishment of all may have been revitalizing what he called "the American Spirit." Manufacturing confidence was at an all-time record high, and optimism among consumers and businesses had skyrocketed.

Reading this, you may think that some, or much, or perhaps almost all of Trump's first-year policies were bad. But in spite of all of the mayhem, it's hard to deny that he was getting things—even some big things—done. And for a wide swath of the country, it was more than they ever thought possible. They may have bristled at the tweets. They may not have always liked the methods. They probably felt like the White House had turned into some kind of bizarre reality television show. And in this, of course, they wouldn't be entirely off base. But they also probably had more money in their bank accounts. Their 401(k)s were going through the roof. Their wages were rising. And we were experiencing a time of relative peace around the globe, even if not in the West Wing.

I wasn't proud of everything the President had done, said, or tweeted. I wasn't always proud of the way I had conducted myself, either. It's impossible to deny how absolutely out of control the White House staff—again, myself included—was at times. But I *was* proud of what we had somehow accomplished, often in spite of ourselves. I was reminded again of Kellyanne's line from the darkest moments of the campaign: "There's a difference . . . between what offends you and what affects you." I truly believe we were affecting people's lives in a positive way. And I wanted to keep going.

— 13 —

FRENEMIES OF THE PEOPLE

Monday morning, November 27, 2017, most Americans were dispassionately making their way back to work, still stuffed full of turkey and dressing after a long Thanksgiving weekend of family and football. The President was in the White House residence soaking in, and occasionally stewing over, the latest news coverage.

It will likely come as no surprise to anyone that he was a voracious consumer of news—even the "fake news" he sometimes claimed he didn't read. His routine generally involved reading *The New York Times*, *The Wall Street Journal*, and *The Washington Post* front-to-back, and then bouncing around to various TV morning shows, which he saved on his highly prized super TiVo. This put extraordinary pressure on his aides, particularly those of us in communications, to be aware of every story—because *he* definitely would be.

During the campaign, comms aides Kaelan Dorr and Steven Cheung would stay up deep into the night or rise before dawn to organize press clippings and collect newspaper stories that they could use to brief senior communications adviser Jason Miller. Jason also had to be up early so that he could read and consider them all prior to his morning phone call with the boss. Sometimes Kaelan would even throw out anticipated questions from Trump on some particular story or media narrative, so that Jason could practice his responses. But as much as you tried, you could never know for certain what would tick off the candidate or grab his interest.

And so every morning, Jason would sit anxiously by the phone, waiting for the call. He would start by giving Trump a rundown of the coverage, and then Trump would pepper him with questions. *Did you see what Maggie wrote in the* Times *this morning? Did you see what Hannity said about Crooked Hillary? What'd you think about that first* Morning Joe *segment?* Those were predictable, but what made the job harder was that he also might ask about an article by some guy no one had ever heard of, buried thirty pages into *The Wall Street Journal.*

On top of that, he might decide on the fly, without any sort of formalized strategy, what the campaign's message of the day was going to be.

All of this was a test. If Jason was on top of the news stories and had a good plan for pushing back on the negative ones, he passed. If he almost instantly got people on TV to parrot Trump's "news of the day," Jason passed again. Usually Jason would scramble to call a reporter like NBC's Hallie Jackson to give her the scoop on what Trump was thinking. She would then be able to go on the next segment of *Morning Joe* and say, "According to sources close to Mr. Trump, he plans to . . ." If Trump saw that, A+.

But if Jason failed this sometimes-impossible test, Trump would take matters into his own hands and, well, I don't have to tell you what those days were like. You saw the tweets. What was amazing—and is just a fact of life now—was how easily Trump could say or tweet anything and change the news coverage almost instantaneously. This was a power that I don't think any presidential candidate ever had—and Trump was not shy about using it, sometimes for a purpose and sometimes just for the fun of it.

Unfortunately, the scheduled morning calls stopped happening once we made it into the White House, mainly because Miller—whom Trump referred to affectionately as "my Jace"—was gone and his relationship with Sean Spicer, well, it wasn't quite the same. Early in the administration, then, various aides—myself included on rare occasions—funneled articles or other information directly to Trump because there was no official process for putting things in front of him. Sometimes aides took advantage of the lax oversight to feed him articles that painted internal rivals in an unflattering light. Other times they did it to advance a policy argument or thwart someone else's. I did it for one reason only: to tell him he had been right about something. If there was a topic he was frequently talking about and I came across an article that supported or verified his point, I'd print it out, write a little note on it that said, "You were right about this.—Cliff," then give it to him at the end of the day. Once I asked Madeleine Westerhout, his executive assistant, to include an article and note in his nightly briefing book because I

wasn't going to see him. I saw it later sitting on Sean Spicer's desk—
Madeleine was an RNC alumnus, after all—so I didn't do that again.

On this particular post-Thanksgiving morning, one story in the Lifestyle
section of *The Washington Post* was garnering some buzz. "The hosts of
MSNBC's *Morning Joe* did the usual day-after Thanksgiving kibitzing on
the air on Friday morning, telling viewers about their turkey dinners and
mentioning the big football game the night before," wrote *Post* media reporter Paul Farhi. "One problem: None of those things had actually happened
at the time Joe Scarborough, Mika Brzezinski and Co. started talking about
them. The program that aired Friday morning was taped Wednesday, but
made to look and sound as if it was airing live." Farhi went on to write that
the whole thing was "cooked up to appear as if it was happening in real time."

Even though I wasn't there when he read this, I have no trouble envision-
ing the mischievous grin that slowly formed across the President's face. There
was nothing—nothing—he loved more than members of the media getting
caught up in some embarrassment, and then rubbing their noses in it. Unable
to resist, Trump fired off a tweet about the *Morning Joe* gaffe: "The good
news is that their ratings are terrible, nobody cares!" Trump loved to claim
that any media outlet he felt was out to get him had terrible ratings, whether
it was true or not. To the President, the former TV producer, there was no
bigger insult than to tell someone nobody was watching you.

That tweet made his morning. Feeling inspired, he hatched an idea which
of course he likely shared with no one before announcing it on Twitter.
"We should have a contest as to which of the Networks, plus CNN and not
including Fox, is the most dishonest, corrupt and/or distorted in its political
coverage of your favorite President (me)," he tweeted. "They are all bad.
Winner to receive the FAKE NEWS TROPHY!" In an instant, a sleepy post-
Thanksgiving Twitter feed was brought to life—with eye rolls, outrage, and
aggrieved commentary from members of the media. Mission accomplished.

That afternoon, the President hosted an event in the Oval Office with three
of the thirteen surviving Navajo Code Talkers, who were integral to U.S. military communication during World War II. Those inspiring, heroic stories
might have moved the President, I'm not sure. What I do know is that right
after the event, he saw me helping the audio-video crew take the podium and
other equipment out of the Oval Office, and waved me over.

His thoughts were, as it turned out, not consumed by the Navajo.

"What'd you think about the fake news trophy?" he asked, barely concealing his amusement over his tweet and the reaction.

Now, if you're looking for a voice of reason when it came to the tweets, I was generally not your guy. Sure, I—and plenty of others—would occasionally debate with the President about whether to tweet certain things, or how various tweets should be worded. Sometimes I think he just wanted to voice his displeasure about something, then be talked down from actually tweeting about it. But most of the time I was just in favor of what was going to happen anyway. In other words, the tweets were going out regardless of what anyone thought or said, so why burn capital with the boss arguing over them?

So when the President asked me about his latest salvo against the media, I told him I thought it was hilarious. This had the benefit of being true. I mean, seriously, deconstruct that tweet. He had somehow invented a Twitter syntax all his own. I also viewed this type of tweet as the humorous, mostly harmless side of a coin that, when flipped over, featured the much darker, and more dangerous, phrase "Enemy of the People."

Unlike most people working in the Trump White House, I had been a journalist and seen the world through their eyes. I had written tough stories, including some that helped take down a once-popular Republican governor in my home state. I didn't always get things right—I could be guilty of the same things that frustrated me about White House reporters—but I had done my best to be accurate. I felt like most members of the White House press corps tried to do the same.

To be sure, there was a lot I disliked about the press corps. Many reporters I knew personally could be pretentious, self-absorbed, self-righteous, blinded by ideology, biased toward controversy, and far too slow to admit when they were wrong. Like many Republicans, who had felt with some justification that the media was biased against them for decades, I cheered as hard as anyone when Trump took on the media establishment, which had become just as much a part of the swamp culture as the politicians it was covering. It was clear that many reporters covering Trump had become advocates against him and his supporters, in ways that would have seemed totally inappropriate even a few years earlier. Their view was that Trump's extreme behavior justified these departures from the norm. I didn't think that was a good enough excuse. Regardless, calling journalists enemies of the people was a bridge too far for me; the connotation was too loaded.

During the French Revolution, Robespierre had called for "enemies of the people" to be put to death. Lenin had labeled opponents of the Soviet Communist Party "enemies of the people" and "outlaws," and called for them to be "arrested immediately." Mao ominously warned of "enemies of the people" seeking to "sabotage" his "socialist revolution." I doubt Trump was aware of the history of the phrase. Then again, maybe he was fully aware and used it anyway, knowing it would spark outrage. Regardless, it made me squirm. But I never told Trump that, or tried to explain this, which was a failing on my part.

So if the choice was between calling reporters enemies of the United States or mocking their errors—and it was—I was all in for the Fake News Awards.

"I think we should do it," he told me. "I'll give you a hundred dollars. Go buy a trophy—a nice, little trophy." He was moving his hands out in front of him, as if measuring the trophy in the air. He could see it now. I imagined it looking something like an Emmy (for which he'd been nominated twice for his work on *The Apprentice*).

"And get a little engraving on there," he ordered. "CNN—Fake News Network of the Year."

I didn't comment that he'd already prejudged the winner of this "contest." Instead, I laughed as I walked back toward the a/v crew. "I'll see what we can put together," I said with a smile. Then I didn't give it much additional thought.

As everyone working for Donald Trump knew, there were generally two kinds of presidential requests—ones you acted on and ones you ignored unless he brought it up again. I figured this was the latter. A little over a month went by without him saying anything else about it, at least to me. But late on New Year's Day of 2018, I got a text from a friend traveling back from Mar-a-Lago with the President on Air Force One. "POTUS is back to talking about the Fake News Awards. He wants to host an awards show and hand out trophies." The text ended with the emoji character that's laughing so hard it's crying.

Shortly after I received that text, the President tweeted, "I will be announcing THE MOST DISHONEST & CORRUPT MEDIA AWARDS OF THE YEAR on Monday at 5:00 o'clock. Subjects will cover Dishonesty & Bad Reporting in various categories from the Fake News Media. Stay tuned!"

Immediately after seeing that, I texted Hope Hicks, "Well, we've got an awards show to put together."

Hope responded right away: "I think we should have someone hand Sarah an envelope in the briefing, then say it was too tough to choose and give them all little participation trophies."

We were both joking—sort of—but there was no avoiding this now. The show would go on.

The rest of the staff was divided on the entire concept, much less producing some type of awards show with multiple categories. The White House Counsel's Office was adamantly opposed, as attorneys tend to be when there's fun involved. President Obama's former ethics czar even tweeted out a stern warning that if White House staff helped with the awards, we would "risk violating §§ 702, 704 & 705 forbidding use of gov time & $$$ to harm some media & aid others."

In the end, Trump was begrudgingly talked into allowing the Republican National Committee to release an online list, titled "The Highly-Anticipated 2017 Fake News Awards," that he could tweet out. This was anticlimactic, and the RNC web page didn't even work at first. But I must admit, seeing some of the most egregious reporting errors of 2017 all in one place was actually pretty striking. For all the justifiable criticism of the Trump administration's credibility issues—and there were plenty of them—the media gave the President numerous opportunities to throw that charge back at them.

The list included *The New York Times* predicting Trump's election would destroy the economy, when in reality the stock market boomed and unemployment plummeted. It included an erroneous ABC News story claiming Trump's former National Security Advisor was prepared to testify against him in the Russia probe. The story tanked the stock market for a day, but was later found to be false, earning the reporter a suspension and demotion. It included three CNN employees having to resign after publishing, then retracting, another false Russia-related story. Then there was the time *Newsweek* falsely reported that the Polish First Lady refused to shake Trump's hand. And another time when CNN deceptively edited a video of Trump and the Japanese prime minister feeding fish—yes, feeding fish. The video made it look like Trump had just dumped out all of the food, unprompted, when in reality he was following the lead of the Japanese Prime Minister, his host.

Trump was unusually diligent in pointing out these mistakes, of course. And he was effective. According to a Gallup survey released in January 2018, less than half of Americans could name an "objective news source"—not a single one. The effect of this was that the more the "fake news" attacked Trump, the tighter his supporters clung to him.

But behind the scenes, the relationship between the press and the White House was more complicated—and sometimes more incestuous—than either side wanted to admit.

Trump sincerely held most members of the media in low regard—that wasn't for show. But what he didn't like to admit was that he also craved their approval. Decades in the New York City tabloids had convinced him that being the topic of conversation—whether positive or negative—was what really mattered. Nothing was more a focus of his attention in this regard than *The New York Times*. It was his hometown paper, after all. During a dinner with evangelical leaders in the Blue Room, Trump named the exact number of occasions he had been on the front page of the *Times* during his career as a businessman. It was only a handful. "Now I'm on there almost every day," he observed, though usually not in the way he would have liked. He added, with a mix of pride and irritation, that Ivanka, who was also in the room, still got better coverage in the *Times* than he did.

But if Trump held the media in low esteem, members of the media clearly felt the same way. Yet, thanks to him, they were also having the time of their lives. There had never been this much news in Washington, D.C., and they had never gotten this much attention. Politics had seldom been the go-to conversation at office water coolers and around the family dinner table, but it was now. And journalists were becoming stars in their own right. Some of them were satirized on *Saturday Night Live,* right along with the Trumps, Kellyanne, Sean, Jared, and Steve. Almost all of them were now recognizable in public, pausing to take selfies with fans for the first time in their lives.

To the public, Trump versus the press was a bitter war. But behind the scenes, it was much more like professional wrestling. The reporters needed Trump and his team to leak to them and give them information or they couldn't break news. By contrast, Trump and his team needed them to get information out, or misinformation, or serve as a powerful and effective political foil. They also served two almost completely separate audiences—the press often seemed to be writing stories to get clicks from the Trump haters while the White House used those same stories to rile up the media haters. *Wash, rinse, repeat.*

Never was this more evident than on August 2, 2017, when Senior Policy Advisor Stephen Miller was brought into the White House Press Briefing Room to discuss an immigration bill that the President had just endorsed. The WWE nature of the entire proceeding was clear right from the beginning. Everyone knew what was going to happen. Everyone had their unofficially assigned roles.

"I'd like to hand it over to Stephen Miller," Sarah Sanders said with a smile. "I know you guys will have a lot of fun."

Miller swaggered over to the podium in his perfectly tailored suit and skinny tie, like he had been pulled straight off the set of *Mad Men*. In his rather off-putting, dogmatic, weirdly self-confident style, he launched into an explanation of various controversial components of the bill as if he were discussing a bread recipe. Then after a lengthy round of questions, Miller said he would take one more, from the Trump White House's favorite media villain—CNN's Jim Acosta.

"The Statue of Liberty says, 'Give me your tired, your poor, your huddled masses yearning to breathe free,'" Acosta said with seeming conviction, his head cocked slightly to the right. "Aren't you trying to change what it means to be an immigrant coming into this country . . . ?" Acosta didn't answer his own question—though clearly his answer would be yes—but he didn't have to. He had perfected the seemingly earnest expression that many White House reporters tried to don. He was just an impartial fact gatherer like the rest of the press—even though his questions, tone, and temperament just happened to suggest that he believed Stephen Miller, his policies, his views, his colleagues, and his president were irredeemable racists. But that's what Acosta's audience wanted. And that's, as it turned out, what we wanted, too.

Miller tried to suppress a grin, but the corners of his mouth subtly betrayed the excitement welling up inside of him. This was exactly what he had been hoping for. A TV moment.

As it happened, I was in Sarah's office just before she and Miller went into the briefing. I told Miller that someone—probably Acosta—was going to bring up the "The New Colossus" poem, which was mounted on the Statue of Liberty's pedestal almost two decades after it was erected. I knew this because the subject had come up with a caller on my radio program the year before.

"I don't want to get off into a whole thing about history here, but the Statue of Liberty is . . . a symbol of American liberty lighting the world," Miller said. "The poem that you're referring to, that was added later, is not actually a part of the original Statue of Liberty." He tried to complete his point, but Acosta cut him off.

"You're saying that that does not represent what the country has always thought of as immigration coming into this country? That sounds like some National Park revisionism."

Reporters chuckled. The game was on. The two bantered back and forth, neither allowing the other to finish a sentence, much less complete a full thought. Acosta seemed particularly irked at the idea of scaling back the total number of legal immigrants coming into the country each year, which Miller pointed out had fluctuated over time.

"Jim, let's talk about this," Miller said, still barely concealing his glee. He knew that there was nothing President Trump would like more than for Miller to go to battle with Acosta, a reporter Trump probably loathed more than any other human being in the entire capital. Except maybe Jim Comey. If the Acosta-Miller exchange had descended into a physical brawl, the President would have run into the room with a bowl of popcorn and a diet soda. "In 1970, when we let in three hundred thousand people a year, was that violating or not violating the Statue of Liberty law of the land? In the 1990s, when it was half a million a year, was it violating or not violating the Statue of Liberty law of the land?"

Acosta tried to jump back in, but Miller pressed on.

"Tell me what years meet Jim Acosta's definition of the Statue of Liberty poem law of the land," he demanded. "So you're saying a million a year is the Statue of Liberty number? Nine hundred thousand violates it? Eight hundred thousand violates it?" I imagined Donald Trump—who loved to watch these briefings in real time—jumping up from the private dining room table and pumping his fist in jubilation.

For seven minutes Miller and Acosta sparred in front of the entire country. And as he wrapped it, his final words from the podium were: "I think that went exactly as planned. I think that's what Sarah was hoping would happen. I think that's exactly what we were hoping to have happen."

He was laughing as he said it, but actually, it kind of was. Everything Miller said about the poem and the statue was historically accurate because he'd gamed it out in advance. He'd thought through how he would respond. Both sides knew what was coming, the staging and timing were preset, and everyone played their part. *How is this any different from professional wrestling?*

I met Miller in the hallway between the Briefing Room and the Press Secretary's office right after he'd come offstage, and he literally high-fived me. We got what we wanted—a confrontation that allowed the White House to take a hard line on immigration. Acosta got what he wanted—a confrontation that CNN could air on a loop for the rest of the day, and sound bites their panelists could dissect with righteous indignation. The American people got—what, exactly? I have no idea. And that's how I felt most days after the press briefings.

I'm not sure there has ever been a time when on-camera briefings were productive. The Clinton administration was the first to give them a shot, but a couple of weeks in they shut them down. "The briefing is more an opportunity to exchange ideas and to have a conversation about what's happening," explained Clinton Press Secretary Dee Dee Myers. "That wasn't really happening as productively as we had hoped."

I know exactly what she meant. The reason productive exchanges rarely take place during on-camera briefings is because they create perverse incentives for both sides. Grandstanding TV correspondents try to manufacture *gotcha* moments, confrontations that make their producers happy and look dramatic on screen. Whether they actually glean any useful information in the process is a much lesser concern. And under-siege spokespeople resort to condescension and witty one-liners that go viral on social media, get the base riled up, and please the boss, who's almost always watching. Whether they provide relevant, accurate information on the news of the day is, again, a lesser priority.

Reporters publicly decried the White House for holding fewer and fewer briefings, but privately conceded that they were mostly useless theater. Print journalists loathed the TV grandstanders in the Briefing Room because the spectacle didn't provide them with anything useful to fill column space. In fact, some of the most widely respected White House reporters, like Maggie Haberman from *The New York Times* and Jonathan Swan from *Axios*, rarely showed their faces in the Briefing Room. Why bother? They were busy talking to dozens of sources throughout the building, hustling for the real scoop while their competitors crowded into a room to ask the same questions and get the same nonanswers.

For the most part we all carried on like the good frenemies that we were—publicly bashing one another's brains out while privately acknowledging that each side needed the other. The Jim Acostas of the world needed to attract the White House's ire, making them heroes to "the resistance." And the White House needed them to be foils, Fake News mascots for the conservative base.

Leaning over the phone in the Oval Office, arms crossed in front of him with his elbows sitting on the Resolute desk, Trump was trying to cut a deal. But it wasn't with a congressman or senator haggling over details of legislation. It wasn't a foreign head of state, debating a trade accord. Nor was it a major corporate CEO who Trump was trying to persuade to expand operations in the United States. It was a reporter.

"Who gave you this story?" Trump asked playfully. "I'd just be curious to know who told you this."

The reporter laughed somewhat nervously, saying they obviously could not reveal their sources.

"Well, I guess that's fine," Trump replied. "But of course you know I could give you so much better stories—so much better."

After a little more unsuccessful coaxing Trump relented, and the reporter hung up without a hot scoop from "a source close to the President."

Privately Trump acknowledged that interacting, even brawling, with reporters was one of his favorite aspects of the job—it was like a sport to him. Early in the administration, after a tense back-and-forth with Acosta during a press conference in the East Room, Trump came back to the West Wing enthused and playing media critic. "I actually think Jim handled himself well there," he said. "Sometimes he's so defensive—just so defensive. Not today. Very calm. Very professional. I thought he was good. I got the better of him, of course—they're fake news, as we know—but he was good, Jim was good."

That's not to say that Trump's press criticisms were insincere. Far from it. As with pretty much everything else, what he said publicly closely mirrored what he said in private.

On January 31, 2018, I had organized a meeting with the President and seven workers whose employers had given them pay raises as a result of the Trump tax cuts. As was our routine, the press pool was brought in to cover some casual remarks by the President and his guests. As the event concluded, reporters shouted questions at the President before being ushered out of the room. This was normal and totally reasonable. Sometimes the President would answer them, sometimes he wouldn't. In this particular instance, Trump chose not to engage, sending Acosta into a fit of anger. "Are you a racist?" he demanded to know. The two press wranglers, young ladies in their early twenties whose job it was to escort the press in and out of such meetings, immediately looked at me like deers in headlights. "Thank you, press! Thank you, press!" they said louder and louder, trying to drown out the belligerent Acosta and nudge the reporters to leave the room. Eventually they succeeded.

"Sorry about that," the President said as the press were finally gone and the door was closed behind them. "Comes with the territory." The room was filled with nervous laughter, then William Harmon, an African American man in his late twenties from Muscogee County, Georgia, spoke up.

"I just want you to know that we see through all of them," he said. "They're going to keep throwing stuff at you. Don't let it bother you. There are millions of us all over the country who support you and want you to succeed. You make us all proud to be Americans."

"Thank you, William, thank you very much," the President said with sincere appreciation.

After the meeting broke up and the guests were escorted out, the President sat down behind the Resolute desk and I asked him if he was pleased with the event.

"I thought it was perfect," Treasury Secretary Steven Mnuchin interjected. "Having you surrounded by those workers is great optics and great messaging."

The President nodded in agreement. "Yeah," he said, looking back at Mnuchin, "but we've gotta do something about this lunatic Jim Acosta screaming at everyone in the Oval Office. Can't we suspend him, or something?"

"It's a lack of decorum, is what it is," Mnuchin added.

Sarah Sanders, who had walked up just in time to hear the President expressing this familiar frustration, said she didn't think it was worth worrying about. "There's not much we can do, sir. If we kick him out, they'll just accuse us of being like China, like we're suppressing the free press. It'll end up being more trouble than it's worth."

"But who cares?" Trump retorted. "They lie about everything else. Our people don't care what they say."

Turning to me, he said, "What do you think?"

"I think it's reasonable to expect everyone at the White House to have a certain level of decorum, especially in the Oval," I told him. "If Acosta can't hold himself together, I say we suspend him for the next time CNN is in the press pool, but let them send another reporter in his place." That way CNN could still have a reporter there, but the event wouldn't be pointlessly derailed by Acosta's attention-seeking belligerence. The President seemed to like this idea, pursing his lips and nodding in approval.

"Well, somebody needs to do something, because he's out of control," Trump concluded. "So talk about it and do something. I don't care what, but it needs to be something."

This was an ongoing debate among senior press aides, and occasionally even the Chief of Staff's office when the President got really spun up. But during my time in the West Wing, the decision was always made to let it go, rather than exacerbate our already contentious relationship with the press.

He consumed TV like the late Roger Ebert must have watched movies. I imagine that, after being a film critic for almost a half century, it was difficult for Ebert to enjoy a movie just for the fun of it. He must have always been analyzing the plotline, character development, and cinematography. Trump was the same way about network news programming. He commented on the sets, the graphics, the wardrobe choices, the lighting, and just about every other visual component of a broadcast. Sure, he liked to hear pundits saying nice things about him or White House officials defending him from attacks, but everything came back to *how does it look?* With that in mind, the most Trumpian tactic the comms team employed was arguing with TV networks about the "chyrons," the words displayed at the bottom of the screen that act as headlines for whatever the commentators are discussing.

"People watch TV on mute," the President told me, "so it's those words, those sometimes beautiful, sometimes nasty little words that matter." He had mastered television as a communications medium, and this was one of his smartest insights. Steven Cheung, the White House Director of Strategic Response, was effective at getting negative or unfair chyrons changed. He had developed that skill—and the TV network relationships to implement it—while working sixteen-hour days in Trump Tower during the campaign. He continued to work his magic in the White House, perhaps most notably during the confirmation hearings for Secretary of State Mike Pompeo.

When the President would deliver a speech somewhere outside of D.C., the research team would take screenshots of all the chyrons that aired while he was speaking. Then, adding those images to headlines and tweets from influential reporters and pundits, they would race to print out a packet before Trump made it back to the White House. The goal was for Sarah or Hope or me—or whoever hadn't traveled with him—to meet him on the ground floor of the residence and hand him the packet to review mere moments after Marine One landed on the South Lawn.

And once he got upstairs to the residence, you could bet that he was going to watch the replays and commentary from his favorite prime-time lineup on Fox. After all, Trump undoubtedly loved the fight, but he loved being, well, loved even more. And there were few places he felt the love more than on Fox.

Sean Hannity, the network's biggest star, was one of the few people outside the White House who spoke to the President as much as the media seemed to think he did. Most people inflated their access to Trump; Hannity didn't have to. The President loved that he had "the most highly rated show of them all," and the two discussed everything from personnel matters to communications strategy. Trump also loved to watch Tucker Carlson embarrass his hapless guests and would occasionally call to congratulate him on his performance. Laura Ingraham was the Fox host most ideologically aligned with Trump on his signature issue, immigration, but she did not share the close rapport with Trump that others did, in part because some of the people around Trump found her difficult to deal with. During one "radio row" event in the East Room, Ingraham went so far over her allotted time interviewing the President that Hope Hicks had to step in and apologetically but forcefully end the conversation because Trump was so late for his next interview. Trump didn't mind, though. She had been one of his earliest supporters, so she could have a few extra minutes if it made her happy. But no one in the Fox lineup held a place closer to Trump's heart than Lou Dobbs.

In July 2017, Kellyanne Conway appeared on Dobbs's Fox Business Network show. Dobbs, a protectionist on trade and a "build the wall" hard-liner on immigration, loved Trump and supported him relentlessly. In contrast, he frequently derided Republican leaders in Congress, whom he viewed as feckless and incapable of walking and chewing gum at the same time, much less legislating.

It was the summer of Trump's first year in office, and a debate was raging over the GOP's longtime promise to "repeal and replace" Obamacare. Dobbs was frustrated that Republicans—who had voted dozens of times to repeal Obamacare while in the minority—suddenly couldn't pull it off with majorities in both chambers. Calling out both Senate Majority Leader Mitch McConnell and House Speaker Paul Ryan by name, Dobbs unloaded from his studio as Kellyanne stood and listened on the North Lawn of the White House.

"There's no toughness, there's no intelligence, and there is very little beyond pure flaccidity on the part of the Republican leadership," he declared. "It's time to make something happen, isn't it?"

He assumed Kellyanne would echo his frustrations, but she didn't. "I'm going to push back on this," she replied. "There's a very serious effort here to make good on repealing and replacing Obamacare."

As she continued defending Republican congressional leaders, Dobbs grew increasingly irritated. "Kellyanne, I can't believe you're filibustering me! . . . You've got to be straight with this audience," he finally said in exasperation. "What is the Republican leadership up to? Why in the world isn't the White House responding with greater force and direction?"

The following day, I was in the Oval Office showing the President a draft of a video we'd recently recorded when he saw Kellyanne through the doorway.

"Kellyanne, come on in here," he called out. Then he shouted at his secretary. "Madeleine, get me the great Lou Dobbs on the phone." I'm pretty sure by this point Madeleine had this guy on speed dial.

Kellyanne gave me a kiss on the cheek as she walked in and stood behind one of the wooden chairs in front of the President's desk.

Within a matter of moments, Dobbs was patched into the Oval Office. Trump immediately put him on speakerphone and leaned forward so he could be heard clearly.

"One hell of a show last night, Lou," the President said, grinning.

"Well, thank you, Mr. President. I certainly appreciate it," Dobbs said.

"Lou, I've been thinking a lot about it and I really think you might be the best."

Dobbs tried to interject, but Trump wouldn't have it.

"No, I'm serious. Honest to God, Lou, I think you're the best who's ever done it. You've got a certain way that you do things. Now you know Hannity— Sean is wonderful, so good. But I honestly think you may be better. And you know why? It's not just information, Lou. It's great information but it's more than that; it's entertainment. People forget about that. You can't just inform them. They won't listen to you for long if you put them to sleep! You've got to entertain them. You're a hell of an entertainer, Lou. That's why I just keep watching and watching."

I'd heard Trump praise many of his media allies before, but with Dobbs there was no doubting his sincerity. Maybe it was in part because they were close to the same age, but Donald Trump was an unabashed Lou Dobbs fanboy. This, of course, meant that Lou Dobbs had the most secure job at Fox News for the duration.

"That's very kind of you to say, Mr. President," Dobbs said with a humility bordering on shyness. "I do my best, and I hope it's helpful in getting some other Republicans to do what they're supposed to do."

Trump looked up at Kellyanne with a waggish glint in his eye. Clearly he had something in mind.

"Oh, you're doing great, Lou. But I couldn't believe it last night. Kellyanne was on there defending Paul Ryan! Who would have imagined? My Kellyanne taking Paul Ryan's side over ours!"

Kellyanne rolled her eyes as Trump muted the phone and laughed. Dobbs, unaware that she was in the room, laughed sheepishly and sidestepped the previous night's conflict. Part of the fun in this type of game for Trump was that you really didn't know what the person on the other end of the line would say. What if Lou had lit Kellyanne up? I suspect Trump would have loved every moment. But of course it would have put Lou in an awkward spot.

Instead he just chuckled. "She's great. Kellyanne does a great job."

Trump unmuted the phone and filled him in on the joke. "She's right here, Lou! She's listening to every word. I'm kidding, but not really, she was really on there defending him. You had to set her straight."

"Love you, Lou," Kellyanne said. "Keep up the great work."

"Lou, you're the greatest," Trump concluded, and hung up the phone with a giant smile on his face. I'm not sure if Trump had genuine affection for much of anyone outside of his family. But if he did, it was for the people who defended him day after day on television.

Bob Novak, a syndicated columnist in hundreds of newspapers before he passed away in 2009, was famous inside the Beltway for having some kind of scoop in every column. In his autobiography, he shed some light on his superhuman ability to pry information out of people by noting that aides understood that they were either "a source or a target."

As a former journalist, I understand where he was coming from. If you were willing to play ball, I wouldn't necessarily bury stories you didn't like, but I wouldn't go out of my way to ding you, either. On the other hand, if you tried to ignore me—as Alabama Governor Robert Bentley's office did after I wrote a series of damaging (but accurate) articles—that meant it was open season to tee off. Rewarding sources can be a useful trade-off to gain access. But it's foolish to think that just being nice to people is going to make you a go-to reporter for aides looking to off-load inside information. The best reporters spend a disproportionate amount of their time with sources building actual relationships that are deeper than just "I'll scratch your back if you scratch mine." The most press-savvy aides did the same.

In the Trump White House, the fear of being a target—of both hungry reporters and, perhaps of greater concern, your colleagues—was the most powerful motivator to talk to journalists. The thought process went something like this: *If I can maintain close relationships with reporters, I can at least avoid gratuitous hit pieces planted by my rivals.*

I experienced this myself for the first time in May 2017.

Jared Kushner and Steve Bannon, usually staunch adversaries, had grown so frustrated with Spicer's bumbling communications operation that they joined forces in an attempt to overhaul it.

"Put a plan together," Bannon snarled at a handful of us. "Weaponize everything. We're going back to war."

"We're taking this back to campaign-style," Jared added enthusiastically.

Piling into a secluded EEOB office to sketch out a plan to bolster the operation were four former campaign aides: Andy Surabian, Steven Cheung, Andy Hemming, and myself. For the next four hours, we brainstormed, analyzed the communications operation, and debated how to best address its problems. Unfortunately, Hemming was out of his office so long that his direct supervisor, Raj Shah, came looking for him. He needed an excuse, but Bannon and Kushner didn't want other people in the building knowing what we were actually up to. So Hemming told Raj that we were working on a plan to better respond to the onslaught of Russia-related stories.

Within a matter of hours, Surabian and I were contacted by Lachlan Markay and Asawin Suebsaeng from *The Daily Beast*, who said they had White House sources telling them that we were leading an effort to set up a "Russia War Room."

Neither Surabian nor I had a relationship with the two reporters, and we made the mistake of ignoring them, thinking they were just out on a fishing expedition. We couldn't have done anything about it anyway. We couldn't tell them the truth on background, because Bannon and Kushner wanted it kept confidential.

Later that afternoon, *The Daily Beast* published a story, based on information provided by anonymous White House sources, saying that "ground-level operations" for a "Russia War Room" would be run by "senior White House communications hands. . . . Cliff Sims, the director of White House message strategy, and deputy policy strategist Andrew Surabian."

We were livid. First of all, it wasn't true. But more concerning was that being connected to anything Russia-related opened up the possibility of legal bills that could easily be more than a year's salary in the White House. My frustrations culminated months later in a near brawl in the Trump Hotel lobby when I confronted Asawin Suebsaeng and we both had to be restrained by mutual friends. We would later laugh it all off.

This story illustrates a fundamental reality of life inside Trump's White House—there was a deep, often justified, feeling of paranoia engulfing the entire building. Seeing a reporter's name pop up on the screen could send your heart racing with adrenaline that this might be the assassin approaching, ready to carry out a hit put out by a colleague.

I didn't have a full appreciation of this until May 2017, when I saw the American Sniper of West Wing marksmen practicing her craft firsthand. As I watched Kellyanne Conway in operation over our time in the White House, my view of her sharpened. It became hard to look long at her without getting the sense that she was a cartoon villain brought to life. Her agenda—which was her survival over all others, including the President—became more and more transparent. Once you figured that out, everything about her seemed so calculated; every statement, even a seemingly innocuous one, seemed poll tested by a focus group that existed inside her mind. She seemed to be perennially cloaked in an invisible fur coat, casting an all-knowing smile, as if she'd already collected ninety-eight Dalmatians with only three more to go.

The hosts of MSNBC's *Morning Joe* were accusing Kellyanne of being two-faced when it came to Donald Trump. Mika Brzezinski claimed that when she came on their show during the campaign, she would lavish Trump with praise, and then "the camera would be turned off, the microphone would be taken off, and she would say, 'Blech, I need to take a shower,' because she disliked her candidate so much." The other cohost, Joe Scarborough, asserted that Kellyanne had only taken the Trump gig because it would pay off financially. And they both said they had decided to no longer book her on the show because she lacked credibility.

Kellyanne had developed pretty thick skin, and normally she would let this kind of stuff go. So I was a little surprised when she called me upstairs to her office to discuss issuing a response. I assumed this was because she feared Trump would believe the charges, which might threaten her plum White House position of doing whatever it was she wanted whenever she felt like it. Whatever her reasoning, she wanted to fire back and asked if I would help her draft a statement.

Kellyanne's office was one of the largest in the West Wing. On the top floor, above Bannon's and Kushner's offices below, it was about twice as long as it was wide. On the south end of the room, where her desk sat, she had the most valuable commodity in the West Wing: two fairly large, square external windows. On the opposite end of the room she had a small conference table that could comfortably seat six. In between there was a sitting area with a couch and two chairs positioned on opposite sides of an oval coffee table. The office had been set up this same way when Valerie Jarrett occupied it during the Obama years. Just outside her door, in a tiny reception area, sat her executive assistant, who handled her calendar, and her body man, who shadowed her every move and catered to her needs.

I had not brought my work laptop upstairs with me when she called, so Kellyanne pointed over to her personal MacBook sitting on the conference table on the other side of the room.

"Just use that and type something up for me," she said.

I sat down and started slowly pecking out a statement. While working in the White House I found that I'd grown so accustomed to writing in Trump's voice that writing for other people had become somewhat harder than it normally would have been. I was already getting off to a slow start, but I was also getting distracted by the nonstop stream of iMessages popping up on the screen. At that point, personal phones had not yet been banned in the West Wing, so Kellyanne was sitting at her desk texting away. And since her iMessage account was tied to both her phone and her laptop, which she must not have even considered, I could inadvertently see every conversation she was having.

Over the course of twenty minutes or so, she was having simultaneous conversations with no fewer than a half-dozen reporters, most of them from outlets the White House frequently trashed for publishing "fake news." Journalists from *The New York Times, The Washington Post,* CNN, *Politico,* and Bloomberg were all popping up on the screen. And these weren't policy conversations, or attempts to fend off attacks on the President. As I sat there trying to type, she bashed Jared Kushner, Reince Priebus, Steve Bannon, and Sean Spicer, all by name. She also recounted private conversations she'd had with the President during which, at least in her telling, she'd convinced him to see things her way, which she said was a challenge when you're dealing with someone so unpredictable and unrestrained. She wasn't totally trashing the President, at least as the *Morning Joe* crew described it, but she definitely wasn't painting him in the most favorable light. She was talking about him like a child she had to set straight. I was sitting there, watching this, totally bewildered. I was supposed to be writing a statement defending her against accusations that she had done almost exactly what I was watching her do that very moment.

Author Ronald Kessler would later write in his book *The Trump White House: Changing the Rules of the Game* that Kellyanne was the "No. 1 leaker" in the administration. Kessler, whose book was generally favorable toward Trump, claimed Kellyanne "said the most mean, cutting and obviously untrue things about Reince" and "also lit into Jared and Ivanka."

When Fox News host Abby Huntsman asked Kellyanne about Kessler's claims, she sidestepped the question, only saying that "leakers get great press" and adding that "one day, Abby, I will have my say."

278 | TEAM OF VIPERS

From what I saw on her computer, she was having her say all day long. She was playing a double game—putting a foot in both worlds—telling Trump and his supporters on Fox one thing while bad-mouthing them to the "mainstream" media in private. It didn't hurt matters with the latter group that her husband, George, was an increasingly frequent critic of the President on Twitter. If the Trump administration was the *Titanic,* as many outsiders routinely claimed, then Kellyanne seemed determined to play the role of the Unsinkable Molly Brown. She wasn't going to go down with this ship.

But while Kellyanne stood in a class of her own in terms of her machinations—I had to admire her sheer gall—it would be unfair to pretend that Kellyanne was a complete anomaly. I myself had dozens of reporter relationships, going all the way back to the campaign. We worked in communications, after all. And calling her the "No. 1 leaker" wasn't fair, either, because all leaks are not created equal. Sure, the staff-on-staff backstabbing was a distraction and contributed to the toxic work environment, but the real-world damage those leaks inflicted paled in comparison to the national security leaks. And Kellyanne didn't have anything to do with those. On top of that, the President at times benefited greatly from our collective press relationships, which allowed us to shape stories to his advantage or push back on negative story lines. But the unspoken reality inside the Trump White House was that everyone had relationships with journalists, not just the press and comms teams.

One night at the Woodward Table restaurant on the ground floor of my apartment building, I saw the White House's top ethics attorney having dinner with a CNN reporter. On another night, across the street at Joe's Seafood, I saw Rob Porter—who had angrily accused Peter Navarro of leaking—having dinner with a different CNN reporter. At various times I saw countless White House officials outside the comms team buddying up to journalists. I saw the Chief Digital Officer meeting with a reporter at a coffee shop. Another reporter bragged that even the President's personal aide Jordan Karem had asked to meet up clandestinely on the weekend to avoid being seen.

These meetings weren't necessarily nefarious, although I can't really think of a good reason for the President's body man to buddy up with reporters. Karem's predecessor, Johnny McEntee, certainly never would have violated the President's trust like that. But the point is, everyone wanted to stop everyone else from talking to the press, while continuing to talk to the press themselves. And since that wasn't realistic, aides and reporters both developed weblike information networks.

The Trump White House staff was famously factionalized—RNC vs. campaign loyalists, establishment vs. MAGA, globalists vs. nationalists, free traders vs. protectionists. But less well known is that the press was, too. Every West Wing faction had its favored reporters.

Early on, former RNC aides seemed to leak the most to Josh Dawsey (*Politico* and later *The Washington Post*), Zeke Miller (*Time* and later the Associated Press), and Paul Bedard (*Washington Examiner*). They also aired their personal grievances with the President through Lachlan Markay and Asawin Suebsaeng of *The Daily Beast*. Aides who wanted to take shots at Spicer knew they'd be well received by the *Politico* duo of Tara Palmeri and Alex Isenstadt, both of whom had been targets of Spicer's ire. NEC aides who wanted to undermine the President's protectionist trade instincts liked to leak to *Politico*'s Andrew Restuccia. NSC aides opposed to National Security Advisor H. R. McMaster found willing enablers at *Breitbart News*. Reporters joked that senior aides seemed to save their "best" leaks for Maggie Haberman of *The New York Times,* because of her reputation and the *Times*'s massive platform—and also because the President read everything she wrote (even though he once called her a "third-rate flunky" who he never talked to). *The Washington Post*'s team of Phil Rucker and Ashley Parker also seemed to cross the various factions, and later they became go-to reporters for staffers taking shots at General Kelly. *The Wall Street Journal* seemed to have the most rigorous reporting standards, which made it much more difficult for aides to take anonymous shots at one another. On the opposite extreme, *Politico* was generally the outlet of choice for any staffer trying to stab a colleague because its entire content strategy revolved around stoking White House palace intrigue. But *Politico*'s coverage didn't drive the conversation in the White House like it did on Capitol Hill, where they had some of the best reporters in town. The West Wing—and much of D.C.—woke up to *Axios*'s morning email blast, written by longtime Washington insider Mike Allen. Between Allen and his protégé Jonathan Swan, the behind-the-scenes details they unearthed made it feel like *Axios* had someone sitting in the corner of our meetings taking notes.

Reporters were relentless in their source-development methods. They knew they couldn't come in through the front door—our official email addresses or phone numbers—so they tried the back door, our personal cell phones. Or, they found their way into the house through cracks, like direct messages on Twitter, Facebook, Instagram, LinkedIn, or, for the millennial aides, Snapchat. And most of the time they were successful.

As a former journalist, I respected the hustle, but as time went by, I became more and more alarmed at the overall low quality of some of the coverage. At their best, journalists present facts within their proper context to provide readers and viewers with the information they need to develop informed opinions. In the age of Twitter journalism, where every minor development (scooplet!) was met with breathless outrage or analysis, context nearly disappeared. Reporters obsessed over the process, rather than the substance, and the palace-intrigue stories were justified by reporters analyzing what it all "meant." In short, when everything matters, nothing matters. This actually worked to Trump's advantage in some ways, because there was so much "news" happening that damaging stories either couldn't break through or were in the spotlight so briefly that they didn't inflict lasting damage. Most Americans couldn't follow the play-by-play; they had actual lives to live.

On top of all that, many reporters were so personally offended by Trump's broadsides that they essentially became what he was accusing them of being: the opposition party. I can understand how difficult it must have been to endure his withering criticisms of their profession. But over time I saw once-decent reporters subconsciously devolve into anti-Trump protesters, some because they took it all so personally, others because it was the quickest way to build their profile, while for still others it was some of both.

Reporters' other main problem was their overreliance on anonymous sources and their willingness to regurgitate whatever they were told, as if they were absolved from any responsibility over whether or not it was actually true. The President was convinced the sources were made up, that they didn't exist. Reporters responded to this assertion with righteous indignation. But even though I was confident these anonymous sources were indeed real, that did not make up for the fact that what they were saying was often untrue, or at least only part of the story.

In March 2018, I got a text from my comms team colleague Steven Cheung. "We need to pay attention to CNN, because I think something bad might be about to happen," he said. I joked that such a statement could apply to almost any moment. But in this particular instance, Cheung explained that one of our former campaign colleagues was mad at Sarah Sanders—he wasn't entirely clear why—and was sending Cheung cryptic texts that he "had something coming for her on CNN."

Sure enough, an article popped up on CNN's website shortly thereafter with the headline TRUMP UPSET WITH SANDERS.

"President Donald Trump is upset with White House Press Secretary Sarah Sanders over her responses regarding his alleged affair with porn star Stormy Daniels, a source close to the White House tells CNN," Jim Acosta wrote.

"POTUS is very unhappy," the source was quoted as saying. Acosta then went out on TV and dramatically described the deteriorating relationship between the President and his once-beloved Press Secretary.

All of this, of course, was based on a single anonymous source. But unlike the public, we knew this source went around town convincing people—journalists and clients alike—that he maintained a close relationship with the President. In reality, Trump couldn't have picked him out of a lineup. He had completely made up the story about the President being mad at Sarah. Acosta had run the single-sourced story, apparently unconcerned about whether it was true or not. And that's how your CNN news was programmed for the day.

Now, you might think to yourself, *Okay, fine, Jim Acosta's no Bob Woodward. That's not exactly breaking news.* But what if I told you that Bob Woodward is no Bob Woodward, either, at least the way his legend is portrayed?

In Woodward's book on the Trump White House, *Fear,* the famed journalist describes a scene in Trump Tower after Steve Bannon had first joined the campaign as its CEO. Bannon takes the elevators up to the fourteenth floor and enters the war room, the nerve center of the campaign, and is stunned to find just one person sitting there: Andy Surabian. Bannon peppers Surabian with questions, taken aback by the lack of people working on a weekend. It's all very cinematic. Bannon—the campaign's savior—fully realizes the challenge that lies ahead of him. The empty war room illustrates the ragtag nature of the campaign and implies a contrast between the skeleton crew in Trump Tower and the Clinton machine headquartered a few miles away in Brooklyn. It's all quite interesting. Except it never happened; the entire scene is a total fabrication, presented by the country's most esteemed journalist as if he had been sitting there observing it all himself.

Now, in a sense, the scene is not misleading. The underlying points being illustrated were generally correct. But the actual interaction and dialogue literally never took place. There were only two people in the scene: Steve Bannon and Andy Surabian. And yet, according to Surabian, Woodward never called him to verify the story. Surabian laughed upon reading the excerpt with his name in it. He wasn't mad—it wasn't like the story was damaging to him, or to anyone else, for that matter. He just couldn't believe that Bob Woodward of Watergate fame was printing fictionalized accounts made up out of thin air without even making a cursory attempt to confirm their veracity.

Large chunks of the book are recitations of one-on-one conversations between Trump's senior aides and the President. When the book came out, Woodward was very public about the fact that he had not talked to Trump while writing the book. So obviously he was entirely reliant on single sources for many of these conversations. Unsurprisingly, the individuals in these scenes almost always come across as nearly heroic. And since I'd spent countless hours with many of the people portrayed in the book, I knew much of the dialogue sounded nothing like the way they actually spoke—to the President or to one another.

Throughout the book, Woodward quotes various people who "told an associate" this, that, or the other. Readers are left wondering who this mystery associate is, or what ax they may have to grind. Assessing the credibility of sources is a very real challenge for members of the press. Sources inflate their access and knowledge. They have agendas. Reporters have to attempt to assess what's true and what's not. As for readers, they have no idea how trustworthy these sources are.

I know firsthand the value of anonymous sources. A series of stories I broke in Alabama—all based on information provided to me by anonymous sources—ultimately helped take down a corrupt governor. These stories included audio recordings, bank records, and other evidence of wrongdoing. Woodward is a legend as the result of anonymous sources who helped him and his colleagues take down Nixon. But now we have reporters relying on anonymous sources to tell their readers about pretty much everything, including the President's "mood" at a given moment. It's a joke.

14

BLACK EYES AND BROKEN GLASS

By the third week of January 2018, the West Wing was finally settling into a post-holiday routine. After the health-care failure and tax reform success of 2017, our second-year legislative agenda was shaping up to be decidedly less ambitious. For Trump, this just meant looking for more opportunities to take executive actions wherever he felt inclined. During his first year in office, nothing made him happier than slashing executive branch regulations on business. He rolled back the most in history. In his second year, trade wars were his new favorite pastime.

On the afternoon of January 23, 2018, Trump was in a great mood after slapping tariffs on imported residential washing machines and solar products, something he had been wanting to do for a long time. But when Kellyanne Conway and I walked into the Oval Office that afternoon, we were coming to discuss another issue that needed additional attention: the opioid crisis.

Over two million Americans were suffering from an addiction to opioids, which were now killing more people on an annual basis than car accidents. Trump had campaigned on doing something about this epidemic, which he had already declared a national health emergency. Kellyanne was the White House's point person on opioids—the rare occasion when she had a defined responsibility—and she was pushing for a massive public affairs campaign to raise awareness.

"We're creating a website," Kellyanne told the President, "and the centerpiece of it will be a video of you encouraging people to submit their personal stories about how the crisis has affected them, their family, or their friends."

Trump thought about this concept for a moment, and then shook his head.

"This isn't going to work," he said. "Me telling people to sign up on a website isn't going to do anything."

Kellyanne defended the idea, noting that it was a small part of a much bigger plan, but Trump was unmoved. He liked the idea of doing videos, but he had something much different in mind.

"We need to scare kids so much that they will never touch a single drug in their entire life," he began, leaning back and rocking slowly. "What about ads? Can't we make ads? I want to make ads. Just give this to Cliff and let him make the most horrifying ads you've ever seen. Could you do that?"

He looked at me and I just nodded. *Sure, I mean, yeah, I could do that.*

"No, I mean it," he said, suddenly sitting up straight with a scowl across his face. "We need people dying in a ditch. I want bodies stacked on top of bodies."

Whoa, that escalated quickly.

"Do it like they did with cigarettes," he continued. "They had body bags piled all over the streets and ugly people with giant holes in their faces and necks."

He leaned back in his chair again, like a confident attorney resting his case.

"Next thing you know, the kids don't want to be 'cool' and smoke anymore," he concluded. "If we don't do that, then I don't even know what we're doing this for."

The President was attuned to how the public reacted viscerally to certain images. His rhetoric often conjured up terrifying pictures of violent gang members, terrorists—and even scheming, biting snakes. The media recoiled at his appeals to the country's basest instincts, but he was talking to Middle America the way that Middle America talked. And if there was any issue Middle America was struggling with, it was opioids.

He begrudgingly walked with me over to the residence to record the toned-down video Kellyanne was asking for, and he spent most of the walk railing to me about how drug kingpins should get the death penalty because "they're killing way more people than one guy with a knife." We would have to come back to this conversation later, though, because the White House was about to descend into a crisis of our own.

That evening, I got a phone call from a White House reporter working at one of the country's largest newspapers. He had heard something so outrageous he didn't believe it was true. But it was also salacious enough that he felt like he had to ask around anyway.

"So, have you heard anything disturbing about Rob Porter?"

Porter was the White House Staff Secretary and may have been second only to the Chief of Staff in terms of day-to-day proximity to the President. Every piece of paper the President saw was supposed to first go through Porter's office. In a famously non-process-oriented White House, Porter viewed his operation as the thin line between controlled chaos and total anarchy. Senior aides sometimes griped that Porter was exceeding his mandate and becoming too overbearing. But everyone would concede that he was highly competent, and his team was one of the few in the building that had succeeded in developing some semblance of structure.

By all outward appearances, Porter was "central casting," to borrow Trump's favorite phrase. He was a clean-cut guy from a prominent Mormon family. His father had been a senior aide to President George H. W. Bush before becoming a professor at Harvard. His mom had been a faculty dean at Harvard prior to passing away in May 2017. Porter himself had done a two-year stint as a Mormon missionary in London between earning two degrees from Harvard and one from Oxford. He was a blue blood—a card-carrying member of the Ivy League elite. His hair was always gelled and crisply parted from left to right.

Handsome, Harvard, Oxford. Elite. There weren't any more bells you could ring to receive star status from the President.

From the perspective of a coworker who didn't know anything about Porter's personal life, like me, he seemed like the most buttoned-up, low-key player in a White House full of oversized characters. But that was far from what the reporter was hearing.

"Look, man, I have no idea if this is true," he said, hesitating. "In fact, I feel weird even saying it because it just seems like a nasty rumor."

"Spit it out, dude," I said, jokingly. "It's Porter—it can't be that bad."

"Well, actually, it is—at least what I've been told," he replied, clearing his throat. "Here's the thing: I've been told that Porter abused his ex-wives, and that's why they both divorced him. I was also told that this abuse popped up on his background check, so he hasn't been able to get a full security clearance."

My immediate reaction was, "Whoa, man. Definitely didn't expect you to say that. I didn't even know Rob had ever been married."

I told the reporter off the record that it all sounded really far-fetched—the kind of rumor that could only be dreamt up by the demented minds of D.C. political operatives. "But more than that," I said, "how could the guy do that job without a clearance? I mean, I don't think they'd let someone like that work in the White House at all, much less that close to the President. It just doesn't sound plausible."

He agreed. "That's what I thought, too. It's probably not true. But the weird thing is that I trust the source I heard it from. Like, normally what they tell me turns out to be legit."

The D.C. rumor mill can be like a cutthroat version of the old children's game of "telephone"—the one where the first kid whispers something to the second, who whispers it to the third, and so on until it reaches the end of the line. The last kid then says the statement as he heard it, and everyone bursts out laughing because it's unrecognizable from its original form. When I got off the phone with the reporter, that's what I assumed was going on.

Meanwhile, on the other side of the country, another Trump ally was facing much more public accusations of his own. Billionaire casino mogul Steve Wynn was the focus of a shocking *Wall Street Journal* exposé detailing "a decades-long pattern of sexual misconduct by Mr. Wynn" that included accusations of "pressuring employees to perform sex acts." Wynn was a former casino-business rival of Trump's, but the President considered him a good friend. And since Trump had taken office, Wynn had become the Republican National Committee's finance chairman.

The Wynn story broke in the midst of a national movement exposing powerful men for abusing their positions, especially in the workplace, to commit acts of sexual harassment and assault. Activists encouraged other women to share such stories online using the hashtag #MeToo.

A few days after the Wynn story came to light, Trump mentioned it to a handful of aides lingering in the Oval after an event. "You see this thing with Wynn?" he asked. We all had, of course. "Who knows, maybe he was out there forcing women into all kinds of stuff. If he did, well, then, that's that. But I've gotta tell you, I've got friends—many friends, good guys, you would know them—and they're scared to death about this 'Me Too,' as they're calling it." As was by now a common occurrence, the President was citing friends he would never name as validators of what he believed. In this case, I had no doubt he was reflecting genuine concerns. "There was a time in America when you were innocent until proven guilty. Now all it takes is for one anonymous person to say one disgusting thing and you're finished." He added, "Well, unless you pay them a fortune. Then when the lawyers find out you're paying out, they find three or four more women to come after you. It's a dirty business." He didn't mention Stormy Daniels, though I wouldn't be surprised if the name crossed a few more minds in the room than my own.

Working himself up, the President continued, "So I'm telling you, this 'Me Too' thing might backfire, if you want to know the truth. Because now women aren't getting the opportunities sometimes because the men are scared to death they're gonna be marks. It's a shame. No one will say it, but it's true." Trump would later express these sentiments publicly and acknowledge that his views were heavily influenced by his personal experiences with such allegations. But at the time we were glad he was just venting about it privately.

The Wynn story and my day-to-day work in the West Wing had put out of my mind the reporter's phone call about Rob Porter. But not for long, because on February 1, the day after Trump's #MeToo riff in the Oval, news broke publicly that Porter and Hope Hicks were dating. The *Daily Mail*, a U.K.-based tabloid that also dabbled in political coverage, released paparazzi-style photos of Porter and Hicks "canoodling" and "kissing in the back seat of a cab." Their relationship was known to a small group of people in the White House, but would now be the talk of D.C., a famously chatty town, even when there aren't pictures of a model involved.

I was bummed for Hope. Even though there wasn't anything scandalous about two single adults going out on a date, no one wants to be clandestinely photographed and then wake up to find the pictures all over the internet. But she was more annoyed than angry, rolling her eyes at the office the next morning and shrugging it off. *What can ya do, ya know?*

But not long after the tabloid spread hit the internet, I got a call from another reporter. She described in gut-wrenching detail a story of Porter's past domestic abuse. The story, she explained, had been relayed to her by a "somewhat trustworthy source," but she had not yet seen any tangible proof that it was true or had any success getting it confirmed.

For a second time I dismissed the rumors as absurd, telling the reporter that it sounded like someone had an ax to grind. At this point, though, I was wrestling with what to do. Hope was plenty tough enough to take care of herself, but I felt a sense of loyalty—even affection—for her and everyone else with whom I'd been in a foxhole for well over a year now. I thought she should at least know what people were saying. I didn't believe any of it, so I wasn't concerned for her well-being as much as I just wanted to alert her that someone clearly had it out for Rob, and maybe her, too.

Sitting in a Cheesecake Factory in suburban D.C., I finally decided to call Josh Raffel. Josh was a former top-tier PR executive who had handled both the Trump and Kushner accounts for his firm. Like Kushner, and an earlier version of Trump himself, he had been a Democrat. He had supported Hillary Clinton, even donating to her campaign less than a month before Election Day. But once he agreed to enter the White House, no one was more fierce in his defense of the President, the White House, or the staff. His close relationship with many of the so-called Trump loyalists, myself included, was definitive proof in my mind that our biggest problem with so many of the former RNC aides was not their past lapses in loyalty, it was that they were awful at their jobs. Josh, on the other hand, was far and away the most experienced crisis communications manager in the administration, which earned him the unenviable task of handling some of the most difficult incoming stories. Ivanka—and all of us, really—almost always followed his guidance. He also happened to be Hope's closest friend. I thought something like this would be better received coming from him.

Two reporters, I explained, had called with the same salacious story. Even they agreed that it seemed far-fetched. I had no idea if there was any truth to it and no sense of where it was coming from.

"Are they working on stories or just fishing?" he asked. I told him I thought they were just fishing, for now, and that I'd swatted down the gossip as best I could.

The following Monday morning, I was sitting at my desk in the West Wing press office when Porter came in. He walked across the room with purpose, looking me squarely in the eyes, reached over the computer screen, and held out his hand. "Thank you," he said quietly, not adding any further explanation. I reached up and shook his hand and gave him a quick, downward head nod as if to say, *Of course, this is what teammates do.*

There was always foot traffic coming through the West Wing press office—staff, reporters, visitors—but by this point I could tell whenever there was a crisis situation unfolding. The routine of preparing Sarah for the press brief-ing was interrupted. Standing meetings were canceled without explanation. Senior press aides rushed in and out of Sarah's office without knocking. And the following evening, on February 6, 2018, we were in comms crisis mode again. I watched my press colleagues like they were trapped inside of a snow globe. Someone had shaken it up and everything was swirling around them.

I was on the outside looking in, sitting comfortably at my desk, eating green apple slices and peanut butter and planning out some events the Presi-dent would be traveling for in the coming months. Then I saw a flustered Rob Porter dart into Sarah's office and quickly close the door behind him.

Well, that's not normal, I thought. *Could this be about . . . ?*

Shortly after 7 P.M., the *Daily Mail* published on-the-record accounts from Porter's two ex-wives, both claiming that he had abused them. The ar-ticle included detailed descriptions and documentation to support the accu-sations.

"He was verbally, emotionally and physically abusive and that is why I left," said Porter's first wife, Colbie Holderness. His second wife, Jennifer Wil-loughby, claimed "Porter pulled her naked from the shower by the shoulders and yelled at her." Both wives described unpredictable fits of rage. They called him "oppressive," and Willoughby produced a protective order she had ob-tained when Porter "punched in the glass" on her front door after she repeat-edly asked him to leave.

I suddenly remembered I had once actually seen a flash of Porter's anger—when he had berated Peter Navarro, accusing him of leaking to the press. When Navarro tried to defend himself, Porter began shouting.

"You're a f—ing liar, Peter! You're a f—ing liar and everyone knows it!" Tiny strands of his meticulously managed hair broke away from the pack as his head jerked around. A vein bulged on his temple as the blood rushed to his face.

Cooler heads ultimately prevailed, and Porter called me down to his of-fice later that day to apologize for his "unprofessional behavior." I laughed it off, told him not to worry about it. At that time it seemed to be an isolated incident in a tense working environment. What these women were alleging went well beyond that.

In the face of this sensational news, Porter was indignant. "I will not comment about these matters, beyond stating that many of these allegations are slanderous and simply false," he told the *Daily Mail.*

Many? Not all? Yikes.

Everyone in the Trump White House had been buffeted by so many outrageous news stories and allegations—a fair number of them false or only partially true—that the temptation was to deny everything first and revise as needed. The President seemed to do that himself with some regularity. Also, since Porter was personally well-liked among most of the senior staff, they seemed to readily dismiss such awful allegations and to offer Rob their support without hesitation.

"Rob Porter is a man of true integrity and honor, and I can't say enough good things about him," General Kelly said in an on-the-record statement. "He is a friend, a confidant, and a trusted professional. I am proud to serve alongside him."

Sarah backed Porter up, too. "I have worked directly with Rob Porter nearly every day for the last year and the person I know is someone of the highest integrity and exemplary character."

I wasn't sure if Porter had lied to Kelly and Sarah and they were acting on false information, or if they even truly believed what they were saying. I would soon learn the answer, and it wasn't the same for both of them.

I was not high-profile enough for my support to have mattered, but I was nonetheless relieved I wasn't asked to give it. No one wants to believe that a person they work with could have a dark side hidden just beneath their public persona. Then again, not all monsters look the part. In any event, I didn't know Rob well enough to have an opinion on whether he was capable of what he was being accused of. I didn't want to believe it—I had dismissed the rumors early on—but these accusations sure seemed credible to me. The allegations, Porter's denial, and questions about his security clearance were the top story lines on cable news that evening. But the story didn't really explode until late that night—at 12:53 A.M.—when Ryan Grim, a reporter for *The Intercept,* tweeted photos provided by Porter's first wife, showing her with a black eye that she claimed Porter had given her.

Lying in bed, unable to sleep and scrolling through Twitter, I sat up when I saw the picture, startling our dog, who had been sleeping peacefully between Megan and me. The image was shocking. Porter's then-wife was looking straight into the camera, her big brown eyes defiant, not betraying the pain she must be feeling from the crescent-shaped, purple-and-light-brown bruise swelling beneath her right eye.

Some of Porter's closest friends in the White House began advising him that it was time to resign. Notably, however, General Kelly was not among them. "You should stay and fight," he kept saying. The Chief seemed to be letting his personal relationship with Porter cloud his judgment. But I could also see why he found that impulse tempting. He viewed Porter as a sober, trustworthy deputy in a White House full of flighty, naïve, and sometimes nefarious characters.

However, what Kelly seemed to be forgetting in the moment was that our job as White House aides was to always put the President's interests first. How did it serve the President to insist on keeping a credibly accused wife beater on staff? We didn't have to go out of our way to kick the guy while he was down, but surely he couldn't be allowed to stick around and drag the entire White House down with him. This was my view, but I didn't share it with the President. That would have been veering too far out of my lane, a lesson I'd tried to learn from my earlier mistakes. Kelly had insisted on day one that the staff was his responsibility now. These decisions were on him.

The Chief seemed willing to keep propping Porter up, but Porter himself wasn't cooperating. Perhaps in deference to the President, perhaps because he thought there might be more coming, perhaps out of guilt, he had come to the decision that it was time for him to step down. To make this announcement, the press team decided to bring in four reporters from top-tier news outlets. Each of them was chasing the story that Porter was on the brink of resigning. The idea was to allow him to tell his side of the story in his own words. So the following morning, Mike Bender from *The Wall Street Journal*, Josh Dawsey from *The Washington Post*, Maggie Haberman from *The New York Times*, and Jonathan Swan from *Axios* were all invited into the Press Secretary's office.

When they walked in, Porter was there waiting for them. Haberman, Swan, and Dawsey sat down on the couch beneath a shelving unit that held pictures of Sanders's family and a bottle of "Warrior Whiskey." She displayed the bottle as a show of support for veterans—the company was founded by a Navy SEAL—but on days like this I'm sure she was tempted to crack it open. Bender sat down in a chair adjacent to the couch, across from Porter, and Sanders and Raffel laid out the ground rules. Porter would share his story—the "real" story—off the record. Then the press staff would provide background information and quotes they could use for their stories.

With the formalities out of the way, Porter was given the floor to explain himself. The stakes were high. These were four of the most influential journalists in Washington. If Porter could lay out a convincing case that he was not the terrible person he was being portrayed as, it wouldn't save his job but could have a significant impact on his future prospects. He eased into the conversation, thanking the reporters for coming. He spoke methodically, as if each word needed to be precise and measured. He wasn't a perfect person, he explained slowly. He had endured two failed marriages and bore much of the blame for their failures. As reported, he had indeed called his wife a "f—ing b—" on their honeymoon. He'd lashed out during verbal arguments. But he'd never been physically abusive.

Everyone in the room listened in complete silence. Rob's body language made it seem like it was physically painful for him to concede that he had been verbally abusive. But he must have thought that admitting he had been a less-than-ideal husband might add credibility to his other denials. He haltingly continued on.

The allegations were part of a coordinated smear campaign, he intoned. The forces arrayed against him included disgruntled people in his personal life as well as political foes who were angry he was in the White House and they weren't. While he didn't name these people to the reporters, behind the scenes he had been much more direct in his conspiracy theorizing. At the top of the list was a woman named Samantha Dravis, a senior staffer at the Environmental Protection Agency. She and Porter had dated. At one point they had even lived together. Now she was apparently—in his mind at least—a woman scorned.

The other name Porter brought up privately was Corey Lewandowski, Trump's onetime campaign manager who still maintained a place in his orbit. At various points throughout Trump's first year in office, Lewandowski had been rumored to be on the verge of joining the White House staff. It was always hard to tell if there was legitimacy to these rumors or if Corey was just spreading them himself—or perhaps both. But Corey was notorious in media circles for spreading information, sometimes with questionable validity, about various Trump World rivals. By all accounts, he jealously guarded his closeness to the President like a treasure, and there was no denying he held a special place in Trump's heart. Corey was one of his originals, on board in the early days when most other people thought it was a fool's errand. One thing that had not changed in the transition from Reince Priebus to John Kelly was that Corey undercut the Chief of Staff to the President just about every chance he got. *They weren't loyal, they weren't competent,* and—implied in all of the criticisms—they weren't Corey. Porter, being a Kelly acolyte, believed he might be a Lewandowski target as well. Once again, it wasn't entirely clear to me whether Porter's theory had merit or if he was just straining for an explanation.

One of the reporters asked Porter to discuss the photo showing his bruised ex-wife. Porter dismissed it, explaining that he himself had taken the picture to document the results of an unfortunate little accident. Nothing, he claimed, was as it was being portrayed. It was all character assassination, plain and simple.

He was gathered before some of the sharpest reporters in D.C. But it didn't take a genius to wonder what sort of "unfortunate" accident could cause a black eye. One of those present pressed him on that very question.

Porter hesitated for a moment, looking around as if to say, *This is all off the record, right?* Then he leaned in.

He and his wife were vacationing in Venice, Italy, celebrating a birthday, he explained. While shopping one afternoon, they had purchased a fancy Murano glass vase. Once they made it back to their hotel room, an argument ensued. His wife was so angry, he said, that she grabbed the vase and threatened to smash it on the floor. He tried to stop her. There was a tug of war over the vase, and in the struggle she somehow ended up with an unintentional black eye.

The reporters in the room must have been wondering, *How could it have gotten so violent that it led to an "accidental" black eye?*

There was more uneasy silence. Then a reporter asked another question. What about the other accusations, like the restraining order alleging he had punched through the window of his wife's door?

They were living apart at the time, he said. He came to her house and approached the front door, which was wooden on the bottom half with nine glass panes at the top. He tapped on one of the windowpanes with his index finger, and somehow—inexplicably—his hand broke through the glass. He started bleeding and asked if he could come inside to bandage it up. She wouldn't let him, so he left. She called the police to report the incident, which led to the report. He was uncertain if an actual restraining order ever went through.

As the conversation wound down, Porter made it clear that he had not been asked to resign. In fact, he had been encouraged to stay. But out of a sense of duty to the President and the White House, he said, he had decided to remove himself as a distraction. He would not be leaving immediately, but would participate in a smooth and orderly transition of the Staff Secretary's office over the coming days and weeks. With that, Porter exited the room, leaving the small group of reporters and press staff to digest what they had just been told. To my knowledge, it was the first time anyone in the room—staff included— had heard Porter's full, sensational explanation.

Nobody had to say a word because everyone was thinking the same thing anyway. *That was . . . really quite something. And could he possibly expect any of us to believe this?*

I was once again thankful that my job did not require me to publicly explain or defend, well, anything. Sarah Sanders's job, unfortunately, did not afford her that luxury.

Sarah's entire approach to the job was different from Sean Spicer's. The first half of every press secretary's day revolves around preparation for the afternoon press briefing. Sean would have upward of twenty-five staff arrayed around his office, throwing out topics and questions while he chewed and swallowed about thirty-five pieces of gum before lunch. These prep sessions were disorganized free-for-alls, frequently derailed by a combination of Sean's lack of discipline and staffers spitballing random thoughts.

Sarah, by contrast, organized and shrank these sessions to just a handful of people: two of her deputies, Raj Shah and Hogan Gidley, research director Adam Kennedy, and National Security Council spokesman Michael Anton. Hope Hicks and I would come in and out at various times, and Josh Raffel was always there to offer advice during crises—like the Porter situation— but other staff only came in to brief on their areas of expertise. My primary role was to write the prepared remarks Sarah would read at the top of each briefing.

Once she was behind the podium, Sarah's approach continued to diverge from Sean's. His instinct was to always be confrontational. When the temperature was running hot, Sean would crank it up even higher. Sarah, on the other hand, wanted to turn the temperature down, to see cooler heads prevail. That's not to say that she totally shied away from confrontation; she got into her fair share of Briefing Room squabbles. But she was more inclined than Sean was to deflect and disarm, rather than unload. She also set aside time in the office every day to do a quick Bible study. Just before the briefing, she would go into one of the smaller press offices with a devotional book, close the door, and not come out until she had spent time praying. This was her routine even—or perhaps especially—on the most chaotic and stressful days, like during the Porter crisis.

A couple of hours after the sit-down with the four reporters, Sarah took the podium in the White House Briefing Room, where Porter was the only thing reporters wanted to ask about.

"Rob has been effective in his role as Staff Secretary, and the President and Chief of Staff have had full confidence and trust in his abilities and his performance," she said. "He is going to be leaving the White House. It won't be immediate, but he is resigning from the White House, but is going to stay on to ensure that there's a smooth transition moving forward."

NBC's Hallie Jackson was the first reporter called on to ask a question.

"Less than eighteen hours ago, the White House released several statements praising Rob Porter and his service," she began. "Obviously, he's somebody who's very close with the President. So why would the President accept his resignation if the President thinks he did nothing wrong?" Sarah tiptoed around the question. Porter, she said, had made a "personal decision," but was "not pressured" to resign. As the press briefing continued, *The Intercept* published an article revealing that both of Porter's ex-wives had informed the FBI about his abusive past in January 2017, when they were both interviewed as part of his background check to receive a security clearance.

This is how a story gets legs. The press is always searching for the next angle to keep it alive. First there were the accusations. Then there were the images. Now there was evidence that the White House knew about these issues all along, but chose not to do anything—a potential cover-up. Had the White House been aware of these allegations all along? Who made the decision to let him stay, to give him a security clearance, to let him handle some of the U.S. government's most sensitive documents?

Porter retreated to his low-ceilinged office in the basement of the West Wing. He sat in a near catatonic state, contemplating how these events would change the course of his life forever. Senior aides sought to console him.

Maybe he wouldn't resign after all, he said at times. I went down to see him at one point, but the door was closed.

"Pop back by later, or whenever is convenient," one of the staffers told me. "He'll be around for the next couple of weeks, so there's no rush."

But while Porter pondered his future downstairs, the political calculus in other parts of the building was changing rapidly.

General Kelly finally started to feel the heat, and he wanted out of this particular kitchen—the one in which he was all but single-handedly defending an accused wife beater. At 9:31 P.M. that night, he released a new statement. "I was shocked by the new allegations released today against Rob Porter," he said. "There is no place for domestic violence in our society. . . . I accepted his resignation earlier today and will ensure a swift and orderly transition."

The following morning, Porter still showed up to work. But the media pressure had grown so intense that he was told he had to quickly pack up his stuff and leave. There would be no "smooth transition" over the course of days or weeks. His time in the White House had come to an end. His final exit was rushed so that Deputy Press Secretary Raj Shah could say during the next press briefing that Porter had already left the building for good.

But there were still countless unanswered questions. Foremost among them, the media relentlessly pressed for an explanation of what so-called new allegations had surfaced, causing General Kelly to withdraw his staunch support. "So you're saying the initial reports where two former wives accused him of violence, both physical and verbal abuse, were not sufficient?" NBC's Peter Alexander asked, noting that even after that Kelly had called Porter "a man of honor."

The following morning, General Kelly convened a senior staff meeting in the Roosevelt Room and laid out a strict timeline he expected everyone to stick to. With a straight face, according to several people who were there, Kelly claimed that within forty minutes of learning about the abuse allegations against Porter, he had taken action to have him removed from his job. The staff, many of whom had been following the crisis closely throughout the week, knew this was patently false. Several senior aides felt like they were being told to lie—a more generous interpretation was they were being brought into a new, more convenient reality—and the meeting quickly leaked to *The Washington Post*.

To understand why this was an important moment in Kelly's tenure, you have to understand the psychology of leaks. More often than not, such leaks "from inside the room" are a direct reflection of how the staff perceives the person leading the meeting. This is not a hard-and-fast rule, but people tended not to leak against people they respected, even when they disagreed with them. Factionalism certainly contributed to the leakiness of Priebus's and Spicer's tenure in the White House, but it was the fact that no one respected them that made leaking so widespread. Leaks with details from internal meetings had slowed significantly under Kelly's leadership, and to my recollection his senior staff meeting had never leaked—until then.

Kelly's standing with the staff plummeted. Even long after the Porter saga moved off the front pages, he never fully regained the respect he had once engendered. His morale-building turn defending the President in the White House Briefing Room was now a distant memory.

And no one was buying his story—inside or outside the administration. "[Kelly's] version of events contradicts both the public record and accounts from numerous other White House officials in recent days as the Porter drama unfolded," the *Post* reported. Then, to make matters worse, FBI Director Christopher Wray testified before Congress and publicly contradicted the White House's timeline on when they became aware of issues in Porter's background check. The FBI, Wray said, had submitted a partial report on Porter in March 2017, then completed their investigation in July 2017. So, according to the Federal Bureau of Investigation, for at least seven months the White House—or at least *somebody* in the White House—had total visibility on the Porter allegations and supporting evidence, but did nothing.

Sarah Sanders was shell-shocked. Anyone could see that. Porter had been a close personal friend. She had been completely blindsided by the abuse allegations. Then she had defended him, without all the facts, based on their relationship and his word. She had been burned. And now she was being sent out to defend the White House and Kelly, whom she was uncertain was being truthful.

The Chief remained defiant, even as it looked like his mishandling of the Porter situation could cost him his job. He later told me that everything that had been reported about his actions during the Porter crisis had been wrong. He blamed it all on a miscommunication between his office and the press team. Specifically, he blamed Jim Carroll, one of his deputies who had been acting as a liaison between the Chief's office and the crisis communications team. When he put his name on the original statement defending Porter, Kelly said he intended for it to make clear that Porter was resigning, only adding in as a side note that he had never witnessed Porter conduct himself unprofessionally in any way. But somewhere between his office and the press shop, Carroll had failed to accurately articulate his intentions. Of course, that didn't explain why he went out of his way to call Porter, who stood credibly accused of abusing multiple women, a man of integrity and honor. Maybe Jim Carroll got that wrong, too. For a Marine—and someone whom I had deeply respected up until that point—he sure did have a lot of excuses; it was everyone's fault but his.

Regardless, Kelly never trusted the press team again. When he would personally come under fire in the future, he would circumvent the press office by sending his personal aide, Zach Fuentes, to defend him on the record instead. The Chief never wavered from his position that he had acted decisively. Soon thereafter he even shipped Jim Carroll out of the White House to work instead in the Office of National Drug Control Policy.

Porter's credibility had been eviscerated. Kelly, a four-star Marine general, was watching his credibility be tarnished beyond repair. And Sarah sensed that hers was not far behind. She couldn't get clear information on when Kelly, White House Counsel Don McGahn, and Deputy Chief of Staff Joe Hagin, who oversaw the Personnel Security Division, knew about the Porter allegations.

Many of us believed that Porter had been given a pass simply because he was "one of them"—the type of staffer that Kelly and Hagin in particular wished they could fill the White House with instead of the rest of us losers. And yet Sarah was expected to go out and defend them all? She couldn't endure it any longer. Her frustration had finally reached a boiling point.

I know people out there—many people—have no sympathy for Sarah Sanders. In their view, she willingly excused, covered up for, and lied about the actions of the Trump administration. Sometimes spokespeople in any White House knowingly give misleading statements, other times they're just left out of the loop or sent out with false or incomplete information to unwittingly bend the truth on someone else's behalf. In my experience, Sarah typically endured the latter. But not always. Sometimes she knew she was being sent out to talk to the press with information that would likely prove to be inaccurate. She didn't press as hard as she could have for the rock-bottom truth. That intentional lack of rigor allowed her to go out and tell reporters things like "That's all I have" or "I've given you the best information I've got" or "I haven't talked to the President about that in detail." These gymnastics with the truth would tax even the nimblest of prevaricators, and Sarah was not that. She was not a natural liar and, I believe, in most cases she was not an intentional one.

During Spicer's tenure behind the podium, the effects of this pirouette wore on him professionally—he was just holding on to his job for dear life as his decades of public affairs experience were being wiped from memory. For Sarah, it felt much more personal—the enduring questions about her character and trustworthiness hit her in a much deeper way. I believed—and still believe—she was a good person doing an impossible job. But on the other hand, everyone reserves the right to resign at any moment. The Porter situation could well have been one of those moments, but it wasn't. Instead it pushed her boundaries in ways I wouldn't fully appreciate until the days and weeks went on.

On the second floor of the West Wing, she confronted White House Counsel Don McGahn. She made it clear that she was no longer going to be fed to the wolves with inaccurate or partial information. The door to the White House Counsel's Office is solid. It's outfitted with a keypad lock and reinforced to make it one of the most secure rooms in the building. As the tense conversation came to a head, Sarah stormed out and slammed the heavy door behind her with a thunderous clap. From that point forward a representative from the White House Counsel's Office attended all prep sessions for any spokespeople who might be forced to defend the White House's handling of the Porter scandal.

We may never know the full truth. Had senior White House aides covered up the Porter allegations, assuming they would never be made public? That appears likely, but remains somewhat murky. What we do know is this: a story that started with a paparazzi-style photo spread of Washington, D.C.'s new "power couple" ended as the single most damaging hit to the White House's credibility of the early Trump presidency—and it basically had nothing to do with the President. Even the media never really attempted to rope him into it. This was Kelly's debacle—his lapse of judgment. And, increasingly, it looked like it was his job on the line.

One of the reasons that nothing—no scandal, no outrageous comment, etc.—ever seemed to stick to Trump was that the news cycle shifted too rapidly for anything to fully take hold. The average person casually following the news couldn't keep up. Sometimes the outrage of the moment would be supplanted by something even more outrageous. Other times Trump would simply find a way to change the subject. That was the real power of his Twitter account—being able to seize control of the national conversation at any moment.

But with the Porter scandal, Trump was largely silent, letting it play out on its own. And there didn't appear to be anything on the horizon that might change the subject. Kelly was dangling from a rope, and the tree limb was slowly bending, lowering him closer and closer to the snapping jaws of the press alligators below.

At 2:19 P.M. on Wednesday, February 14, 2018—a week after the Porter scandal first broke—I was in the Oval Office, where the President was hosting a working session on "Opportunity Zones," a provision in the new tax law that was designed to drive investment into distressed communities. After he had remained silent on the Porter situation for the past week, the media had started pressing Trump to make a statement about domestic violence. We were planning to bring the press in for part of the Opportunity Zones meeting and knew at least one reporter would shout a question that would give Trump an opportunity to comment. Sure enough, right before the press was ushered out of the room, one of them called out, "Why have you not spoken out against domestic violence?"

Trump was ready for this, held his hand up to quiet the room, and made his statement. "I am opposed to domestic violence, and everybody here knows that," he said. "I am totally opposed to domestic violence of any kind. Everyone knows that, and it almost wouldn't even have to be said. So, now you hear it, but you all know it."

Trump was visibly annoyed, not because he wasn't opposed to domestic violence or anything like that, but because he loathed being dragged into commenting on issues he wasn't directly involved with, at least from his perspective. Commenting was the right thing to do, a point that he would begrudgingly concede, but he also knew it would have the effect of prolonging the Porter story—and Kelly's complicity in it—yet another day.

Kelly was already starting to lose his luster with the President anyway, as anyone who was getting credit for "managing" him eventually would. It wouldn't have mattered to Trump much, or at all, if the Porter issue sent Kelly packing, too.

Except it didn't, because at the moment the narrative changed in a shocking fashion.

Unbeknownst to us, at the exact moment we were standing in the Oval that day, a nineteen-year-old gunman had just opened fire on students and staff members at Marjory Stoneman Douglas High School in Parkland, Florida. When the carnage finally came to an end, seventeen people had lost their lives in the deadliest high school massacre in U.S. history. When I returned to my desk after the Oval Office event, horrifying images of children frantically running out of the school had just started to hit our television screens.

I never considered this until I worked in the West Wing, but staff in the White House experience such events much the same as the general public. Lines of communication are opened up between the administration and law enforcement officials on the ground, and the President is briefed with whatever information is available at the time, but it's not like we have real-time visibility on every crisis situation as it happens. During such events, the Situation Room circulates regular email updates, but most of them include information from "open source intelligence" (OSINT), like news reports.

Staffers in the Homeland Security offices downstairs hustle to quickly gather whatever information they can, but most of us stand speechless in front of our TVs, watching in horror like millions of other Americans in homes and offices around the country. We would come to find out that a former student, who had previously threatened to carry out such an attack, had finally decided to do it.

The following morning, the President addressed the nation from the Diplomatic Reception Room on the ground floor of the White House. I stood in the back of the room, just behind a line of press and television cameras, dozens of cables snaking around my feet, and watched him deliver lines that would overwhelm the emotions of most parents if they tried to say them out loud.

"Our entire nation, with one heavy heart, is praying for the victims and their families," he said. "To every parent, teacher, and child who is hurting so badly, we are here for you—whatever you need, whatever we can do, to ease your pain. We are all joined together as one American family, and your suffering is our burden also. No child, no teacher, should ever be in danger in an American school. No parent should ever have to fear for their sons and daughters when they kiss them good-bye in the morning. . . . I want to speak now directly to America's children, especially those who feel lost, alone, confused, or even scared: I want you to know that you are never alone and you never will be. You have people who care about you, who love you, and who will do anything at all to protect you. If you need help, turn to a teacher, a family member, a local police officer, or a faith leader. Answer hate with love; answer cruelty with kindness."

There's a certain amount of detachment that any speaker has to take on to keep from breaking down while delivering remarks that are that emotionally charged. That was hard even for an unsentimental man like the President. But as he spoke, I could feel his deep sympathy for the victims and their families.

After he was done speaking, he walked out of the Diplomatic Reception Room and back into the Center Hall that runs the length of the residence's ground floor. Turning left, he passed the Map Room and saw a small group of senior aides watching his remarks on a small television in the White House doctor's office. There's a slight delay in even "live" broadcasts, so he'd often stop in there to see the end of his remarks being aired. The entire team then walked with the President through the Palm Room and down the West Colonnade, parting ways as he and the Vice President turned left to go to the Oval, and everyone else continued straight into the West Wing.

I lagged behind the rest of the group and was the last staffer still outside when the President suddenly realized he had something he needed to say. Turning around, he saw me about twenty yards away.

"I'm going to Florida tomorrow," he said emphatically. "I don't care what they have to do. I'm going to Florida, okay? I want you to go right now, find Tony, and you tell him that I'm going to Florida. I'm sick of them telling me no. I want to go to Parkland. I want to see these people. And you go tell them right now that they better figure it out. Okay? That's it."

I nodded. "Yes, sir."

He turned around without saying another word and walked toward the Oval with the Vice President.

I knew immediately that the "Tony" he was referring to was Tony Ornato, the head Secret Service agent on the President's protective detail. As I would come to find out, the Secret Service was trying to pump the brakes on the President visiting Parkland. They were hoping to give themselves a little more time to iron out the logistical and security details. It's a herculean task to move the President and his team safely and smoothly. The Secret Service are total pros, and the President treated them all with the utmost respect. But he would occasionally grow frustrated when he couldn't do what he wanted on short notice. In this case, he was itching to show the people of Parkland that their President cared about them in their darkest hour.

I walked over to the Secret Service office in the Eisenhower Executive Office Building and delivered the message.

"He's adamant about going tomorrow," I told the agents on duty. "He said he doesn't care what has to be done, he just wants to be on a plane to Parkland tomorrow afternoon."

"Roger that," one of them replied. "We're on it." They delivered, as they always did.

As the Parkland shooting justifiably consumed the news, a colleague quietly made an observation that no one else had yet stopped to consider. "This is one of the saddest things I've ever seen," he began, "so I don't want anyone to take this the wrong way. But the fact that this will dominate news coverage for the foreseeable future could end up having the effect of saving Kelly his job." This was the kind of comment that, while true, could only come out of the mouth of a political operative who had been conditioned to suppress human reactions and focus on cold political realities.

But as awful as it was to contemplate, especially at a moment like that, he was right. The Porter scandal would never again be the focus of media obsession the way it initially was.

In the coming days, the President held emotional listening sessions with students, teachers, parents, and other survivors. During my time in the White House, I saw him empathize with Gold Star families, survivors of natural disasters, crime victims, and countless others. It wasn't always smooth—every interaction was conducted in his own unique, Trumpian way. But he was always sincere. Then, almost exactly two weeks later, another story would supplant the Parkland shooting. One far more personal to the President.

Hope Hicks had been spending hours preparing to testify before the House Intelligence Committee over Russian interference in the 2016 election. On

Tuesday, February 27, she spent over nine hours in a secure committee meeting room being peppered with question after question.

I have no idea what happened during her testimony. One of the few hard-and-fast rules that everyone seemed to abide by was that no one dared discuss anything related to any investigations. We didn't want to be subpoenaed next. However, nothing could stop members of the congressional committees from leaking about whatever happened behind closed doors, so once again most White House staffers were watching the drama unfold on TV, just like everyone else.

For Hope, the entire month of February was difficult on a deeply personal level. She had met a tall, brilliant, nice guy and was quietly experiencing the ride of a lifetime with him, working together during the day and walling themselves off from the world in the evenings. She was so private that she hadn't even shared their relationship with most of her friends in the White House. Next thing she knew, her pictures were spread all over the television, magazines, and newspapers, paparazzi were staking out her apartment, and her boyfriend was being accused of some of the most vile abuses imaginable. On top of that she was enduring another round of blistering press coverage of her testimony, during which media reports claimed she had admitted to occasionally telling "white lies" on the President's behalf. That was no revelation, not really—nearly everyone in a press role told "white lies" in this White House (and probably other White Houses, too).

She had also been considering for quite a while whether it was time for her to move on to a new adventure. Hope had not even turned thirty and she had seen more, experienced more—endured more—than most people would in a lifetime. But while being at the center of it all was exciting, even addicting, she also seemed to feel like it might be time for her to leave it all behind—to return to some sense of normalcy, even if anonymity was no longer possible.

I walked over to her office just outside the Oval one evening after most of the staff had gone home. I found her there sitting at her desk, leaning back in her office chair and staring at a muted television screen as the talking heads dissected everything from her relationship to her fashion choices to whether she might just be a traitor to her country.

"Are you okay?" I asked her.

She smiled faintly, never diverting her eyes from the TV.

"I'm fine," she said. "DJT and I talked about all of this coverage today and he just told me, you know, 'If you're going to be someone in this world, if you're going to do something with your life, there are always going to be people who try to drag you down.'"

The changing images on the television screen were splashing different colors across Hope's face in the dimly lit room. "I mean, just look at what he deals with," she continued. "He's done this for decades. Constant press, constant stories, people digging into his life, his family. If he can make it through all of that, I can deal with this. It's little, it's nothing."

Mirroring is a phenomenon in which people subconsciously mimic each other in social settings—their body language, posture, and gestures. In Trump World, mirroring took on a life of its own. At home, I'd find myself repositioning my silverware the same way Trump would at the dinner table. While making speeches I would realize—sometimes in the moment, sometimes while watching video after the fact—that I was using certain Trumpian mannerisms. All of us on staff seemed to have adopted his counterpunching mentality, at various times deploying it against the press, our political adversaries, and even our colleagues. As I listened to Hope speak, I sensed her inherent toughness—she had been a college lacrosse player, after all—but also couldn't help but see her mirroring Trump's unflinching belief that he could endure anything, overcome any attack, and thrive in the midst of chaos that made others wilt.

But unlike the President, she still had almost her entire life ahead of her. There was so much more to do, so much left to experience, to preserve some energy for.

On February 28, three weeks after the Porter story hit the news, Hope resigned.

Trump was accustomed to staff turnover—we all were. I usually couldn't tell if he cared at all when people came and went, even his closest aides. He maintained an unnatural emotional detachment from it all. But this was different, more personal. Hope wasn't staff; she was family. I also got the sense that Trump was starting to look around and realize, *There aren't many of us left*. The "loyalists" were slowly leaving, one by one.

The next day, after he had delivered remarks at an event in the East Room, I broached the subject with him for the first and only time. "Not going to be the same without Hope," I said. "End of an era."

For the first time ever, I sensed the slightest tinge of, I don't know, almost sadness in the President's demeanor. Which was something no one I knew had ever seen in Donald Trump.

"Hopey was the best," he said, looking away. What was interesting to me was that Hope wasn't gone quite yet, but he was already talking about her in the past tense.

15

DISPOSABLE

"You can go on in," Chief of Staff John Kelly's executive assistant told me. "He'll join you shortly."

I walked into the Chief's office and made my way over to the conference table running along the far wall. By West Wing standards, the office was downright palatial. The half-dozen floor-to-ceiling windows were covered by sheer—almost translucent—white curtains, allowing the outside light to stream into the room. That, combined with the fifteen-foot-tall ceilings, made it one of the few spaces in the building that actually felt open and airy. The chief typically worked behind an L-shaped desk, with the computer elevated, allowing him to stand as he scanned his emails. The north end of the room included built-in shelving and one of the West Wing's finest old fireplaces. A large flat-screen TV hung on the wall above it, with a spacious sitting area out in front. French doors on the south side of the room opened out onto a patio, which led down to a large swimming pool with a standalone pool house. It was good to be the Chief.

It was March 2018, and Kelly seemed like he was finally emerging from the Porter scandal to catch his second wind, even though he would never again be revered by the staff. He had called me in to discuss a job opening he was looking to fill—Director of the Office of Public Liaison (OPL). This was the role that Priebus had blocked Scaramucci from filling in the early days of the administration. In a highly functioning White House, OPL leads the effort to build coalitions of support for the President and his agenda. Needless to say, we weren't a highly functioning White House, and OPL had been a virtual nonentity to that point.

The Chief walked into the room, along with his deputy Zach Fuentes and Johnny DeStefano, a former aide to House Speaker John Boehner who was now Counselor to the President, overseeing the White House political and external affairs operation. Kelly was relaxed. He maintained an air of confidence—perhaps arrogance—that was reminiscent of a small-town high school quarterback who wasn't quite as good as he thought he was. Normally he liked to get right to the point, but on this particular day he wanted to chat— about the inept press and communications teams, the Porter debacle, the media, and how much he hated his job.

"What do you think is wrong with the comms shop?" he asked, seemingly baffled by the dysfunction. I told him I saw two primary issues. First, due to a failure of leadership early on, warring factions had never jelled into a single team. And even though the old leaders were long gone, the bad blood remained. Second, I told him we were victims of the "tyranny of the urgent," as the late author Charles Hummel called it. Everyone was sucked into the crisis of the moment, and no one was planning ahead, strategizing, or really thinking through how to win the battle of ideas. Addressing those two issues is what made our tax "tiger team" successful, while the day-to-day operations remained a disaster.

Now he was intrigued. He set his pen down on the table, pushed his chair back slightly, and crossed one leg over the other. "So what would you have done differently with the Rob Porter issue?"

This question was trickier. I was very interested in the OPL job, and the last thing I wanted to do in that moment was re-litigate all of the ways I thought the Chief had mishandled the situation. As I've mentioned, I knew he blamed everyone in the building but himself, and at this point it wouldn't do anything for me to suggest otherwise.

"Well, unfortunately, the public will never be able to fully understand how that played out behind the scenes," I said. This was true, but also ambiguous enough to be safe ground. And to my great relief, Kelly jumped back in before I had to elaborate further.

"Everything that's been reported about that was a lie," he grumbled, furrowing his brow even more than usual. "I took immediate action. Within an hour of learning about the issue, it was addressed, he was gone. The only problem was miscommunication." I wasn't sure if he was telling me what he actually thought or what I was supposed to believe from here on out. Probably both. Of course, this comment was absurd on its face. *Miscommunication? You mean putting your name on a statement praising the character and integrity of a credibly accused wife beater? Or do you mean telling him to "stay and fight," then turning around twenty-four hours later and saying his resignation was effective immediately?*

Of course, I didn't say any of that, but it was impossible not to think it.

"This is the worst f—ing job I've ever had," Kelly continued in a sudden spurt of exasperation. "People apparently think that I care when they write that I might be fired. If that ever happened, it would be the best day I've had since I walked into this place. And the President knows it, too. It's a liberating feeling when no one has any power over you—when you don't care if you get fired."

On one hand I understood where he was coming from. Working in the West Wing had been the most trying professional experience of my life as well—by far. But I was struck by the disdain he seemed to harbor for both the extraordinary honor he had been given and even for the President himself. It also was clear despite his bravado that he did care what people wrote about him—who wouldn't?

But I tried to relate, in my own way. I told him that in my experience, people in Washington tended to be defined by their job. It becomes much more than what they do—it becomes *who they are*. I told him I struggled with that, too, but that I ultimately knew my identity was found in my faith. *So, yeah, there is liberty in knowing who you are, regardless of what your job is.*

The Chief nodded earnestly; he at least seemed to agree with the sentiment. From there we spent the next twenty minutes working through what I would do with OPL, if I was named director.

I told him the first priority would be to lead organizational change, to motivate team members to become a highly functioning unit that produced top-quality results. We would focus on "keeping the turnstiles spinning," I explained, a reference to the southwest entrance where guests entered. There would not be a single day when the White House didn't engage with key outside groups or host working sessions, policy and communications briefings, or meet and greets. I ran through how we would coordinate with other White House offices to develop deep support among influential parts of the Trump coalition, like conservatives, the faith community, veterans, and law enforcement groups, among others. And I told him we had to make a serious effort to reach various ethnic groups that had either been ignored or spurned by earlier bad experiences. To measure our progress, I told him we would develop key performance indicators, like the number of groups and individuals we had engaged, the number of sessions we had hosted, and particularly how we were engaging on the President's top agenda items.

I closed with a list of eight core values that would guide everything we did:

1. We are people of character.
2. We never settle for anything less than excellence.
3. We deliver a consistent experience.
4. We take extreme ownership of our responsibilities.
5. We always present a unified front.
6. We put our agendas aside, because the President's agenda is the only one that matters.
7. We are humbled by our small role in shaping the course of history.
8. We never quit.

I wanted to show Kelly—the military man—that I understood that everything rises and falls on leadership. This was something I believed deep in my bones, and it also happened to be at the core of every frustration I experienced in the White House. I thought this was something he would connect with.

When our meeting finished, DeStefano called me up to his office upstairs. "That was really impressive, man," he said. "No matter what ends up happening with OPL, that was good for you. You made a big impression."

I went home that evening feeling good. I told my wife, Megan, that I was ready to move on from the daily nightmares of the White House communications team. For the first time since we passed tax reform, I felt like there was light at the end of the tunnel—*I may survive this after all.*

Oh, how wrong I would be.

A little over a week after my meeting with the Chief about OPL, his deputy Zach Fuentes asked me to come down to his new office—the one that Steve

Bannon once occupied. It was almost unrecognizable. The dark lord's lair had been turned into a run-of-the-mill West Wing office instead of HQ for a historic insurrection against global elites. Fuentes and DeStefano were in there waiting for me.

"So here's the thing," Fuentes said. "You blew the Chief away in your meeting with him. I mean, really blew him away. He's brought it up several times since then. But we think we've come up with a better idea for you than OPL."

"Yeah, I agree," DeStefano chimed in. "We're going to give OPL to Justin Clark," who at that point was Director of Intergovernmental Affairs. "You don't want it," he continued. "Believe me, it's a huge mess and you're just going to get yourself shot up if you move over there."

I liked Justin. He was a great guy, a staunch Trump loyalist from the campaign, hardworking and competent. *But where's this going? And why am I already being sold so hard on whatever it is being better than what I wanted?*

"We've got a much better spot for you," Fuentes said, jumping back in. "What do you think about being Assistant Secretary of Veterans Affairs? It's the second biggest government department, and it needs someone the President trusts to go in and help fix it."

Whoa, I didn't see this coming.

At the time, the VA Secretary, Dr. David Shulkin, was in hot water for using taxpayer money to cover his wife's airfare to fly with him to Europe. Once they got there, they had improperly accepted tickets to the Wimbledon tennis tournament. The VA's internal watchdog uncovered the impropriety and was accusing Shulkin's Chief of Staff of making false statements to try to cover it all up. Meanwhile, Shulkin's current Assistant Secretary, a former Trump campaign staffer, was openly trying to orchestrate his ouster. My immediate reaction was to point out that the VA was making the West Wing look tame by comparison. "I just don't know if that's a situation I want to get into the middle of right now," I said.

"That's going to take care of itself very soon," Fuentes said. I didn't know it at the time, but he was right about that. Shulkin would get pushed out, along with many of the other appointees, in a matter of weeks. "Think about it. You can go over there and build it back up. The vets need someone who knows what they're doing."

I spent the weekend mulling it over. I called Jared Kushner that Sunday afternoon to see what he thought about it. He had taken a keen interest in overhauling the VA, and he was one of the few people in the West Wing who I trusted to have a confidential conversation. He was surprised by Kelly's offer, but said he'd support the move. He said he knew how frustrated I had become in my current role and thought it might be a massive undertaking that I could really own. I did feel flattered that they thought I was up to the task. But ultimately I just couldn't get excited about the challenge.

On Monday morning, I told the Chief my decision.

"I'm honored you guys thought of me for this," I said. "But I didn't come to Washington to work for the government, I came here to work for the President." He told me he was disappointed but understood. "We'll keep coming up with ideas," he said.

But before they even had a chance, a new idea landed in my lap a couple of days later.

The President was bringing in economist and longtime CNBC host Larry Kudlow to replace Gary Cohn, who had announced he was resigning as Trump's top economic adviser. We had a lot of mutual friends, and once we met we hit it off right away. He knew I had run the messaging on tax reform, and he made it clear that he wanted me on his team. Within a few hours of meeting for the first time, he offered me a job as Deputy Director of the National Economic Council, where my job would be coordinating communications on the President's entire economic agenda, across the whole administration.

This is perfect, I thought to myself. *I already know all of these issues. I can get out of the mess in the comms shop. I can once again work alongside my old tax teammate Tony Sayegh at Treasury. And I'll still be close to the President.*

"The President told me I can hire whoever I want," Larry said. "You're my guy."

I accepted the job without hesitation. But there was another, unspoken reason why I thought this was a good job for me: Larry didn't know it yet, but he was going to need a knife fighter in his corner.

Larry had seen a lot. He had worked in the Reagan White House three decades before, albeit at a much lower level. He had fought addictions to cocaine and alcohol in the mid-1990s, crediting his Catholic faith with saving him. He had made himself a legend in conservative—"supply-side"—economics. And he had become a regular TV commentator. He was the sweetest, most genuinely kind man I had met since coming to the White House, and he was so grateful to be back there himself and so excited to work for Trump that he rekindled the feeling that I had when I had walked into the West Wing for the first time—before I let *the game* suck the joy out of the job. I vowed to myself to protect him from that game.

I realized in that moment that Larry was like a minnow going for a happy little swim in what was—unbeknownst to him—a tank full of hungry piranhas. I barely knew him, but I already felt protective. I knew what it took to survive in this place—at least I did to that point. And in that moment, I decided that I would metaphorically bite the head off anyone who threatened to steal a single moment of Larry's enjoyment in the White House.

I once again went home that evening and told Megan the good news. Everything had come together perfectly. This was a far better fit for me than either the OPL or VA job would have been.

On the afternoon of Thursday, March 29, I was sitting in the back hallway of the West Wing, outside Jared's office, waiting to fill him in on my impending move to the NEC. The President was in Richfield, Ohio, announcing plans to "rebuild America's crumbling infrastructure," so in his absence, the West Wing was uncharacteristically quiet. But since he was flying straight from Ohio to Mar-a-Lago for a long Easter weekend, most of the staff had stayed behind, including General Kelly and Deputy Chief of Staff Joe Hagin.

The back hallway of the West Wing is a roughly twenty-five-yard straight shot from the Oval on one end to the Vice President's suite on the other. Working your way down the hallway from the Oval, on the left side was the President's private dining room, Jared's office, then the Chief's suite. On the right side were the Roosevelt Room; the scheduler, Michael Haidet; and Hagin. This was the most prime real estate in the entire building. In an environment where proximity to the President was power, this was the inner sanctum. The hallway was lined with the usual combination of historical paintings, antique cabinetry, and famous busts and sculptures. The ceiling was slightly curved, like the top of the number zero. While the upper press office, where I worked, was the bustling center of activity, not to mention accessible to the media, this place was almost serene.

About fifteen feet down the hallway from where I was sitting, I could hear the TV inside the Chief's suite airing coverage from Trump's Ohio event, which was set to begin any minute. Hagin sauntered out of his office and across the hall, where he found Kelly standing in front of the TV with a couple of other close aides. Though I hadn't intended to, I overheard their entire, unguarded conversation.

"I talked to the President on the plane and he swore to me that he wouldn't announce anything about Syria," Kelly said, in an exasperated tone. I knew immediately what he was talking about. The President had for some time been privately expressing a desire to pull U.S. troops out of Syria. I wasn't involved in the national security decision-making process, but his inclination to pull out was well known throughout the building. Top military officials were urging him to keep a couple of thousand troops in the country to clear out the last remnants of the so-called Islamic State. To that point he had begrudgingly acquiesced, but his patience was running thin. Kelly clearly was expecting him to say something about the topic anyway.

"We won't know until he walks offstage," Hagin replied with a resigned chuckle. This was a common sentiment among staffers who bristled at Trump's tendency to go off script during his remarks. It also happened to be what made him interesting to watch—no one knew what he would say, not even the staff.

"He d— well better know not to screw us on this," Kelly growled. I was taken aback by this brief but revealing exchange, which seemed to encapsulate Kelly's view of his job and of the President himself: which was that Trump was a missile of chaos and Kelly was the general trying to keep him in the silo. Many reporters over the years reported that this was Kelly's view of the job—to various denials from the White House—but we all knew it was true.

In fact, there was a pervasive view among some of the President's most senior aides that there was something patriotic about undermining Trump's most disruptive impulses. I know that many people reading this will say, "Thank God." And if I give them the benefit of the doubt, it may have been a sincere effort to do what they thought was in the best interest of the country. But whether they were sincere or not, I found it cowardly. There's nothing patriotic about being a part of "the resistance" inside the building. Imagine the arrogance of saying, "I know sixty-three million of my fellow Americans voted for this guy, but I'm going to sabotage him anyway because I know better."

At that moment, Jared popped his head out of his office and nodded his head back, signaling me to come in. So I wasn't around to hear Kelly's reaction a few minutes later when Trump told the Ohio crowd, "We'll be coming out of Syria, like, very soon."

Once in Jared's office, I grabbed a silver-wrapped Hershey's Kiss out of the bowl on his conference table, which took up about half the room. He had the closest office to the Oval, but what it had in proximity it lacked in size. I told Jared about Kudlow's offer for me to join his NEC team and he was immediately enthusiastic. "This is going to be great and the President is going to love it," he said. "But are you sure they're not going to try to stop it?" He nodded his head in the direction of Kelly's office next door. He had grown deeply distrustful of the Kelly regime. A month earlier, Kelly had downgraded Jared's security clearance, a slight that Jared viewed as an unnecessary power play designed to embarrass him. He was quietly fuming about it, and knowing Jared, I figured he would one day extract his pound of flesh. But not until the timing was just right.

"I don't know why they would," I said. "The Chief can fully hand over the comms operation to Mercedes and I can go about my business in another part of the building. The President will be happy with it. Everyone wins."

He nodded. "Well, I hope that's true," he said. But he was skeptical.

A couple of days later, Larry Kudlow called me back upstairs. When I got to his office suite—which he was sharing with Gary Cohn, who had resigned but not yet departed—he looked worried. He had just come from the Oval, he explained, and the President was railing against a "special deal" Amazon was getting from the U.S. Postal Service that he wanted Kudlow to somehow stop. This "deal" was one of Trump's perennial hobbyhorses. Someone had told him that Amazon, personified by presidential nemesis Jeff Bezos, the Amazon CEO, was getting some perk from the government that the company didn't deserve. And Trump just couldn't let it go.

As Larry recounted the conversation and Trump's order to "do something" about Amazon, Gary laughed loudly. "Welcome to the White House," he said, shaking Larry's hand. Larry, for his part, appeared totally confused.

"It's total bulls—," Gary told him. A giant smile spread across his face, as if he was silently saying *Thank goodness I don't have to deal with this nonsense anymore.* "He's been trying to get me to do something about this for months," Cohn explained. "Amazon's not getting some special deal. USPS is mandated to go to every house, every day, no matter what. The Amazon contract is paying them extra to take their packages 'the last mile' from the distro center to the front door. They'd have to go to these houses anyway." Shaking his head, he finished, "Amazon may actually be saving the Postal Service, not killing it."

Then Cohn got to the real motivation behind this latest Trump obsession. "He's just mad at Bezos for owning *The Washington Post*."

That explanation didn't help Kudlow any. He'd just been given a direct order from the President of the United States. You'd better believe that back in the day, if Ronald Reagan had told young Kudlow to jump in a lake, he'd be treading water until Reagan told him to get out.

"So . . ." Larry replied hesitantly, "I shouldn't do anything about this?"

I could see what he was thinking: *Is this how it always works around here?*

"Don't worry about it," Gary told him. "Cliff will help you figure it out. But now you know why I'm so happy to be leaving."

For now, anyway, Amazon would have to wait. After that perplexing encounter, Kudlow pulled me into his private office and closed the door. The wood-paneled walls were now bare. Gary's pictures, paintings, and other personal items had been removed, and Larry had not yet made the space his own. He had a grim look on his face.

"You're not going to be able to work for me on NEC," he said.

I shot him a confused look. *Wasn't this already worked out?*

He explained that he'd met with Sarah Sanders and Mercedes Schlapp and brought up my move. It had not gone over well, especially with Mercedes. "She said, 'He doesn't play well with the other children and can't be trusted,'" he continued.

This was the same Mercedes who, to my face, called me "the President's spirit animal" and raved about how no one "got the President" or his "voice" like I did. Which, in hindsight, was my undoing.

Kudlow, the poor guy, had no idea about the vicious infighting in the press office, but I knew what was really going on. That morning, the *Washington Examiner* had published a story about Mercedes and my tax team colleague Tony Sayegh both angling to succeed the outgoing Hope Hicks as White House comms director. In the story, anonymous sources claimed that Tony had a tendency to "boss people around" and to "manipulate others for his own benefit." They also said he was a "terrible bully," and one "senior administration official" said "such behavior has been particularly noticeable in Sayegh's interactions with female staff." I thought back to Mercedes's blowup on Tony in the Treasury Dining Room months before, where I'd been an innocent bystander. Was I now catching shrapnel because she wanted to blow up Tony and anyone close to him? *All of this for a stupid job title?*

The accusations against Tony were particularly malicious, even by Trump White House standards. Not only were they untrue—to the point of absurdity—they more than implied that Tony had a problem with women, at a time when there was a heightened sensitivity about such allegations. I remained close to Tony after tax reform, and while turning down the VA job, I had told Fuentes and DeStefano I thought he would be a great choice to succeed Hope. Hope happened to agree with this assessment. Since I was a fan of Tony's, I instantly became an enemy of Mercedes.

It also didn't help matters that I was friends with Hope, who, for her part, didn't have much use for Mercedes, either. She viewed Mercedes as a self-promoter, especially after CNN published an article praising her for being "the adult in the room" and "a godsend" for a chaotic comms department. In reality, although my desk was ten feet from Mercedes's, I had no idea what occupied most of her time. She had exasperated the entire West Wing by hosting a weekly "planning meeting," during which decisions would supposedly be made on the President's calendar. But nothing decided in the meeting ever seemed to come to fruition. And there was no rhyme or reason—no discernible strategy—to what the "Director of Strategic Communications" was doing.

The President could not have cared less about what Mercedes had to say. But weirdly, he left these sorts of personnel decisions almost entirely to Kelly, even when he vehemently disagreed with him. And the Chief was a different story.

Larry went on to tell me that the day after he met with Mercedes and Sarah, he also met with Kelly and Hagin. Mercedes and Hagin had served together in the Bush White House—and all the Bushies stuck together. So when Kudlow brought up bringing me in as his deputy on the NEC, Kelly and Hagin shot it down. Whatever new respect I'd won with Kelly hadn't amounted to much.

"Kelly told me, 'Nope, that's not going to happen,'" a bewildered Kudlow said. "I told him, 'Well, the President said I could hire my people,' and he said, 'Not this one you can't.'"

Kudlow was clearly annoyed by this, and a little embarrassed that he'd offered me a job he wasn't allowed to bestow. But he wasn't going to fight the Chief of Staff over it. I understood that. "I'm so sorry," he said. "This was a perfect fit, and I don't know all the backstory. I just know there's nothing I can do about it."

As I walked back down the West Wing's narrow stairwell, I tried to make sense of the animosity, especially Joe Hagin's. I'd barely even talked to the guy in the past year. Then I suddenly remembered that the only substantive interaction I'd had with him was during the Scaramucci debacle. Hagin was Mooch's polar opposite—a low-key, do-it-by-the-book, process-oriented professional. *Is he holding it against me that I was Mooch's guy?* If he was, it wasn't entirely unreasonable. But it still felt petty. And how did it come to this so quickly with the Chief, after he had been so "blown away" by my OPL interview?

That's when it really hit me.

Paradoxically, one of the advantages I had enjoyed in past turf wars was that I had always "punched up." I maintained a low enough public profile that my enemies had a hard time convincing reporters to waste their time writing hit pieces on someone whose name their readers wouldn't recognize. They also couldn't go to the President directly, mainly because he would view it as weakness, but also because my good relationship with him was well known. This was a source of resentment in some corners of the building, but it was also the ultimate air cover for me.

I had ruffled some feathers by carving out such a large role for myself in the tax reform push, but I was still just a comms staffer who wasn't threatening to move too far into other people's territory. Either the OPL job or the NEC job would be different. I would have a bigger title to match my standing with the President—more latitude to spread my wings. So when word got around that I was in consideration for these jobs, the knives came out for me. I just wasn't perceptive enough—and probably too arrogant—to realize it at first.

Later that day, I was in the East Wing venting my frustrations to members of the First Lady's staff when I got a cryptic phone call from Sarah Sanders, asking me to come meet with her and Hope in her office. When I arrived, the mood was strange, almost somber. The good humor that I was accustomed to was nonexistent.

The two women were there with a warning.

Sarah was a different person since the Porter debacle. She appeared more resigned, more beaten down by the impossible demands of her job. I could see that now in her expression, which was both weary and wary. "We know how frustrated you are," Sarah began. "But there's just no way you're going to rise any higher in the West Wing. You're going to keep getting blocked."

Then Hope, my friend, jumped in. She was finished with this place, too, before it ruined her. "I've always done everything I could to protect you," she said. "But I'm going to be gone soon and I just don't want you to be left in here totally fending for yourself. They're going to come for you."

Well, that sounds ominous.

I knew Hope had my best interests at heart. I wasn't so sure about Sarah. I didn't necessarily think she had it out for me, but I also knew she wouldn't go to bat for me the way Hope would. Then again, maybe I was letting the paranoia that had built up over the last year finally consume me. I was perplexed. I had played a major leadership role in the White House's only long-term communications success: tax reform. The President loved me. *What's the deal? Who's got it out for me?*

Sarah finally conceded it was Joe Hagin. "He claims people told him you aren't trustworthy and that you've been in rooms you shouldn't have been in," she said. On the first point I told her I thought it was nonsense that such an ambiguous accusation could somehow be held against me. On the second, I noted that no one had ever said a word to me about being in any room or meeting, and I got the impression that while he—or whoever else—might not want me there, the President obviously did. And that's probably what the real problem was. Regardless, I thought I deserved a chance to answer whatever specific accusations were being made against me. This was how dangerous and toxic the Trump White House had become. Outright hostility between various factions was standard. Any false rumor or sometimes even the whisper of a rumor could sink anyone at any time.

"It could be a silly misunderstanding," I said. "Or maybe I genuinely did somebody wrong and I need to make it right. Either way, it's unprofessional to handle it this way." This was obvious to everyone in the room. But there was little anyone could do.

Still, I had to try. I asked Sarah if she would set up a conversation between Hagin and me, and she said she would. In the meantime, Hope and

Sarah both asked me to run comms on CIA Director Mike Pompeo's nomination for Secretary of State. Rex Tillerson had been fired in March 2018—and Kelly had inexplicably leaked to the press that Tillerson was sitting on the toilet when he called to tell him he was being pushed out.

Months before, I had told Hope that State was the only department I would seriously considering moving to—but only for the right job. "Go work with Pompeo for a few weeks and see what you think," she said. "And that'll give some time for all of this to work itself out."

I agreed, but only if I was doing it as a White House employee just temporarily detailed to State. I would still have my desk in the West Wing and go back and forth between the two buildings as needed. With that agreed upon, there was one more thing I needed to make clear: "The Alabama football team is coming here on the tenth to celebrate their national championship," I said. "I'm writing the President's remarks, and I'm going to be there for that, no matter what else is going on." Everyone laughed and agreed, ending the meeting on a light note.

When April 10, 2018, arrived, just a few days later, I woke up in my apartment with a rare sense of excitement. I had invited over fifty guests from my home state to attend the Alabama event, so with great anticipation, I put on my crimson tie and socks and made the five-minute walk from my apartment to the East Gate of the White House complex. Upon entering, I could already see preparations being made for the event, which would take place on the South Lawn. Every presidential event is a massive logistical undertaking. This one was no exception. No fewer than two dozen staffers were involved in the planning and execution of the event.

I had obsessed over the President's remarks. In fact, of all the untold thousands of words I had drafted for him—from speeches to talking points to tweets, and everything in between—I don't think there were any remarks on which I spent more time per word. But what I spent the most time considering was what deeper lesson or meaning I could include in the remarks that would make them more than just a rehashing of a great team's on-field exploits.

The idea I came up with was very personal to me. I titled it "Work While You Wait."

During one of my darkest nights in the White House, I stumbled across a video while scrolling through my Twitter feed that completely changed my perspective. In the video, University of Louisiana baseball coach Tony Robichaux expressed dismay at the culture surrounding modern youth sports.

"Most people—even in their personal life—they stop working until the door opens," he explained. "Then they want to work again now that the door's open. . . . But you've got to work while you wait.

"That's why the [current youth baseball model] is such a bad model," he continued. "Nobody sits the bench. But in high school you're going to sit the bench. Then in college you're going to sit the bench. And in rookie ball you're going to sit the bench. And in low-A and high-A you're going to sit the bench. In double-A you're going to sit the bench. In triple-A you're going to sit the bench. And at the big-league level you're going to sit the bench. Why would we go down and create a stupid model that doesn't allow people to sit the bench, when every other model after that you're going to sit the bench?

"That's why so many kids quit," he concluded. "That's also why they stop working while they wait, because somebody created a model that promised them that they would never sit. And then they get out into the real world— they get out of 'Daddy Ball'—and they get into big-boy baseball and they can't handle it."

The fiery coach went on to praise a player on his team who had maintained his work ethic, even while sitting the bench, and then rose to the occasion when he was given an opportunity.

"He had to work while he waited," he said, "and he finally had a chance to get in and try to do some damage, and he did it. . . . Be a warrior, not a worrier."

I've generally found Twitter to be a vitriolic place where time is wasted and constructive public discourse goes to die. But that short video, which I randomly stumbled across at just the right moment, totally changed my mindset. And I watched it come true for someone else during Alabama's national championship game.

Down 13–0 at halftime, Alabama's head football coach, Nick Saban, made an extraordinary decision to bench his starting quarterback, Jalen Hurts, the reigning SEC offensive player of the year. Sitting on the bench behind Hurts all year had been Tua Tagovailoa, a freshman phenom from Hawaii with a big arm and an even bigger faith in Jesus Christ. Tua had not started a game all year, and pretty much all of his playing time had come late in games where the team was blowing out its opponent.

But on January 8, 2018, Tua was suddenly thrust into the middle of the action, on the biggest stage in college football. And as the old Louisiana baseball coach said, "He finally had a chance to get in and try to do some damage, and he did it." Alabama roared back and ultimately won the game in overtime on a game-winning pass by—you guessed it—Tua Tagovailoa.

Andrew Giuliani, the son of former New York City Mayor Rudy Giuliani, was in charge of championship team visits to the White House. Trump loved the guy, having had a close personal relationship with him that preceded Trump's rise in politics. When Rudy and his wife Donna Hanover, Andrew's mother, went through a messy and very public divorce in the early 2000s, Trump took Andrew under his wing. The two played hundreds of rounds of golf together in subsequent years—Andrew was at one point a professional golfer—and Trump perked up every time he walked into the room. Perhaps unsurprisingly, none of this sat well with General Kelly, who loathed anyone whose access to the President seemed disproportionate to their station. A couple of months later, Trump would explicitly order for Andrew to be promoted. Kelly would respond by doing the exact opposite and revoking Andrew's coveted blue White House badge, which granted access to the West Wing. This relegated him to the EEOB, where he wouldn't ever see the President. Kelly seemed to think such moves projected his total power over staffing decisions. And maybe they did. But most of us thought it just made him look like a small, petty man. Strangest of all, though, was that the President seemed wholly unwilling to confront his Chief over his insubordination.

In any event, knowing that I was an Alabama grad, Andrew had made sure I was included in the group going into the Oval with the coaches and team captains.

As we walked from the residence to the West Wing with the group, I grabbed a football that the team and coaches had autographed so that the President could sign it as well. It was intended to be a gift to the Alabama Governor, since she couldn't attend the event in person. We laughed that we couldn't decide whether it was a kind gesture by us and the university, or an epic troll, since she was a graduate and fan of 'Bama's sworn enemy, Auburn University.

A few minutes later we were in the Roosevelt Room, waiting to be brought into the Oval, and I had a few minutes to talk to Coach Saban. Indisputably one of the greatest coaches of all time, he had developed a reputation as the no-nonsense builder of a college football dynasty and as a molder of men. In spite of the countless times I'd seen him explode on the sideline during games—on referees, players, and coaches alike—I found him to be quiet, almost shy in person. He was walking around with an easy smile and placid demeanor, perhaps because he was being accompanied by his wife, the legendary "Miss Terry," as she was known in Alabama.

Lieutenant General Keith Kellogg, the Chief of Staff of the National Security Council, saw us chatting and walked over to meet Saban.

"What is it that you think has made you so successful?" Kellogg asked Saban. "I don't mean this year; I mean year after year after year. Plenty of coaches have a special team and everything happens to go their way one season, but you do it over and over. How? What's different about what you do?"

Seeming slightly embarrassed by the praise, Saban politely said, "Well, I don't really know, because I don't know what other people do.

"But one thing I did learn working for [New England Patriots coach] Bill Belichick," he continued, "is that everyone in an organization has to have clear roles, clear objectives, and they have to be held accountable. It was like that for everyone in the organization, top to bottom—the ball boys to the star quarterback. You've got to have that. Everyone in an organization has to know exactly what is expected of them. We try to do that."

General Kellogg and I shot each other a knowing glance and he thanked Coach Saban, congratulated him on his success, and went back to work. Alone with Saban, I told him what had gone unsaid by General Kellogg.

"What you just explained is the exact opposite of what happens here," I said, testing the bounds of how candid Saban might get with me.

"It sounds simple, but it's not easy," he replied without hesitation. "But working here, with everything you guys deal with, it's a learning experience, man, no matter what. It'll pay off for the rest of your life. It will have been worth it."

He was right about this, but I wouldn't fully realize it until long after I walked out of the West Wing for the last time.

"Yeah, but from a leadership perspective—particularly at the staff level—this has been a master class in what *not* to do," I replied with a chuckle.

He smiled and shrugged. "Well, that counts as learning, too."

Moments later we were called into the Oval Office. Saban led the way with a beautiful golden putter, ready to be gifted to the golfer in chief. But as we walked in, Jordan Karem, the President's body man, stopped me.

"There are enough people in here already, you need to get out," he said quietly.

"What?" I whispered back. "What's your deal? I was invited to this, and we've had three times this many people in here before. Plus you know the President won't care one bit if I'm in here."

Karem ignored my response and took the football out of my hands.

"What's this for?" he said in an unusually angry tone.

"It's for the President to sign, what do you think?" I snapped back.

"We can't do this right now," he said, turning around and taking the ball with him.

This was a bizarre interaction, for numerous reasons. I'd gotten dozens of things signed by the President during my time in the White House. I had also gone out of my way to do this by the book—the ultimate rarity in the Trump White House. I had received approval from the White House Counsel's Office to get the ball signed for the Governor, and Andrew Giuliani, who was in charge of the event, had included me on the list of people coming into the Oval.

But rather than press the issue, I watched for a few minutes from the Outer Oval, then headed out to the South Lawn, where the President would soon deliver remarks to the team and hundreds of Alabama fans.

While I had never before had any type of run-in with Karem, I was aware of his personal animus toward me.

He had replaced Johnny McEntee, who had been with the President a long time and had known his likes and dislikes. He understood who Trump wanted to see and who he wanted to avoid at any given moment. I never abused the fact that I could ask Johnny to bring me in to see the President. But the fact that I had that direct pipeline bred resentment among some of the staff.

As noted, when General Kelly became Chief of Staff, one of his first orders of business was to choke off all direct access to the President. I kept my head down, but others—including the President himself—chafed at the sudden clampdown. Trump, one of the world's most social creatures, began going around Kelly's blockade by making calls to friends and allies after hours and from his cell phone. And McEntee, his trusted personal aide, was one of the primary conduits for circumventing the Kelly system.

As a result, the Kelly regime got rid of him the first chance they got.

Less than a month earlier, McEntee had been frog-marched out of the White House after being accused of having issues with his background check. He'd been by Trump's side for years, from the campaign to the White House, but was suddenly deemed untrustworthy. And rather than do it quietly, Kelly publicly humiliated him, then leaked to CNN that Johnny was "under investigation by the Department of Homeland Security for serious financial crimes."

Those of us who knew Johnny—and even many casual observers—viewed the event as a disgraceful and callous abuse of power. Reporters were telling me that even Stephen Miller, who typically buddied up to whatever regime was empowered, was telling them off the record that they should call out Kelly and Hagin for bullying McEntee and manipulating the President. But Kelly and Hagin got what they wanted: Johnny gone and the opportunity to plug their own spy—Jordan Karem—into that job. By any historical measure, he was a strange fit for the role, which usually goes to a single young man in his twenties. Karem was in his mid-thirties and recently married. But he fit the one description that Kelly and Hagin cared about: he was loyal to them over the President. He kept them updated on the President's movements, conversations, and activities. He also eliminated the casual interactions with trusted friends and aides that the President thrived on.

Finally out on the South Lawn, the President entertained the crowd like only he could.

"They are extraordinary and they're going to be very rich!" he said of the massive football players standing behind him as the entire crowd broke into laughter.

"Anyone who wants to know how Alabama does it should study Coach Saban's simple philosophy. It's called 'The Process.' Coach tells his players, 'Don't look at the scoreboard; don't look at any external factors.' Just focus 'all your efforts, all your toughness, and all your discipline' on executing . . . one play at a time. And by doing that, by focusing on 'The Process,' the outcome—winning—will take care of itself. It's a great philosophy.

"In the national championship game, you stuck to 'The Process,' even when it was looking pretty tough. . . . On the first play of overtime, Georgia sacked Tua for a big loss. . . . But the Crimson Tide never gave in—never even a little bit. . . . On the very next play, Tua dropped back to pass, launched the ball from near midfield . . . and DeVonta Smith caught that ball for the win. . . .

"Every moment of hard work and preparation for Alabama paid off," Trump concluded.

Work while you wait, I thought.

As the event finished up and everyone began to leave, JK Scott, the team's All-American punter, asked the President if he could pray for him, which Trump readily agreed to. It was a perfect conclusion, or at least it could have been. Unfortunately, the day's events weren't over for me.

Upon returning to the West Wing, I got a phone call from the Chief's office saying Kelly wanted to see me immediately. When I walked into his office, he was standing at his conference table with his back to the door.

"Hey, Chief," I said. The camaraderie from a few weeks before—when he was friendly and considering me for an array of jobs—was gone. The room seemed darker and colder—although the darkness and the chill were more of a feeling than an actuality.

"Cliff, in the past forty years, I don't think I've ever had a subordinate whose reputation is worse than yours. In every single context that your name comes up, it's always negative—always. It's going to follow you for the rest of your life. Allow me to give you some advice. Take this to heart, from an old guy to a young guy, 'cause I've been around a lot longer than you have. Reputation is all we have in this world. That's it. All we have is our reputation."

Wow. I was reeling. He fired off words at me like bullets from an M4 rifle. I had the worst reputation of anyone he'd ever known? In forty years?

He apparently had a complete lack of awareness that his own reputation was in tatters.

I held my shoulders back and stood my ground. I told him I thought that his assessment was unfair and misinformed. I told him it made no sense that I had sat in this very office less than a month before and won his praise, only to see his opinion changed by cowardly gossip. And so quickly.

"Well, then, what the hell is this football thing?" he shot back. "Jordan's already told me all about you trying to force your way into the Oval."

By the way he said it, you would have thought I'd kneecapped a Secret Service agent, clotheslined Jordan, and thrown the football at the President's face. But it was pointless to explain. I remembered Hope's warning, "They are coming for you." He was just looking for a reason—any reason. It was personal, and I no longer felt like I had anything to lose.

"This all boils down to two things," I said. "Number one, resentment over my personal relationship with the President. And number two, the lack of clearly defined roles and responsibilities in this White House."

I realized in the moment that he was likely to take number two as a direct shot at his leadership, but he didn't immediately respond. So I recounted my conversation with Coach Saban from earlier in the day and explained how the lack of clearly defined roles in the White House had led to people veering in and out of different lanes, sparking territorial disputes and breeding rivalries. I conceded that I had been an active participant in some of those disputes, but I was far from unique in that.

Kelly was now fuming even more. I had just confessed to bad-mouthing Kelly's management style to the most revered college football coach in America.

"If I had been here from the beginning, it never would have been like this," he retorted, his jaw flexing. Then he bemoaned his own fate, which he had done repeatedly, it seemed, to anyone who would listen. "I should have stayed at DHS and never come to this place. Either that or I should have been brought here right from the beginning. Everything would be different." Why he was sharing this with me—the most reprehensible character he'd encountered in forty years—was just another mystery to add to a long list of them in the Trump White House.

This was much deeper than whatever problem he had with me. He was in denial about his own failures. And he was now fully consumed by the culture he had been brought in to change. In that moment, something about this exchange made me no longer care a whit what he did to me. He was a damaged character, and many of his wounds were self-inflicted. His scowl and dominating demeanor masked an obvious and deep insecurity. I suddenly didn't fear him anymore.

"Do you want my resignation?" I asked him. The words seemed to just jump out of my mouth, without any real forethought. But at that moment I was more than ready to tender it. I didn't need this insanity anymore. Strangely enough, that offer seemed to break the tension.

"No, no, don't do that," he replied, softening his tone. "No one believes resignations around here. Everyone will assume you were fired." I thought he *was* firing me—or at least wanted to. None of this conversation made any sense. People told me all the time that staying in Trump World too long would make anyone crazy. I started to wonder if that was what had happened to John Kelly, who was now paranoid, easily angered, at war with everyone, and whining to a staff member he apparently didn't even like. He was a shell of the man I'd first encountered a year and a half earlier.

"Just go to the State Department for a couple of weeks, get Pompeo confirmed, and see what happens," he concluded. "But don't forget what I told you; reputation is everything."

We shook hands and I left his office. He was wrong about me, but there was no use in pressing the issue. He had a small group of aides around him that he trusted implicitly. He couldn't delve into the details of every disagreement or the backstory of every frayed relationship, so he had to just take their word for it. If they said I was a problem, I was a problem. And I already fit the description of someone he wouldn't like—a Trump loyalist who disregarded the traditional hierarchy because my relationship with the President was closer than my title should have allowed.

In any conversation like the one I had with Kelly, there are always things you think of later that you wish you had said in the moment. In this instance, it hit me about ten minutes after I left. As I walked along the north front of the White House, through a ground-floor hallway typically used by Secret Service agents and culinary staff, I realized he wasn't just wrong about me personally; he was wrong about the entire premise of his "advice." Reputation is not, in fact, the most important thing. As famed UCLA basketball coach John Wooden once explained: "Be more concerned with your character than your reputation, because your character is what you really are, while your reputation is merely what others think you are."

I found solace in those words, and for the next several weeks I threw myself into the daunting task of getting Mike Pompeo confirmed to be the country's seventieth Secretary of State. It shouldn't have been a heavy lift. Pompeo had graduated first in his class at West Point. He patrolled the Iron Curtain during the Cold War as an Army cavalry officer. He was elected to Congress and served as a member of the House Intelligence Committee. The President then appointed him his first CIA Director, and had trusted him with some of his most sensitive national security and foreign policy issues. On top of that, secretaries of state are typically confirmed by wide, bipartisan majorities, because national security is the one area in which Democrats and Republicans typically put politics aside. But this wasn't a typical time in American politics.

We had a razor-thin GOP majority in the Senate, and libertarian-leaning Republican Rand Paul was holding out his vote for Pompeo, citing Pompeo's past support for the Iraq War and the "failed" policy of "regime change" in the Middle East.

With that in mind, our strategy was simple: let the President handle Senator Paul, and we'd go after the handful of red-state Democrats who were facing difficult reelections in states that Trump had won. That meant flooding regional media markets in states like North Dakota, West Virginia, Indiana, Missouri, Florida, Maine, and Alabama.

A handful of White House aides, including Director of Legislative Affairs Marc Short, who was leading the overall confirmation effort, Sarah Sanders, the deputy press secretaries, and myself fanned out to do media hits on targeted local and regional news outlets.

The President, meanwhile, turned up the heat on Senator Paul.

"I will say this about Rand Paul: he's never let me down," the President told reporters. "Rand Paul is a very special guy as far as I'm concerned. He's never let me down and I don't think he'll let us down again. So let's see what happens."

While that was happening, Brett O'Donnell, Pompeo's longtime political adviser, and I pushed back on negative stories and worked to shape the overall press coverage. The clown show in the West Wing was the furthest thing from my mind. I was having a blast. On the day of Pompeo's confirmation hearing, I led a staff of about a dozen in a makeshift war room in the State Department, monitoring coverage on television and online, and working to build momentum from Pompeo's masterful performance.

Ultimately, our plan worked exactly how we hoped it would, with a little help from the news of the day. A week before his confirmation vote *The Washington Post* broke the blockbuster story that Pompeo had conducted a secret mission to North Korea to meet with the country's leader, Kim Jong-un. While we did not leak the story—in fact, Pompeo was frustrated by its release—it worked to our advantage. The President already had entrusted Pompeo to go on the most sensitive diplomatic mission in recent memory; how was anyone going to say he shouldn't be Trump's Secretary of State? The safety and security of the entire world was on the line. We cranked up the heat on red-state Democrats even further. Brett O'Donnell, Marc Short, fellow Legislative Affairs aide Mary Elizabeth Taylor, State Department press staffer Matt Lloyd, and I sat in the gallery of the Senate and watched as Pompeo was confirmed by a 57–42 vote.

Coming after tax reform, it was the second major legislative victory in which I had played a significant part. *At least they can never take this moment away from me,* I thought. And for the first time, I really started considering what life might look like after the White House.

Right on cue, Secretary Pompeo asked to see me in his new, mahogany-paneled office on the seventh floor of the State Department.

The Secretary of State's suite makes the West Wing truly look like a dump by comparison. There were receiving rooms, conference rooms, and waiting rooms that led into lobbies. Every space was well appointed—everything just *felt* important. A large wooden door slid open to reveal the Secretary waiting for me behind it, like Willy Wonka—and I was a wide-eyed kid from Alabama with a golden ticket. My name had been beautifully written on a card and placed neatly on a small table beside the chair where I was to sit. The Secretary greeted me with a firm handshake and a smile, and invited me to sit down with him. A small bottle of water was waiting for me, with the State Department seal imprinted on its white label.

He had a role in mind for me on his senior staff, he explained. But before he offered me a job, he wanted to know why I wanted to leave the White House for State.

This was an easy question to answer. I had two main reasons, I explained.

First of all, it was an incredible time to be working in foreign policy and international affairs. We were angling for a breakthrough with North Korea that could literally change the course of history. The President's decision to move the U.S. embassy in Israel to Jerusalem was sparking new challenges and opportunities in the Middle East. We had to figure out how to counter China's aggressive rise. We were wiping ISIS off the face of the earth while facing an uncertain future in Syria. The President was preparing to withdraw from the Iran nuclear deal, setting up another high-stakes showdown in the Gulf tinderbox. Our European allies were still adjusting to Trump's disruptive approach. The list could go on and on.

Second—and I didn't hold back on this one—I was ready to turn the page on fifteen months in the most cutthroat, toxic, mean-spirited, draining working environment I had ever encountered. (As I've noted, I was part of this problem—a willing combatant, too.) I wanted to be a part of a team with a strong esprit de corps. I wanted to play an important leadership role. I wanted to be a part of something special, something I could look back on and be proud of, a winning culture.

Pompeo got it immediately. A self-described "talent hawk," he said he was bringing in his own team of killers to fill the upper ranks of the State Department. He had heard all he needed to hear, and he'd seen my work during his confirmation. He wanted me on his team. I'd be a senior adviser to the Secretary with a portfolio focusing on strategic communications. My office would be right next to his. He offered me the job and I accepted it on the spot.

I was elated. I was so close to escaping the Trump White House relatively unscathed and moving on to one of the most coveted jobs in U.S. national security and foreign policy. But as I checked my email to see what I'd missed while inside the State Department—where cell phone signals go to die—my heart sank. In my in-box was a curt email from Deputy White House Counsel Uttam Dhillon explaining that he needed to meet with me immediately about an issue that had arisen in my background check. I had heard this before. This is the same thing they'd said to Johnny McEntee and other Trump loyalists right before they kicked them off campus before the President could find out and intervene.

I'd had one interaction with Dhillon before. After the Rob Porter debacle, security clearances were a hot topic. Since the security clearance process could take many months, it was not unusual for senior White House aides to start their tenure with a provisional clearance, giving them access to classified information even though they hadn't been fully cleared. What was unusual, however, was that top aides like Porter—who handled sensitive information constantly—had not received their permanent clearance (or been let go for not being able to obtain one) even *a year* into the administration.

The buzz about clearances made me wonder about my own. I had completed my "Standard Form 86," the questionnaire everyone seeking a clearance must fill out. I had sat for a lengthy interview with FBI investigators. Federal agents had conducted my background check investigation, which I knew because they talked to numerous people from my past. Over a year had gone by, but no one had said anything else to me about it. I assumed this meant everything was fine. After all, although I wasn't working in national security policy, I was in plenty of meetings in classified settings, including in the Situation Room and Oval Office. But after the Chief had revoked Jared Kushner's security clearance and gotten rid of several other Trump loyalists because of supposed issues in their background checks, I wanted some peace of mind. So I emailed the White House Counsel's office.

An assistant emailed me back and asked me to come upstairs in the West Wing to meet with Uttam Dhillon. When I got there, he brusquely informed me that I did not have a security clearance, like, *at all*—neither provisional nor permanent. I asked him how on earth that could even be possible.

He told me they—it was unclear who "they" were—had "just never activated" my clearance, and told me I shouldn't be involved in any more classified discussions from that point forward. I was rattled, and I wasn't sure what to say. I knew what I thought, though:

Okay, so for the past year I've been in numerous bilateral meetings with foreign leaders, sat next to the Deputy National Security Advisor during an Oval Office meeting with the Secretary General of NATO, been around the President nearly every day and heard him discuss just about every topic under the sun, and now you tell me this? Could the White House really work this way?

"You will need to be debriefed on whatever classified information you heard," he told me, with a tone suggesting that somehow this was all my fault. As I was walking out, he asked me to keep the conversation between the two of us. Not to protect me, I realized. But to protect himself, or perhaps whoever "they" were.

It took me a while to figure out what was *really* going on, though I could never prove it. I suspected that certain White House officials whose purview included the murky world of background checks and security clearances were abusing this power to manipulate personnel decisions in the administration. This potentially dangerous game did not come into full view for me until long after I left the White House. In late 2018, *The Wall Street Journal* broke a bombshell story that Dhillon "had urged several candidates for Drug Enforcement Administration chief to withdraw from consideration, citing concerns about their background checks. Then he accepted the job himself." During the selection process, he had handled candidate vetting, then personally "called multiple candidates to inform them they were out of the running or to encourage them to withdraw from the process," a move that was described as "unusual for someone in Mr. Dhillon's role." And he apparently did all of this to get them out of the way so he could take the job himself.

But at the time I received my email to meet Dhillon, the *Journal* story was months away from publication. And even though I was suspicious of what had been done to some of my colleagues, it was difficult in the moment to make sense of it all.

No matter, I thought. *I'm leaving anyway, regardless of what nonsense they're trying to pull.* Dhillon and I exchanged a couple of emails and agreed to meet several hours later.

In the meantime, I typed out a brief resignation letter:

> Serving the President in the White House for the past 15 months has been an extraordinary privilege. I will cherish the time I have been honored to spend working alongside the team here.
>
> However, today I have been presented with another opportunity to serve that I feel I must pursue. Therefore, it is incumbent upon me to submit my resignation from the White House, with a heavy heart.
>
> I will, of course, assist in any way I can to ensure a smooth transition.
>
> Respectfully,
> Cliff Sims
> Special Assistant to the President for Communications

I walked into Sarah's office and submitted it. She congratulated me—she knew what I'd been through. This was the third big job I had been offered in the past month, and it looked like the third time was going to be the charm. But I also told her about the email I had received from the Deputy White House Counsel, and noted with trepidation that I was going to meet with him shortly.

When I walked into a ground floor office of the Eisenhower Executive Office Building, Uttam Dhillon was waiting for me. And he wasn't alone; he was flanked by three Secret Service agents.

"You guys know I already resigned from the White House, right?" I joked. They didn't laugh.

"Take a seat," Dhillon said. "These gentlemen have some questions they'd like to ask you."

With that, one of the agents, a tall, well-built man in his late thirties who, as the President would say, looked like he was straight out of central casting, asked me why I had recently emailed a video file from my government email address to my personal Gmail.

I paused, confused. *What in the world is this guy talking about?* Then I realized what he must be referencing.

"You mean the video of me briefing the President?" I asked.

"Yes, that's the one," he replied. "Talk to me about what that was, where it came from, and why you emailed it to a personal email address."

A great sense of relief washed over me. *If this is what you've brought me here for, then I know it's not a big deal.*

Among my various responsibilities in the White House, I explained, was briefing the President before certain public events. One such event took place on January 24, when mayors from all over the country were assembled in the East Room to hear remarks from the President.

Waiting just down the hall in the Green Room, I chatted with one of the residence staff who was raving about the kind and generous treatment he received from the Trump family. I told him my experience had always been the same, and remarked how incredible it would be to one day tell my kids about interacting with the President. It was the rare time when I mentally stepped back and considered just how dang cool it all was. The butler agreed, but pointed out that the staff had an advantage because we got our pictures taken with the President, so at least we had mementos. The residence staff didn't really get that opportunity. "I'd love to have a picture or a video or something with him," he said.

I did have a lot of pictures of us together, but I told him I didn't have a video. In fact, I thought I'd take that opportunity to take one that I could hold on to for posterity. So with President Trump coming down the corridor toward us, I pulled out my government cell phone, propped it up, and recorded a short video of the pre-event briefing. Like the dozens of such mundane interactions we'd had before, this one included me telling him his prepared remarks were in a binder, rather than on a teleprompter. I handed him a note card with the names of three people he'd be recognizing, and explained why they were important. Then I laid out a quick run of show—how he'd be announced, where he'd walk, and how he'd exit the room at the end. The President then noted that he was going to make a comment about "sanctuary cities," since they had been in the news so much recently. We agreed this was a good idea. The whole conversation lasted about ninety seconds. And with that, the President was introduced and left the room, and I walked over and picked up my cell phone.

Walking back to the West Wing later, I showed a clip from the video to the President's personal aide, prompting the President to ask what we were looking at. I told him what it was. He nodded and pivoted the conversation to other topics.

I didn't even think about the video until about three months later when I accepted the job at State. Knowing I was preparing to leave the White House, I looked through my government cell phone to see if there were any images I wanted to preserve before turning it back in. Seeing the video of the briefing, I emailed it to my personal email account.

After that explanation, the Secret Service agents spent another few minutes peppering me with questions.

"Have you ever recorded any other interactions with the President?"

No.

"Did you share this video with anyone outside of the White House, other than emailing it to yourself?"

No.

"Do you understand why you shouldn't have recorded this and sent it to a personal email?"

I told them that while it did not even cross my mind at the time, I understood why they needed to check into this kind of stuff. And I told them that, in hindsight, I should not have done it. What if he had said something controversial or sensitive and my phone had been hacked? I voluntarily deleted the video from my personal phone and email account as they watched.

The agents told me they believed I had been honest and forthcoming with them. We exchanged a few jokes about the Alabama-Auburn football rivalry, with me saying that they could grill me as long as they wanted but I would never say "War Eagle," and the meeting came to an end. That was it. It wasn't very dramatic. It was clear to them that my intentions weren't nefarious, and they wished me well in my new job.

In the spirit of openness and transparency, I informed Secretary Pompeo about the incident and included it on my updated security clearance forms. He wasn't concerned; it was no big deal.

When I walked out of the White House that day, it was the best I had felt in months. I was reinvigorated and ready to tackle a new challenge. I was going to get a couple of weeks off while the State Department paperwork was processed. And then I'd hit the ground running. I was already helping Pompeo with his introductory speech to the State Department staff.

But first, since this was the Trump White House, it was only a matter of hours before the news of my departure leaked to the press.

In spite of early attempts by anonymous sources inside the White House to frame my departure as me being "forced out," most of the reports were relatively neutral. I preferred for my name to never appear in the news—I had been pretty successful in keeping it that way for months—but this wasn't that bad.

But a few days later I read a line in *The New York Times* that jumped out at me.

There was "a crackdown" after an "aide was found to be taping meetings with Mr. Trump and playing them to impress friends," the *Times*'s Maggie Haberman wrote.

My immediate reaction, much like everyone else's, was "Whoa, is this true? Who did that?!" But then my second reaction was, "Wait, is that supposed to be about me?" I called Sarah, who confirmed my suspicion and apologized.

"The Chief said that in senior staff the other day," she said, clearly annoyed. "He didn't say your name, but of course what he said leaked almost immediately."

Whether he said my name or not, it was an outlandish misrepresentation of what had actually happened. In addition to that, making that remark in a room full of other staff shows just how flippant Kelly was about besmirching other people's character.

I realized then, if I hadn't fully before, that Kelly was bent on my demise. His—or his minions'—next move was to leak the bizarre Alabama football story to *Politico,* framing it as if I had been fired over it. This backfired on them in a way, because the story quoted former chiefs of staff belittling Kelly for involving himself in such petty squabbles.

As the Kelly regime spread lies about me in the press, Sarah went on the record in my defense, telling *Alabama Daily News* that I "was a valuable member of President Trump's team on the campaign and for 15 months in the White House. I worked with him on both and he is talented, smart, and worked hard for the President. We hated to see him resign from the White House, but know he will continue to be a loyal supporter for the President and impactful for him in the future."

But ultimately Kelly & Co. got what they wanted.

On a rainy afternoon several weeks after I'd left the White House, Ulrich Brechbühl, Pompeo's former West Point classmate turned State Department Counselor, called me with the last bad news I'd ever have to endure in the Trump administration.

"We've been working this from every possible angle," he explained, "but at every turn they're putting up roadblocks to you coming in here. There's just nothing else we can do about it. I'm sorry—and the Secretary is very disappointed—but we're just not going to be able to make it happen."

When we hung up the phone, I sat back on my couch and closed my eyes. I wasn't angry, but I did feel crushed. My first thought was that Kelly had been fully consumed by the darkness. He had become everything he claimed to hate about this administration—vindictive, unhinged, and prone to abuse his power. There was zero chance he had discussed this with the President. He didn't care what he thought about it anyway. He had been totally neutered in his role as Trump's self-appointed babysitter, but he still maintained massive power because of the President's aversion to actually managing the staff. I never wanted to bring Trump into my fights, but this was the one time I decided to call him.

When the White House switchboard operator answered, she told me the President was on the other line, but added something I'd never heard before: I was now on a "screen" list that required her to refer my calls "to staff." I told her not to bother. I had plenty of other ways to get to him anyway. Over the next few weeks, several of his closest friends, advisers, and even family members spoke to him about my situation. According to each of them, he repeated the same basic thing. I'd stuck with him through a lot. Kelly had told him I was untrustworthy. But he didn't know whether to believe him because I'd always been so loyal.

All he had to do was say, "Hey, leave Cliff alone, okay? He's going to State, he's out of your hair. But he's my guy. So let him go."

But he chose not to do that. And not just for me. This wasn't personal to him. And in a way I didn't take it personally, either. He hadn't lifted a finger for countless loyal aides before me, and I'm sure he wouldn't for countless loyal aides to come. It was well known that in Trump World, loyalty was mostly a one-way street. But it's one thing to know that, another thing entirely to experience it firsthand—to be unceremoniously abandoned by the President of the United States. I had let my personal relationship with the President blind me to the one unfailing truth that applied to anyone with whom he didn't share a last name: we were all disposable.

EPILOGUE: OUTSIDE THE BUBBLE

Late in the summer of 2018, several weeks after I left the White House, I was in a taxicab making my way to a meeting at Trump's Washington hotel. Downtown D.C. seemed to be in a state of almost total gridlock, and my taxi's air-conditioning wasn't working very well. I was starting to get carsick, so I got out and walked the remaining few blocks.

As I got closer to the Trump Hotel, I realized what was going on. The Secret Service had created a perimeter around the building and shuttered the roughly five-block stretch of Pennsylvania Avenue from the White House complex to the hotel. The President would be arriving soon.

As I walked toward the perimeter, hoping there was at least one entrance open so I could make it to my meeting on time, I was repeatedly blocked by D.C. police officers. There was no way in. About thirty yards away from me, though, I saw a Secret Service agent I had gotten to know while working in the White House. A few minutes later he looked in my direction and I flagged him down. He jogged over with a big smile on his face, shook my hand, and asked how I was doing.

"I'm good, man," I said. "Just trying to get in there 'cause I've got a meeting, but you guys have it locked down. Any chance I could . . ."

The agent laughed apologetically. "You know better than that," he said, smiling. "Welcome to life outside the bubble."

A few minutes later the President's motorcade rumbled by. Supporters cheered and strained to catch a glimpse of Trump. Protesters waved impeachment signs and held up their middle fingers. I soaked it all in like a dramatic, slow-motion scene in a movie. *Life outside the bubble.*

Working in the White House gives you the sense that you are at the center of the universe. You casually walk through the world's most heavily guarded gates as tourists watch and wonder what you must do inside those walls. Your work plays out on television screens around the world. Everyone you meet wants to hear "what it's like." For the first couple of months I was on the outside, I would glance at TV screens in restaurants or airports, see the latest crisis playing out at the White House, and get depressed. *What must I be missing?* But over time this feeling faded away. Other than scrolling through my Twitter feed, I quit following along with the play-by-play. One of the remarkable things about the Trump era is that if you unplug for a week, you'll miss a dozen wild plot twists, and nothing, all at the same time.

It took some time, but eventually I remembered that for most Americans the White House is not the center of their universe. That distinction is held by their family dinner table, their kids' Little League games, their church, their community, their jobs—*real life*. And that's how it should be. After a while, I remembered what it was like for my life to be my own. I stayed up late watching movies and slept in on weekdays whenever I felt like it. I traveled. Megan and I laughed that we spent more time together in the two months after I left the White House than we had in the entire two whirlwind years before.

Every now and then I would get sucked back in. A White House aide would call for feedback on how they were handling a certain issue with the press or the President. A journalist would ask if I could offer any insight into the way the President thought about a certain person or policy. And occasionally a reporter would call to ask for a comment on a ridiculous hit piece one of my former colleagues had tried to plant on me (some things never change).

Then I started getting approached with job offers and consulting requests. I turned down the former but decided to launch a consulting firm to take advantage of the latter. And the money being thrown around quickly made me realize why so many people who come to D.C. end up getting stuck in the swamp. But I wanted something more for my life; I wanted to do something meaningful, something with a purpose. However, I first needed closure on the Trump season of my life. I wanted to spend time deeply considering what it all meant and where I wanted to go from there. That's where this book comes in. I wrote it cover-to-cover over a roughly two-month span in the fall of 2018.

So what did I learn? What did it all mean? To some extent, I still don't know. Would a single significant outcome have been different had I not been there? Would some meaningful accomplishment have been left just out of reach? It's impossible to say, but I tend to doubt it. I do know that I am proud to have worked in the White House, to have served my country. I'm proud to have worked for the President of the United States. And in spite of the frustrations and misgivings laid out in this book, I'm proud that the president I served was Donald Trump.

In a sense, my time in the White House could serve as a cautionary tale of the corrosive effects of power. I do believe that power can corrupt, that our moral compass becomes less trustworthy the closer it gets to the magnetic pole of absolute power. But the further removed I am from the West Wing, the more convinced I become that what power really does, more than corrupt, is *reveal*— it exposes our true colors, uncovers or magnifies the flaws that already existed. As the nineteenth-century orator Robert G. Ingersoll wrote, reflecting on the legacy of Abraham Lincoln, "Most people can bear adversity. But if you wish to know what a man really is, give him power. This is the supreme test."

My test results revealed that while I was by disposition a polite person, I was not by nature a kind one. I was quick to seek revenge and slow to offer forgiveness. I had a warrior spirit, but lacked a servant heart. I was too quick to pass judgment on the motives of my "enemies," while granting myself moral superiority in the process. None of this would have made my family or friends proud. It didn't make me proud of myself, that's for sure. And worst of all, I knew it didn't please my God, from whom I spent less and less time seeking direction. I continued to wrestle with these moral failings, even long after leaving the White House. On the other hand, I took the fact that I wrestled with these shortcomings at all as a sign that I did not totally lose myself in it all. I learned from it. And because of these experiences—and a lot of self-reflection—I will be far better prepared for the next test, perhaps a bigger one.

On a practical level, the greatest takeaway from working in the White House was that I want to make sure my life's priorities are in order. God created work. I know it is a huge part of his plan for my life and he can be glorified in it and through it. But I don't want to be consumed by it. Bronnie Ware, a nurse who spent years of her life caring for patients in their final days and wrote a book titled *The Top Five Regrets of the Dying*, found that many of them simply wished they had not been so consumed by their careers. "They missed their children's youth and their partner's companionship," she explained. "All of the men I nursed deeply regretted spending so much of their lives on the treadmill of a work existence." The first time I read that, I wondered if Donald Trump will one day feel that way, too.

When I'd occasionally stumble across one of his rally speeches on TV or streaming online, I'd feel the adrenaline flow again. I'd remember how it felt in Trump Tower when we were a gang of bandits with nothing to lose. And I'd sense the tension that I believe nags Trump the most, at least subconsciously: nothing about *being* President has ever reached the high of *becoming* President. This is one of the reasons he loves to relive Election Night 2016 over and over again.

There is a vague sense of dissatisfaction—of hollowness—that sometimes accompanies what most of the world views as success. There will always be something missing. I personally believe there's a God-shaped void inside us all—one that only he can fill. But I've also come to believe that it's the journey, the long ride between milestones, where life really happens. I plan to enjoy that journey more in the future.

As for my friends, most of them have moved on from Trump World, replaced by a new cast of characters. As the President looks around, the familiar faces—the ones who were with him before the presidency—are fewer and fewer. Jared and Ivanka, of course, stayed in the West Wing and may end up being in there until Trump takes his last flight on Marine One. Dan Scavino became the last remaining one of the "originals," the small group of staff who were with Trump when he launched his campaign and rode the wave all the way into the White House.

Through it all, my perception of the President has remained largely unchanged—a man of extraordinary talents and stunning shortcomings. But anyone who attempts to deny his accomplishments in office—whether they are in spite of or because of his methods—at this point cannot be taken seriously. His greatest accomplishment of all may be somehow getting his opponents to expose themselves to be—or to turn themselves into—exactly what he says they are. Members of Congress largely proved to be the spineless opportunists he had always contended—putting their loyalty or opposition to Trump ahead of doing their jobs. The "fake news" media has gotten so outraged at his broadsides—and committed to showing Trump to be unfit for office—that they peddle half-truths and manufactured narratives. The "deep state" bureaucrats, especially in the Justice Department, were so offended by his rise that they actually abused their power in ham-handed attempts to take him down. The "mob" of left-wing activists resorted to openly calling for anyone associated with Trump to never again be allowed to live in peace. Even Hillary Clinton said in October 2018, "You cannot be civil with a political party that wants to destroy what you stand for, what you care about," barely concealing the underlying assertion—that Trump, his allies, and his supporters must be stopped by whatever tactics are necessary. It's almost like the entire nation has descended into an ends-justify-the-means dystopia.

The country has always swung back and forth—left to right, party to party—ever since the Democratic Republicans crushed the Federalists in the election of 1800, in what Thomas Jefferson viewed as tantamount to a second American revolution. While reflecting on this later in life, Jefferson wrote John Adams, "Every one takes his side in favor of the many, or of the few." Trump, like Bernie Sanders on the other side of the aisle, played to "the many." In 2016, they both tapped into the feeling—shared by millions of Americans across party lines—that our economic and political systems are stacked against them. Where they diverge is in the solution to this problem: individual freedom and less government intervention vs. collectivism and centralized control.

There is nothing wrong with honest populism. But people often forget that while the Founders were repulsed by monarchy, they feared pure democracy. There are some hints of Trump in Alexander Hamilton's description of a dangerous man who would "mount the hobby horse of popularity," take opportunities to "embarrass the General Government and bring it under suspicion" and "throw things into confusion that he may ride the storm and direct the whirlwind." Self-government is an experiment that is not immune to failure. Watching Trump undermine long-standing institutions has been uncomfortable at times. But he also exposed what we already suspected: many of them were rotten to their core. The question is, does he have it in him to build them back up, or will that task be left to whoever comes next? That remains to be seen. But to paraphrase Jefferson again, I prefer this dangerous freedom over peaceful slavery.

Prior to Trump's rise, Republican Party leaders were convinced that abandoning the so-called culture wars was the only way the party could survive. As usual, Trump took the opposite approach; now everything is a culture war. Looking toward 2020, this will likely continue.

In September 2017, the President seized upon protests by some NFL players who refused to stand for the national anthem to raise awareness about racial injustices and police treatment of African Americans. "Wouldn't you love to see one of these NFL owners, when somebody disrespects our flag, to say, 'Get that son of a b— off the field right now. Out. He's fired. He's fired!'" Trump said during a rally in my home state of Alabama. "You know, some owner is going to do that. He's going to say, 'That guy that disrespects our flag, he's fired.' And that owner, they don't know it. They don't know it. They'll be the most popular person, for a week. They'll be the most popular person in this country."

The media backlash was predictably severe. At the height of the furor, I got a phone call from Jim McLaughlin, a pollster who, along with his brother John, had known Trump for decades. Jim explained that public polling on the issue was starting to come out and it was very positive for the President's position. "The country overwhelmingly agrees with him on this," Jim said. "They just want to watch sports. They want it to be an escape from the nonsense. And next thing you know they've got to watch people kneeling for the national anthem. It's offensive, and that's what the polling numbers show."

At the end of an afternoon video recording session in the Diplomatic Reception Room, I pulled the President aside, told him what Jim had said, and showed him some of the polling numbers.

"Of course I'm right about this," the President said, his voice dripping with righteous indignation. "I knew it from the moment I said it; everyone's going to agree with me on this—most everyone. It's about our country. People are sick of their country being disrespected." He then switched gears, and with a wily grin began considering how this would play out during his reelection campaign.

"The Democrats—you watch—they're going to nominate a kneeler," he crowed. "They're going to nominate a kneeler and I'm going to beat the hell out of them." He bit his bottom lip as he slowly punched the air with his right hand, like a champion boxer readying for another match. "You can't win a Democrat primary anymore unless you're a kneeler. But you can't win a general election if you hate the flag and the national anthem."

We walked off down the hallway back toward the West Wing and he tied a bow on his line of thought. "2020 will be fun, that I can tell you—a lot of fun," he said. "The kneelers! Just watch."

Just watch.

I will. And so will you. Because the fact of the matter is, when it comes to Trump, we just can't look away.

ACKNOWLEDGMENTS

I never would have been able to complete this book without the support of so many people—family, friends, mentors, and colleagues alike.

My wife, Megan, endured years of me working deep into the night, even long before writing this book consumed my every waking moment. Thank you for your loving encouragement and unfailing belief in me. To my family—especially my mom, dad, and brother, Brian—thank you for always supporting me as I pursued one dream after another. Thank you to the Parks family (and the Icasianos, Olveras, and Lukers!) for your never-ending kindness and for entrusting Megan to me. To B.J. and Courtney Ellis, you will always be like a brother and a sister to me. Thank you to our incredible friends from The Church at Brook Hills. Megan and I could feel your prayers during difficult times, even from the other side of the country. To Jim and Betty Warren, you will never fully understand the impact you've had on us all. Likewise, David and Heather Platt.

To the Yellowhammer team—especially John and Allison Ross and Tim Howe—thank you for carrying on the torch. And to Walker Miller, you were the first hire I ever made, and the best one (sorry, B.J.). There are numerous mentors who have invested their time and energy in me over the years, namely men like Andy Andrews, Freddy Ard, Dexter Day, Joe Fine, Bob Geddie, Tim Gillis, Johnny Johns, Billy Joy, Barry Moore, Gary Palmer, Dale Rice, Jeff Roberts, Jay Sanders, Jeff Sessions, Richard Shelby, Swaid Swaid . . . The list could go on and on. Thank you for pouring your wisdom and experience into me.

To my friends from the campaign and the White House, I won't name you here so that you won't have to answer for anything I've written, but you know who you are. We walked through the fire together and will forever share a special bond. I hope what I've written in these pages captures our shared experience.

Matt Latimer and Keith Urbahn of Javelin were the best agents a first-time author could ever have. Thank you both for pushing me to be honest and to write a book that will stand the test of time. If we are fortunate enough to achieve that goal, it will be because of your efforts. You improved every piece of this project that you touched. Matt, thank you in particular for the countless hours you spent reading through every word, refining every draft, and for being a 24/7 sounding board for every idea and concern.

The team at Thomas Dunne Books and St. Martin's Press was all in from day one. In particular, I would like to thank Tom Dunne for allowing me to tell my story. Thank you to my editor, Stephen S. Power, and assistant editor Samantha Zukergood for giving great feedback and for tending to my fragile ego. Greg Villepique and Michael Cantwell improved the manuscript in countless ways. Thank you to Tracey Guest and Gabi Gantz for making sure the world was aware of this book.

Finally, to the state of Alabama: I traveled the world, met kings, conversed with princes, dined with diplomats, and shook hands with some of the wealthiest people in human history. And all the while I couldn't wait to come home to you. I hope you will welcome back a weary traveler.

INDEX